A CLASSICAL DICTIONARY OF

HINDU MYTHOLOGY AND RELIGION GEOGRAPHY, HISTORY, AND LITERATURE

A CLASSICAL DICTIONARY

OF

HINDU MYTHOLOGY AND RELIGION GEOGRAPHY, HISTORY, AND LITERATURE

JOHN DOWSON

GYAN

Published by

GYAN

Gyan Publishing House
5, Ansari Road
Daryaganj, New Delhi-110002
Phone: 011-47034999, 9811692060
E-mail: books@gyanbooks.com

Distribution Network
gyanbooks.com
India, USA, Canada, UK, Australia, France

ISBN : 978-81-212-3251-7 (PB)
First Published, 1879

2nd Impression 2020

Printed at: Gyan Press, Delhi.

A
Classical Dictionary
Author: John Dowson

A

CLASSICAL DICTIONARY

OF

HINDU MYTHOLOGY AND RELIGION, GEOGRAPHY, HISTORY, AND LITERATURE.

BY

JOHN DOWSON, M.R.A.S.

LATE PROFESSOR OF HINDUSTANI, STAFF COLLEGE.

LONDON:

TRÜBNER & CO., LUDGATE HILL.

1879.

A

CLASSICAL DICTIONARY

OF

HINDU MYTHOLOGY AND RELIGION GEOGRAPHY, HISTORY, AND LITERATURE

JOHN DOWSON

ASIAN EDUCATIONAL SERVICES
NEW DELHI ★ CHENNAI ★ 2004

ASIAN EDUCATIONAL SERVICES

- 31, HAUZ KHAS VILLAGE, NEW DELHI - 110016
  Tel 2656-0187, 2656-8594 Fax 011-2649-4946, 2685-5499
  e-mail asian_jj@vsnl com / aes_publications@yahoo co in

- 5, SRIPURAM FIRST STREET, CHENNAI - 600 014
  Tel 2811-5040 Fax 044-2811-1291
  e-mail asianeds@md3 vsnl.net in

www asianeds com

First Published London, 1879
AES Reprint New Delhi, 2004
ISBN 81-206-1786-X

Published by J Jetley
for ASIAN EDUCATIONAL SERVICES
31 Hauz Khas Village, New Delhi - 110 016
Processed by AES Publications Pvt Ltd New Delhi-110016
Printed at Chaudhary Offset Process DELHI - 110 051

PREFACE.

In this work an endeavour has been made to supply the long-felt want of a Hindu Classical Dictionary. The late Professor Wilson projected such a work, and forty years ago announced his intention of preparing one for the Oriental Translation Fund, but he never accomplished his design. This is not the first attempt to supply the void. Mr. Garrett, Director of Public Instruction in Mysore, published in India a few years ago a "Classical Dictionary of India," but it is of a very miscellaneous character, and embraces a good deal of matter relating to the manners and customs of the present time. It has not obtained favour in Europe, and it cannot be considered as any obstacle in the way of a more complete and systematic work.

The main portion of this work consists of mythology, but religion is bound up with mythology, and in many points the two are quite inseparable. Of history, in the true sense, Sanskrit possesses nothing, or next to nothing, but what little has been discovered here finds its place. The chief geographical names of the old writers also have received notice, and their localities and identifications are described so far as present knowledge extends. Lastly, short descriptions have been given of the most frequently mentioned Sanskrit books, but only of such books as are likely to be found named in the works of European writers.

It must be understood from the first that this work is derived entirely from the publications of European scholars. I have not resorted to original Sanskrit authorities. My remaining span of life would at the best be quite insufficient for an investigation of their manifold and lengthy volumes. But I have gleaned from many European writers, and have sought to present a summary of the present condition of our knowledge of the religion and mythology of Ancient India.

The work is no doubt very defective. The full harvest of Sanskrit learning has not yet been gathered in, but the knowledge which has been stored by former labourers ought to be made readily available for the service of their successors, to lighten their labours and strengthen them for onward progress. There is nothing in this book for which authority is not to be found in some one or more of the many works upon Hindu literature and religion, but the aim has been to condense and bring together in a compact form that information which lies scattered in many volumes. Hindu mythology is so extensive, and the authorities are often so at variance with each other, that I cannot but feel diffident of the success of my labours. I have worked diligently and carefully, I hope also intelligently, but mistakes have no doubt been made, and it may be that matters have been passed over which ought to have been recorded, and others have been printed which might well have been left unnoticed. But while I have no expectation of any near approach to perfection, I do hope that a good beginning has been made, and that a basis has been laid on which a greater and more worthy structure may hereafter be raised. If the work is received with anything like favour, I shall be constantly on the watch to improve it, and honest criticism will be welcomed and carefully considered.

The book would be more valuable and interesting were it well illustrated with plates and cuts, but the work is a speculative one, and does not directly appeal to a large field of students and readers. The expense of befitting illustrations would be heavy, too great to be at once ventured upon. But if the work is approved, and illustrations are desired, an attempt will be made to supply the want by a series of plates containing a selection of subjects from the stores of our museums and from other sources.

It is unnecessary to specify all the works that have been used in the compilation of this book. Some have been referred to occasionally, but the mainstays throughout have been the "Original Sanskrit Texts" of Dr. Muir and the works of the late Professor H. H. Wilson, including his translation of the *Ri*g-veda, and more especially that of the Vish*n*u Purā*n*a, republished with additional notes by Dr. FitzEdward Hall. I have also levied numerous contributions from the writings of Williams, Max Müller, Roth, Böhthlingk, Lassen, Weber, Whitney, Wollheim da Fonseca, and many others too numerous to mention.

INTRODUCTION.

THE Āryan settlers on the banks of the Indus and in the land of the Five Rivers were possessors of a large number of hymns addressed to the elements and powers of nature. Some of these hymns they no doubt brought from their earlier homes to the West, but others were composed after they had reached the land of their adoption. These ancient hymns cover a long period, the length and the era of which can only be conjectured, but fifteen hundred years before Christ is about the mean of the various ages assigned to them. The hymns form what is called the *Ṛig*-veda Sanhitā, a collection which embraces all the extant compositions of the early Āryans. It is the *Ṛig*-veda which is of primary importance in Hindu religion and mythology; the other Vedas are later in date, and the second and third Vedas consist almost exclusively of hymns derived from the *Ṛig*, but specially arranged for religious purposes. The fourth or Atharva-veda borrows less from the *Ṛig*-veda, but it is considerably later in date, and is of a different character.

The Āryan hymns of the Veda embody the ideas of the Indian immigrants. These ideas were inherited from their forefathers. They were originally the property of the united progenitors of the Āryan races, and the offshoots of this great human stock have spread their primitive ideas over a large portion of the earth. In the Vedic hymns the ideas and myths appear in their simplest and freshest forms, directly connected with the sources from which they sprang by clear ties of language. Comparative philology and mythology go hand in hand; and as the language of the Vedas has proved the great critical instrument in the construction of the science of philology, so the simple myths of the Vedic hymns furnish many clues for unravelling the science of mythology. For where the etymology of a mythic name or term yields a distinct sense of its meaning, the origin of the myth is not far to seek. The language of the Vedas has in many instances supplied this clue, and led to a definite comprehension of what was previously hidden and obscure. The Vedic hymns have preserved the myths in their primitive forms, and, says Max Müller, "Nowhere is the wide distance which separates the ancient poems of India from the most ancient literature of Greece more clearly felt than when we compare the growing myths of the Veda with the full-grown and decayed myths on which the poetry of Homer is founded. The Veda is the real Theogony of the Āryan races, while that of Hesiod is a distorted caricature of the original image."

The Āryan settlers were a pastoral and agricultural people, and they were keenly alive to those influences which affected their prosperity and comfort. They knew the effects of heat and cold, rain and drought, upon their crops and herds, and they marked the influence of warmth and cold, sunshine and rain, wind and storm, upon their own personal comfort. They invested these benign and evil influences with a personality; and behind the fire, the sun, the cloud, and the other powers of nature, they saw beings who directed them in their beneficent and evil operations. To these imaginary beings they addressed their praises, and to them they put up their prayers for temporal blessings. They observed also the movements of the sun and moon, the constant succession of day and night, the intervening periods of morn and eve, and to these also they gave personalities, which they invested with poetical clothing and attributes. Thus observant of nature in its various changes and operations, alive to its influences upon themselves, and perceptive of its beauties, they formed for themselves deities in whose glory and honour they exerted their poetic faculty. They had no one god in particular, no superior deity guiding and controlling the rest, but they paid the tribute of their praise to the deity whose bounties they enjoyed, or whose favours they desired for bodily comfort. They lauded also in glowing language the personifications of those beauties of nature which filled their minds with delight and kindled the poetic fire. So each of the deities in turn received his meed of praise, and each in his turn was the powerful god, able to accomplish the desires of his votary or to excite a feeling of awe or admiration.

Thus there were many distinct deities, and each of them had some general distinctive powers and attributes; but their attributes and characters were frequently confounded, and there was a constant tendency to elevate now this one now that one to the supremacy, and to look upon him as the Great Power. In course of time a pre-eminence was given to a triad of deities, foreshadowing the Tri-mūrti or Trinity of later days. In this triad Agni (Fire) and Sūrya (the Sun) held a place, and the third place was assigned either to Vāyu (the Wind) or to Indra (god of the sky). Towards the end of the *Ri*g-veda Sanhitā, in the hymns of the latest date, the idea of one Supreme Being assumed a more definite shape, and the Hindu mind was perceiving, even if it had not distinctly realised, the great conception.

As the Vedic hymns grew ancient, ritual developed and theological inquiry awoke. Then arose what is called the Brāhma*n*a portion of the Veda. This consists of a variety of compositions, chiefly in prose, and attached to the different Mantras. Ritual and liturgy were the chief objects of these writings, but traditions were cited to enforce and illustrate, and speculation was set at work to explain, the allusions of the hymns. The simplicity of the Vedic myths gradually became obscured, the deities grew more personal, and speculations as to the origin of the world and of the human race invested them with new attributes. Later on, in the Āra*n*yakas and Upanishads, which form part of the collective Brāhma*n*a, a further development took place, but principally in a philosophical direction.

Between the times of the Sanhitā and of the Brāhma*n*a the conception of a Supreme Being had become established. The Brāhma*n*as recognise one Great Being as the Soul of the Universe, and abound with philosophical speculations as to the work of creation and the origin of man. A golden egg was produced in the universal waters, from which in course of time came forth Prajāpati, the progenitor—or, the quiescent Universal Soul,

Brahma, took a creative form as Brahmā the Prajāpati. From the Prajāpati, or great progenitor, there was produced a daughter, and by her he was the father of the human race. The explanations and details of this connection vary, but there is a general accord that the Prajāpati was the progenitor of all mankind by a female produced from himself. Before the times of the Brāhmanas some of the old myths of the hymns had crystallised, the personifications had become more distinct, and the ideas from which they had been developed had grown hazy or were quite forgotten. Philosophy speculated as to the origin of the world, theories were founded upon etymologies, and legends were invented to illustrate them. These speculations and illustrations in course of time hardened into shape, and became realities when the ideas which gave them birth were no longer remembered and understood. The priestly order had advanced in power, and had taken a more prominent and important position, but the Kshatriya or second class held a high place, and asserted something like an equality with the Brāhmans even in matters of learning.

Another interval elapsed between the days of the Brāhma*n*a and of Manu. The theory of the golden egg is held by Manu, and he calls the active creator who was produced from it Brahmā and Nārāyana, the latter name being one which was afterwards exclusively appropriated by Vish*n*u. But the most remarkable change observable in Manu is in the condition of the people, in the great advancement of the Brahmanical caste, the establishment of the four great castes, and the rise of a number of mixed castes from cross intercourse of these four. In a hymn called Purusha-sūkta, one of the latest hymns of the *Ri*g-veda, there is a distinct recognition of three classes, Brāhmans, Kshatriyas, and Vai*s*yas, and these appear more distinctly in the Brāhma*n*a, but no mention of the Sūdras and mixed castes has been found before the work of Manu.

The Rāmāya*n*a and Mahā-bhārata are poems of the heroic age, and though they are full of marvels, they deal more with the actions of mortal men and romantic creations than the might and majesty of the gods. The old deities of the Vedas have retired into the background, and some have disappeared altogether. Indra retains a place of some dignity; but Brahmā, *S*iva, and Vish*n*u have, in the Epics, risen to the chief place. Even of these three, the first is comparatively insignificant. His work of creation was over, and if he was ever an object of great adoration, he had ceased to be so. Vish*n*u and *S*iva both appear in these poems; and although Vish*n*u is the god who holds the most prominent place, still there are many passages in which *S*iva is elevated to the supreme dignity. The Vish*n*u who, in the Vedas, was the friend and companion of Indra and strode over the universe, has become the great deity of preservation, and the terrible and howling Rudra is now *S*iva, the deity of destruction and renovation. Each of these two gods in his turn contends with and subdues the other; now this, now that, receives the homage of his rival, and each in turn is lauded and honoured as the chief and greatest of gods.

The Avatāras or incarnations of Vish*n*u assume a prominent place in the poems, and still more so in the Purā*n*as. The first three, the Fish, the Tortoise, and the Boar, have a cosmical character, and are foreshadowed in the hymns of the Vedas. The fourth, or Man-lion, seems to belong to a later age, when the worship of Vish*n*u had become established. The fifth, or Dwarf, whose three strides deprived the Asuras of the dominion of heaven and earth, is in its character anterior to the fourth Avatāra, and the three strides are attributed to Vish*n*u in the Veda. The fifth, sixth, and seventh, Para*s*u-rāma, Rāma-chandra, and K*ri*sh*na*, are mortal heroes, whose exploits are celebrated in these poems so fervently as to raise the heroes to the rank of gods. The ninth Avatāra, Buddha, is manifestly and avowedly the offspring of the preaching of Buddha; and the tenth, Kalki, is yet to come.

When we reach the Purā*n*as there is found a very different condition of things. The true meaning of the Vedic myths is entirely lost, their origin is forgotten, and the signification and composition of many of the mythic names are unknown. Marvellous legends have gathered round the favourite divinities, and many more have been built upon fanciful etymologies of the old names. The simple primitive fancies suggested by the operations of nature have disappeared, and have been supplanted by the wild imaginings of a more advanced civilisation, but of a more corrupt state of society and religion. The Tri-mūrti or triad of deities has assumed a distinct shape, and while Brahmā has quite fallen into obscurity, Vishnu and Siva have each become supreme in the belief of their respective followers. Vishnu, in his youthful form Krishna, is the object of a sensuous and joyous worship. The gloomy and disgusting worship of Siva, in his terrible forms, has grown side by side with it. The worship of his fierce consort, Devī, has become established, and the foundation has been laid of the obscene and bloody rites afterwards developed in the Tantras.

The Veda, in modern Hinduism, is a mere name,—a name of high authority, often invoked and highly reverenced,—but its language is unintelligible, and its gods and rites are things of the past. The modern system is quite at variance with the Vedic writings out of which it grew, and the descendant bears but few marks of resemblance to its remote ancestor.

The Purānas and later writings are the great authorities of modern Hinduism; their mythology and legends fill the popular mind and mould its thoughts. The wonderful tales of the great poems also exercise a great influence. The heroes of these poems are heroes still; their exploits, with many embellishments and sectarial additions, are recounted in prose and verse, and the tales of Rāma and the Pāndavas, of Hanumat and Rāvana, are still read and listened to with wonder and delight. A host of legends has grown up around the hero Krishna; they attend him from his cradle to his pyre; but the stories of his infancy and his youth are those which are most popular, and interest all classes, especially women and young people. The mild and gentle Rāma, "the husband of one wife," pure in thought and noble in action, is in many places held in the highest honour, and the worship paid to him and his faithful wife Sītā is the purest and least degrading of the many forms of Hindu worship.

This later mythology, with its wonders and marvels, and its equally marvellous explanations of them, is the key to modern Hinduism. It is curious to trace its descent, to contrast such legends as are traceable with their simple beginnings in the Vedic hymns, and so to follow the workings of the mind of a great people through many centuries. Such a survey supplies important and interesting matter for the history of religion, and gives a clear and complete view of the degradation of a mythology. But for the purposes of comparative mythology the Pauranik legends are of trifling importance. The stories of the Epic poems even are of no great value. It may be, as has been maintained, that they "are simply different versions of one and the same story, and that this story has its origin in the phenomena of the natural world and the course of the day and the year;" but still they are of later date, and afford no direct clue for unravelling the mythology of the Āryan nations.

The most ancient hymns of the *Rig*-veda are the basis upon which comparative mythology rests, and they have already supplied the means of unfolding the real source and signification of several Greek and Zoroastrian myths. The science is young, and has a wide field before it. Some of its results are beyond doubt, but there are other deductions which have not advanced as yet beyond conjecture and speculation. In the present work some of the more obvious identifications, or proposed identifications, have been mentioned as occasion offered; in a work of reference like this it would be out of place to have done more. The reader who wishes to pursue the study must consult the writings of Max Müller and the "Aryan Mythology" of the Rev. Sir George Cox. In them and in the books to which they refer he will find ample information, and plenty of materials for investigation and comparison.

TRANSLITERATION AND PRONUNCIATION.

If this work answers the purpose for which it is intended, it will be used by students who are acquainted with the alphabet in which Sanskrit is written, and by readers to whom that alphabet is unknown. Its system of transliteration ought then to be such as to enable a student to restore any word to its original letters, but the ordinary reader ought not to be embarrassed with unnecessary diacritical points and distinctions. The alphabet of the Sanskrit is represented on the following plan :—

VOWELS.

Short.	Long.
a as in America.	ā as in last.
i ,, pin.	ī ,, police.
u ,, put.	ū ,, rule.
ri ,, rill.	*rī* ,, chagrin.

The vowel *lri* will not be met with.

DIPHTHONGS.

e as in ere or fête.
ai ,, aisle.
o ,, so.
au as ou in house.

CONSONANTS.

Guttural	k	kh	g	gh	n
Palatal	ch	chh	j	jh	n
Cerebral	*t*	*th*	*d*	*dh*	*n*
Dental	t	th	d	dh	n
Labial	p	ph	b	bh	m
Semi-vowels	y	r	l	v, w	
Sibilants	*s*	sh, s	Aspirate h	Visarga *h*	Anuswāra n

To the uninitiated Englishman the chief difficulty lies in the short 'a,' the primary inherent vowel of the Sanskrit, pronounced as in the word 'America.' The English alphabet has no distinct letter for this sound, but uses every one of its vowels in turn, and some even of its double vowels to represent it; so it is the 'a' and 'e' in 'servant,' the 'i' in 'bird,' the 'o' in 'word,' the 'u' in 'curd,' the 'y' in 'myrtle,' and the 'ea' in 'heard.' The Sanskrit short 'a' has this sound invariably, and unaffected by any combination of consonants; so Sanskrit '*barn*' must be pronounced not as the English 'barn' but as 'burn.' The pronunciation of the other vowels is sufficiently obvious. The vowel '*ri*' is represented in italics to distinguish it from the consonants 'r' and 'i.'

Of the consonants, the cerebral letters '*t*,' '*th*,' '*d*,' '*dh*,' and '*n*,' the palatal sibilant '*s*,' and the visarga '*h*,' are represented in italics. Practically these are the only distinctions necessary. The guttural nasal is used only in combination with a guttural letter ('nk' or 'ng'); the palatal nasal is used only with palatals ('nch' and 'nj'), and no other nasal can be combined with these letters. The anuswāra, and the anuswāra only, is used before the sibilants and 'h,' so in 'ns,' 'nsh,' 'ns,' and 'nh,' the nasal is the anuswāra. The letter m before a semi-vowel may be represented either by m or anuswāra. In all these instances the combinations distinctly indicate the proper nasal, and no discriminative sign is necessary.

Of the pronunciation of the nasals it is only necessary to notice the anuswāra. This, with a sibilant, is a simple n, but before h it is like ng or the French n in *bon;* so the Sanskrit *Sinha*, in the modern derivative tongues, is written and pronounced Singh.

The aspirates are simple aspirations of their respective consonants, and make no other change of their sounds; so 'th' is to be pronounced as in the words 'at home,' and 'ph' as in 'uphill,' never as in 'thine' and in 'physic.' The letter 'g' is always hard as in 'gift.' The palatals are the simple English sounds of 'ch' and 'j' as in 'church' and 'just.' The cerebrals and the dentals are similar letters, but the former are drawn from the roof of the mouth and the latter from the tips of the teeth. In 'train' and 'drain' we have cerebrals; in 'tin' and 'due' we have dentals, or an approach to them. The ordinary English 't' and 'd' are more cerebral than dental, and the natives of India in transcribing English names use the cerebrals for our 't' and 'd.' The palatal sibilant '*s*' has a sound intermediate between 's' and 'sh,' resembling the double 'ss' in 'session.' The visarga, the final '*h*,' has no distinct enunciation, but it is nevertheless a real letter, and changes in certain positions into 's' and 'r.' Thus the name *S*una*hs*ephas is sometimes written *S*una*ss*ephas.

[In French the palatal 'ch' is represented by 'tch' and the 'j' by 'dj.' In German the 'ch' is expressed by 'tsch' and the 'j' by 'dsch.' These very awkward combinations have induced Max Müller and others to use an italic '*k*' and '*g*' instead of them.]

Some words will be found with varying terminations, as 'Hanumat' and 'Hanumān,' 'Sikha*nd*in' and 'Sikha*nd*ī.' The explanation of this is that Sanskrit nouns have what is called a crude form or stem independent of case termination, and the nominative case very frequently differs from it. So 'Hanumat' and 'Sikha*nd*in' are crude forms; 'Hanumān' and 'Sikha*nd*ī' are their nominative cases. There are other such variations which need not be noticed.

The letters b and v are often interchanged, so words not found under the one letter should be sought for under the other.

HINDU CLASSICAL DICTIONARY.

ĀBHĀSWARAS. A class of deities, sixty-four in number, of whose nature little is known.

ABHIDHĀNA. A dictionary or vocabulary. There are many such works. One of the oldest of them is the *Abhidhāna ratna-mālā* of Halāyudha Bhat*t*a (circa 7th cent.), and one of the best is the *Abhidhāna Chintā-mani* of Hema-chandra, a Jaina writer of celebrity (13th cent.). The former has been edited by Aufrecht; the latter by Colebrooke and by Böhtlingk and Rieu.

ABHIMĀNĪ. Agni, the eldest son of Brahmā. By his wife Swāhā he had three sons, Pāvaka, Pavamāna, and *S*uchi. "They had forty-five sons, who, with the original son of Brahmā and his three descendants, constitute the forty-nine fires." *See* Agni.

ABHIMANYU. Son of Arjuna by his wife Su-bhadrā, and known by the metronymic Saubhadra. He killed Lakshma*n*a, the son of Dur-yodhana, on the second day of the great battle of the Mahā-bhārata, but on the thirteenth day he himself fell fighting heroically against fearful odds. He was very handsome. His wife was Uttarā, daughter of the Rāja of Virāta. His son, Parīkshit, succeeded to the throne of Hastināpura.

ABHĪRA, ĀBHĪRA. A cowherd; according to Manu the offspring of a Brāhman by a woman of the Ambash*t*ha or medical tribe. A people located in the north of India along the Indus. There has been a good deal of misapprehension respecting this people. Hindu writers have described them as living in the north and in the west, the quarter varying according to the locality of the writer, and translators have mixed them up with a neighbouring people, the *S*ūdras, sometimes called *S*ūras, with whom they are generally associated, and have called them Sūrābhīras. Their modern representatives are the Ahīrs, and perhaps there is something more than identity of locality in their association with the *S*ūdras. It has been suggested that the country or city of the Abhīras is the *Ophir* of the Bible.

ABHIRĀMA-MA*N*I. A drama in seven acts on the history of Rāma, written by Sundara Misra in 1599 A.D. "The composition possesses little dramatic interest, although it has some literary merit."—*Wilson.*

ĀCHĀRA. 'Rule, custom, usage.' The rules of practice of castes, orders, or religion. There are many books of rules which have this word for the first member of their titles, as *Āchāra-chandrikā*, 'moonlight of customs,' on the customs of the *S*ūdras; *Āchārādarsa*, 'looking-glass of customs;' *Āchāra-dīpa*, 'lamp of customs,' &c., &c.

ĀCHĀRYA. A spiritual teacher or guide. A title of Dro*n*a, the teacher of the Pā*n*davas.

ACHYUTA. 'Unfallen;' a name of Vish*n*u or K*r*ish*n*a. It has been variously interpreted as signifying "he who does not perish with created things," in the Mahā-bhārata as "he who is not distinct from final emancipation," and in the Skanda Purā*n*a as "he who never declines (or varies) from his proper nature."

ADBHUTA-BRĀHMA*N*Ā. 'The Brāhma*n*a of miracles.' A Brāhma*n*a of the Sāma-veda which treats of auguries and marvels. It has been published by Weber.

ADHARMA. Unrighteousness, vice; personified as a son of Brahmā, and called "the destroyer of all beings."

ADHIRATHA. A charioteer. The foster-father of Kar*n*a, according to some he was king of Anga, and according to others the charioteer of King Dh*r*itarāsh*t*ra; perhaps he was both.

ADHWARYU. A priest whose business it is to recite the prayers of the Yajur-veda.

ADHYĀTMAN. The supreme spirit, the soul of the universe.

ADHYĀTMA RĀMĀYA*N*A. A very popular work, which is considered to be a part of the Brahma*n*da Purā*n*a. It has been printed in India. *See* Rāmāya*n*a.

ĀDI-PURAṆA. 'The first Purāṇa,' a title generally conceded to the Brahma Purāṇa.

ADITI. 'Free, unbounded.' Infinity; the boundless heaven as compared with the finite earth; or, according to M. Müller, "the visible infinite, visible by the naked eye; the endless expanse beyond the earth, beyond the clouds, beyond the sky." In the *Ṛig*-veda she is frequently implored "for blessings on children and cattle, for protection and for forgiveness." Aditi is called Deva-mātṛi, 'mother of the gods,' and is represented as being the mother of Daksha and the daughter of Daksha. On this statement Yāska remarks in the Nirukta:—"How can this be possible? They may have had the same origin; or, according to the nature of the gods, they may have been born from each other, have derived their substance from one another." "Eight sons were born from the body of Aditi; she approached the gods with seven but cast away the eighth, Mārttāṇḍa (the sun)." These seven were the Ādityas. In the Yajur-veda Aditi is addressed as "Supporter of the sky, sustainer of the earth, sovereign of this world, wife of Vishṇu;" but in the Mahābhārata and Rāmāyaṇa, as well as in the Purāṇas, Vishṇu is called the son of Aditi. In the Vishṇu Purāṇa she is said to be the daughter of Daksha and wife of Kaśyapa, by whom she was mother of Vishṇu, in his dwarf incarnation (wherefore he is sometimes called Āditya), and also of Indra, and she is called "the mother of the gods" and "the mother of the world." Indra acknowledged her as mother, and Vishṇu, after receiving the adoration of Aditi, addressed her in these words: "Mother, goddess, do thou show favour unto me and grant me thy blessing." According to the Matsya Purāṇa a pair of ear-rings was produced at the churning of the ocean, which Indra gave to Aditi, and several of the Purāṇas tell a story of these ear-rings being stolen and carried off to the city of Prāg-jyotisha by the Asura king Naraka, from whence they were brought back and restored to her by Kṛishṇa. Devakī, the mother of Kṛishṇa, is represented as being a new birth or manifestation of Aditi. *See* Max Müller's *Rig Veda*, i. 230; Muir's *Texts*, iv. 11, v. 35.

ĀDITYA. In the early Vedic times the Ādityas were six, or more frequently seven, celestial deities, of whom Varuṇa was chief, consequently he was *the* Āditya. They were sons of Aditi, who had eight sons, but she approached the gods with seven, having cast away the eighth, Mārttā*n*da (the sun). In after-times the number was increased to twelve, as representing the sun in the twelve months of the year. Āditya is one of the names of the sun. Dr. Muir quotes the following from Professor Roth:—"There (in the highest heaven) dwell and reign those gods who bear in common the name of Ādityas. We must, however, if we would discover their earliest character, abandon the conceptions which in a later age, and even in that of the heroic poems, were entertained regarding these deities. According to this conception they were twelve sun-gods, bearing evident reference to the twelve months. But for the most ancient period we must hold fast the primary signification of their name. They are the inviolable, imperishable, eternal beings. Aditi, eternity, or the eternal, is the element which sustains or is sustained by them. . . . The eternal and inviolable element in which the Ādityas dwell, and which forms their essence, is the celestial light. The Ādityas, the gods of this light, do not therefore by any means coincide with any of the forms in which light is manifested in the universe. They are neither sun, nor moon, nor stars, nor dawn, but the eternal sustainers of this luminous life, which exists, as it were, behind all these phenomena."

The names of the six Ādityas are Mitra, Aryaman, Bhaga, Varu*n*a, Daksha, and An*s*a. Daksha is frequently excluded, and Indra, Savit*r*i (the sun), and Dhāt*ri* are added. Those of the twelve Ādityas are variously given, but many of them are names of the sun.

ĀDITYA PURĀ*N*A. One of the eighteen Upa-purā*n*as.

AGASTI, AGASTYA. A *R*ishi, the reputed author of several hymns in the *R*ig-veda, and a very celebrated personage in Hindu story. He and Vasish*th*a are said in the *R*ig-veda to be the offspring of Mitra and Varu*n*a, whose seed fell from them at the sight of Urva*s*ī; and the commentator Sāya*n*a adds that Agastya was born in a water-jar as "a fish of great lustre," whence he was called Kala*si*-suta, Kumbha-sambhava, and Gha*t*odbhava. From his parentage he was called Maitrā-varu*n*i and Aurva*s*īya; and as he was very small when he was born, not more than a span in length, he was called Māna. Though he is thus associated in his birth with Vasish*th*a, he is evidently later in date, and he is not one of the Prajāpatis. His name.

Agastya, is derived by a forced etymology from a fable which represents him as having commanded the Vindhya mountains to prostrate themselves before him, through which they lost their primeval altitude; or rather, perhaps, the fable has been invented to account for his name. This miracle has obtained for him the epithet Vindhya-kū*t*a; and he acquired another name, Pītābdhi, or Samudra-chuluka, 'Ocean drinker,' from another fable, according to which he drank up the ocean because it had offended him, and because he wished to help the gods in their wars with the Daityas when the latter had hidden themselves in the waters. He was afterwards made regent of the star Canopus, which bears his name. The Purā*n*as represent him as being the son of Pulastya, the sage from whom the Rākshasas sprang. He was one of the narrators of the Brahma Purā*n*a and also a writer on medicine.

The Mahā-bhārata relates a legend respecting the creation of his wife. It says that Agastya saw his ancestors suspended by their heels in a pit, and was told by them that they could be rescued only by his begetting a son. Thereupon he formed a girl out of the most graceful parts of different animals and passed her secretly into the palace of the king of Vidarbha. There the child grew up as a daughter of the king, and was demanded in marriage by Agastya. Much against his will the king was constrained to consent, and she became the wife of the sage. She was named Lopā-mudrā, because the animals had been subjected to loss (*lopa*) by her engrossing their distinctive beauties, as the eyes of the deer, &c. She was also called Kau*s*ītakī and Vara-pradā. The same poem also tells a story exhibiting his superhuman power, by which he turned King Nahusha into a serpent and afterwards restored him to his proper form. *See* Nahusha.

It is in the Rāmāya*n*a that Agastya makes the most distinguished figure. He dwelt in a hermitage on Mount Kunjara, situated in a most beautiful country to the south of the Vindhya mountains, and was chief of the hermits of the south. He kept the Rākshasas who infested the south under control, so that the country was "only gazed upon and not possessed by them." His power over them is illustrated by a legend which represents him as eating up a Rākshasa named Vātāpi who assumed the form of a ram, and as destroying by a flash of his eye the

Rākshasa's brother, Ilvala, who attempted to avenge him. (*See* Vātāpi.) Rāma in his exile wandered to the hermitage of Agastya with Sītā and Lakshma*n*a. The sage received him with the greatest kindness, and became his friend, adviser, and protector. He gave him the bow of Vish*n*u; and when Rāma was restored to his kingdom, the sage accompanied him to Ayodhyā.

The name of Agastya holds a great place also in Tamil literature, and he is "venerated in the south as the first teacher of science and literature to the primitive Drāvi*d*ian tribes;" so says Dr. Caldwell, who thinks "we shall not greatly err in placing the era of Agastya in the seventh, or at least in the sixth century B.C." Wilson also had previously testified to the same effect: "The traditions of the south of India ascribe to Agastya a principal share in the formation of the Tamil language and literature, and the general tenor of the legends relating to him denotes his having been instrumental in the introduction of the Hindu religion and literature into the Peninsula."

AGHĀSURA. (Agha the Asura.) An Asura who was Kansa's general. He assumed the form of a vast serpent, and K*ri*sh*n*a's companions, the cowherds, entered its mouth, mistaking it for a mountain cavern: but K*ri*sh*n*a rescued them.

AGNĀYĪ. Wife of Agni. She is seldom alluded to in the Veda and is not of any importance.

ĀGNEYA. Son of Agni, a name of Kārttikeya or Mars; also an appellation of the Muni Agastya and others.

ĀGNEYĀSTRA. 'The weapon of fire.' Given by Bharadwāja to Agnivesa, the son of Agni, and by him to Dro*n*a. A similar weapon was, according to the Vish*n*u Purā*n*a, given by the sage Aurva to his pupil King Sagara, and with it "he conquered the tribes of barbarians who had invaded his patrimonial possessions."

ĀGNEYA PURĀ*N*A. *See* Agni Purā*n*a.

AGNI. (Nom. Agnis = Ignis.) Fire, one of the most ancient and most sacred objects of Hindu worship. He appears in three phases—in heaven as the sun, in mid-air as lightning, on earth as ordinary fire. Agni is one of the chief deities of the Vedas, and great numbers of the hymns are addressed to him, more indeed than to any other god. He is one of the three great deities —Agni, Vāyu (or Indra), and Sūrya—who respectively preside over earth, air, and sky, and are all equal in dignity. "He is considered as the mediator between men and gods, as protector of men and their homes, and as witness of their actions; hence his invocation at all solemn occasions, at the nuptial ceremony, &c. Fire has ceased to be an object of worship, but is held in honour for the part it performs in sacrifices." Agni is represented as having seven tongues, each of which has a distinct name, for licking up the butter used in sacrifices. He is guardian of the south-east quarter, being one of the eight lokapalas (q.v.), and his region is called Pura-jyotis.

In a celebrated hymn of the *Ri*g-veda attributed to Vasish*th*a, Indra and other gods are called upon to destroy the Kravyāds 'the flesh-eaters,' or Rakshas enemies of the gods. Agni himself is also a Kravyād, and as such he takes an entirely different character. He is represented under a form as hideous as the beings he is invoked to devour. He sharpens his two iron tusks, puts his enemies into his mouth and swallows them. He heats the edges of his shafts and sends them into the hearts of the Rakshas.

"He appears in the progress of mythological personification as a son of Angiras, as a king of the Pit*ri*s or Manes, as a Marut, as a grandson of *S*a*n*dila, as one of the seven sages or *Ri*shis, during the reign of Tāmasa the fourth Manu," and as a star. In the Mahā-bhārata Agni is represented as having exhausted his vigour by devouring too many oblations, and desiring to consume the whole Khā*nd*ava forest as a means of recruiting his strength. He was prevented by Indra, but having obtained the assistance of K*ri*sh*n*a and Arjuna, he baffled Indra and accomplished his object. In the Vish*n*u Purā*n*a he is called Abhimānī, and the eldest son of Brahmā. His wife was Swāhā; by her he had three sons, Pāvaka, Pavamāna, and *S*uchi, and these had forty-five sons; altogether forty-nine persons, identical with the forty-nine fires, which forty-nine fires the Vāyu Purā*n*a endeavours to discriminate. He is described in the Hari-van*s*a as clothed in black, having smoke for his standard and head-piece, and carrying a flaming javelin. He has four hands, and is borne in a chariot drawn by red horses, and the seven winds are the wheels of his car. He is accompanied by a ram, and sometimes he is represented riding on that animal. The representations of him vary.

The names and epithets of Agni are many—Vahni, Anala, Pāvaka, Vai*s*wānara, son of Vi*s*wānara, the sun; Abja-hasta, 'lotus in hand;' Dhūma-ketu, 'whose sign is smoke;' Hutāsa or Huta-bhuj, 'devourer of offerings;' *S*uchi or *S*ukra, 'the bright;' Rohitāswa, 'having red horses;' Chhāga-ratha, 'ram-rider;' Jāta vedas (q.v.); Sapta-jihva, 'seven-tongued;' Tomara-dhara, 'javelin-bearer.'

AGNI-DAGDHAS. Pit*ri*s, or Manes, who when alive kept up the household flame and presented oblations with fire. Those who did not do so were called *An-agni dagdhas.* *See* Pit*ri*s.

AGNI PURĀ*N*A. This Purā*n*a derives its name from its having been communicated originally by Agni, the deity of fire, to the Muni Vasish*th*a, for the purpose of instructing him in the twofold knowledge of Brahmā. Its contents are variously specified as "sixteen thousand, fifteen thousand, and fourteen thousand stanzas." This work is devoted to the glorification of *S*iva, but its contents are of a very varied and cyclopædical character. It has portions on ritual and mystic worship, cosmical descriptions, chapters on the duties of kings and the art of war, which have the appearance of being extracted from some older work, a chapter on law from the text-book of Yājnawalkya, some chapters on medicine from the Su*s*ruta, and some treatises on rhetoric, prosody, and grammar according to the rules of Pingala and Pā*n*ini. Its motley contents "exclude it from any legitimate claims to be regarded as a Purā*n*a, and prove that its origin cannot be very remote." The text of this Purā*n*a is now in course of publication in the *Bibliotheca Indica,* edited by Rājendra Lāl Mitra.

AGNISHWĀTTAS. Pit*ri*s or Manes of the gods, who when living upon earth did not maintain their domestic fires or offer burnt-sacrifices. According to some authorities they were descendants of Marīchi. They are also identified with the seasons. *See* Pit*ri*s.

AGNIVE*S*A. A sage, the son of Agni, and an early writer on medicine.

AHALYĀ. Wife of the *Ri*shi Gautama, and a very beautiful woman. In the Rāmāya*n*a it is stated that she was the first woman made by Brahmā, and that he gave her to Gautama. She was seduced by Indra, who had to suffer for his adultery. One version of the Rāmāya*n*a represents her as knowing the god and being flattered by his condescension; but another version states that the god assumed the form of her husband, and so deceived her. Another story is that Indra secured the help of the moon, who assumed the form of a cock and crowed at midnight. This roused Gautama to his morning's devotions, when Indra went in and took his place. Gautama expelled Ahalyā from his hermitage, and deprived her of her prerogative of being the most beautiful woman in the world, or, according to another statement, he rendered her invisible. She was restored to her natural state by Rāma and reconciled to her husband. This seduction is explained mythically by Kumārila Bha*tt*a as Indra (the sun's) carrying away the shades of night—the name Ahalyā, by a strained etymology, being made to signify 'night.'

AHI. A serpent. A name of V*ri*tra, the Vedic demon of drought: but Ahi and V*ri*tra are sometimes "distinct, and mean, most probably, differently formed clouds."—*Wilson.*

AHI-CHHATRA, AHI-KSHETRA. A city mentioned in the Mahā-bhārata as lying north of the Ganges, and as being the capital of Northern Panchāla. It is apparently the Adisadra of Ptolemy, and its remains are visible near Rām-nagar.

AINDRI. 'Son of Indra.' An appellation of Arjuna.

AIRĀVATA. 'A fine elephant.' An elephant produced at the churning of the ocean, and appropriated by the god Indra. The derivation of this name is referred to the word Irāvat, signifying 'produced from water.' He is guardian of one of the points of the compass. *See* Loka-pāla.

AITAREYA. The name of a Brāhma*n*a, an Āra*n*yaka, and an Upanishad of the *Rig*-veda. The Brāhma*n*a has been edited and translated by Dr. Haug; the text of the Āra*n*yaka has been published in the *Bibliotheca Indica* by Rājendra Lāla, and there is another edition. The Upanishad has been translated by Dr. Roer in the same series. "The Aitareya Āra*n*yaka consists of five books, each of which is called Āra*n*yaka. The second and third books form a separate Upanishad, and a still further subdivision here takes place, inasmuch as the four last sections of the second book, which are particularly consonant with the doctrines of the Vedānta system, pass as the Aitareyopanishad."—*Weber.*

AJA. 'Unborn.' An epithet applied to many of the gods. A prince of the Solar race, sometimes said to be the son of Raghu, at others the son of Dilīpa, son of Raghu. He was the husband chosen at her swayam-vara by Indumatī, daughter of the Rāja of Vidarbha, and was the father of Da*s*aratha and grandfather of Rāma. The Raghu-vansa relates how on his way to the swayam-vara he was annoyed by a wild elephant and ordered it to be shot. When the elephant was mortally wounded, a beautiful figure issued from it, which declared itself a gandharva who had been transformed into a mad elephant for deriding a holy man. The gandharva was delivered, as it had been foretold to him, by Aja, and he gave the prince some arrows which enabled him to excel in the contest at the swayam-vara. When Dasaratha grew up, Aja ascended to Indra's heaven.

ĀJAGAVA. The 'primitive bow' of *S*iva, which fell from heaven at the birth of P*ri*thu.

AJĀMILA. A Brāhman of Kanauj, who married a slave and had children, of whom he was very fond.

AJĀTA-*S*ATRU. 'One whose enemy is unborn.' 1. A king of Kā*s*ī, mentioned in the Upanishads, who was very learned, and, although a Kshatriya, instructed the Brāhman Gārgya-bālāki. 2. A name of *S*iva. 3. Of Yudhi-sh*th*ira. 4. A king of Mathurā who reigned in the time of Buddha.

AJAYA-PĀLA. Author of a Sansk*ri*t vocabulary of some repute.

AJĪGARTTA. A Brāhman *Ris*hi who sold his son *S*una*h*-*s*ephas to be a sacrifice.

AJITA. 'Unconquered.' A title given to Vish*n*u, *S*iva, and many others. There were classes of gods bearing this name in several Manwantaras.

AKRŪRA. A Yādava and uncle of K*ri*sh*n*a. He was son of *S*wa-phalka and Gāndinī. It was he who took K*ri*sh*n*a and Rāma to Mathurā when the former broke the great bow. He is chiefly noted as being the holder of the Syamantaka gem.

AKSHA. The eldest son of Rāva*n*a, slain by Hanumān. Also a name of Garu*d*a.

AKSHAMĀLĀ. A name of Arundhati (q.v.).

ĀKULI. An Asura priest. *See* Kilātākuli.

AKŪPĀRA. A tortoise or turtle. The tortoise on which the earth rests.

ĀKŪTI. A daughter of Manu Swāyambhuva and *S*ata-rūpā, whom he gave to the patriarch Ruchi. She bore twins, Yajna and Dakshi*n*ā, who became husband and wife and had twelve sons, the deities called Yāmas.

ALAKĀ. The capital of Kuvera and the abode of the

gandharvas on Mount Meru. It is also called Vasu-dhārā, Vasu-sthalī, and Prabhā.

ALAKA-NANDĀ. One of the four branches of the river Gangā, which flows south to the country of Bhārata. This is said by the Vaishnavas to be the terrestrial Gangā which *S*iva received upon his head.

ALAMBUSHA. A great Rākshasa worsted by Sātyaki in the great war of the Mahā-bhārata, and finally killed by Gha*t*otkacha. He is said to be a son of *R*ishya*s*ringa.

ALĀYUDHA. A Rākshasa killed after a fierce combat by Gha*t*otkacha in the war of the Mahā-bhārata (*Fauche*, ix. 278).

AMARA-KA*NT*AKA. 'Peak of the immortals.' A place of pilgrimage in the table-land east of the Vindhyas.

AMARA-KOSHA. This title may be read in two ways—'the immortal vocabulary,' or, more appropriately, 'the vocabulary of Amara or Amara Sinha.' "The oldest vocabulary hitherto known, and one of the most celebrated vocabularies of the classical Sansk*r*it." It has been the subject of a great number of commentaries. The text has been often printed. There is an edition published in India with an English interpretation and annotations by Colebrooke, and the text with a French translation has been printed by Deslongchamps.

AMARA SINHA. The author of the vocabulary called Amara-kosha. He was one of the nine gems of the court of Vikrama. (*See* Nava-ratna.) Wilson inclines to place him in the first century B.C. Lassen places him about the middle of the third century A.D., and others incline to bring him down later.

AMARĀVATĪ. The capital of Indra's heaven, renowned for its greatness and splendour. It is situated somewhere in the vicinity of Meru. It is sometimes called Deva-pura, 'city of the gods,' and Pūsha-bhāsā, 'sun-splendour.'

AMARE*S*WARA. 'Lord of the immortals.' A title of Vish*n*u, *S*iva, and Indra. Name of one of the twelve great *lingas*. *See* Linga.

AMARU-*S*ATAKA. A poem consisting of a hundred stanzas written by a king named Amaru, but by some attributed to the philosopher *S*ankara, who assumed the dead form of that king for the purpose of conversing with his widow. The verses are of an erotic character, but, like many others of the same kind, a religious or philosophical interpretation has been found for them.

There is a translation in French by Apudy with the text, and a translation in German by Rückert.

AMBĀ. 'Mother.' 1. A name of Durgā. 2. The eldest daughter of a king of Kāsī. She and her sisters Ambikā and Ambālikā were carried off by Bhīshma to be the wives of Vichitra-vīrya. Ambā had been previously betrothed to a Rāja of *S*alwa, and Bhīshma sent her to him, but the Rāja rejected her because she had been in another man's house. She retired to the forest and engaged in devotion to obtain revenge of Bhīshma. *S*iva favoured her, and promised her the desired vengeance in another birth. Then she ascended the pile and was born again as *S*ik-ha*nd*in, who slew Bhīshma.

AMBĀLIKĀ. The younger widow of Vichitra-vīrya and mother of Pā*nd*u by Vyāsa. *See* Mahā-bhārata.

AMBARĪSHA. 1. A king of Ayodhyā, twenty-eighth in descent from Ikshwāku. (*See* *S*una*h*sephas.) 2. An appellation of *S*iva. 3. Name of one of the eighteen hells.

AMBASH*T*HA. A military people inhabiting a country of the same name in the middle of the Panjāb; probably the Ἀμβάσται of Ptolemy. 2. The medical tribe in Manu.

AMBIKĀ. 1. A sister of Rudra, but in later times identified with Umā. 2. Elder widow of Vichitra-vīrya and mother of Dh*r*ita-rāsh*t*ra by Vyāsa. *See* Mahā-bhārata.

AMBIKEYA. A metronymic applicable to Ganesa, Skanda, and Dh*r*ita-rāsh*t*ra.

ĀMNĀYA. Sacred tradition. The Vedas in the aggregate.

AM*R*ITA. 'Immortal.' A god. The water of life. The term was known to the Vedas, and seems to have been applied to various things offered in sacrifice, but more especially to the Soma juice. It is also called Nir-jara and Pīyūsha. In later times it was the water of life produced at the churning of the ocean by the gods and demons, the legend of which is told with some variations in the Rāmāya*n*a, the Mahā-bhārata, and the Purā*n*as. The gods, feeling their weakness, having been worsted by the demons, and being, according to one authority, under the ban of a holy sage, repaired to Vish*n*u, beseeching him for renewed vigour and the gift of immortality. He directed them to churn the ocean for the Am*r*ita and other precious things which had been lost. The story as told in the Vish*n*u Purā*n*a has been rendered into verse by Professor Williams thus :—

"The gods addressed the mighty Vish*n*u thus—
'Conquered in battle by the evil demons,
We fly to thee for succour, soul of all;
Pity, and by thy might deliver us!'
Hari, the lord, creator of the world,
Thus by the gods implored, all graciously
Replied—'Your strength shall be restored, ye gods;
Only accomplish what I now command.
Unite yourselves in peaceful combination
With these your foes; collect all plants and herbs
Of diverse kinds from every quarter; cast them
Into the sea of milk; take Mandara,
The mountain, for a churning stick, and Vāsuki,
The serpent, for a rope; together churn
The ocean to produce the beverage—
Source of all strength and immortality—
Then reckon on my aid; I will take care
Your foes shall share your toil, but not partake
In its reward, or drink th' immortal draught.'
Thus by the god of gods advised, the host
United in alliance with the demons.
Straightway they gathered various herbs and cast them
Into the waters, then they took the mountain
To serve as churning-staff, and next the snake
To serve as cord, and in the ocean's midst
Hari himself, present in tortoise-form,
Became a pivot for the churning-staff.
Then did they churn the sea of milk; and first
Out of the waters rose the sacred Cow,
God-worshipped Surabhi, eternal fountain
Of milk and offerings of butter; next,
While holy Siddhas wondered at the sight,
With eyes all rolling, Vāru*n*ī uprose,
Goddess of wine. Then from the whirlpool sprang
Fair Pārijāta, tree of Paradise, delight
Of heavenly maidens, with its fragrant blossoms
Perfuming the whole world. Th' Apsarasas,
Troop of celestial nymphs, matchless in grace,
Perfect in loveliness, were next produced.
Then from the sea uprose the cool-rayed moon,
Which Mahā-deva seized; terrific poison
Next issued from the waters; this the snake-gods
Claimed as their own. Then, seated on a lotus,
Beauty's bright goddess, peerless *S*rī, arose
Out of the waves; and with her, robed in white,
Came forth Dhanwantari, the gods' physician.

High in his hand he bore the cup of nectar—
Life-giving draught—longed for by gods and demons.
Then had the demons forcibly borne off
The cup, and drained the precious beverage,
Had not the mighty Vishnu interposed.
Bewildering them, he gave it to the gods;
Whereat, incensed, the demon troops assailed
The host of heaven, but they with strength renewed,
Quaffing the draught, struck down their foes, who fell
Headlong through space to lowest depths of hell!"

There is an elaborate article on the subject in Goldstücker's *Dictionary*. In after-times, Vishnu's bird Garuda is said to have stolen the Amrita, but it was recovered by Indra.

ANĀDHRISHTI. A son of Ugrasena and general of the Yādavas.

ĀNAKA-DUNDUBHI. 'Drums.' A name of Vasu-deva, who was so called because the drums of heaven resounded at his birth.

ĀNANDA. 'Joy, happiness.' An appellation of Siva, also of Bala-rāma.

ĀNANDA GIRI. A follower of Sankarāchārya, and a teacher and expositor of his doctrines. He was the author of a *Sankara-vijaya*, and lived about the tenth century.

ĀNANDA-LAHARI. 'The wave of joy.' A poem attributed to Sankarāchārya. It is a hymn of praise addressed to Pārvatī, consort of Siva, mixed up with mystical doctrine. It has been translated into French by Troyer as *L'Onde de Beatitude.*

ANANGA. 'The bodiless.' A name of Kāma, god of love.

ANANTA. 'The infinite.' A name of the serpent Sesha. The term is also applied to Vishnu and other deities.

ANARANYA. A descendant of Ikshwāku and king of Ayodhyā. According to the Rāmāyana, many kings submitted to Rāvana without fighting, but when Anaranya was summoned to fight or submit, he preferred to fight. His army was overcome and he was thrown from his chariot. Rāvana triumphed over his prostrate foe, who retorted that he had been beaten by fate, not by Rāvana, and predicted the death of Rāvana at the hands of Rāma, a descendant of Anaranya.

ANARGHA RĀGHAVA. A drama in seven acts by Murāri Misra, possibly written in the thirteenth or fourteenth century. Rāghava or Rāma is the hero of the piece. "It has no dramatic merit, being deficient in character, action, situation, and interest.

As a poem it presents occasionally poetic thoughts, but they are very few, and are lost amid pages of flat commonplace, quaint conceit, hyperbolical extravagance, and obscure mythology."—*Wilson.* It is also called, after its author, Murāri Nā*t*aka.

AN-ĀRYA. 'Unworthy, vile.' People who were not Āryans, barbarians of other races and religion.

ANASŪYĀ. 'Charity.' Wife of the *Ri*shi Atri. In the Rāmāya*n*a she appears living with her husband in a hermitage in the forest south of Chitra-kū*t*a. She was very pious and given to austere devotion, through which she had obtained miraculous powers. When Sītā visited her and her husband, she was very attentive and kind, and gave Sītā an ointment which was to keep her beautiful for ever. She was mother of the irascible sage Durvāsas. A friend of *S*akuntalā.

ANDHAKA. 1. A demon, son of Ka*s*yapa and Diti, with a thousand arms and heads, two thousand eyes and feet, and called Andhaka because he walked like a blind man, although he saw very well. He was slain by *S*iva when he attempted to carry off the Pārijāta tree from Swarga. From this feat *S*iva obtained the appellation Andhaka-ripu, 'foe of Andhaka.' 2. A grandson of Krosh*tri* and son of Yudhājit, of the Yādava race, who, together with his brother V*ri*sh*n*i, is the ancestor of the celebrated family of Andhaka-V*ri*sh*n*is. 3. The name was borne by many others of less note.

ANDHRA, ĀNDHRA. Name of a country and people in the south of India, the country of Telingana. It was the seat of a powerful dynasty, and the people were known to Pliny as *gens Andaræ.*

ANDHRA-BH*RI*TYA. A dynasty of kings that reigned in Magadha somewhere about the beginning of the Christian era. The name seems to indicate that its founder was a native of Andhra, now Telingana.

ANGA. 1. The country of Bengal proper about Bhāgalpur. Its capital was Champā, or Champā-purī. (*See* Anu.) 2. A supplement to the Vedas. *See* Vedānga.

ANGADA. 1. Son of Lakshma*n*a and king of Āngadi, capital of a country near the Himālaya. 2. Son of Gada (brother of K*ri*sh*n*a) by V*ri*hatī. 3. Son of Bālī, the monkey king of Kishkindhyā. He was protected by Rāma, and fought on his side against Rāva*n*a.

ANGIRAS. A *Ri*shi to whom many hymns of the *Rig*-veda are attributed. He was one of the seven Maharshis or great *Ri*shis, and also one of the ten Prajāpatis or progenitors of mankind. In later times Angiras was one of the inspired lawgivers, and also a writer on astronomy. As an astronomical personification he is B*ri*haspati, the regent of the planet Jupiter, or the planet itself. He was also called "the priest of the gods," and "the lord of sacrifice." There is much ambiguity about the name. It comes from the same root as *agni*, 'fire,' and resembles that word in sound. This may be the reason why the name Angiras is used as an epithet or synonyme of Agni. The name is also employed as an epithet for the father of Agni, and it is found more especially connected with the hymns addressed to Agni, Indra, and the luminous deities. According to one statement, Angiras was the son of Uru by Āgneyī, the daughter of Agni, although, as above stated, the name is sometimes given to the father of Agni. Another account represents that he was born from the mouth of Brahmā. His wives were Sm*ri*ti, 'memory,' daughter of Daksha; *S*raddhā, 'faith,' daughter of Kardama; and Swadhā 'oblation,' and Satī, 'truth,' two other daughters of Daksha. His daughters were the *Ri*chas or Vaidik hymns, and his sons were the Manes called Havishmats. But he had other sons and daughters, and among the former were Utathya, B*ri*haspati, and Mārka*nd*eya. According to the Bhāgavata Purā*n*a "he begot sons possessing Brahmanical glory on the wife of Rathī-tara, a Kshatriya who was childless, and these persons were afterwards called descendants of Angiras."

ANGIRASAS, ANGIRASES. Descendants of Angiras. "They share in the nature of the legends attributed to Angiras. Angiras being the father of Agni, they are considered as descendants of Agni himself, who is also called the first of the Angirasas. Like Angiras, they occur in hymns addressed to the luminous deities, and, at a later period, they become for the most part personifications of light, of luminous bodies, of divisions of time, of celestial phenomena, and fires adapted to peculiar occasions, as the full and change of the moon, or to particular rites, as the Aswa-medha, Rāja-sūya, &c."—*Goldstücker.* In the *S*atapatha Brāhma*n*a they and the Ādityas are said to have descended from Prajāpati, and that "they strove together for the priority in ascending to heaven."

Some descendants of Angiras by the Kshatriya wife of a childless king are mentioned in the Purāṇas as two tribes of Angirasas who were Brāhmans as well as Kshatriyas.

The hymns of the Atharva-veda are called Angirasas, and the descendants of Angiras were specially charged with the protection of sacrifices performed in accordance with the Atharva-veda. From this cause, or from their being associated with the descendants of Atharvan, they were called distinctively Atharvāngirasas.

ĀNGIRASAS. A class of Pitṛis (q.v.).

ANILA. 'The wind.' *See* Vāyu.

ANILAS. A gaṇa or class of deities, forty-nine in number, connected with Anila, the wind.

ANIMISHA. 'Who does not wink.' A general epithet of all gods.

ANIRUDDHA. 'Uncontrolled.' Son of Pradyumna and grandson of Kṛishṇa. He married his cousin, Su-bhadrā. A Daitya princess named Ushā, daughter of Bāṇa, fell in love with him, and had him brought by magic influence to her apartments in her father's city of Sonita-pura. Bāṇa sent some guards to seize him, but the valiant youth, taking an iron club, slew his assailants. Bāṇa then brought his magic powers to bear and secured him. On discovering whither Aniruddha had been carried, Kṛishṇa, Bala-rāma, and Pradyumna went to rescue him. A great battle was fought; Bāṇa was aided by Śiva and by Skanda, god of war, the former of whom was overcome by Kṛishṇa, and the latter was wounded by Garuḍa and Pradyumna. Bāṇa was defeated, but his life was spared at the intercession of Śiva, and Aniruddha was carried home to Dwārakā with Ushā as his wife. He is also called Jhashānka and Ushā-pati. He had a son named Vajra.

ANJANA. 1. The elephant of the west or south-west quarter. 2. A serpent with many heads descended from Kadru.

ANJANĀ. Mother of Hanumat by Vāyu, god of the wind.

ANNA-PŪRṆA. 'Full of food.' A form of Durgā, worshipped for her power of giving food *Cf.* the Roman *Anna Perenna.*

ANŚUMAT, ANŚUMĀN. Son of Asamanjas and grandson of Sagara. He brought back to earth the horse which had been carried off from Sagara's Aśwa-medha sacrifice, and he discovered the remains of that king's sixty thousand sons, who had been killed by the fire of the wrath of Kapila.

ANTAKA. 'The ender.' A name of Yama, judge of the dead.

ANTARĪKSHA. The atmosphere or firmament between heaven and earth, the sphere of the Gandharvas, Apsarases, and Yakshas.

ANTARVEDĪ. The Doāb or country between the Ganges and the Jumna.

ANU. Son of King Yayāti by his wife Sarmish*th*ā, a Daitya princess. He refused to exchange his youthful vigour for the curse of decrepitude passed upon his father, and in consequence his father cursed him that his posterity should not possess dominion. Notwithstanding this, he had a long series of descendants, and among them were Anga, Banga, Kalinga, &c., who gave their names to the countries they dwelt in.

ANUKRAMA*N*I, ANUKRAMA*N*IKĀ. An index or table of contents, particularly of a Veda. The Anukrama*n*is of the Vedas follow the order of each Sanhitā, and assign a poet, a metre, and a deity to each hymn or prayer. There are several extant.

ANUMATI. The moon on its fifteenth day, when just short of its full. In this stage it is personified and worshipped as a goddess.

ANU*S*ARA. A Rākshasa or other demon.

ANUVINDA. A king of Ujjayinī. *See* Vinda.

APARĀNTA. 'On the western border.' A country which is named in the Vish*n*u Purā*n*a in association with countries in the north; and the Vāyu Purā*n*a reads the name as Aparita, which Wilson says is a northern nation. The Hari-van*s*a, however, mentions it as "a country conquered by Para*s*u-rāma from the ocean," and upon this the translator Langlois observes: "Tradition records that Para*s*u-rāma besought Varu*n*a, god of the sea, to grant him a land which he might bestow upon the Brāhmans in expiation of the blood of the Kshatriyas. Varu*n*a withdrew his waves from the heights of Gokar*n*a (near Mangalore) down to Cape Comorin" (*As. Researches*, v. 1). This agrees with the traditions concerning Para*s*u-rāma and Malabar, but it is not at all clear how a gift of territory to Brāhmans could expiate the slaughter of the Kshatriyas by a Brāhman and in behalf of Brāhmans.

APAR*N*Ā. According to the Hari-van*s*a, the eldest daughter of Himavat and Menā. She and her two sisters, Eka-par*n*ā and

Eka-pāṭalā, gave themselves up to austerity and practised extraordinary abstinence; but while her sisters lived, as their names denote, upon one leaf or on one pāṭalā (*Bignonia*) respectively, Aparṇā managed to subsist upon nothing, and even lived without a leaf (*a-parṇā*). This so distressed her mother that she cried out in deprecation, 'U-mā,' 'Oh, don't.' Aparṇā thus became the beautiful Umā, the wife of Śiva.

ĀPASTAMBA. An ancient writer on ritual and law, author of Sūtras connected with the Black Yajur-veda and of a Dharma-śāstra. He is often quoted in law-books. Two recensions of the Taittirīya Sanhitā are ascribed to him or his school. The Sūtras have been translated by Bühler, and are being reprinted in the *Sacred Books of the East* by Max Müller.

ĀPAVA. 'Who sports in the waters.' A name of the same import as Nārāyaṇa, and having a similar though not an identical application. According to the Brahma Purāṇa and the Hari-vanśa, Āpava performed the office of the creator Brahmā, and divided himself into two parts, male and female, the former begetting offspring upon the latter. The result was the production of Vishṇu, who created Virāj, who brought the first man into the world. According to the Mahā-bhārata, Āpava is a name of the Prajāpati Vasishṭha. The name of Āpava is of late introduction and has been vaguely used. Wilson says: "According to the commentator, the first stage was the creation of Āpava or Vasishṭha or Virāj by Vishṇu, through the agency of Brahmā, and the next was that of the creation of Manu by Virāj."

APSARAS. The Apsarases are the celebrated nymphs of Indra's heaven. The name, which signifies 'moving in the water,' has some analogy to that of Aphrodite. They are not prominent in the Vedas, but Urvaśī and a few others are mentioned. In Manu they are said to be the creations of the seven Manus. In the epic poems they become prominent, and the Rāmāyaṇa and the Purāṇas attribute their origin to the churning of the ocean. (*See* Amṛita.) It is said that when they came forth from the waters neither the gods nor the Asuras would have them for wives, so they became common to all. They have the appellations of Surānganās, 'wives of the gods,' and Sumad-ātmajās, 'daughters of pleasure.'

> "Then from the agitated deep up sprung
> The legion of Apsarases, so named

That to the watery element they owed
Their being. Myriads were they born, and all
In vesture heavenly clad, and heavenly gems:
Yet more divine their native semblance, rich
With all the gifts of grace, of youth and beauty.
A train innumerous followed ; yet thus fair,
Nor god nor demon sought their wedded love:
Thus Rāghava! they still remain—their charms
The common treasure of the host of heaven."
—(*Rāmāyana*) WILSON.

In the Purā*n*as various ga*n*ās or classes of them are mentioned with distinctive names. The Vāyu Purā*n*a enumerates fourteen, the Hari-van*s*a seven classes. They are again distinguished as being *daivika*, 'divine,' or *laukika*, 'worldly.' The former are said to be ten in number and the latter thirty-four, and these are the heavenly charmers who fascinated heroes, as Urva*s*ī, and allured austere sages from their devotions and penances, as Menakā and Rambhā. The Kā*s*ī-kha*n*da says "there are thirty-five millions of them, but only one thousand and sixty are the principal." The Apsarases, then, are fairylike beings, beautiful and voluptuous. They are the wives or the mistresses of the Gandharvas, and are not prudish in the dispensation of their favours. Their amours on earth have been numerous, and they are the rewards in Indra's paradise held out to heroes who fall in battle. They have the power of changing their forms; they are fond of dice, and give luck to whom they favour. In the Atharva-veda they are not so amiable; they are supposed to produce madness (love's madness?), and so there are charms and incantations for use against them. There is a long and exhaustive article on the Apsarases in Goldstücker's *Dictionary*, from which much of the above has been adapted. As regards their origin he makes the following speculative observations:—"Originally these divinities seem to have been personifications of the vapours which are attracted by the sun and form into mist or clouds; their character may be thus interpreted in the few hymns of the *R*ig-veda where mention is made of them. At a subsequent period . . . (their attributes expanding with those of their associates the Gandharvas), they became divinities which represent phenomena or objects both of a physical and ethical kind closely associated with that life" (the elementary life of heaven).

ĀRA*N*YAKA. 'Belonging to the forest.' Certain religious

and philosophical writings which expound the mystical sense of the ceremonies, discuss the nature of God, &c. They are attached to the Brāhmanas, and intended for study in the forest by Brāhmans who have retired from the distractions of the world. There are four of them extant: 1. Brihad; 2. Taittirīya; 3. Aitareya; and 4. Kaushītaki Āranyaka. The Āranyakas are closely connected with the Upanishads, and the names are occasionally used interchangeably: thus the Brihad is called indifferently Brihad Āranyaka or Brihad Āranyaka Upanishad; it is attached to the Satapatha Brāhmana. The Aitareya Upanishad is a part of the Aitareya Brāhmana, and the Kaushītaki Āranyaka consists of three chapters, of which the third is the Kaushītaki Upanishad. "Traces of modern ideas (says Max Müller) are not wanting in the Āranyakas, and the very fact that they are destined for a class of men who had retired from the world in order to give themselves up to the contemplation of the highest problems, shows an advanced and already declining and decaying society, not unlike the monastic age of the Christian world." "In one sense the Āranyakas are old, for they reflect the very dawn of thought; in another they are modern, for they speak of that dawn with all the experience of a past day. There are passages in these works unequalled in any language for grandeur, boldness, and simplicity. These passages are the relics of a better age. But the generation which became the chronicler of those Titanic wars of thought was a small race; they were dwarfs, measuring the footsteps of departed giants."

ARANYĀNĪ. In the Rig-veda, the goddess of woods and forests.

ARBUDA. Mount Ābu. Name of the people living in the vicinity of that mountain.

ARBUDA. 'A serpent.' Name of an Asura slain by Indra.

ARDHA-NĀRĪ. 'Half-woman.' A form in which Siva is represented as half-male and half-female, typifying the male and female energies. There are several stories accounting for this form. It is called also Ardhanārīsa and Parāngada.

ARISHTA. A Daitya, and son of Bali, who attacked Krishna in the form of a savage bull, and was slain by him.

ARJUNA. 'White.' The name of the third Pāndu prince. All the five brothers were of divine paternity, and Arjuna's father was Indra, hence he is called Aindri. A brave warrior, high-minded, generous, upright, and handsome, the most prominent and the most amiable and interesting of the five brothers. He was taught the use of arms by Drona, and was his favourite pupil. By his skill in arms he won Draupadi at her Swayamvara. For an involuntary transgression he imposed upon himself twelve years' exile from his family, and during that time he visited Parasu-rāma, who gave him instruction in the use of arms. He at this period formed a connection with Ulūpī, a Nāga princess, and by her had a son named Irāvat. He also married Chitrāngadā, the daughter of the king of Manipura, by whom he had a son named Babhru-vāhana. He visited Krishna at Dwārakā, and there he married Su-bhadrā, the sister of Krishna. (*See* Su-bhadrā.) By her he had a son named Abhimanyu. Afterwards he obtained the bow Gāndīva from the god Āgni, with which to fight against Indra, and he assisted Āgni in burning the Khāndava forest. When Yudhi-shthira lost the kingdom by gambling, and the five brothers went into exile for thirteen years, Arjuna proceeded on a pilgrimage to the Himālayas to propitiate the gods, and to obtain from them celestial weapons for use in the contemplated war against the Kauravas. There he fought with Siva, who appeared in the guise of a Kirāta or mountaineer; but Arjuna, having found out the true character of his adversary, worshipped him, and Siva gave him the pāsupata, one of his most powerful weapons. Indra, Varuna, Yama, and Kuvera came to him, and also presented him with their own peculiar weapons. Indra, his father, carried him in his car to his heaven and to his capital Amarāvatī, where Arjuna spent some years in the practice of arms. Indra sent him against the Daityas of the sea, whom he vanquished, and then returned victorious to Indra, who "presented him with a chain of gold and a diadem, and with a war-shell which sounded like thunder." In the thirteenth year of exile he entered the service of Rāja Virāta, disguised as a eunuch, and acted as music and dancing master, but in the end he took a leading part in defeating the king's enemies, the king of Trigarta and the Kaurava princes, many of whose leading warriors he vanquished in single combat. Preparations for the great struggle with the Kauravas now began. Arjuna obtained the personal assistance of Krishna, who acted as his charioteer, and, before the great battle began, related to him the Bhagavad-gītā. On the tenth day of the battle he mortally wounded Bhīshma; on the twelfth he defeated Susarman and his four brothers; on the fourteenth he killed Jayadratha; on the seventeenth, he was so stung by some reproaches of his brother, Yudhi-sh*t*hira, that he would have killed him had not K*ri*sh*n*a interposed. On the same day he fought with Kar*n*a, who had made a vow to slay him. He was near being vanquished when an accident to Kar*n*a's chariot gave Arjuna the opportunity of killing him. After the defeat of the Kauravas, A*s*watthāman, son of Dro*n*a, and two others, who were the sole survivors, made a night attack on the camp of the Pa*nd*avas, and murdered their children. Arjuna pursued A*s*watthāman, and made him give up the precious jewel which he wore upon his head as an amulet. When the horse intended for Yudhi-sh*t*hira's A*s*wa-medha sacrifice was let loose, Arjuna, with his army, followed it through many cities and countries, and fought with many Rājas. He entered the country of Trigarta, and had to fight his way through. He fought also against Vajradatta, who had a famous elephant, and against the Saindhavas. At the city of Ma*n*ipura he fought with his own son, Babhrū-vāhana, and was killed; but he was restored to life by a Nāga charm supplied by his wife Ulūpī. Afterwards he penetrated into the Dakshi*n*a or south country, and fought with the Nishādas and Drāvi*d*ians: then went westwards to Gujarāt, and finally conducted the horse back to Hastināpura, where the great sacrifice was performed. He was subsequently called to Dwārakā by K*ri*sh*n*a amid the internecine struggles of the Yādavas, and there he performed the funeral ceremonies of Vasudeva and of K*ri*sh*n*a. Soon after this he retired from the world to the Himālayas. (*See* Mahā-bhārata.) He had a son named Irāvat by the serpent nymph Ulūpī; Babhru-vāhana, by the daughter of the king of Ma*n*ipura, became king of that country; Abhimanyu, born of his wife Su-bhadrā, was killed in the great battle, but the kingdom of Hastināpura descended to his son Parīkshit. Arjuna has many appellations: Bībhatsu, Gu*d*ā-ke*s*a, Dhananjaya, Jish*n*u, Kirī*t*in, Pāka-*s*ā*s*ani, Phālguna, Savya-sāchin, *S*weta-vāhana, and Pārtha.

ARJUNA. Son of K*ri*ta-vīrya, king of the Haihayas. He is better known under his patronymic Kārta-vīrya (q.v.).

ARTHA-*S*ĀSTRA. The useful arts. Mechanical science.

ARU*N*A. 'Red, rosy.' The dawn, personified as the charioteer of the sun. This is of later origin than the Vedic Ushas (q.v.). He is said to be the son of Kasyapa and Kadru. He is also called Rumra, 'tawny,' and by two epithets of which the meaning is not obvious, An-uru, 'thighless,' and Āsmana, 'stony.'

ARUNDHATĪ. The morning star, personified as the wife of the *Ri*shi Vasish*th*a, and a model of conjugal excellence.

ARUSHA, ARUSHĪ. 'Red.' 'A red horse.' In the *Rig*-veda the red horses or mares of the sun or of fire. The rising sun.

ARVAN, ARVĀ. 'A horse.' One of the horses of the moon. A fabulous animal, half-horse, half-bird, on which the Daityas are supposed to ride.

ARVĀVASU. *See* Raibhya.

ĀRYA, ĀRYAN. 'Loyal, faithful.' The name of the immigrant race from which all that is Hindu originated. The name by which the people of the *Rig*-veda "called men of their own stock and religion, in contradistinction to the Dasyus (or Dasas), a term by which we either understand hostile demons or the rude aboriginal tribes" of India, who were An-āryas.

ĀRYA-BHA*T*A. The earliest known Hindu writer on algebra, and, according to Colebrooke, "if not the inventor, the improver of that analysis," which has made but little advance in India since. He was born, according to his own account, at Kusuma-pura (Patna), in A.D. 476, and composed his first astronomical work at the early age of twenty-three. His larger work, the *Ārya Siddhānta*, was produced at a riper age. He is probably the Andubarius (Ardubarius?) of the *Chronichon Paschale*, and the Arjabahr of the Arabs. Two of his works, the *Dasāgīti-sūtra* and *Āryāshtasata*, have been edited by Kern under the title of Āryabha*t*īya. See Whitney in *Jour. Amer. Or. Society* for 1860, Dr. Bhau Dājī in *J. R. A. S.* for 1865, and Barth in *Revue Critique* for 1875. There is another and later astronomer of the same name, distinguished as Laghu Ārya-bha*t*a, *i.e.*, Ārya-bha*t*a the Less.

ARYAMAN. 'A bosom friend.' 1. Chief of the Pit*ri*s. 2. One of the Ādityas. 3. One of the Viswe-devas.

ĀRYA SIDDHĀNTA. The system of astronomy founded by Ārya-bha*t*a in his work bearing this name.

ĀRYĀVARTA. 'The land of the Āryas.' The tract between the Himālaya and the Vindhya ranges, from the eastern to the western sea.—*Manu.*

ASAMANJAS. Son of Sagara and Kesinī. He was a wild and wicked young man, and was abandoned by his father, but he succeeded him as king, and, according to the Hari-vansa, he was afterwards famous for valour under the name of Panchajana.

ĀSANGA. Author of some verses in the *Rig*-veda. He was son of Playoga, but was changed into a woman by the curse of the gods. He recovered his male form by repentance and the favour of the *Ri*shi Medhātithi, to whom he gave abundant wealth, and addressed the verses preserved in the Veda.

Ā*S*ARA. A Rākshasa or other demon.

ASH*T*ĀVAKRA. A Brāhman, the son of Kaho*d*a, whose story is told in the Mahā-bhārata. Kaho*d*a married a daughter of his preceptor, Uddālaka, but he was so devoted to study that he neglected his wife. When she was far advanced in her pregnancy, the unborn son was provoked at his father's neglect of her, and rebuked him for it. Kaho*d*a was angry at the child's impertinence, and condemned him to be born crooked; so he came forth with his eight (*ashta*) limbs crooked (*vakra*); hence his name. Kaho*d*a went to a great sacrifice at the court of Janaka, king of Mithilā. There was present there a great Buddhist sage, who challenged disputations, upon the understanding that whoever was overcome in argument should be thrown into the river. This was the fate of many, and among them of Kaho*d*a, who was drowned. In his twelfth year Ashtāvakra learned the manner of his father's death, and set out to avenge him. The lad was possessed of great ability and wisdom. He got the better of the sage who had worsted his father, and insisted that the sage should be thrown into the water. The sage then declared himself to be a son of Varu*n*a, god of the waters, who had sent him to obtain Brāhmans for officiating at a sacrifice by overpowering them in argument and throwing them into the water. When all was explained and set right, Kaho*d*a directed his son to bathe in the Samangā river, on doing which the lad became perfectly straight. A story is told in the Vish*n*u Purā*n*a that Ashtāvakra was standing in water performing penances when he was seen by some celestial nymphs and worshipped by them. He was pleased, and told them to ask a boon. They asked for the best of men as a husband. He came out of the water and offered himself. When they saw him, ugly and crooked in eight places, they laughed in derision. He was angry, and as he could not recall his blessing, he said that, after obtaining it, they should fall into the hands of thieves.

ASIKNĪ. The Vedic name of the Chināb, and probably the origin of the classic Akesines.

A-*S*IRAS. 'Headless.' Spirits or beings without heads.

A*S*MAKA. Son of Madayantī, the wife of Kalmāsha-pāda or Saudāsa. See Kalmāsha-pāda.

A*S*OKA. A celebrated king of the Maurya dynasty of Magadha, and grandson of its founder, Chandra-gupta. "This king is the most celebrated of any in the annals of the Buddhists. In the commencement of his reign he followed the Brahmanical faith, but became a convert to that of Buddha, and a zealous encourager of it. He is said to have maintained in his palace 64,000 Buddhist priests, and to have erected 84,000 columns (or topes) throughout India. A great convocation of Buddhist priests was held in the eighteenth year of his reign, which was followed by missions to Ceylon and other places." He reigned thirty-six years, from about 234 to 198 B.C., and exercised authority more or less direct from Afghānistān to Ceylon. This fact is attested by a number of very curious Pāli inscriptions found engraven upon rocks and pillars, all of them of the same purport, and some of them almost identical in words, the variations showing little more than dialectic differences. That found at Kapur-di-giri, in Afghānistān, is in the Bactrian Pāli character, written from right to left; all the others are in the India Pāli character, written from left to right. The latter is the oldest known form of the character now in use in India, but the modern letters have departed so far from their prototypes that it required all the acumen and diligence of James Prinsep to decipher the ancient forms. These inscriptions show a great tenderness for animal life, and are Buddhist in their character, but they do not enter upon the distinctive peculiarities of that religion. The name of A*s*oka never occurs in them; the king who set them up is called Piyada*s*i (Sans. Priya-dar*s*ī), 'the beautiful,' and he is entitled Devānam-piya, 'the beloved of the gods.' Buddhist writings identify this Piyada*s*i with A*s*oka, and little or no doubt is entertained of the two names representing the same person. One of the most curious passages in these inscriptions refers to the Greek king Antiochus, calling him and three others "Turamāyo, Antakana, Mako, and Alikasunari," which represent Ptolemy, Antigonus, Magas, and Alexander. "The date of Asoka is not exactly that of Antiochus the Great, but it is not very far different; and the corrections required to make it correspond are no more than the inexact manner in which both Brahmanical and Buddhist chronology is preserved may well be expected to render necessary." See Wilson's note in the Vishnu Purāna, his article in the *Journal of the Royal Asiatic Society*, vol. xii., Max Müller's *Ancient Sanskrit Literature*, and an article by Sir E. Perry in vol. iii. of the *Journal of the Bombay Asiatic Society*.

ĀSRAMA. There are four stages in the life of a Brāhman which are called by this name. See Brāhman.

ĀSTĪKA. An ancient sage, son of Jarat-kāru by a sister of the great serpent Vāsuki. He saved the life of the serpent Takshaka when Janamejaya made his great sacrifice of serpents, and induced that king to forego his persecution of the serpent race.

ASURA. 'Spiritual, divine.' In the oldest parts of the *Ṛig-veda* this term is used for the supreme spirit, and is the same as the Ahura of the Zoroastrians. In the sense of 'god' it was applied to several of the chief deities, as to Indra, Agni, and Varuna. It afterwards acquired an entirely opposite meaning, and came to signify, as now, a demon or enemy of the gods. The word is found with this signification in the later parts of the *Ṛig*-veda, particularly in the last book, and also in the Atharva-veda. The Brāhmanas attach the same meaning to it, and record many contests between the Asuras and the gods. According to the Taittirīya Brāhmana, the breath (*asu*) of Prajāpati became alive, and "with that breath he created the Asuras." In another part of the same work it is said that Prajāpati "became pregnant. He created Asuras from his abdomen." The Satapatha Brāhmana accords with the former statement, and states that "he created Asuras from his lower breath." The Taittirīya Āranyaka represents that Prajāpati created "gods, men, fathers, Gandharvas, and Apsarases" from water, and that the Asuras, Rākshasas, and Pisāchas sprang from the drops which were spilt. Manu's statement is that they were created by the Prajāpatis. According to the Vishnu Purāna, they were produced from the groin of Brahmā (Prajāpati). The account of the Vāyu Purāna is: "Asuras were first produced as sons from his (Prajāpati's) groin. *Asu* is declared by Brāhmans to mean breath. From it these beings were produced; hence they are Asuras." The word has long been used as a general name for the enemies of the gods, including the Daityas and Dānavas and other descendants of Kasyapa, but not including the Rākshasas descended from Pulastya. In this sense a different derivation has been found for it: the source is no longer *asu*, 'breath,' but the initial *a* is taken as the negative prefix, and *a-sura* signifies 'not a god;' hence, according to some, arose the word *sura*, commonly used for 'a god.' *See* Sura.

ĀSURI. One of the earliest professors of the Sānkhya philosophy.

ĀSWALĀYANA. A celebrated writer of antiquity. He was pupil of Saunaka, and was author of Srauta-sūtras, Grihya-sūtras, and other works upon ritual, as well as founder of a Sākhā of the *Rig*-veda. The Sūtras have been published by Dr. Stenzler, and also in the *Bibliotheca Indica.*

ASWA-MEDHA. 'The sacrifice of a horse.' This is a sacrifice which, in Vedic times, was performed by kings desirous of offspring. The horse was killed with certain ceremonies, and the wives of the king had to pass the night by its carcase. Upon the chief wife fell the duty of going through a revolting formality which can only be hinted at. Subsequently, as in the time of the Mahā-bhārata, the sacrifice obtained a high importance and significance. It was performed only by kings, and implied that he who instituted it was a conqueror and king of kings. It was believed that the performance of one hundred such sacrifices would enable a mortal king to overthrow the throne of Indra, and to become the ruler of the universe and sovereign of the gods. A horse of a particular colour was consecrated by the performance of certain ceremonies, and was then turned loose to wander at will for a year. The king, or his representative, followed the horse with an army, and when the animal entered a foreign country, the ruler of that country was bound either to fight or to submit. If the liberator of the horse succeeded in obtaining or enforcing the submission of all the countries over which it passed, he returned in triumph with the vanquished Rājas in his train; but if he failed, he was disgraced and his pretensions ridiculed. After the successful return a great festival was held, at which the horse was sacrificed, either really or figuratively.

ASWA-MUKHA. 'Horse faced.' *See* Kinnara.

ASWA-PATI. 'Lord of horses.' An appellation of many kings.

ASWATTHĀMAN. Son of Drona and Kripā, and one of the generals of the Kauravas. Also called by his patronymic Draunāyana. After the last great battle, in which Dur-yodhana was mortally wounded, Aswatthāman with two other warriors, Kripa and Krita-varman, were the sole survivors of the Kaurava host that were left effective. Aswatthāman was made the commander. He was fierce in his hostility to the Pāndavas, and craved for revenge upon Dhrishta-dyumna, who had slain his father, Drona. These three surviving Kauravas entered the Pāndava camp at night. They found Dhrishta-dyumna asleep, and Aswatthāman stamped him to death as he lay. He then killed Sikhandin, the other son of Drupada, and he also killed the five young sons of the Pāndavas and carried their heads to the dying Dur-yodhana. He killed Parikshit, while yet unborn in the womb of his mother, with his celestial weapon Brahmāstra, by which he incurred the curse of Krishna, who restored Parikshit to life. On the next morning he and his comrades fled, but Draupadī clamoured for revenge upon the murderer of her children. Yudhi-shthira represented that Aswatthāman was a Brāhman, and pleaded for his life. She then consented to forego her demand for his blood if the precious and protective jewel which he wore on his head were brought to her. Bhīma, Arjuna, and Krishna then went in pursuit of him. Arjuna and Krishna overtook him, and compelled him to give up the jewel. They carried it to Draupadī, and she gave it to Yudhi-shthira, who afterwards wore it on his head.

ASWINS, ASWINAU (dual), ASWINĪ KUMĀRAS. 'Horsemen.' Dioskouroi. Two Vedic deities, twin sons of the sun or the sky. They are ever young and handsome, bright, and of golden brilliancy, agile, swift as falcons, and possessed of many forms; and they ride in a golden car drawn by horses or birds, as harbingers of Ushas, the dawn. "They are the earliest bringers of light in the morning sky, who in their chariot hasten onwards before the dawn and prepare the way for her."—*Roth.* As personifications of the morning twilight, they are said to be children of the sun by a nymph who concealed herself in the form of a mare; hence she was called Aswinī and her sons Aswins. But inasmuch as they precede the rise of the sun, they are called his parents in his form Pūshan. Mythically they are the parents of the Pā*nd*u princes Nakula and Sahadeva. Their attributes are numerous, but relate mostly to youth and beauty, light and speed, duality, the curative power, and active benevolence. The number of hymns addressed to them testify to the enthusiastic worship they received. They were the physicians of Swarga, and in this character are called Dasras and Nāsatyas, Gadāgadau and Swar-vaidyau; or one was Dasra and the other Nāsatya. Other of their appellations are Abdhijau, 'ocean born;' Pushkara-srajau, 'wreathed with lotuses;' Bā*d*aveyau, sons of the submarine fire, Bā*d*ava. Many instances are recorded of their benevolence and their power of healing. They restored the sage Chyavana to youth, and prolonged his life when he had become old and decrepit, and through his instrumentality they were admitted to partake of the libations of soma, like the other gods, although Indra strongly opposed them. (*See* Chyavana.) The A*s*wins, says Muir, "have been a puzzle to the oldest commentators," who have differed widely in their explanations. According to different interpretations quoted in the Nirukta, they were "heaven and earth," "day and night," "two kings, performers of holy acts." The following is the view taken of them by the late Professor Goldstücker, as printed in Muir's *Texts*, vol. v. :—

"The myth of the A*s*wins is, in my opinion, one of that class of myths in which two distinct elements, the cosmical and the human or historical, have gradually become blended into one. It seems necessary, therefore, to separate these two elements in order to arrive at an understanding of the myth. The historical or human element in it, I believe, is represented by those legends which refer to the wonderful cures effected by the A*s*wins, and to their performances of a kindred sort; the cosmical element is that relating to their luminous nature. The link which connects both seems to be the mysteriousness of the nature and effects of the phenomena of light and of the healing art at a remote antiquity. That there might have been some horsemen or warriors of great renown, who inspired their contemporaries with awe by their wonderful deeds, and more especially by their medical skill, appears to have been also the opinion of some old commentators mentioned by Yāska [in the Nirukta], for some 'legendary writers,' he says, took them for 'two kings, performers of holy acts,' and this view seems likewise borne out by the legend in which it is narrated that the gods refused the A*s*wins admittance to a sacrifice on the ground that they had been on too familiar terms with men. It would appear, then, that these A*s*wins, like the *Ri*bhus, were originally renowned mortals, who, in the course of time, were translated into the companionship of the gods. . . .

"The luminous character of the A*s*wins can scarcely be matter of doubt, for the view of some commentators, recorded by Yāska, according to which they are identified with 'heaven and earth,' appears not to be countenanced by any of the passages known to us. Their very name, it would seem, settles this point, since A*s*wa, the horse, literally 'the pervader,' is always the symbol of the luminous deities, especially of the sun. . . .

"It seems to be the opinion of Yāska that the A*s*wins represent the transition from darkness to light, when the intermingling of both produces that inseparable duality expressed by the twin nature of these deities. And this interpretation, I hold, is the best that can be given of the character of the cosmical A*s*wins. It agrees with the epithets by which they are invoked, and with the relationship in which they are placed. They are young, yet also ancient, beautiful, bright, swift, &c.; and their negative character, the result of the alliance of light with darkness, is, I believe, expressed by *dasra*, the destroyer, and also by the two negatives in the compound *nāsatya* (na + a-satya); though their positive character is again redeemed by the ellipsis of 'enemies, or diseases' to *dasra*, and by the sense of *nāsatya*, not untrue, *i.e.*, truthful."

ATHARVA, ATHARVAN. The fourth Veda. *See* Veda.

ATHARVAN. Name of a priest mentioned in the *Rig*-veda, where he is represented as having "drawn forth" fire and to have "offered sacrifice in early times." He is mythologically represented as the eldest son of Brahmā, to whom that god revealed the Brahma-vidyā (knowledge of God), as a Prajāpati, and as the inspired author of the fourth Veda. At a later period he is identified with Angiras. His descendants are called Atharvanas, and are often associated with the Angirasas.

ATHARVĀNGIRASAS. This name belongs to the descendants of Atharvan and Angiras, or to the Angirasas alone, who are especially connected with the Atharva-veda, and these names are probably given to the hymns of that Veda to confer on them greater authority and holiness.

ĀTMA-BODHA. 'Knowledge of the soul.' A short work attributed to *S*ankarāchārya. It has been printed, and a translation of it was published in 1812 by Taylor. There is a French version by Néve and an English translation by Kearns in the *Indian Antiquary*, vol. v.

ĀTMAN, ĀTMA. The soul. The principle of life. The supreme soul.

ĀTREYA. A patronymic from Atri. A son or descendant of Atri; a people so called.

ATRI. 'An eater.' A *R*ishi, and author of many Vedic hymns. "A Maharshi or great saint, who in the Vedas occurs especially in hymns composed for the praise of Agni, Indra, the A*s*wins, and the Vi*s*wa-devas. In the epic period he is considered as one of the ten Prajāpatis or lords of creation engendered by Manu for the purpose of creating the universe; at a later period he appears as a mind-born son of Brahmā, and as one of the seven *R*ishis who preside over the reign of Swāyambhuva, the first Manu, or, according to others, of Swārochisha, the second, or of Vaivaswata, the seventh. He married Anasūyā, daughter of Daksha, and their son was Durvāsas."—*Goldstücker*. In the Rāmāya*n*a an account is given of the visit paid by Rāma and Sītā to Atri and Anasūyā in their hermitage south of Chitrakū*t*a. In the Purā*n*as he was also father of Soma, the moon, and the ascetic Dattātreya by his wife Anasūyā. As a *R*ishi he is one of the stars of the Great Bear.

AURVA. A *R*ishi, son of Urva and grandson of Bh*ri*gu. He is described in the Mahā-bhārata as son of the sage Chyavana by his wife Ārushī. From his race he is called Bhārgava. The Mahā-bhārata relates that a king named K*ri*ta-vīrya was very liberal to his priests of the race of Bh*ri*gu, and that they grew rich upon his munificence. After his death, his descendants, who had fallen into poverty, begged help from the Bh*ri*gus, and met with no liberal response. Some of them buried their money, and when this was discovered the impoverished Kshatriyas were so exasperated that they slew all the Bh*ri*gus down to the children in the womb. One woman concealed her unborn child in her thigh, and the Kshatriyas being informed of this, sought the child to kill it, but the child "issued forth from its mother's thigh with lustre and blinded the persecutors. From being produced from the thigh (*uru*), the child received the name of Aurva. The sage's austerities alarmed both gods and men, and he for a long time refused to mitigate his wrath against the Kshatriyas, but at the persuasion of the Pit*ri*s, he cast the fire of his anger into the sea, where it became a being with the face of a horse called Haya-*s*iras. While he was living in the forest he prevented the wife of King Bāhu from burning herself with her husband's corpse. Thus he saved the life of her son, with whom she had been pregnant seven years. When the child was born he was called Sagara (ocean); Aurva was his preceptor, and bestowed on him the Āgneyāstra, or fiery weapon with which he conquered the barbarians who invaded his country. Aurva had a son named *Ri*chīka, who was father of Jamadagni. The Hari-van*s*a gives another version of the legend about the offspring of Aurva. The sage was urged by his friends to beget children. He consented, but he foretold that his progeny would live by the destruction of others. Then he produced from his thigh a devouring fire, which cried out with a loud voice, "I am hungry; let me consume the world." The various regions were soon in flames, when Brahmā interfered to save his creation, and promised the son of Aurva a suitable abode and maintenance. The abode was to be at Ba*d*avā-mukha, the mouth of the ocean; for Brahmā was born and rests in the ocean, and he and the newly produced fire were to consume the world together at the end of each age, and at the end of time to devour all things with the gods, Asuras, and Rākshasas. The name Aurva thus signifies, shortly, the submarine fire. It is also called Ba*d*avānala and Samvarttaka. It is represented as a flame with a horse's head, and is also called Kāka-dhwaja, from carrying a banner on which there is a crow.

AU*S*ANA, or AU*S*ANASA PURĀ*N*A. *See* Purā*n*a.

AUTTAMI. The third Manu. *See* Manu.

AVANTĪ, AVANTIKĀ. A name of Ujjayinī, one of the seven sacred cities.

AVATĀRA. 'A descent.' The incarnation of a deity, especially of Vish*n*u. The first indication, not of an Avatāra, but of what subsequently developed into an Avatāra, is found in the *Ri*g-veda in the "three steps" of "Vish*n*u, the unconquerable preserver," who "strode over this (universe)," and "in three places planted his step." The early commentators understood the "three places" to be the earth, the atmosphere, and the sky; that in the earth Vishnu was fire, in the air lightning, and in the sky the solar light. One commentator, Aurnavābha, whose name deserves mention, took a more philosophical view of the matter, and interpreted "the three steps" as being "the different positions of the sun at his rising, culmination, and setting." Sāyana, the great commentator, who lived in days when the god Vishnu had obtained pre-eminence, understood "the three steps" to be "the three steps" taken by that god in his incarnation of Vāmana the dwarf, to be presently noticed. Another reference to "three strides" and to a sort of Avatāra is made in the Taittirīya Sanhitā, where it is said, "Indra, assuming the form of a she-jackal, stepped all round the earth in three (strides). Thus the gods obtained it."

Boar Incarnation.—In the Taittirīya Sanhitā and Brāhmana, and also in the Satapatha Brāhmana, the creator Prajāpati, afterwards known as Brahmā, took the form of a boar for the purpose of raising the earth out of the boundless waters. The Sanhitā says, "This universe was formerly waters, fluid. On it Prajāpati, becoming wind, moved. He saw this (earth). Becoming a boar, he took her up. Becoming Viswakarman, he wiped (the moisture from) her. She extended. She became the extended one (Prithvī). From this the earth derives her designation as 'the extended one.'" The Brāhmana is in accord as to the illimitable waters, and adds, "Prajāpati practised arduous devotion (saying), How shall this universe be (developed)? He beheld a lotus leaf standing. He thought, There is somewhat on which this (lotus leaf) rests. He, as a boar—having assumed that form—plunged beneath towards it. He found the earth down below. Breaking off (a portion of her), he rose to the surface. He then extended it on the lotus leaf. Inasmuch as he extended it, that is the extension of the extended one (the earth). This became (*abhūt*). From this the earth derives its name of Bhūmi." Further, in the Taittirīya Āranyaka it is said that the earth was "raised by a black boar with a hundred arms." The Satapatha Brāhmana states, "She (the earth) was only so large, of the size of a span. A boar called Emūsha raised her up. Her lord, Prajāpati, in consequence prospers him with this pair and makes him complete." In the Rāmāyana also it is stated that Brahmā "bebecame a boar and raised up the earth."

Kūrma or Tortoise.—In the Satapatha Brāhmana it is said that "Prajāpati, having assumed the form of a tortoise (*kūrma*), created offspring. That which he created he made (*akarot*); hence the word Kūrma."

Fish Incarnation.—The earliest mention of the fish Avatāra occurs in the Satapatha Brāhmana, in connection with the Hindu legend of the deluge. Manu found, in the water which was brought to him for his ablutions, a small fish, which spoke to him and said, "I will save thee" from a flood which shall sweep away all creatures. This fish grew to a large size, and had to be consigned to the ocean, when he directed Manu to construct a ship and to resort to him when the flood should rise. The deluge came, and Manu embarked in the ship. The fish then swam to Manu, who fastened the vessel to the fish's horn, and was conducted to safety. The Mahā-bhārata repeats this story with some variations.

The incarnations of the boar, the tortoise, and the fish are thus in the earlier writings represented as manifestations of Prajāpati or Brahmā. The "three steps" which form the germ of the dwarf incarnation are ascribed to Vishnu, but even these appear to be of an astronomical or mythical character rather than glorifications of a particular deity. In the Mahā-bhārata Vishnu has become the most prominent of the gods, and some of his incarnations are more or less distinctly noticed; but it is in the Purānas that they receive their full development. According to the generally received account, the incarnations of Vishnu are ten in number, each of them being assumed by Vishnu, the great preserving power, to save the world from some great danger or trouble.

1. Matsya. 'The fish.' This is an appropriation to Vishnu of the ancient legend of the fish and the deluge, as related in the Satapatha Brāhmana, and quoted above. The details of this Avatāra vary slightly in different Purānas. The object of the incarnation was to save Vaivaswata, the seventh Manu, and progenitor of the human race, from destruction by a deluge. A small fish came into the hands of Manu and besought his protection. He carefully guarded it, and it grew rapidly until

nothing but the ocean could contain it. Manu then recognised its divinity, and worshipped the deity Vish*n*u thus incarnate. The god apprised Manu of the approaching cataclysm, and bade him prepare for it. When it came, Manu embarked in a ship with the *R*ishis, and with the seeds of all existing things. Vish*n*u then appeared as the fish with a most stupendous horn. The ship was bound to this horn with the great serpent as with a rope, and was secured in safety until the waters had subsided. The Bhāgavata Purā*n*a introduces a new feature. In one of the nights of Brahmā, and during his repose, the earth and the other worlds were submerged in the ocean. Then the demon Haya-grīva drew near, and carried off the Veda which had issued from Brahmā's mouth. To recover the Veda thus lost, Vish*n*u assumed the form of a fish, and saved Manu as above related. But this Purā*n*a adds, that the fish instructed Manu and the *R*ishis in "the true doctrine of the soul of the eternal Brahmā;" and, when Brahmā awoke at the end of this dissolution of the universe, Vish*n*u slew Haya-grīva and restored the Veda to Brahmā.

2. Kūrma. 'The tortoise.' The germ of this Avatāra is found in the *S*atapatha Brāhma*n*a, as above noticed. In its later and developed form, Vish*n*u appeared in the form of a tortoise in the Satya-yuga, or first age, to recover some things of value which had been lost in the deluge. In the form of a tortoise he placed himself at the bottom of the sea of milk, and made his back the base or pivot of the mountain Mandara. The gods and demons twisted the great serpent Vāsuki round the mountain, and, dividing into two parties, each took an end of the snake as a rope, and thus churned the sea until they recovered the desired objects. These were—(1.) Am*r*ita, the water of life; (2.) Dhanwantari, the physician of the gods and bearer of the cup of Am*r*ita; (3.) Lakshmī, goddess of fortune and beauty, and consort of Vish*n*u; (4.) Surā, goddess of wine; (5.) Chandra, the moon; (6.) Rambhā, a nymph, and pattern of a lovely and amiable woman; (7.) Uchchai*h*-*s*ravas, a wonderful and model horse; (8.) Kaustubha, a celebrated jewel; (9.) Pārijāta, a celestial tree; (10.) Surabhi, the cow of plenty; (11.) Airāvata, a wonderful model elephant; (12.) *S*ankha, a shell, the conch of victory; (13.) Dhanus, a famous bow; and (14.) Visha, poison.

3. Varāha. 'The boar.' The old legend of the Brāhmanas concerning the boar which raised the earth from the waters has been appropriated to Vishnu. A demon named Hiranyāksha had dragged the earth to the bottom of the sea. To recover it Vishnu assumed the form of a boar, and after a contest of a thousand years he slew the demon and raised up the earth.

4. Nara-sinha, or Nri-sinha. 'The man-lion.' Vishnu assumed this form to deliver the world from the tyranny of Hiranya-kasipu, a demon who, by the favour of Brahmā, had become invulnerable, and was secure from gods, men, and animals. This demon's son, named Prahlāda, worshipped Vishnu, which so incensed his father that he tried to kill him, but his efforts were all in vain. Contending with his son as to the omnipotence and omnipresence of Vishnu, Hiranya-kasipu demanded to know if Vishnu was present in a stone pillar of the hall, and struck it violently. To avenge Prahlāda, and to vindicate his own offended majesty, Vishnu came forth from the pillar as the Nara-sinha, half-man and half-lion, and tore the arrogant Daitya king to pieces.

These four incarnations are supposed to have appeared in the Satya-yuga, or first age of the world.

5. Vāmana. 'The dwarf.' The origin of this incarnation is "the three strides of Vishnu," spoken of in the *Rig*-veda, as before explained. In the Tretā-yuga, or second age, the Daitya king Bali had, by his devotions and austerities, acquired the dominion of the three worlds, and the gods were shorn of their power and dignity. To remedy this, Vishnu was born as a diminutive son of Kasyapa and Aditi. The dwarf appeared before Bali, and begged of him as much land as he could step over in three paces. The generous monarch complied with the request. Vishnu took two strides over heaven and earth; but respecting the virtues of Bali, he then stopped, leaving the dominion of Pātāla, or the infernal regions, to Bali.

The first five incarnations are thus purely mythological; in the next three we have the heroic element, and in the ninth the religious.

6. Parasu-rāma. 'Rāma with the axe.' Born in the Tretā, or second age, as son of the Brāhman Jamadagni, to deliver the Brāhmans from the arrogant dominion of the Kshatriyas. See Parasu-Rāma.

7. Rāma or Rāma-chandra. 'The moon-like or gentle Rāma,' the hero of the Rāmāyana. He was the son of Dasaratha, king of Ayodhyā, of the Solar race, and was born in the Treta-yuga, or second age, for the purpose of destroying the demon Rāvana.

8. Krishna. 'The black or dark coloured.' This is the most popular of all the later deities, and has obtained such pre-eminence, that his votaries look upon him not simply as an incarnation, but as a perfect manifestation of Vishnu. When Krishna is thus exalted to the full godhead, his elder brother, Bala-rāma takes his place as the eighth Avatāra. *See* Krishna and Bala-rāma.

9. Buddha. The great success of Buddha as a religious teacher seems to have induced the Brāhmans to adopt him as their own, rather than to recognise him as an adversary. So Vishnu is said to have appeared as Buddha to encourage demons and wicked men to despise the Vedas, reject caste, and deny the existence of the gods, and thus to effect their own destruction.

10. Kalkī or Kalkin. 'The white horse.' This incarnation of Vishnu is to appear at the end of the Kali or Iron Age, seated on a white horse, with a drawn sword blazing like a comet, for the final destruction of the wicked, the renovation of creation, and the restoration of purity.

The above are the usually recognised Avatāras, but the number is sometimes extended, and the Bhāgavata Purāna, which is the most fervid of all the Purānas in its glorification of Vishnu, enumerates twenty-two incarnations:—(1.) Purusha, the male, the progenitor; (2.) Varāha, the boar; (3.) Nārada, the great sage; (4.) Nara and Nārāyana (q.v.); (5.) Kapila, the great sage; (6.) Dattātreya, a sage; (7.) Yajna, sacrifice; (8.) Rishabha, a righteous king, father of Bharata; (9.) Prithu, a king; (10.) Matsya, the fish; (11.) Kūrma, the tortoise; (12 and 13.) Dhanwantari, the physician of the gods; (14.) Nara-sinha, the man-lion; (15.) Vāmana, the dwarf; (16.) Parasu-rāma; (17.) Veda-Vyāsa; (18.) Rāma; (19.) Bala-rāma; (20.) Krishna; (21.) Buddha; (22.) Kalkī. But after this it adds—"The incarnations of Vishnu are innumerable, like the rivulets flowing from an inexhaustible lake. Rishis, Manus, gods, sons of Manus, Prajāpatis, are all portions of him."

AVATĀRANA. An abode of the Rākshasas.

AYODHYĀ. The modern Oude. The capital of Ikshwāku,

the founder of the Solar race, and afterwards the capital of Rāma. It is one of the seven sacred cities. The exact site has not been discovered.

ĀYUR-VEDA. 'The Veda of life.' A work on medicine, attributed to Dhanwantari, and sometimes regarded as a supplement to the Atharva-veda.

AYUS. The first-born son of Purūravas and Urvasī, and the father of Nahusha, Kshattra-vriddha, Rambha, Raji, and Anenas.

BABHRŪ-VĀHANA. Son of Arjuna by his wife Chitrāngadā. He was adopted as the son of his maternal grandfather, and reigned at Manipura as his successor. He dwelt there in a palace of great splendour, surrounded with wealth and signs of power. When Arjuna went to Manipura with the horse intended for the Aswa-medha, there was a quarrel between Arjuna and King Babhrū-vāhana, and the latter killed his father with an arrow. Repenting of his deed, he determined to kill himself, but he obtained from his step-mother, the Nāga princess Ulūpī, a gem which restored Arjuna to life. He returned with his father to Hastināpura. The description of this combat has been translated from the Mahā-bhārata by Troyer in his *Rāja Taranginī*, tome i. p. 578.

BĀDARĀYANA. A name of Veda Vyāsa, especially used for him as the reputed author of the Vedānta philosophy. He was the author of the Brahma Sūtras, published in the *Bibliotheca Indica.*

BADARĪ, BADARĪKĀSRAMA. A place sacred to Vishnu, near the Ganges in the Himālayas, particularly in Vishnu's dual form of Nara-Nārāyana. Thus, in the Mahā-bhārata, Siva, addressing Arjuna, says, "Thou wast Nara in a former body, and, with Nārāyana for thy companion, didst perform dreadful austerity at Badarī for many myriads of years." It is now known as Badarī-nātha, though this is properly a title of Vishnu as lord of Badarī.

BADAVĀ. 'A mare, the submarine fire.' In mythology it is a flame with the head of a horse, called also Haya-siras, 'horse-head.' *See* Aurva.

BĀHĪKAS. People of the Panjāb, so called in Pānini and the Mahā-bhārata. They are spoken of as being impure and out of the law.

BĀHU, BĀHUKA. A king of the Solar race, who was vanquished and driven out of his country by the tribes of Haihayas and Tālajanghas. He was father of Sagara.

BĀHUKA. The name of Nala when he was transformed into a dwarf.

BAHULĀS. The K*ri*ttikās or Pleiades.

BAHV*RI*CHA. A priest or theologian of the *Rig*-veda.

BALA-BHADRA. *See* Bala-rāma.

BĀLA-GOPĀLA. The boy K*ri*sh*n*a.

BALA-RĀMA. (Bala-bhadra and Bala-deva are other forms of this name.) The elder brother of K*ri*sh*n*a. When K*ri*sh*n*a is regarded as a full manifestation of Vish*n*u, Bala-rāma is recognised as the seventh Avatāra or incarnation in his place. According to this view, which is the favourite one of the Vaish*n*avas, K*ri*sh*n*a is a full divinity and Bala-rāma an incarnation; but the story of their birth, as told in the Mahā-bhārata, places them more upon an equality. It says that Vish*n*u took two hairs, a white and a black one, and that these became Bala-rāma and K*ri*sh*n*a, the children of Devakī. Bala-rāma was of fair complexion, K*ri*sh*n*a was very dark. As soon as Bala-rāma was born, he was carried away to Gokula to preserve his life from the tyrant Kan*s*a, and he was there nurtured by Nanda as a child of Rohinī. He and K*ri*sh*n*a grew up together, and he took part in many of K*ri*sh*n*a's boyish freaks and adventures. His earliest exploit was the killing of the great Asura Dhenuka, who had the form of an ass. This demon attacked him, but Bala-rāma seized his assailant, whirled him round by his legs till he was dead, and cast his carcase into a tree. Another Asura attempted to carry off Bala-rāma on his shoulders, but the boy beat out the demon's brains with his fists. When K*ri*sh*n*a went to Mathurā, Bala-rāma accompanied him, and manfully supported him till Kan*s*a was killed. Once, when Bala-rāma was intoxicated, he called upon the Yamunā river to come to him, that he might bathe; but his command not being heeded, he plunged his ploughshare into the river, and dragged the waters whithersoever he went, until they were obliged to assume a human form and beseech his forgiveness. This action gained for him the title Yamunā-bhid and Kālindī-karsha*n*a, breaker or dragger of the Yamunā. He killed Rukmin in a gambling brawl. When *S*āmba, son of K*ri*sh*n*a, was detained as a prisoner at Hastināpur by Dur-yodhana, Bala-rāma demanded his release, and, being refused, he thrust his ploughshare under the ramparts of the city, and drew them towards him, thus compelling the Kauravas to give up their prisoner. Lastly, he killed the great ape Dwivida, who had stolen his weapons and derided him.

Such are some of the chief incidents of the life of Bala-rāma, as related in the Purā*n*as, and as popular among the votaries of K*r*ish*n*a. In the Mahā-bhārata he has more of a human character. He taught both Dur-yodhana and Bhīma the use of the mace. Though inclining to the side of the Pā*nd*avas, he refused to take an active part either with them or the Kauravas. He witnessed the combat between Dur-yodhana and Bhīma, and beheld the foul blow struck by the latter, which made him so indignant that he seized his weapons, and was with difficulty restrained by K*r*ish*n*a from falling upon the Pā*nd*avas. He died just before K*r*ish*n*a, as he sat under a banyan tree in the outskirts of Dwārakā.

Another view is held as to the origin of Bala-rāma. According to this he was an incarnation of the great serpent *S*esha, and when he died the serpent is said to have issued from his mouth.

The "wine-loving" Bala-rāma (Madhu-priya or Priya-madhu) was as much addicted to wine as his brother K*r*ish*n*a was devoted to the fair sex. He was also irascible in temper, and sometimes quarrelled even with K*r*ish*n*a: the Purā*n*as represent them as having a serious difference about the Syamantaka jewel. He had but one wife, Revatī, daughter of King Raivata, and was faithful to her. By her he had two sons, Nis*a*t*h*a and Ulmuka. He is represented as of fair complexion, and, as Nīla-vastra, 'clad in a dark-blue vest.' His especial weapons are a club (*khetaka* or *saunanda*), the ploughshare (*hala*), and the pestle (*musala*), from which he is called Phāla and Hāla, also Halāyudha, 'plough-armed;' Hala-bh*r*it, 'plough-bearer;' Lāngali and Sankarsha*n*a, 'ploughman;' and Musalī, 'pestle-holder.' As he has a palm for a banner, he is called Tāla-dhwaja. Other of his appellations are Gupta-chara, 'who goes secretly;' Kāmpāla and Samvartaka.

BĀLA-RĀMĀYA*N*A. A drama by Rāja-*s*ekhara. It has been printed.

BĀLEYA. A descendant of Bali, a Daitya.

BĀLHI. A northern country, Balkh. Said in the Mahābhārata to be famous for its horses, as Balkh is to the present time.

BĀLHĪKAS, BĀHLĪKAS. "Always associated with the people of the north, west, and ultra-Indian provinces, and usually considered to represent the Bactrians or people of Balkh."—*Wilson.*

BALI. A good and virtuous Daitya king. He was son of Virochana, son of Prahlāda, son of Hira*n*ya-ka*s*ipu. His wife was Vindhyāvalī. Through his devotion and penance he defeated Indra, humbled the gods, and extended his authority over the three worlds. The gods appealed to Vish*n*u for protection, and he became manifest in his Dwarf Avatāra for the purpose of restraining Bali. This dwarf craved from Bali the boon of three steps of ground, and, having obtained it, he stepped over heaven and earth in two strides; but then, out of respect to Bali's kindness and his grandson Prahlāda's virtues, he stopped short, and left to him Pātāla, the infernal regions. Bali is also called Mahā-bali, and his capital was Mahā-bali-pura. The germ of the legend of the three steps is found in the *Rig*-veda, where Vish*n*u is represented as taking three steps over earth, heaven, and the lower regions, typifying perhaps the rising, culmination, and setting of the sun.

BĀLĪ, BĀLIN. The monkey king of Kishkindhyā, who was slain by Rāma, and whose kingdom was given to his brother Su-grīva, the friend and ally of Rāma. He was supposed to be the son of Indra, and to have been born from the hair (*bāla*) of his mother, whence his name. His wife's name was Tārā, and his sons Angada and Tāra.

BĀ*N*A. A Daitya, eldest son of Bali, who had a thousand arms. He was a friend of *S*iva and enemy of Vish*n*u. His daughter Ūshā fell in love with Aniruddha, the grandson of K*ri*sh*n*a, and had him conveyed to her by magic art. K*ri*sh*n*a, Bala-rāma, and Pradyumna went to the rescue, and were resisted by Bā*n*a, who was assisted by *S*iva and Skanda, god of war. *S*iva was overpowered by K*ri*sh*n*a; Skanda was wounded; and the many arms of Bā*n*a were cut off by the missile weapons of K*ri*sh*n*a. *S*iva then interceded for the life of Bā*n*a, and K*ri*sh*n*a granted it. He is called also Vairochi.

BANGA. Bengal, but not in the modern application. In ancient times Banga meant the districts north of the Bhāgīrathī —Jessore, K*ri*sh*n*agar, &c. *See* Anu.

BARBARAS. Name of a people. "The analogy to 'barbarians' is not in sound only, but in all the authorities these are classed with borderers and foreigners and nations not Hindu." —*Wilson.*

BARHISHADS. A class of Pit*ri*s, who, when alive, kept up the household flame, and presented offerings with fire. Some authorities identify them with the months. Their dwelling is Vaibhrāja-loka. *See* Pit*ri*s.

BAUDHĀYANA. A writer on Dharma-*s*āstra or law. He was also the author of a Sūtra work.

BHADRĀ. Wife of Utathya (q.v.).

BHADRACHĀRU. A son of K*ri*sh*n*a and Rukminī.

BHADRA-KĀLĪ. Name of a goddess. In modern times it applies to Durgā.

BHADRĀ*S*WA. 1. A region lying to the east of Meru. 2. A celebrated horse, son of Uchchai*h*-sravas.

BHAGA. A deity mentioned in the Vedas, but of very indistinct personality and powers. He is supposed to bestow wealth and to preside over marriage, and he is classed among the Ādityas and Vi*s*wedevas.

BHAGA-NETRA-GHNA (or -HAN). 'Destroyer of the eyes of Bhaga.' An appellation of *S*iva.

BHAGAVAD-GĪTĀ. 'The song of the Divine One.' A celebrated episode of the Mahā-bhārata, in the form of a metrical dialogue, in which the divine K*ri*sh*n*a is the chief speaker, and expounds to Arjuna his philosophical doctrines. The author of the work is unknown, but he "was probably a Brāhman, and nominally a Vaish*n*ava, but really a philosopher and thinker, whose mind was cast in a broad mould." This poem has been interpolated in the Mahā-bhārata, for it is of much later date than the body of that epic; it is later also than the six Dar*s*a*n*as or philosophical schools, for it has received inspiration from them all, especially from the Sānkhya, Yoga, and Vedānta. The second or third century A.D. has been proposed as the probable time of its appearance. K*ri*sh*n*a, as a god, is a manifestation of Vish*n*u; but in this song, and in other places, he is held to be the supreme being. As man, he was related to both the Pā*nd*avas and the Kauravas, and in the great war between these two families he refused to take up arms on either side. But he consented to act as the Pā*nd*ava Arjuna's charioteer. When the opposing hosts were drawn up in array against each other, Arjuna, touched with compunction for the approaching slaughter of kindred and friends, appeals to K*r*ish*n*a for guidance. This gives the occasion for the philosophical teaching. "The poem is divided into three sections, each containing six chapters, the philosophical teaching in each being somewhat distinct," but "undoubtedly the main design of the poem, the sentiments expressed in which have exerted a powerful influence throughout India for the last 1600 years, is to inculcate the doctrine of Bhakti (faith), and to exalt the duties of caste above all other obligations, including those of friendship and kindred." So Arjuna is told to do his duty as a soldier without heeding the slaughter of friends. "In the second division of the poem the Pantheistic doctrines of the Vedānta are more directly inculcated than in the other sections. K*r*ish*n*a here, in the plainest language, claims adoration as one with the great universal spirit pervading and constituting the universe." The language of this poem is exceedingly beautiful, and its tone and sentiment of a very lofty character, so that they have a striking effect even in the prose translation. It was one of the earliest Sansk*r*it works translated into English by Wilkins; but a much more perfect translation, with an excellent introduction, has since been published by Mr. J. Cockburn Thompson, from which much of the above has been borrowed. There are several other translations in French, German, &c.

BHĀGAVATA PURĀ*N*A. The Purā*n*a "in which ample details of duty are described, and which opens with (an extract from) the Gāyatrī; that in which the death of the Asura V*r*itra is told, and in which the mortals and immortals of the Sāraswata Kalpa, with the events that then happened to them in the world, are related, that is celebrated as the Bhāgavata, and consists of 18,000 verses." Such is the Hindu description of this work. "The Bhāgavata," says Wilson, "is a work of great celebrity in India, and exercises a more direct and powerful influence upon the opinions and feelings of the people than perhaps any other of the Purā*n*as. It is placed fifth in all the lists, but the Padmá ranks it as the eighteenth, as the extracted substance of all the rest. According to the usual specification, it consists of 18,000 *s*lokas, distributed amongst 332 chapters, divided into twelve skandhas or books. It is named Bhāgavata from its being dedicated to the glorification of Bhāgavata or Vish*n*u." The most popular and characteristic part of this

Purāna is the tenth book, which narrates in detail the history of Krishna, and has been translated into perhaps all the vernacular languages of India. Colebrooke concurs in the opinion of many learned Hindus that this Purāna is the composition of the grammarian Vopadeva, who lived about six or seven centuries ago at the court of Hemādri, Rāja of Deva-giri (Deogurh or Daulatābād), and Wilson sees no reason for calling in question the tradition which assigns the work to this writer. This Purāna has been translated into French by Burnouf, and has been published with the text in three volumes folio, and in other forms.

BHĀGĪRATHĪ. The Ganges. The name is derived from Bhagīratha, a descendant of Sagara, whose austerities induced Siva to allow the sacred river to descend to the earth for the purpose of bathing the ashes of Sagara's sons, who had been consumed by the wrath of the sage Kapila. Bhagīratha named the river Sāgara, and after leading it over the earth to the sea, he conducted it to Pātāla, where the ashes of his ancestors were laved with its waters and purified.

BHAIRAVA (mas.), BHAIRAVĪ (fem.). 'The terrible.' Names of Siva and his wife Devī. The Bhairavas are eight inferior forms or manifestations of Siva, all of them of a terrible character:—(1.) Asitānga, black limbed; (2.) Sanhāra, destruction; (3.) Ruru, a dog; (4.) Kāla, black; (5.) Krodha, anger; (6.) Tāmra-chūdā, red crested; (7.) Chandra-chūdā, moon crested; (8.) Mahā, great. Other names are met with as variants: Kapāla, Rudra, Bhīshana, Un-matta, Ku-pati, &c. In these forms Siva often rides upon a dog, wherefore he is called *Swāswa*, 'whose horse is a dog.'

BHĀMATĪ. A gloss on Sankara's commentary upon the Brahma Sūtras by Vāchaspati Misra. It is in course of publication in the *Bibliotheca Indica.*

BHĀNUMATĪ. Daughter of Bhānu, a Yādava chief, who was abducted from her home in Dwārakā, during the absence of her father, by the demon Nikumbha.

BHARADWĀJA. A Rishi to whom many Vedic hymns are attributed. He was the son of Brihaspati and father of Drona, the preceptor of the Pāndavas. The Taittirīya Brāhmana says that "he lived through three lives" (probably meaning a life of great length), and that "he became immortal and ascended to the heavenly world, to union with the sun." In the Mahābhārata he is represented as living at Hardwār; in the Rāmāyana he received Rāma and Sītā in his hermitage at Prayāga, which was then and afterwards much celebrated. According to some of the Purānas and the Hari-vansa, he became by gift or adoption the son of King Bharata, and an absurd story is told about his birth to account for his name: His mother, the wife of Utathya, was pregnant by her husband and by Brihaspati. Dīrgha-tamas, the son by her husband, kicked his half-brother out of the womb before his time, when Brihaspati said to his mother, 'Bhara-dwā-jam,' 'Cherish this child of two fathers.'

BHĀRADWĀJA. 1. Drona. 2. Any descendant of Bharadwāja or follower of his teaching. 3. Name of a grammarian and author of Sūtras.

BHARATA. 1. A hero and king from whom the warlike people called Bhāratas, frequently mentioned in the *Rig*-veda, were descended. The name is mixed up with that of Viswāmitra. Bharata's sons were called Viswāmitras and Viswāmitra's sons were called Bharatas.

2. An ancient king of the first Manwantara. He was devoted to Vishnu, and abdicated his throne that he might continue constant in meditation upon him. While at his hermitage, he went to bathe in the river, and there saw a doe big with young frightened by a lion. Her fawn, which was brought forth suddenly, fell into the water, and the sage rescued it. He brought the animal up, and becoming excessively fond of it, his abstraction was interrupted. "In the course of time he died, watched by the deer with tears in its eyes, like a son mourning for his father; and he himself, as he expired, cast his eyes upon the deer and thought of nothing else, being wholly occupied with one idea." For this misapplied devotion he was born again as a deer with the faculty of recollecting his former life. In this form he lived an austere retired life, and having atoned for his former error, was born again as a Brāhman. But his person was ungainly, and he looked like a crazy idiot. He discharged servile offices, and was a palankin bearer; but he had true wisdom, and discoursed deeply upon philosophy and the power of Vishnu. Finally he obtained exemption from future birth. This legend is "a sectarial graft upon a Paurānik stem."

3. Son of Dasaratha by his wife Kaikeyī, and half-brother of Rāma-chandra. He was educated by his mother's father, Aswa-pati, king of Kekaya, and married Māndavī, the cousin of Sītā. His mother, through maternal fondness, brought about the exile of Rāma, and endeavoured to secure her own son's succession to the throne, but Bharata refused to supplant his elder brother. On the death of his father Bharata performed the funeral rites, and went after Rāma with a complete army to bring him back to Ayodhyā and place him on the throne. He found Rāma at Chitra-kūta, and there was a generous contention between them as to which should reign. Rāma refused to return until the period of his exile was completed, and Bharata declined to be king; but he returned to Ayodhyā as Rāma's representative, and setting up a pair of Rāma's shoes as a mark of his authority, Bharata ruled the country in his brother's name. "He destroyed thirty millions of terrible gandharvas" and made himself master of their country.

4. A prince of the Puru branch of the Lunar race. Bharata was son of Dushyanta and Sakuntalā. Ninth in descent from him came Kuru, and fourteenth from Kuru came Sāntanu. This king had a son named Vichitra-vīrya, who died childless, leaving two widows. Krishna Dwaipāyana was natural brother to Vichitra-vīrya. Under the law he raised up seed to his brother from the widows, whose sons were Dhrita-rāshtra and Pāndu, between whose descendants, the Kauravas and Pāndavas, the great war of the Mahā-bhārata was fought. Through their descent from Bharata, these princes, but more especially the Pāndavas, were called Bhāratas.

5. A sage who is the reputed inventor of dramatic entertainments.

6. A name borne by several others of less note than the above.

BHĀRATA. A descendant of Bharata, especially one of the *Pāndu* princes.

BHĀRATA-VARSHA. India, as having been the kingdom of Bharata. It is divided into nine Khandas or parts: Indra-dwīpa, Kaserumat, Tāmra-varna, Gabhastimat, Nāga-dwīpa, Saumya, Gāndharva, Vāruna.

BHĀRATĪ. A name of Saraswatī.

BHĀRGAVA. A descendant of Bhrigu, as Chyavana, Saunaka, Jamad-agni, but more especially used for the latter and Parasu-rāma.

BHARTRI-HARI. A celebrated poet and grammarian, who is said to have been the brother of Vikramāditya. He wrote three Satakas or Centuries of verses, called—(1.) Sringāra-sataka, on amatory matters; (2.) Nīti-sataka, on polity and ethics; (3.) Vairāgya-sataka, on religious austerity. These maxims are said to have been written when he had taken to a religious life after a licentious youth. He was also author of a grammatical work of high repute called Vākya-padīya, and the poem called Bhatti-kāvya is by some attributed to him. The moral verses were translated into French so long ago as 1670. A note at the end of that translation says, "Trad. par le Brahmine Padmanaba en flamand et du flamand en français par Th. La Grue." The text with a Latin translation was printed by Schiefner and Weber. There is a translation in German by Bohlen and Schütz, in French by Fauche, and of the erotic verses by Regnaud; in English by Professor Tawney in the *Indian Antiquary*.

BHĀSHA-PARICHCHHEDA. An exposition of the Nyāya philosophy. There are several editions.

BHĀSKARĀCHĀRYA. (Bhāskara + Āchārya.) A celebrated mathematician and astronomer, who was born early in the eleventh century A.D. He was author of the Bīja-ganita on arithmetic, the Līlāvatī on algebra, and the Siddhānta Siromani on astronomy. It has been claimed for Bhāskara that he "was fully acquainted with the principle of the Differential Calculus." This claim Dr. Spottiswoode considers to be overstated, but he observes of Bhāskara: "It must be admitted that the penetration shown by Bhāskara in his analysis is in the highest degree remarkable; that the formula which he establishes, and his method of establishing it, bear more than a mere resemblance—they bear a strong analogy—to the corresponding process in modern astronomy; and that the majority of scientific persons will learn with surprise the existence of such a method in the writings of so distant a period and so distant a region."—*Jour. R. A. S.*, 1859.

BHATTĀCHĀRYA. *See* Kumārila Bhatta.

BHATTI-KĀVYA. A poem on the actions of Rāma by Bhatti. It is of a very artificial character, and is designed to illustrate the laws of grammar and the figures of poetry and rhetoric. The text has been printed with a commentary, and part has been translated into German by Schütz.

BHAUMA. Son of Bhūmi (the earth). A metronymic of the Daitya Nāraka.

BHAUTYA. The fourteenth Manu. *See* Manu.

BHAVA. 1. A Vedic deity often mentioned in connection with *S*arva the destroyer. 2. A name of Rudra or *S*iva, or of a manifestation of that god. *See* Rudra.

BHAVA-BHŪTI. A celebrated dramatist, the author of three of the best extant Sansk*ri*t dramas, the Mahā-vīra Charita, Uttara Rāma Charita, and Mālatī Mādhava. He was also known as *S*rī-kan*th*a, or 'throat of eloquence.' He was a Brāhman, and was a native either of Beder or Berar, but Ujjayinī or its neighbourhood would seem, from his vivid descriptions of the scenery, to have been the place of his residence. The eighth century is the period at which he flourished. His three plays have been translated by Wilson in blank verse, who says of Mālatī Mādhava, "The author is fond of an unreasonable display of learning, and occasionally substitutes the phraseology of logic or metaphysics for the language of poetry and nature. At the same time the beauties predominate over the defects, and the language of the drama is in general of extraordinary beauty and power."

BHAVISHYA PURĀ*N*A. "This Purā*n*a, as its name implies, should be a book of prophecies foretelling what will be." The copies discovered contain about 7000 stanzas. The work is far from agreeing with the declared character of a Purā*n*a, and is principally a manual of rites and ceremonies. Its deity is *S*iva. There is another work, containing also about 7000 verses, called the Bhavishyottara Purā*n*a, a name which would imply that "it was a continuation or supplement of the former," and its contents are of a similar character.—*Wilson.*

BHAVISHYOTTARA PURĀ*N*A. *See* Bhavishya Purā*n*a.

BHAWĀNĪ. One of the names of the wife of *S*iva. *See* Devī.

BHELA. An ancient sage who wrote upon medicine.

BHIKSHU. A mendicant. The Brāhman in the fourth and last stage of his religious life. *See* Brāhman.

Any mendicant, especially, in its Pāli form, Bhikkhu, a Buddhist mendicant.

D

BHĪMA, BHĪMA-SENA. 'The terrible.' The second of the five Pāndu princes, and mythically son of Vāyu, 'the god of the wind.' He was a man of vast size, and had great strength. He was wrathful in temper, and given to abuse, a brave warrior, but a fierce and cruel foe, coarse in taste and manners, and a great feeder, so that he was called Vrikodara, 'wolf's belly.' Half of the food of the family was allotted to him, and the other half sufficed for his four brothers and their mother. The weapon he generally used was a club, which suited his gigantic strength, and he had been trained in the use of it by Drona and Bala-rāma. His great strength excited the envy of his cousin Dur-yodhana, who poisoned him and threw his body into the Ganges; but it sank to the realm of the serpents, where it was restored to health and vigour, and Bhīma returned to Hastinā-pura. At the passage of arms at Hastināpura, he and Dur-yodhana engaged each other with clubs; but the mimic combat soon turned into a fierce personal conflict, which Drona had to put an end to by force. It was at this same meeting that he reviled Karna, and heaped contempt upon him, increasing and converting into bitter hatred the enmity which Karna had previously entertained against the Pāndavas. When he and his brothers were in exile, and an attempt was made, at the instigation of Dur-yodhana, to burn them in their house, it was he who barricaded the house of Purochana, the director of the plot, and burnt him as he had intended to burn them. Soon after this he met the Asura Hidimba, whom he killed, and then married his sister Hidimbā. He also slew another Asura named Vaka, whom he seized by the legs and tore asunder; afterwards he killed his brother, Kirmīra, and other Asuras. This brought the Asuras to submission, and they engaged to refrain from molesting mankind. After the Pāndu princes were established at Indraprastha, Bhīma fought in single combat with Jarāsandha, king of Magadha, who had refused to recognise their supremacy. As 'son of the wind,' Bhīma was brother of Hanumān, and was able to fly with great speed. By this power of flight, and with the help of Hanumān, he made his way to Kuvera's heaven, high up in the Himālayas. When Jayadratha failed in his attempt to carry off Draupadī, he was pursued by Arjuna and Bhīma. The latter overtook him, dragged him by the hair from his chariot to the ground, and kicked him till he became senseless. At Arjuna's remonstrance Bhīma refrained from killing him; but he cut off all his hair except five locks, and compelled him to acknowledge publicly that he was the slave of the Pā*nd*avas. Bhīma refused to listen to his brother's plea for Jayadratha's release, but at Draupadī's intercession he let him go free. In the second exile of the Pā*nd*avas, they went to the Rāja of Virā*t*a, whose service they entered. Bhīma, holding a ladle in one hand and a sword in the other, undertook the duties of cook; but he soon exhibited his prowess by fighting with and killing a famous wrestler named Jīmūta. Draupadī had entered into the service of the queen as a waiting-maid, and attracted the admiration of the king's brother-in-law, Kīchaka. When she rejected his advances, he insulted and brutally assaulted her. Her husbands did not seem disposed to avenge her, so she appealed to Bhīma, as she was wont when she sought revenge. Draupadī made an assignation with Kīchaka, which Bhīma kept, and after a sharp struggle with the disappointed gallant, he broke his bones to atoms, and made his body into a large ball of flesh, so that no one could tell how he had been killed or who had killed him. Draupadī was judged to have had a share in his death, and was condemned to be burnt alive; but Bhīma drew his hair over his face, so that no one could recognise him, and, tearing up a large tree for a club, he rushed to the rescue. He was taken for a mighty Gandharva, the crowd fled, and Draupadī was released. Kīchaka had been the general of the forces of Virā*t*a and the mainstay of the king. After his death, Su-*s*arman, king of Trigartta, aided and abetted by the Kauravas and others, determined to attack Virā*t*a. The Rāja of Virā*t*a was defeated and made prisoner, but Bhīma pursued Su-*s*arman and overcame him, rescued the prisoner, and made the conqueror captive. In the great battle between the Kauravas and Pa*nd*avas, Bhīma took a very prominent part. On the first day he fought against Bhīshma; on the second he slew the two sons of the Rāja of Magadha, and after them their father, killing him and his elephant at a single blow. In the night between the fourteenth and fifteenth day of the battle, Bhīma fought with Dro*n*a until the rising of the sun; but that redoubted warrior fell by the hand of Dh*r*ish*t*a-dyumna, who continued the combat till noonday. On the seventeenth day he killed Duh-*s*āsana, and drank his blood, as he had long before vowed to do, in retaliation of the insults Duh-*s*āsana had offered to Draupadī. On the eighteenth and last day of the battle Dur-yodhana fled and hid himself in a lake. When he was discovered, he would not come out until he had received a promise that he should not have to fight with more than one man at a time. Even then he delayed until he was irritated by the abuse and the taunts of the Pā*nd*avas. Bhīma and. Dur-yodhana fought as usual with clubs. The battle was long and furious; the parties were equally matched, and Bhīma was getting the worst of it, when he struck an unfair blow which smashed Dur-yodhana's thigh, and brought him to the ground. Thus he fulfilled his vow and avenged Draupadī. In his fury Bhīma kicked his prostrate foe on the head, and acted so brutally that his brother Yudhi-sh*t*hira struck him in the face with his fist, and directed Arjuna to take him away. Bala-rāma was greatly incensed at the foul play to which Bhīma had resorted, and would have attacked the Pā*nd*avas had he not been mollified by K*r*ish*n*a. He declared that Bhīma should thenceforward be called Jihma-yodhin, 'the unfair fighter.' After the conclusion of the war, the old king, Dh*r*ita-rāsh*t*ra, asked that Bhīma might be brought to him. K*r*ish*n*a, who knew the blind old man's sorrow for his son, whom Bhīma had killed, and suspecting his intention, placed before him an iron statue, which Dh*r*ita-rāsh*t*ra crushed in his embrace. Dh*r*ita-rāsh*t*ra never forgave Bhīma, and he returned the ill feeling with insults, which ended in the old king's retiring into the forest. Bhīma's last public feat was the slaughter of the horse in the sacrifice which followed Yudhi-sh*t*hira's accession to the throne. Apart from his mythological attributes, the character of Bhīma is natural and distinct. A man of burly form, prodigious strength, and great animal courage, with coarse tastes, a gluttonous appetite, and an irascible temper; jovial and jocular when in good humour, but abusive, truculent, and brutal when his passions were roused. His repartees were forcible though coarse, and he held his own even against K*r*ish*n*a when the latter made personal remarks upon him. *See* Mahā-bhārata.

By his Asura wife Hi*d*imbā he had a son named Gha*t*otkacha; and by his wife Balandharā, princess of Kā*s*ī, he also had a son named Sarvatraga or Sarvaga. Other appellations of Bhīma are Bhīma-sena, Bāhu-sālin, 'the large armed,' Jarāsandha-jit, 'vanquisher of Jarāsandha.'

BHĪMA. Name of the father of Damayantī. A name of Rudra or of one of his personifications. *See* Rudra.

BHĪMA *S*ANKARA, BHĪME*S*WARA. Name of one of the twelve great Lingas. *See* Linga.

BHĪMA-SENA. A name of Bhīma.

BHĪSHMA. 'The terrible.' Son of King *S*āntanu by the holy river goddess Gangā, and hence called *S*āntanava, Gāngeya, and Nadi-ja, 'the river-born.' When King *S*āntanu was very old he desired to marry a young and beautiful wife. His son *S*āntanava or Bhīshma found a suitable damsel, but her parents objected to the marriage because Bhīshma was heir to the throne, and if she bore sons they could not succeed. To gratify his father's desires, he made a vow to the girl's parents that he would never accept the throne, nor marry a wife, nor become the father of children. *S*āntanu then married the damsel, whose name was Satyavatī, and she bore him two sons. At the death of his father, Bhīshma placed the elder son upon the throne, but he was headstrong and was soon killed in battle. The other son, named Vichitra-vīryya, then succeeded, and Bhīshma acted as his protector and adviser. By force of arms Bhīshma obtained two daughters of the king of Kā*s*ī and married them to Vichitra-vīryya, and when that prince died young and childless, Bhīshma acted as guardian of his widows. By Bhīshma's arrangement, K*ri*sh*n*a Dwaipāyana, who was born of Satyavatī before her marriage, raised up seed to his half-brother. The two children were Pā*nd*u and Dh*ri*ta-rāsh*t*ra. Bhīshma brought them up and acted for them as regent of Hastinā-pura. He also directed the training of their respective children, the Pā*nd*avas and Kauravas. On the rupture taking place between the rival families, Bhīshma counselled moderation and peace. When the war began he took the side of the Kauravas, the sons of Dh*ri*ta-rāsh*t*ra, and he was made commander-in-chief of their army. He laid down some rules for mitigating the horrors of war, and he stipulated that he should not be called upon to fight against Arjuna. Goaded by the reproaches of Dur-yodhana, he attacked Arjuna on the tenth day of the battle. He was unfairly wounded by *S*ikhandin, and was pierced with innumerable arrows from the hands of Arjuna, so that there was not a space of two fingers' breadth left unwounded in his whole body, and when he fell from his chariot he was upheld from the ground by the arrows and lay as on a couch of darts. He was mortally wounded, but he had obtained the power of fixing the period of his death, so he survived fifty-eight days, and delivered several long didactic discourses. Bhîshma exhibited throughout his life a self-denial, devotion, and fidelity which remained unsullied to the last. He is also known by the appellation Tarpa*n*echchhu, and as Tāla-ketu, 'palm banner.' *See* Mahā-bhārata.

BHÎSHMAKA. 1. An appellation of *S*iva. 2. King of Vidarbha, father of Rukmin and of Rukminî, the chief wife of K*ri*sh*na*.

BHOGAVATÎ. 'The voluptuous.' The subterranean capital of the Nāgas in the Nāga-loka portion of Pātāla. Another name is Pūt-kārî.

BHOJA. A name borne by many kings. Most conspicuous among them was Bhoja or Bhoja-deva, king of Dhār, who is said to have been a great patron of literature, and probably died before 1082 A.D. 2. A prince of the Yādava race who reigned at M*ri*ttikavatî on the Par*n*āsa river in Mālwa; he is called also Mahā-bhoja. 3. A tribe living in the Vindhya mountains. 4. A country; the modern Bhojpur, Bhāgalpur, &c.

BHOJA-PRABANDHA. A collection of literary anecdotes relating to King Bhoja of Dhār, written by Ballāla. The text has been lithographed by Pavie.

BH*RI*GU. A Vedic sage. He is one of the Prajāpatis and great *Ri*shis, and is regarded as the founder of the race of the Bh*ri*gus or Bhārgavas, in which was born Jamad-agni and Para*s*u Rāma. Manu calls him son, and says that he confides to him his Institutes. According to the Mahā-bhārata he officiated at Daksha's celebrated sacrifice, and had his beard pulled out by *S*iva. The same authority also tells the following story:—It is related of Bh*ri*gu that he rescued the sage Agastya from the tyranny of King Nahusha, who had obtained superhuman power. Bh*ri*gu crept into Agastya's hair to avoid the potent glance of Nahusha, and when that tyrant attached Agastya to his chariot and kicked him on the head to make him move, Bh*ri*gu cursed Nahusha, and he was turned into a serpent. Bh*ri*gu, on Nahusha's supplication, limited the duration of his curse.

In the Padma Purā*n*a it is related that the *Ri*shis, assembled at a sacrifice, disputed as to which deity was best entitled to the homage of a Brāhman. Being unable to agree, they resolved to send Bh*ri*gu to test the characters of the various gods, and he accordingly went. He could not obtain access to *S*iva because that deity was engaged with his wife; "finding him, therefore, to consist of the property of darkness, Bh*ri*gu sentenced him to take the form of the Linga, and pronounced that he should have no offerings presented to him, nor receive the worship of the pious and respectable. His next visit was to Brahmā, whom he beheld surrounded by sages, and so much inflated with his own importance as to treat Bh*ri*gu with great inattention, betraying his being made up of foulness. The Muni therefore excluded him from the worship of the Brāhmans. Repairing next to Vish*n*u, he found the deity asleep, and, indignant at his seeming sloth, Bh*ri*gu stamped upon his breast with his left foot and awoke him; instead of being offended, Vish*n*u gently pressed the Brāhman's foot and expressed himself honoured and made happy by its contact; and Bh*ri*gu, highly pleased by his humility, and satisfied of his being impersonated goodness, proclaimed Vish*n*u as the only being to be worshipped by men or gods, in which decision the Munis, upon Bh*ri*gu's report, concurred."—*Wilson.*

BH*RI*GUS. 'Roasters, consumers.' "A class of mythical beings who belonged to the middle or aerial class of gods."—*Roth.* They are connected with Agni, and are spoken of as producers and nourishers of fire, and as makers of chariots. They are associated with the Angirasas, the Atharvans, *Ri*bhus, &c.

BHŪ, BHŪMI. The earth. *See* P*ri*thivī.

BHŪR. *See* Vyāh*ri*ti.

BHŪRI-*S*RAVAS. A prince of the Bālhīkas and an ally of the Kauravas, who was killed in the great battle of the Mahābhārata.

BHUR-LOKA. *See* Loka.

BHŪTA. A ghost, imp, goblin. Malignant spirits which haunt cemeteries, lurk in trees, animate dead bodies, and delude and devour human beings. According to the Vish*n*u Purā*n*a they are "fierce beings and eaters of flesh," who were created by the Creator when he was incensed. In the Vāyu Purā*n*a their mother is said to have been Krodhā, 'anger.' The Bhūtas are attendants of *S*iva, and he is held to be their king.

BHŪTESA, BHŪTESWARA. 'Lord of beings or of created things.' A name applied to Vish*n*u, Brahmā, and K*r*ish*n*a; as 'lord of the Bhūtas or goblins,' it is applied to *S*iva.

BHUVANES*W*ARA. A ruined city in Orissa, sacred to the worship of *S*iva, and containing the remains of several temples. It was formerly called Ekāmra-kānana.

BHUVAR. *See* Vyāh*r*iti.

BHUVAR-LOKA. *See* Loka.

BĪBHATSU. 'Loathing.' An appellation of Arjuna.

BINDUSĀRA. The son and successor of Chandra-gupta.

BRAHMA, BRAHMAN (neuter). The supreme soul of the universe, self-existent, absolute, and eternal, from which all things emanate, and to which all return. This divine essence is incorporeal, immaterial, invisible, unborn, uncreated, without beginning and without end, illimitable, and inappreciable by the sense until the film of mortal blindness is removed. It is all-pervading and infinite in its manifestations, in all nature, animate and inanimate, in the highest god and in the meanest creature. This supreme soul receives no worship, but it is the object of that abstract meditation which Hindu sages practise in order to obtain absorption into it. It is sometimes called Kala-hansa.

There is a passage in the *S*atapatha Brāhma*n*a which represents Brahma (neut.) as the active creator. *See* Brahmā.

The Veda is sometimes called Brahma.

BRAHMĀ (masculine). The first member of the Hindu triad; the supreme spirit manifested as the active creator of the universe. He sprang from the mundane egg deposited by the supreme first cause, and is the Prajāpati, or lord and father of all creatures, and in the first place of the *R*ishis or Prajāpatis.

When Brahmā has created the world it remains unaltered for one of his days, a period of 2,160,000,000 years. The world and all that is therein is then consumed by fire, but the sages, gods, and elements survive. When he awakes he again restores creation, and this process is repeated until his existence of a hundred years is brought to a close, a period which it requires fifteen figures to express. When this period is ended he himself expires, and he and all the gods and sages, and the whole universe are resolved into their constituent elements. His name is invoked in religious services, but Pushkara (*hodie* Pokhar), near Ājmīr, is the only place where he receives worship, though Professor Williams states that he has heard of homage being paid to him at Īdar.

Brahmā is said to be of a red colour. He has four heads; originally he had five, but one was burnt off by the fire of *S*iva's central eye because he had spoken disrespectfully. Hence he is called Chatur-ānana or Chatur-mukha, 'four-faced,' and Ash*t*a-kar*n*a, 'eight-eared.' He has four arms; and in his hands he holds his sceptre, or a spoon, or a string of beads, or his bow Parivīta, or a water jug, and the Veda. His consort is Saraswatī, goddess of learning, also called Brāhmī. His vehicle is a swan or goose, from which he is called Hansa-vāhana. His residence is called Brahma-v*ri*ndā.

The name Brahmā is not found in the Vedas and Brāhma*n*as, in which the active creator is known as Hira*n*ya-garbha, Prajāpati, &c.; but there is a curious passage in the *S*atapatha Brāhma*n*a which says: "He (Brahma, neuter) created the gods. Having created the gods, he placed them in these worlds: in this world Agni, Vāyu in the atmosphere, and Sūrya in the sky." Two points connected with Brahmā are remarkable. As the father of men he performs the work of procreation by incestuous intercourse with his own daughter, variously named Vāch or Saraswatī (speech), Sandhyā (twilight), *S*ata-rūpā (the hundred-formed), &c. Secondly, that his powers as creator have been arrogated to the other gods Vish*n*u and *S*iva, while Brahmā has been thrown into the shade. In the Aitareya Brāhma*n*a it is said that Prajāpati was in the form of a buck and his daughter was Rohit, a deer. According to the *S*atapatha Brāhma*n*a and Manu, the supreme soul, the self-existent lord, created the waters and deposited in them a seed, which seed became a golden egg, in which he himself was born as Brahmā, the progenitor of all the worlds. As the waters (*nara*) were "the place of his movement, he (Brahmā) was called Nārāya*n*a." Here the name Nārāya*n*a is referred distinctly to Brahmā, but it afterwards became the name of Vish*n*u. The account of the Rāmāya*n*a is that "all was water only, in which the earth was formed. Thence arose Brahmā, the self-existent, with the deities. He then, becoming a boar, raised up the earth and created the whole world with the saints, his sons. Brahmā, eternal and perpetually undecaying, sprang from the ether; from him was descended Marīchi; the son of Marīchi was Kasyapa. From Kasyapa sprang Vivaswat, and Manu is declared to have been Vivaswat's son." A later recension of this poem alters this passage so as to make Brahmā a mere manifestation of Vishnu. Instead of "Brahmā, the self-existent, with the deities," it substitutes for the last three words, "the imperishable Vishnu." The Vishnu Purāna says that the "divine Brahmā called Nārāyana created all beings," that Prajāpati "had formerly, at the commencement of the (previous) kalpas, taken the shape of a fish, a tortoise, &c., (so now), entering the body of a boar, the lord of creatures entered the water." But this "lord of creatures" is clearly shown to be Vishnu, and these three forms, the fish, the tortoise, and the boar, are now counted among the Avatāras of Vishnu. (*See* Avatāra.) This attribution of the form of a boar to Brahmā (Prajāpati) had been before made by the Satapatha Brāhmana, which also says, "Having assumed the form of a tortoise, Prajāpati created offspring." The Linga Purāna is quite exceptional among the later works in ascribing the boar form to Brahmā. The Mahābhārata represents Brahmā as springing from the navel of Vishnu or from a lotus which grew thereout; hence he is called Nābhi-ja, 'navel-born;' Kanja, 'the lotus;' Sarojin, 'having a lotus;' Abja-ja, Abja-yoni, and Kanja-ja, 'lotus-born.' This is, of course, the view taken by the Vaishnavas. The same statement appears in the Rāmāyana, although this poem gives Brahmā a more prominent place than usual. It represents Brahmā as informing Rāma of his divinity, and of his calling him to heaven in "the glory of Vishnu." He bestowed boons on Rāma while that hero was on earth, and he extended his favours also to Rāvana and other Rākshasas who were descendants of his son Pulastya. In the Purānas also he appears as a patron of the enemies of the gods, and it was by his favour that the Daitya King Bali obtained that almost universal dominion which required the incarnation of Vishnu as the dwarf to repress. He is further represented in the Rāmāyana as the creator of the beautiful Ahalyā, whom he gave as wife to the sage Gautama. Brahmā, being thus inferior to Vishnu, is represented as giving homage and praise to Vishnu himself and to his form Krishna, but the Vaishnava authorities make him superior to Rudra, who, they say, sprang from his forehead. The Saiva authorities make Mahā-deva or Rudra to be the creator of Brahmā, and represent Brahmā as worshipping the Linga and as acting as the charioteer of Rudra.

Brahmā was the father of Daksha, who is said to have sprung from his thumb, and he was present at the sacrifice of that patriarch, which was rudely disturbed by Rudra. Then he had to humbly submit and appease the offended god. The four Kumāras, the chief of whom was called Sanat-kumāra or by the patronymic Vaidhātra, were later creations or sons of Brahmā.

Brahmā is also called Vidhi, Vedhās, Druhi*n*a, and Srash*t*ri, 'creator;' Dhāt*ri* and Vidhāt*ri*, 'sustainer;' Pitāmaha, 'the great father;' Loke*s*a, 'lord of the world;' Paramesh*t*a, 'supreme in heaven;' Sanat, 'the ancient;' Ādi-kavi, 'the first poet;' and Drū-gha*n*a, 'the axe or mallet.'

BRAHMACHĀRĪ. The Brāhman student. *See* Brāhman.

BRAHMĀDIKAS. The Prajāpatis (q.v.).

BRAHMA-GUPTA. An astronomer who composed the Brahma-gupta Siddhānta in A.D. 628.

BRAHMA-LOKA. *See* Loka.

BRĀHMAN. The first of the four castes; the sacerdotal class, the members of which may be, but are not necessarily, priests. A Brāhman is the chief of all created beings; his person is inviolate; he is entitled to all honour, and enjoys many rights and privileges. The *S*atapatha Brāhma*n*a declares that "there are two kinds of gods; first the gods, then those who are Brāhmans, and have learnt the Veda and repeat it: they are human gods." The chief duty of a Brāhman is the study and teaching of the Vedas, and the performance of sacrifices and other religious ceremonies; but in modern times many Brāhmans entirely neglect these duties, and they engage in most of the occupations of secular life. Under the law of Manu, the life of a Brāhman was divided into four āsramas or stages:—

1. *Brahmachārī.*—The student, whose duty was to pass his days in humble and obedient attendance upon his spiritual preceptor in the study of the Vedas.

2. *Grihastha.*—The householder; the married man living with his wife as head of a family engaged in the ordinary duties of a Brāhman, reading and teaching the Vedas, sacrificing and assisting to sacrifice, bestowing alms and receiving alms.

3. *Vānaprastha.*—The anchorite, or "dweller in the woods,"

who, having discharged his duties as a man of the world, has retired into the forest to devote himself to self-denial in food and raiment, to mortifications of various kinds, to religious meditation, and to the strict performance of all ceremonial duties.

4. *Sannyāsī.*—The religious mendicant, who, freed from all forms and observances, wanders about and subsists on alms, practising or striving for that condition of mind which, heedless of the joys and pains, cares and troubles of the flesh, is intent only upon the deity and final absorption.

The divisions and subdivisions of the Brāhman caste are almost innumerable. It must suffice here to notice the great divisions of north and south, the Pancha Gau*d*a and the Pancha Drāvi*d*a. The five divisions of Gau*d*a, or Bengal, are the Brāhmans of—1. Kanyakubja, Kanauj; 2. Sāraswata, the north-west, about the Saraswatī or Sarsūti river; 3. Gau*d*a; 4. Mithila, North Bihar; 5. Utkala, Orissa. The Pancha Drāvi*d*a are the Brāhmans of—1. Mahā-rāsh*t*ra, the Mahratta country; 2. Telinga, the Telugu country; 3. Drāvi*d*a, the Tamil country; 4. Karnā*t*a, the Canarese country; 5. Gūrjjara, Guzerat.

BRĀHMA*N*A. 'Belonging to Brāhmans.' Works composed by and for Brāhmans. That part of the Veda which was intended for the use and guidance of Brāhmans in the use of the hymns of the Mantra, and therefore of later production; but the Brāhma*n*a, equally with the Mantra, is held to be *S*ruti or revealed word. Excepting its claim to revelation, it is a Hindu Talmud. The Brāhma*n*a collectively is made up of the different Brāhma*n*as, which are ritualistic and liturgical writings in prose. They contain the details of the Vedic ceremonies, with long explanations of their origin and meaning; they give instructions as to the use of particular verses and metres; and they abound with curious legends, divine and human, in illustration. In them are found "the oldest rituals we have, the oldest linguistic explanations, the oldest traditional narratives, and the oldest philosophical speculations." As literary productions they are not of a high order, but some "striking thoughts, bold expressions, sound reasoning, and curious traditions are found among the mass of pedantry and grandiloquence." Each of the Sanhitās or collection of hymns has its Brāhma*n*as, and these generally maintain the essential character of the Veda to which they belong. Thus the Brāhmanas of the *Rig* are specially devoted to the duties of the Hotri, who recites the richas or verses, those of the Yajur to the performance of the sacrifices by the Adhwaryu, and those of the Sāman to the chaunting by the Udgātri. The *Rig* has the Aitareya Brāhmana, which is perhaps the oldest, and may date as far back as the seventh century B.C. This is sometimes called Āswalāyana. It has another called Kaushītaki or Sānkhāyana. The Taittirīya Sanhitā of the Yajur-veda has the Taittirīya Brāhmana, and the Vājasaneyī Sanhitā has the Satapatha Brāhmana, one of the most important of all the Brāhmanas. The Sāma-veda has eight Brāhmanas, of which the best known are the Praudha or Pancha-vinsa, the Tāndya, and the Shad-vinsa. The Atharva has only one, the Gopatha Brāhmana. In their fullest extent the Brāhmanas embrace also the treatises called Āranyakas and Upanishads.

BRAHMANASPATI. A Vedic equivalent of the name Brihaspati.

BRAHMANDA PURĀNA. "That which has declared, in 12,200 verses, the magnificence of the egg of Brahmā, and in which an account of the future kalpas is contained, is called the Brahmanda Purāna, and was revealed by Brahmā." This Purāna, like the Skanda, is "no longer procurable in a collective body," but is represented by a variety of Khandas and Māhātmyas professing to be derived from it. The Adhyātma Rāmāyana, a very popular work, is considered to be a part of this Purāna.

BRAHMĀNĪ. The female form, or the daughter of Brahmā, also called Sata-rūpā (q.v.).

BRAHMĀ-PURA. The city of Brahmā. The heaven of Brahmā, on the summit of Mount Meru, and enclosed by the river Gangā.

BRAHMA PURĀNA. In all the lists of the Purānas the Brahma stands first, for which reason it is sometimes entitled the Ādi or "First" Purāna. It was repeated by Brahmā to Marīchi, and is said to contain 10,000 stanzas, but the actual number is between 7000 and 8000. It is also called the Saura Purāna, because "it is, in great part, appropriated to the worship of Sūrya, the sun." "The early chapters give a description of the creation, an account of the Manwantaras, and the history of the Solar and Lunar dynasties to the time of Krishna in a summary manner, and in words which are common to it and several other Purānas. A brief description of the universe succeeds; and then come a number of chapters relating to the holiness of Orissa, with its temples and sacred groves, dedicated to the sun, to Siva, and Jagan-nātha, the latter especially. These chapters are characteristic of this Purāna, and show its main object to be the promotion of the worship of Krishna as Jagan-nātha. To these particulars succeeds a life of Krishna, which is word for word the same as that of the Vishnu Purāna; and the compilation terminates with a particular detail of the mode in which Yoga or contemplative devotion, the object of which is still Vishnu, is to be performed. There is little in this which corresponds with the definition of a Pancha-lakshana Purāna, and the mention of the temples of Orissa, the date of the original construction of which is recorded, shows that it could not have been compiled earlier than the thirteenth or fourteenth century." This Purāna has "a supplementary or concluding section called the Brahmottara Purāna, which contains about 3000 stanzas. This bears still more entirely the character of a Māhātmya or local legend, being intended to celebrate the sanctity of the Balajā river, conjectured to be the same as the Banās in Marwar. There is no clue to its date, but it is clearly modern, grafting personages and fictions of its own invention on a few hints from older authorities."—*Wilson.*

BRAHMARSHI-DESA. "Kurukshetra, the Matsyas, the Panchālas, and the Surasenas. This land, which comes to Brahmāvartta, is the land of Brahmarshis."—*Manu.*

BRAHMARSHIS. *R*ishis of the Brāhman caste, who were the founders of the gotras of Brāhmans, and dwell in the sphere of Brahmā. *See Rishi.*

BRAHMA-SĀVARNI. The tenth Manu. *See* Manu.

BRAHMA SŪTRAS. Aphorisms on the Vedānta philosophy by Bādarāyana or Vyāsa. They are also called Brahma Mīmānsā Sūtrās. They are in course of translation by the Rev. K. M. Banerjea in the *Bibliotheca Indica.*

BRAHMA VAIVARTA PURĀNA. "That Purāna which is related by Sāvarni to Nārada, and contains the account of the greatness of Krishna, with the occurrences of the Rathantara-kalpa, where also the story of Brahma-varāha is repeatedly told, is called the Brahma Vaivarta Purāna, and contains 18,000 stanzas." The copies known rather exceed this number of stanzas, but the contents do not answer to this description. "The character of the work is so decidedly sectarial, and the sect to which it belongs so distinctly marked—that of the worshippers of the juvenile K*ri*sh*n*a and Rādhā, a form of belief of known modern origin"—that it must be a production of a comparatively late date. A specimen of the text and translation has been published by Stenzler.

BRAHMĀVARTTA. "Between the two divine rivers, Saraswatī and D*ri*shadwatī, lies the tract of land which the sages have named Brahmāvartta, because it was frequented by the gods."—*Manu*, ii. 17.

BRAHMA-VEDA. A name given to the Atharvan or fourth Veda, the Veda of prayers and charms.

BRAHMA-YUGA. 'The age of Brāhmans.' The first or K*ri*ta-yuga. *See* Yuga.

BRAHMOTTARA PURĀ*N*A. *See* Brahma Purā*n*a.

B*RI*HAḌ ĀRA*N*YAKA, B*RI*HAD UPANISHAD. The B*ri*had Āra*n*yaka Upanishad belongs to the *S*atapatha Brāhma*n*a, and is ascribed to the sage Yājnawalkya. It has been translated by Dr. Roer, and published in the *Bibliotheca Indica*. *See* Āra*n*yaka and Yājnawalkya.

B*RI*HAD-DEVATĀ. An ancient work in slokas by the sage *S*aunaka, which enumerates and describes the deity or deities to which each hymn and verse of the *Ri*g-veda is addressed. It frequently recites legends in support of its attributions.

B*RI*HAD-RATHA. The tenth and last king of the Maurya dynasty, founded by Chandragupta.

B*RI*HAN NĀRADĪYA PURĀ*N*A. *See* Nārada Purā*n*a.

B*RI*HASPATI. In the *Ri*g-veda the names B*ri*haspati and Brahmanaspati alternate, and are equivalent to each other. They are names "of a deity in whom the action of the worshipper upon the gods is personified. He is the suppliant, the sacrificer, the priest, who intercedes with gods on behalf of men and protects mankind against the wicked. Hence he appears as the prototype of the priests and priestly order; and is also designated as the Purohita (family priest) of the divine community. He is called in one place 'the father of the gods,' and a widely extended creative power is ascribed to him. He is also designated as 'the shining' and 'the gold-coloured,' and as 'having the thunder for his voice.'"

In later times he is a *R*ishi. He is also regent of the planet Jupiter, and the name is commonly used for the planet itself. In this character his car is called Nīti-ghosha and is drawn by eight pale horses. He was son of the *R*ishi Angiras, and he bears the patronymic Āngirasa. As preceptor of the gods he is called Animishāchārya, Chakshas, Ijya, and Indrejya. His wife, Tārā, was carried off by Soma, the moon, and this gave rise to a war called the Tārakā-maya. Soma was aided by U*s*anas, Rudra, and all the Daityas and Dānavas, while Indra and the gods took the part of B*ri*haspati. "Earth, shaken to her centre," appealed to Brahmā, who interposed and restored Tārā to her husband. She was delivered of a son which B*ri*haspati and Soma both claimed, but Tārā, at the command of Brahmā to tell the truth, declared Soma to be the father, and the child was named Budha. There is an extraordinary story in the Matsya and Bhāgavata Purā*n*as of the *R*ishis having milked the earth through B*ri*haspati. (*See* Vish*n*u Purā*n*a, i. pp. 188, 190.) B*ri*haspati was father of Bharadwāja by Mamatā, wife of Utathya. (*See* Bharadwāja.) An ancient code of law bears the name of B*ri*haspati, and he is also represented as being the Vyāsa of the "fourth, Dwāpara age." There was a *R*ishi of the name in the second Manwantara, and one who was founder of an heretical sect. Other epithets of B*ri*haspati are Jīva, 'the living,' Dīdivis, 'the bright,' Dhisha*n*a, 'the intelligent,' and, for his eloquence, Gīsh-pati, 'lord of speech.'

B*RI*HAT-KATHĀ. A large collection of tales, the original of the Kathā-sarit-sāgara (q.v.).

B*RI*HAT-SANHITĀ. A celebrated work on astronomy by Varāha Mihira. It has been printed by Kern in the *Bibliotheca Indica*, who has also published a translation in *Jour. R. A. S.* for 1870 and following years.

BUDDHA. Gotama Buddha, the founder of Buddhism. Vish*n*u's ninth incarnation. *See* Avatāra.

BUDHA. 'Wise, intelligent.' The planet Mercury, son of Soma, the moon, by Rohi*n*ī, or by Tārā, wife of B*ri*haspati. (*See* B*ri*haspati.) He married Ilā, daughter of the Manu Vaivaswata, and by her had a son, Purūravas. Budha was author of a hymn in the *Ri*g-veda. (*See* Ilā.) From his parents he is called

Saumya and Rauhineya. He is also called Praharsha*n*a, Rodhana, Tunga, and *S*yāmānga, 'black-bodied.' The intrigue of Soma with Tārā was the cause of a great quarrel, in which the gods and the Asuras fought against each other. Brahmā compelled Soma to give up Tārā, and when she returned to her husband she was pregnant. A son was born, who was so beautiful that B*ri*haspati and Soma both claimed him. Tārā for a long time refused to tell his paternity, and so excited the wrath and nearly incurred the curse of her son. At length, upon the command of Brahmā, she declared Soma to be the father, and he gave the boy the name of Budha. This name is distinct from Buddha.

CHAITANYA-CHANDRODAYA. 'The rise of the moon of Chaitanya.' A drama in ten acts by Kavi-kar*n*a-pura. It is published in the *Bibliotheca Indica.* Chaitanya was a modern Vaish*n*ava reformer, accounted an incarnation of K*ri*sh*n*a.

CHAITRA-RATHA. The grove or forest of Kuvera on Mandara, one of the spurs of Meru; it is so called from its being cultivated by the gandharva Chitra-ratha.

CHAKORA. A kind of partridge. A fabulous bird, supposed to live upon the beams of the moon.

CHAKRA-VARTĪ. A universal emperor, described by the Vish*n*u Purā*n*a as one who is born with the mark of Vish*n*u's discus visible in his hand; but, Wilson observes, "the grammatical etymology is, 'He who abides in or rules over an extensive territory called a Chakra.'"

CHĀKSHUSHA. The sixth Manu. *See* Manu.

CHAMPA. Son of P*ri*thu-lāksha, a descendant of Yayāti, through his fourth son, Anu, and founder of the city of Champā.

CHAMPĀ, CHAMPĀVATĪ, CHAMPA-MĀLINĪ, CHAMPĀ-PURI. The capital city of the country of Anga. Traces of it still remain in the neighbourhood of Bhāgalpur. It was also called Mālinī, from its being surrounded with champaka trees as with a garland (*mālā*). It is said to have derived its name from Champa, its founder, but the abundant champaka trees may assert a claim to its designation.

CHĀMU*N*D*Ā*. An emanation of the goddess Durgā, sent forth from her forehead to encounter the demons Cha*n*d*a* and Mu*n*d*a*. She is thus described in the Mārka*n*deya Purā*n*a :—

"From the forehead of Ambikā (Durgā), contracted with wrathful frowns, sprang swiftly forth a goddess of black and formidable aspect, armed with a scimitar and noose, bearing a ponderous mace, decorated with a garland of dead corses, robed in the hide of an elephant, dry and withered and hideous, with yawning mouth, and lolling tongue, and bloodshot eyes, and filling the regions with her shouts." When she had killed the two demons, she bore their heads to Durgā, who told her that she should henceforth be known, by a contraction of their names, as Chāmu*nd*ā.

CHĀ*N*AKYA. A celebrated Brāhman, who took a leading part in the destruction of the Nandas, and in the elevation of Chandra-gupta to their throne. He was a great master of finesse and artifice, and has been called the Machiavelli of India. A work upon morals and polity called Chā*n*akya Sūtra is ascribed to him. He is the chief character in the drama called Mudrā-rākshasa, and is known also by the names Vish*n*u-gupta and Kau*t*ilya. His maxims have been translated by Weber.

CHA*ND*Ā, CHA*ND*Ī. The goddess Durgā, especially in the form she assumed for the destruction of the Asura called Mahisha.

CHA*ND*Ī-MĀHĀTMYA, CHA*ND*IKĀ-MĀHĀTMYA. The same as the Cha*nd*īpā*t*ha.

CHA*ND*ĪPĀ*T*, CHA*ND*ĪPĀ*T*HA. A poem of 700 verses, forming an episode of the Mārka*nd*eya Purā*n*a. It celebrates Durgā's victories over the Asuras, and is read daily in the temples of that goddess. The work is also called Devī-māhātmya. It has been translated by Poley and by Burnouf.

CHANDRA. The moon, either as a planet or a deity. *See* Soma.

CHANDRA-GUPTA. This name was identified by Sir W. Jones with the Sandracottus or Sandrocyptus mentioned by Arrian and the other classical historians of Alexander's campaign; and somewhat later on as having entered into a treaty with Seleucus Nicator through the ambassador Megasthenes. The identification has been contested, but the chief writers on Indian antiquities have admitted it as an established fact, and have added confirmatory evidence from various sources, so that the identity admits of no reasonable doubt. This identification is of the utmost importance to Indian chronology; it is the only link by which Indian history is connected with that of Greece, and everything in Indian chronology depends upon the date of Chandra-gupta as ascertained from that assigned to Sandracottus by the classical writers. His date, as thus discovered, shows that he began to reign in 315 B.C., and as he reigned twenty-four years, his reign ended in 291 B.C. Chandra-gupta is a prominent name in both Brāhmanical and Buddhist writings, and his accession to the throne is the subject of the drama Mudrā-rākshasa.

When Alexander was in India, he learned that a king named Xandrames reigned over the Prasii (Prāchyas) at the city of Palibothra, situated at the confluence of the Ganges and another river called Erranaboas (the Sone). At this time, Sandracottus was young, but he waged war against Alexander's captains, and he raised bands of robbers, with whose help he succeeded in establishing freedom in India.

Hindu and Buddhist writers are entirely silent as to Alexander's appearance in India, but they show that Chandra-gupta overthrew the dynasty of the Nandas, which reigned over Magadha, and "established freedom in India by the help of bands of robbers." He established himself at Pā*t*ali-putra, the capital of the Nandas, which is identical with the Greek Palibothra, and this has been shown to be the modern Patna. That town does not now stand at the confluence of two rivers, but the rivers in the alluvial plains of Bengal frequently change their courses, and a change in the channel of the Sone has been established by direct geographical evidence. There is a difficulty about Xandrames. This is no doubt the Sansk*ri*t Chandramas, which some consider to be only a shorter form of the name Chandra-gupta, while others point out that the Greek references indicate that Xandrames was the predecessor of Sandracottus, rather than Sandracottus himself.

The dynasty of the Nandas that reigned over Magadha are frequently spoken of as the "nine Nandas," meaning apparently nine descents; but according to some authorities the last Nanda, named Mahā-padma, and his eight sons, are intended. Mahā-padma Nanda was the son of a *S*ūdra, and so by law he was a *S*ūdra himself. He was powerful and ambitious, cruel and avaricious. His people were disaffected; but his fall is represented as having been brought about by the Brāhman Chā*n*akya.

Chandra-gupta was then raised to the throne and founded the Mauryan dynasty, the third king of which was the great A*s*oka, grandson of Chandra-gupta. The Brāhmans and Buddhists are widely at variance as to the origin of the Maurya family. The drama Mudrā-rākshasa represents Chandra-gupta as being related to Mahā-padma Nanda, and the commentator on the Vish*n*u Purā*n*a says that he was a son of Nanda by a woman of low caste named Murā, wherefore he and his descendants were called Mauryas. This looks very like an etymological invention, and is inconsistent with the representation that the low caste of Nanda was one cause of his deposition; for were it true, the low-caste king would have been supplanted by one of still lower degree. On the other hand, the Buddhists contend that the Mauryas belonged to the same family as Buddha, who was of the royal family of the *S*ākyas. The question of the identification of Sandracottus and Chandra-gupta has been discussed at length by Wilson in the preface to the Mudrā-rākshasa in his *Hindu Theatre*, and in the Vish*n*u Purā*n*a, vol. iv. p. 185; also by Max Müller in his *History of Ancient Sanskrit Literature.*

CHANDRA-HĀSA. A prince of the south, who lost his parents soon after his birth, and fell into a state of destitution, but after going through a variety of adventures came to the throne. *See* Wheeler, vol. i. p. 522.

CHANDRA-KĀNTA. 'The moon-stone.' A gem or stone supposed to be formed by the congelation of the rays of the moon; a crystal is perhaps meant. It is supposed to exercise a cooling influence. So in the Megha-dūta—

> "The moon's white rays the smiling night illume,
> And on the moon-gem concentrated fall,
> That hangs in woven nets in every hall;
> Whence cooling dews upon the fair descend,
> And life renewed to languid nature lend."

It is also called Ma*n*ī-chaka.

CHANDRA-KETU. 1. A son of Lakshma*n*a. 2. A king of the city of Chakora. 3. A country near the Himālayas.

CHANDRA-VAN*S*A. The Lunar race. The lineage or race which claims descent from the moon. It is divided into two great branches, the Yādavas and Pauravas, respectively descended from Yadu and Puru. K*ri*sh*n*a belonged to the line of Yadu, and Dushyanta with the Kuru and Pā*n*du princes to the line of Puru. The following is a list of the Lunar race as given in the Vish*n*u Purā*n*a, but the authorities vary :—

THE LUNAR RACE.

Atri, the *Ri*shi.
Soma, the Moon.
Budha, Mercury.
Purūravas.
Āyu, Āyus.

Nahusha (and 3 others).
Yayāti (and 5 others).

Yādavas.

Yadu, eldest.
Krosh*t*u (and 3 others).
V*ri*jinīvat.
Swāhi.
Rushadgu.
Chitraratha.
*S*a*s*abindu.
P*ri*thu*s*ravas (one of a million sons).
Tamas.
U*s*anas.
*S*iteyus.
Rukmakavacha or Ruchaka.
Parāv*ri*t.
Jyāmagha.
Vidarbha.
Kratha.
Kunti.
V*ri*sh*n*i.
Nirv*ri*ti.
Da*s*ārha.
Vyoman.
Jīmūta.
Vik*ri*ti.
Bhīmaratha.
Navaratha.
Da*s*aratha.
*S*akuni.
Karambhi.
Devarāta.
Devakshattra.
Madhu.
Anavaratha.
Kuruvatsa.
Anuratha.
Puruhotra.

Pauravas.

Puru, youngest (and 3 others).
Janamejaya.
Prachinvat.
Pravīra.
Manasyu.
Abhayada.
Sudyumna.
Bahugava.
Samyāti.
Ahamyati.
Raudrā*s*wa.
*Ri*teyu (and 9 others).
Rantināra.
Tan*s*u.
Anila.
Dushyanta.
Bharata.
Bharadwāja or Vitatha } adopted.
Bhavanmanyu.
B*ri*hatkshatra (and many others).
Suhotra.
Hastin (of Hastināpur).
Ajamī*d*ha (and 2 others).
*Ri*ksha (and others).
Samvara*n*a.
Kuru.
Jahnu (and many others).
Suratha.
Vidūratha.
Sārvabhauma.
Jayasena.
Ārāvin.

*Kings of Kā*s*ī.*

Kshatrav*ri*ddha.
Suhotra.
Kā*s*a.
Kā*s*irāja.
Dīrghatamas.
Dhanwantari.
Ketumat.
Bhīmaratha.
Divodāsa.
Pratardana. / Dyumat. / *S*atrujit. / Vatsa. / *Ri*tadhwaja or Kuvalayā*s*wa. }
Alarka.
Sannati or Santati.
Sunītha.
Suketu.
Satyaketu.
Vibhu.
Suvibhu.
Sukumāra.
Dh*ri*sh*t*aketu.

THE LUNAR RACE—*Continued.*

Yādavas.	*Pauravas.*	*Kings of Kāsī.*
Ansu.	Ayutāyus.	Vainahotra.
Satwata.	Akrodhana.	Bhārga.
Andhaka (and 6 others).	Devātithi.	Bhārga-bhūmi.
Bhajamāna.	*R*iksha.	
Vidūratha.	Dilīpa.	
*S*ūra.	Pratīpa.	
*S*āmin.	*S*āntanu (and 2 others).	
Pratikshattra.	Pā*nd*u.*	
Swayambhoja.	Dh*ri*tarāsh*t*ra.	
H*ri*dika.	Yudhi-sh*t*hira.	
Devamī*d*husha.	Parikshit.	
*S*ūra.	Janamejaya.	
Vasudeva (and 9 others).	*S*atānīka.	
K*ri*sh*n*a and Bala-rāma.	A*s*wamedhadatta.	
	Adhisīmak*ri*sh*n*a.	
	Nichakru.	
(*Extinct.*)	Ush*n*a.	
	Chitraratha.	
	V*ri*sh*n*imat.	
	Sushena.	
	Sunītha.	
	*R*icha.	
	N*ri*chakshush.	
	Sukhābala.	
	Pariplava.	
	Sunaya.	
	Medhāvin.	
	N*ri*panjaya.	
	M*ri*du.	
	Tigma.	
	B*ri*hadratha.	
	Vasudāna.	
	*S*atānīka.	
	Udayana.	
	Ahīnara.	
	Kha*nd*apā*n*i.	
	Niramitra.	
	Kshemaka.	

CHĀ*N*ŪRA. A wrestler in the service of Kan*s*a, who was killed by K*ri*sh*n*a.

CHARAKA. A writer on medicine who lived in Vedic times. According to his own statement, he received the materials of his work from Agnive*s*a, to whom they were delivered by Ātreya. A legend represents him as an incarnation of the serpent *S*esha. The work was translated into Arabic before the end of the eighth century. The text has been printed in India.

* See Table under Mahā-bhārata.

CHARAKA. One of the chief schools of the Yajur-veda.

CHARAKA-BRĀHMAṆA. A Brāhmaṇa of the Black Yajur-veda.

CHARAṆA. A Vedic school or society. It is explained by a commentator as "a number of men who are pledged to the reading of a certain Śākhā of the Veda, and who have in this manner become one body."

CHĀRAṆAS. Panegyrists. The panegyrists of the gods.

CHARMAṆVATĪ. The river Chambal.

CHĀRU, CHĀRU-DEHA, CHĀRU-DESHṆA, CHĀRU-GUPTA. Sons of Kṛishṇa and Rukmiṇī.

CHĀRU-DATTA. The Brāhman hero of the drama Mṛich-chhakaṭī.

CHĀRU HĀSINĪ. 'Sweet smiler.' This epithet is used for Rukmiṇī and for Lakshmaṇā, and perhaps for other wives of Kṛishṇa.

CHĀRU-MATĪ. Daughter of Kṛishṇa and Rukmiṇī.

CHĀRVĀKA. 1. A Rākshasa, and friend of Dur-yodhana, who disguised himself as a Brāhman and reproached Yudhi-shṭhira for his crimes, when he entered Hastinā-pura in triumph after the great battle. The Brāhmans discovered the imposture and reduced Chārvāka to ashes with the fire of their eyes. 2. A sceptical philosopher who advocated materialistic doctrines. He probably lived before the composition of the Rāmāyaṇa, and is perhaps identical with the Chārvāka of the Mahā-bhārata. His followers are called by his name.

CHATUR-VARṆA. The four castes. *See* Varṇa.

CHEDI. Name of a people and of their country, the modern Chandail and Boglekhand. The capital was Śukti-matī, and among the kings of this country were Dama-ghosha and Śiśu-pāla.

CHEKIṬĀNA. A son of Dhṛishṭa-ketu, Rāja of the Kekayas, and an ally of the Pāṇḍavas.

CHERA. A kingdom in the south of the peninsula, which was absorbed by its rival the Chola kingdom.

CHHANDAS, CHHANDO. Metre. One of the Vedāngas. The oldest known work on the subject is "the Chhandaḥ-śāstra, ascribed to Pingala, which may be as old as the second century B.C." It is published in the *Bibliotheca Indica*. The subject is one to which great attention has been given by the Hindus from the earliest times.

CHHANDOGA. A priest or chanter of the Sāma-veda.

CHHĀNDOGYA. Name of a Upanishad of the Sāma-veda. (*See* Upanishad.) It has been printed by Dr. Roer, and it has been translated into English by Rājendra Lāl, and published in the *Bibliotheca Indica*. There is also another printed edition of the text. The Chhāndogya Upanishad consists of eight out of ten chapters of the Chhāndogya Brāhma*n*a; the first two chapters are yet wanting. This work is particularly distinguished by its rich store of legends regarding the gradual development of Brahmanical theology.

CHHĀYĀ. 'Shade.' A handmaid of the sun. Sanjnā, wife of the sun, being unable to bear the fervour of her lord, put her handmaid Chhāyā in her place. The sun, believing Chhāyā to be his wife, had three children by her: *S*ani, the planet Saturn; the Manu Sāvar*n*i; and a daughter, the Tapatī river. As mother of Saturn, Chhāyā is known as *S*ani-prasū. The partiality which she showed for these children provoked Yama, the son of Sanjnā, and he lifted his foot to kick her. She cursed him to have his leg affected with sores and worms. This made it clear that she was not Sanjnā and mother of Yama, so the sun went in search of Sanjnā and brought her back. According to one Purā*n*a, Chhāyā was a daughter of Vi*s*wakarma, and sister of Sanjnā, the wife of the sun.

CHINTĀ-MA*N*I. 'The wish-gem.' A jewel which is supposed to have the power of granting all desires. The philosopher's stone. It is said to have belonged to Brahmā, who is himself called by this name. It is also called Divya-ratna.

CHIRA-JĪVIN. 'Long-lived.' Gods or deified mortals, who live for long periods.

CHITRA-GUPTA. A scribe in the abodes of the dead, who records the virtues and vices of men. The recorder of Yama.

CHITRA-KŪ*T*A. 'Bright-peak.' The seat of Vālmīki's hermitage, in which Rāma and Sītā both found refuge at different times. It is the modern Chitrakote, on the river Pi*s*uni, about fifty miles south-east of Banda in Bundelkhand. It is a very holy place, and abounds with temples and shrines, to which thousands annually resort. "The whole neighbourhood is Rāma's country. Every headland has some legend, every cavern is connected with his name."—*Cust in "Calcutta Review."*

CHITRA-LEKHĀ. A picture. Name of a nymph who was skilled in painting and in the magic art. She was the friend and confidante of Ūshā. *See* Ūshā.

CHITRĀNGADA. The elder son of King *S*āntanu, and brother of Bhīshma. He was arrogant and proud, and was killed in early life in a conflict with a Gandharva of the same name.

CHITRĀNGADĀ. Daughter of King Chritra-vāha*n*a of Ma*n*i-pura, wife of Arjuna and mother of Babhru-vāhana.

CHITRA-RATHA. 'Having a fine car.' The king of the Gandharvas. There are many others known by this name.

CHITRA-SENA. 1. One of the hundred sons of Dh*r*itarāsh*t*ra. 2. A chief of the Yakshas.

CHITRA-YAJNA. A modern drama in five acts upon the legend of Daksha. It is the work of a Pa*n*dit named Vaidyanātha Vāchaspati.

CHOLA. A country and kingdom of the south of India about Tanjore. The country was called Chola-ma*nd*ala, whence comes the name Coromandel.

CHYAVANA, CHYAVĀNA. A sage, son of the *R*ishi Bh*r*igu, and author of some hymns.

In the *R*ig-veda it is said that when "Chyavana had grown old and had been forsaken, the A*s*wins divested him of his decrepit body, prolonged his life, and restored him to youth, making him acceptable to his wife, and the husband of maidens." This story is thus amplified in the *S*atapatha Brāhma*n*a :—The sage Chyavana assumed a shrivelled form and lay as if abandoned. The sons of *S*aryāta, a descendant of Manu, found this body, and pelted it with clods. Chyavana was greatly incensed, and to appease him *S*aryāta yoked his chariot, and taking with him his daughter Su-kanyā, presented her to Chyavana. The A*s*wins endeavoured to seduce her, but she remained faithful to her shrivelled husband, and under his direction she taunted them with being incomplete and imperfect, and consented to tell them in what respect they were deficient, if they would make her husband young again. They directed that he should bathe in a certain pond, and having done so, he came forth with the age that he desired. She then informed them that they were imperfect because they were excluded from a sacrifice the other gods were performing.

They departed and succeeded in getting admitted to join the other gods.

According to the Māhā-bhārata, Chyavana besought Indra to allow the A*s*wins to partake of the libations of soma. Indra replied that the other gods might do as they pleased, but he would not consent. Chyavana then commenced a sacrifice to the A*s*wins; the other gods were subdued, but Indra, in a rage, rushed with a mountain in one hand and his thunderbolt in another to crush Chyavana. The sage having sprinkled him with water and stopped him, "created a fearful open-mouthed monster called Mada, having teeth and grinders of portentous length, and jaws one of which enclosed the earth, the other the sky; and the gods, including Indra, are said to have been at the root of his tongue like fishes in the mouth of a sea monster." In this predicament "Indra granted the demand of Chyavana, who was thus the cause of the A*s*wins becoming drinkers of the soma."

In another part of the Mahā-bhārata he is represented as exacting many menial offices from King Ku*s*ika and his wife, but he afterwards rewarded them by "creating a magical golden palace," and predicted the birth of "a grandson of great beauty and heroism (Para*s*u-rāma)."

The Mahā-bhārata, interpreting his name as signifying 'the fallen,' accounts for it by a legend which represents his mother, Pulomā, wife of Bh*ri*gu, as having been carried off by the demon Puloman. She was pregnant, and in her fright the child fell from her womb. The demon was softened, and let the mother depart with her infant.

The version of the story as told in the Mahā-bhārata and Purā*n*as is that Chyavana was so absorbed in penance on the banks of the Narmadā that white ants constructed their nests round his body and left only his eyes visible. Su-kanyā, daughter of King *S*aryāta, seeing two bright eyes in what seemed to be an anthill, poked them with a stick. The sage visited the offence on *S*aryāta, and was appeased only by the promise of the king to give him Su-kanyā in marriage. Subsequently the A*s*wins, coming to his hermitage, compassionated her union with so old and ugly a husband as Chyavana, and tried to induce her to take one of them in his place. When their persuasions failed, they told her they were the physicians of the gods, and would restore her husband to youth and beauty, when she could make her choice between him and one of them. Accordingly the three bathed in a pond and came forth of like celestial beauty. Each one asked her to be his bride, and she recognised and chose her own husband. Chyavana, in gratitude, compelled Indra to admit the A*s*wins to a participation of the soma ceremonial. Indra at first objected, because the A*s*wins wandered about among men as physicians and changed their forms at will. But Chyavana was not to be refused; he stayed the arm of Indra as he was about to launch a thunderbolt, and he created a terrific demon who was on the point of devouring the king of the gods when he submitted.

According to the Mahā-bhārata, Chyavana was husband of Ārushī or Su-kanyā and father of Aurva. He is also considered to be the father of Hārita.

The name is Chyavāna in the *Ri*g-veda, but Chyavana in the Brāhma*n*a and later writings.

DADHYANCH, DADHĪCHA. (Dadhīcha is a later form.) A Vedic *Ri*shi, son of Atharvan, whose name frequently occurs. The legend about him, as it appears in the *Ri*g-veda, is that Indra taught him certain sciences, but threatened to cut off his head if he taught them to any one else. The A*s*wins prevailed upon Dadhyanch to communicate his knowledge to them, and, to preserve him from the wrath of Indra, they took off his own head and replaced it with that of a horse. When Indra struck off the sage's equine head the A*s*wins restored his own to him. A verse of the *Ri*g-veda says, "Indra, with the bones of Dadhyanch, slew ninety times nine V*ri*tras;" and the story told by the scholiast in explanation is, that while Dadhyanch was living on earth the Asuras were controlled and tranquillised by his appearance; but when he had gone to heaven, they overspread the whole earth. Indra inquired for Dadhyanch, or any relic of him. He was told of the horse's head, and when this was found in a lake near Kuru-kshetra, Indra used the bones as weapons, and with them slew the Asuras, or, as the words of the Vedic verse are explained, he "foiled the nine times ninety stratagems of the Asuras or V*ri*tras." The story as afterwards told in the Mahā-bhārata and Purā*n*as is that the sage devoted himself to death that Indra and the gods might be armed with his bones as more effective weapons than thunderbolts for the destruction of Vritra and the Asuras. According to one account he was instrumental in bring about the destruction of "Daksha's sacrifice." *See* Daksha.

DAITYAS. Titans. Descendants from Diti by Kasyapa. They are a race of demons and giants, who warred against the gods and interfered with sacrifices. They were in turn victorious and vanquished. They and the Dānavas are generally associated, and are hardly distinguishable. As enemies of sacrifices they are called Kratu-dwishas.

*D*ĀKINĪ. A kind of female imp or fiend attendant upon Kālī and feeding on human flesh. The *D*ākinīs are also called Asra-pas, 'blood drinkers.'

DAKSHA. 'Able, competent, intelligent.' This name generally carries with it the idea of a creative power. Daksha is a son of Brahmā; he is one of the Prajāpatis, and is sometimes regarded as their chief. There is a great deal of doubt and confusion about him, which of old the sage Parāsara could only account for by saying that "in every age Daksha and the rest are born and are again destroyed." In the *Ri*g-veda it is said that "Daksha sprang from Aditi, and Aditi from Daksha." Upon this marvellous mutual generation Yāska in the Nirukta remarks, "How can this be possible? They may have had the same origin; or, according to the nature of the gods, they may have been born from each other, and have derived their substance from each other." Roth's view is that Aditi is eternity, and that Daksha (spiritual power) is the male energy which generates the gods in eternity. In the *S*atapatha Brāhma*n*a, Daksha is identified with Prajāpati, the creator. As son of Aditi, he is one of the Ādityas, and he is also reckoned among the Viswadevas.

According to the Mahā-bhārata, Daksha sprang from the right thumb of Brahmā, and his wife from that deity's left thumb. The Purā*n*as adopt this view of his origin, but state that he married Prasūti, daughter of Priya-vrata, and grand-daughter of Manu. By her he had, according to various statements, twenty-four, fifty, or sixty daughters. The Rāmāya*n*a and Mahā-bhārata agree in the larger number; and according to Manu and the Mahā-bhārata he gave ten of his daughters to Dharma and thirteen to Kasyapa, who became the mothers of gods and demons, men, birds, serpents, and all living things. Twenty-seven were given in marriage to Soma, the moon, and these became the twenty-seven Nakshatras or lunar mansions. One of the daughters, named Satī, married *S*iva, and killed herself in consequence of a quarrel between her husband and father. The Kā*s*ī Kha*n*da represents that she became a satī and burnt herself.

Another legend of the Mahā-bhārata and Purā*n*as represents Daksha as being born a second time, in another Manwantara, as son of the Prachetasas and Mārishā, and that he had seven sons, "the allegorical persons Krodha, Tamas, Dama, Vik*ri*ta, Angiras, Kardama, and A*s*wa." This second birth is said to have happened through his having been cursed to it by his son-in-law *S*iva. Daksha was in a certain way, by his mother Mārishā, an emanation of Soma, the moon; and as twenty-seven of his daughters were married to that luminary, Daksha is sometimes referred to as being both the father and the offspring of the moon, thus reiterating the duality of his nature.

In the Hari-vansa Daksha appears in another variety of his character. According to this authority, Vish*n*u himself became Daksha, and formed numerous creatures, or, in other words, he became the creator. Daksha, the first of males, by virtue of yoga, himself took the form of a beautiful woman, by whom he had many fair daughters, whom he disposed of in marriage in the manner related by Manu and above stated.

An important event in the life of Daksha, and very frequently referred to, is "Daksha's sacrifice," which was violently interrupted and broken up by *S*iva. The germ of this story is found in the Taittirīya Sanhitā, where it is related that the gods, having excluded Rudra from a sacrifice, he pierced the sacrifice with an arrow, and that Pūshan, attempting to eat a portion of the oblation, broke his teeth. The story is found both in the Rāmāya*n*a and Mahā-bhārata. According to the latter, Daksha was engaged in sacrifice, when *S*iva in a rage, and shouting loudly, pierced the offering with an arrow. The gods and Asuras were alarmed and the whole universe quaked. The *Ri*shis endeavoured to appease the angry god, but in vain. "He ran up to the gods, and in his rage knocked out the eyes of Bhaga with a blow, and, incensed, assaulted Pūshan with his foot and knocked out his teeth as he was eating the offering." The gods and *R*ishis humbly propitiated him, and when he was appeased "they apportioned to him a distinguished share in the sacrifice, and through fear resorted to him as their refuge." In another part of the same work the story is again told with considerable variation. Daksha instituted a sacrifice and apportioned no share to Rudra (*S*iva). Instigated by the sage Dadhīchi, the god hurled his blazing trident, which destroyed the sacrifice of Daksha and fell with great violence on the breast of Nārāya*n*a (Vish*n*u). It was hurled back with violence to its owner, and a furious battle ensued between the two gods, which was not intermitted till Brahmā prevailed upon Rudra to propitiate Nārāya*n*a. That god was gratified, and said to Rudra, "He who knows thee knows me; he who loves thee loves me."

The story is reproduced in the Purā*n*as with many embellishments. Daksha instituted a sacrifice to Vish*n*u, and many of the gods repaired to it, but *S*iva was not invited, because the gods had conspired to deprive him of sacrificial offerings. The wife of *S*iva, the mountain goddess Umā, perceived what was going on. Umā was a second birth of Satī, daughter of Daksha, who had deprived herself of life in consequence of her father's quarrel with herself and her husband, *S*iva. Umā urged her husband to display his power and assert his rights. So he created Vīra-bhadra, "a being like the fire of fate," and of most terrific appearance and powers. He also sent with him hundreds and thousands of powerful demigods whom he called into existence. A terrible catastrophe followed; "the mountains tottered, the earth shook, the winds roared, and the depths of the sea were disturbed." The sacrifice is broken up, and, in the words of Wilson, "Indra is knocked down and trampled on, Yama has his staff broken, Saraswatī and the Māt*r*is have their noses cut off, Mitra or Bhaga has his eyes pulled out, Pūshan has his teeth knocked down his throat, Chandra (the moon) is pummelled, Vahni's (fire's) hands are cut off, Bh*r*igu loses his beard, the Brāhmans are pelted with stones, the Prajāpatis are beaten, and the gods and demigods are run through with swords or stuck with arrows." Daksha then, in great terror, propitiated the wrathful deity and acknowledged his supremacy. According to some versions, Daksha himself was decapitated and his head thrown into the fire. *S*iva subsequently restored him and the other dead to life, and as Daksha's head could not be found, it was replaced by that of a goat or ram. The Hari-vansa, in its glorification of Vishnu, gives a different finish to the story. The sacrifice was destroyed and the gods fled in dismay, till Vishnu intervened, and seizing Siva by the throat, compelled him to desist and acknowledge his master.

"This," says Wilson, "is a legend of some interest, as it is obviously intended to intimate a struggle between the worshippers of Siva and Vishnu, in which at first the latter, but finally the former, acquired the ascendancy."

Daksha was a lawgiver, and is reckoned among the eighteen writers of Dharma-sāstras.

The name Daksha was borne by several other persons.

DAKSHA-SĀVARNA. The ninth Manu. *See* Manu.

DĀKSHĀYANA. Connected with Daksha. A son or descendant of that sage.

DĀKSHĀYANĪ. A name of Aditi as daughter of Daksha.

DAKSHINĀ. A present made to Brāhmans; the honorarium for the performance of a sacrifice. This is personified as a goddess, to whom various origins are assigned.

DAKSHINĀCHĀRĪS. Followers of the right-hand form of Sākta worship. *See* Tantra.

DAMA. A son, or, according to the Vishnu Purāna, a grandson of King Marutta of the Solar race. He rescued his bride Su-manā from his rivals, and one of them, named Vapushmat, subsequently killed Marutta, who had retired into the woods after relinquishing his crown to his son. Dama in retaliation killed Vapushmat and offered his blood in the funeral rites of Marutta, while he made an oblation of part of the flesh, and with the rest fed the Brāhmans who were of Rākshasa descent.

DAMA-GHOSHA. King of Chedi and father of Sisu-pāla.

DAMAYANTĪ. Wife of Nala and heroine of the tale of Nala and Damayantī. She is also known by her patronymic Bhaimī. *See* Nala.

DAMBHODBHAVA. A king whose story is related in the Mahā-bhārata as an antidote to pride. He had an overweening conceit of his own prowess, and when told by his Brāhmans that he was no match for Nara and Nārāyana, who were living as ascetics on the Gandha-mādana mountain, he proceeded thither with his army and challenged them. They endeavoured to dissuade him, but he insisted on fighting. Nara then took a handful of straws, and using them as missiles, they whitened all the air, and penetrated the eyes, ears, and noses of the assailants, until Dambhodbhava fell at Nara's feet and begged for peace.

DĀMODARA. A name given to Kr*ish*n*a* because his foster-mother tried to tie him up with a rope (*dāma*) round his belly (*udara*).

DĀNAVAS. Descendants from Danu by the sage Ka*s*yapa. They were giants who warred against the gods. *See* Daityas.

DA*N*D*A*-DHARA. 'The rod-bearer.' A title of Yama, the god of death.

DA*N*D*A*KA. The ara*n*ya or forest of Da*n*d*a*ka, lying between the Godāvarī and Narmadā. It was of vast extent, and some passages of the Rāmāya*n*a represent it as beginning immediately south of the Yamunā. This forest is the scene of many of Rāma and Sītā's adventures, and is described as "a wilderness over which separate hermitages are scattered, while wild beasts and Rākshasas everywhere abound."

DANTA-VAKTRA. A Dānava king of Karūsha and son of V*r*iddha-*s*arma. He took a side against Kr*ish*n*a*, and was eventually killed by him.

DANU. A Dānava. Also the mother of the Dānavas. The demon Kabandha (q.v.).

DARADA. A country in the Hindu Kush, bordering on Kashmīr. The people of that country, "the Durds, are still where they were at the date of the text (of the Vish*n*u Purā*n*a) and in the days of Strabo and Ptolemy; not exactly, indeed, at the sources of the Indus, but along its course above the Himālaya, just before it descends to India."—*Wilson.*

DARBAS. 'Tearers.' Rākshasas and other destructive demons.

DARDURA. Name of a mountain in the south; it is associated with the Malaya mountain in the Mahā-bhārata.

DAR*S*ANA. 'Demonstration.' The Sha*d*-darsanas or six demonstrations, *i.e.*, the six schools of Hindu philosophy. All these schools have one starting-point, *ex nihilo nihil fit;* and all have one and the same final object, the emancipation of the soul from future birth and existence, and its absorption into the supreme soul of the universe. These schools are :—

1. Nyāya, founded by the sage Gotama. The word *nyāya*

means propriety or fitness, the proper method of arriving at a conclusion by analysis. This school has been called the Logical School, but the term is applicable to its method rather than to its aims. It is also said to represent "the sensational aspect of Hindu philosophy," because it has "a more pointed regard to the fact of the five senses than the others have, and treats the external more frankly as a solid reality." It is the exoteric school, as the Vedānta is the esoteric.

2. Vaiseshika, founded by a sage named Kanāda, who lived about the same time as Gotama. It is supplementary to the Nyāya, and these two schools are classed together. It is called the Atomic School, because it teaches the existence of a transient world composed of aggregations of eternal atoms.

Both the Nyāya and Vaiseshika recognise a Supreme Being.

3. Sānkhya. The Sānkhya and Yoga are classed together because they have much in common, but the Sānkhya is atheistical, while the Yoga is theistical. The Sānkhya was founded by the sage Kapila, and takes its name from its numeral or discriminative tendencies. The Sānkhya-Kārikā, the text-book of this school, has been translated by Colebrooke and Wilson, and part of the aphorisms of Kapila were translated for the *Bibliotheca Indica* by the late Dr. Ballantyne.

4. Yoga. This school was founded by Patanjali, and from his name is also called Pātanjala. It pursues the method of the Sānkhya and holds with many of its dogmas, but it asserts the existence not only of individual souls, but of one all-pervading spirit, which is free from the influences which affect other souls.

5. Pūrva-mīmānsā. 6. Uttara-mīmānsā. The prior and later Mīmānsās. These are both included in the general term Vedānta, but the Pūrva-mīmānsā is commonly known as the Mīmānsā and the Uttara-mīmānsā as the Vedānta, 'the end or object of the Vedas.' The Pūrva-mīmānsā was founded by Jaimini, and the Uttara-mīmānsā is attributed to Vyāsa, the arranger of the Vedas. "The object of both these schools is to teach the art of reasoning with the express purpose of aiding the interpretation of the Vedas, not only in the speculative but the practical portion." The principal doctrines of the Vedānta (Uttara) are that "God is the omniscient and omnipotent cause of the existence, continuance, and dissolution of the universe. Creation is an act of his will; he is both the efficient and the material cause of the

world." At the consummation of all things all are resolved into him. He is "the sole-existent and universal soul," and besides him there is no second principle; he is *adwaita*, 'without a second.' *S*ankarāchārya was the great apostle of this school.

The period of the rise of these schools of philosophy is uncertain, and is entirely a matter of inference, but they are probably later than the fifth century B.C. The Vedānta (Uttara-mīmānsā) is apparently the latest, and is supposed to have been evoked by the teachings of the Buddhists. This would bring it to within three or four centuries B.C. The other schools are to all appearance older than the Vedānta, but it is considered by some that all the schools show traces of Buddhist influences, and if so, the dates of all must be later. It is a question whether Hindu philosophy is or is not indebted to Greek teaching, and the later the date of the origin of these schools the greater is the possibility of Greek influence. Mr. Colebrooke, the highest authority on the subject, is of opinion that "the Hindus were in this instance the teachers, not the learners."

Besides the six schools, there is yet a later system known as the Paurā*n*ik and the Eclectic school. The doctrines of this school are expounded in the Bhagavad-gītā (q.v.).

The merits of the various schools have been thus summed up:— "When we consider the six Dar*s*anas, we shall find that one of them, the Uttara-mīmānsā, bears no title to be ranked by the side of the others, and is really little more than a mystical explanation of the practical injunctions of the Vedas. We shall also admit that the earlier Vedānta, very different from the school of Nihilists now existing under that name, was chiefly a controversial essay, seeking to support the theology of sacred writ, but borrowing all its philosophical portions from the Yoga school, the most popular at the time of its composition. Lastly, the Nyāya is little more than a treatise on logic, introducing the doctrines of the theistic Sānkhya; while the Vai*s*eshika is an essay on physics, with, it is true, the theory of atoms as its distinguishing mark, though even to this we feel inclined to refuse the imputation of novelty, since we find some idea of it lurking obscurely in the theory of subtile elements which is brought forward in Kapila's Sānkhya. In short, the basis of all Indian philosophy, if indeed we may not say the only system of philosophy really discovered in India, is the Sānkhya, and this forms the basis of the doctrines expounded in the Bhagavad-gītā."—*Cockburn Thomson.*

Colebrooke's *Essays* are the great authorities on Hindu philosophy. Ballantyne has translated many of the original aphorisms, and he, Cockburn Thomson, Hall, Banerjea, and others have written on the subject.

DĀRUKA. K*ri*sh*n*a's charioteer, and his attendant in his last days.

DA*S*A-KUMĀRA-CHARITA. 'Tales of the ten princes,' by *S*rī Da*n*d*ī*. It is one of the few Sansk*ri*t works written in prose, but its style is so studied and elaborate that it is classed as a Kāvya or poem. The tales are stories of common life, and display a low condition of morals and a corrupt state of society. The text has been printed with a long analytical introduction by H. H. Wilson, and again in Bombay by Bühler. There is an abridged translation by Jacobs, also a translation in French by Fauche, and a longer analysis in vol. iv. of Wilson's works.

DA*S*ĀNANA. 'Ten faced.' A name of Rāva*n*a.

DA*S*A-RATHA. A prince of the Solar race, son of Aja, a descendant of Ikshwāku, and king of Ayodhyā. He had three wives, but being childless, he performed the sacrifice of a horse, and, according to the Rāmāya*n*a, the chief queen, Kau*s*alyā, remained in close contact with the slaughtered horse for a night, and the other two queens beside her. Four sons were then born to him from his three wives. Kau*s*alyā bore Rāma, Kaikeyī gave birth to Bharata, and Su-mitrā bore Lakshma*n*a and *S*atru-ghna. Rāma partook of half the nature of Vish*n*u, Bharata of a quarter, and the other two shared the remaining fourth. The Rāmāya*n*a, in explanation of this manifestation of Vish*n*u, says that he had promised the gods to become incarnate as man for the destruction of Rāva*n*a. He chose Da*s*a-ratha for his human parent; and when that king was performing a second sacrifice to obtain progeny, he came to him out of the fire as a glorious being, and gave him a vessel full of nectar to administer to his wives. Da*s*a-ratha gave half of it to Kau*s*alyā, and a fourth each to Su-mitrā and Kaikeyī. They all in consequence became pregnant, and their offspring partook of the divine nature according to the portion of the nectar each had drunk. There were several others of the name. *See* Rāma-chandra.

DA*S*ĀRHA, DĀ*S*ĀRHA. Prince of the Da*s*ārhas, a title of K*ri*sh*n*a. The Da*s*ārhas were a tribe of Yādavas.

DA*S*A-RŪPAKA. An early treatise on dramatic composition. It has been published by Hall in the *Bibliotheca Indica.*

DĀSAS. 'Slaves.' Tribes and people of India who opposed the progress of the intrusive Āryans.

DASRAS. 'Beautiful.' The elder of the two A*s*wins, or in the dual (Dasrau), the two A*s*wins.

DASYUS. In the Vedas they are evil beings, enemies of the gods and men. They are represented as being of a dark colour, and probably were the natives of India who contended with the immigrant Āryans. It has, however, been maintained that they were hermits and ascetics of Āryan race. In later times they are barbarians, robbers, outcasts, who, according to some authorities, descended from Vi*s*wāmitra.

DATTAKA-CHANDRIKĀ. A treatise on the law of adoption by Devana Bha*tt*a. Translated by Sutherland.

DATTAKA-MĪMĀNSĀ. A treatise on the law of adoption by Nanda Pa*nd*ita. Translated by Sutherland.

DATTAKA-*S*IROMA*N*I. A digest of the principal treatises on the law of adoption. Printed at Calcutta.

DATTĀTREYA. Son of Atri and Anasūyā. A Brāhman saint in whom a portion of Brahmā, Vish*n*u, and *S*iva, or more particularly Vish*n*u, was incarnate. He had three sons, Soma, Datta, and Dur-vāsas, to whom also a portion of the divine essence was transmitted. He was the patron of Kārta-vīrya, and gave him a thousand arms.

DĀYA-BHĀGA. 'Law of inheritance.' This title belongs especially to the treatise of Jīmūta Vāhana, current in Bengal. Translated by Colebrooke.

DĀYA-KRAMA-SANGRAHA. A treatise on the law of inheritance as current in Bengal, by *S*rī K*r*ish*n*a Tarkālankāra. Translated by Wynch.

DĀYA-TATWA. A treatise on the law of inheritance as current in Bengal, by Raghunandana Bha*tt*āchārya.

DEVA. (Nom. Devas = Deus, from the root *Div*, to shine.) God. A deity. The gods are spoken of as thirty-three in number, eleven for each of the three worlds.

DEVAKA. Father of Devakī and brother of Ugrasena.

DEVAKĪ. Wife of Vasu-deva, mother of K*r*ish*n*a and cousin of Kan*s*a. She is sometimes called an incarnation of

Aditi, and is said to have been born again as P*ri*snī, the wife of King Su-tapas.

DEVALA. A Vedic *Ri*shi, to whom some hymns are attributed. There are several men, of this name; one was author of a code of law, another was an astronomer, and one the grandfather of Pā*n*ini.

DEVĀLĀ. Music, personified as a female.

DEVA-LOKA. The world of the gods, *i.e.*, Swarga, Indra's heaven.

DEVA-MĀT*RI*. 'Mother of the gods.' An appellation of Aditi (q.v.).

DEVA-RĀTA. 1. A royal *Ri*shi of the Solar race, who dwelt among the Videhas, and had charge of *S*iva's bow, which descended to Janaka and was broken by Rāma. 2. A name given to *S*una*h*-sephas.

DEVARSHIS. (Deva-*ri*shis.) *Ri*shis or saints of the celestial class, who dwell in the regions of the gods, such as Nārada. Sages who have attained perfection upon earth and have been exalted as demigods to heaven.

DEVATĀ. A divine being or god. The name Devatās includes the gods in general, or, as most frequently used, the whole body of inferior gods.

DEVATĀDHYĀYA-BRĀHMA*N*A. The fifth Brāhma*n*a of the Sāma-veda. The text has been edited by Burnell.

DEVAYĀNĪ. Daughter of *S*ukra, priest of the Daityas. She fell in love with her father's pupil Kacha, son of B*ri*haspati, but he rejected her advances. She cursed him, and in return he cursed her, that she, a Brāhman's daughter, should marry a Kshatriya. Devayānī was companion to Sarmish*t*hā, daughter of the king of the Daityas. One day they went to bathe, and the god Vāyu changed their clothes. When they were dressed, they began to quarrel about the change, and Devayānī spoke "with a scowl so bitter that Sarmish*t*hā slapped her face, and pushed her into a dry well." She was rescued by King Yayāti, who took her home to her father. *S*ukra, at his daughter's vehement persuasion, demanded satisfaction from Sarmish*t*hā's father, the Daitya king. He conceded Devayānī's demand, that upon her marriage Sarmish*t*hā should be given to her for a servant. Devayānī married King Yayāti, a Kshatriya, and Sarmish*t*hā became her servant. Subsequently Yayāti became enamoured of Sarmish*th*ā, and she bore him a son, the discovery of which so enraged Devayānī that she parted from her husband, and went home to her father, having borne two sons, Yadu and Turvasa or Turvasu. Her father, *S*ukra, cursed Yayāti with the infirmity of old age, but afterwards offered to transfer it to any one of Yayāti's sons who would submit to receive it. Yadu, the eldest, and progenitor of the Yādavas, refused, and so did all the other sons, with the exception of Sarmish*th*ā's youngest son, Puru. Those who refused were cursed by their father, that their posterity should never possess dominion; but Puru, who bore his father's curse for a thousand years, succeeded his father as monarch, and was the ancestor of the Pā*nd*avas and Kauravas.

DEVA-YONI. 'Of divine birth.' A general name for the inferior gods, the Ādityas, Vasus, Viswadevas, and others.

DEVĪ. 'The goddess,' or Mahā-devī, 'the great goddess,' wife of the god *S*iva, and daughter of Himavat, *i.e.*, the Himālaya mountains. She is mentioned in the Mahā-bhārata under a variety of names, and with several of her peculiar characteristics, but she owes her great distinction to the Purā*n*as and later works. As the *S*akti or female energy of *S*iva she has two characters, one mild, the other fierce; and it is under the latter that she is especially worshipped. She has a great variety of names, referable to her various forms, attributes, and actions, but these names are not always used accurately and distinctively. In her milder form she is Umā, 'light,' and a type of beauty; Gaurī, 'the yellow or brilliant;' Pārvatī, 'the mountaineer;' and Haimavatī, from her parentage; Jagan-mātā, 'the mother of the world;' and Bhavānī. In her terrible form she is Durgā, 'the inaccessible;' Kālī and *S*yāmā, 'the black;' Cha*nd*ī and Cha*n*-*d*ikā, 'the fierce;' and Bhairavī, 'the terrible.' It is in this character that bloody sacrifices are offered to her, that the barbarities of the Durgā-pūjā and Charak-pūjā are perpetrated in her honour, and that the indecent orgies of the Tāntrikas are held to propitiate her favours and celebrate her powers. She has ten arms, and in most of her hands there are weapons. As Durgā she is a beautiful yellow woman, riding on a tiger in a fierce and menacing attitude. As Kālī or Kālikā, 'the black,' "she is represented with a black skin, a hideous and terrible countenance, dripping with blood, encircled with snakes, hung round with skulls and human heads, and in all respects resembling a fury rather than a goddess." As Vindhya-vāsinī, 'the dweller in the Vindhyas,' she is worshipped at a place of that name where the Vindhyas approach the Ganges, near Mirzapur, and it is said that there the blood before her image is never allowed to get dry. As Mahā-māyā she is the great illusion.

The Chan*d*ī-māhātmya, which celebrates the victories of this goddess over the Asuras, speaks of her under the following names :—1. Durgā, when she received the messengers of the Asuras. 2. Da*s*a-bhujā. 'Ten-armed,' when she destroyed part of their army. 3. Sinha-vāhinī. 'Riding on a lion,' when she fought with the Asura general Rakta-vīja. 4. Mahisha-mardinī. 'Destroyer of Mahisha,' an Asura in the form of a buffalo. 5. Jagad-dhātri. 'Fosterer of the world,' when she again defeated the Asura army. 6. Kālī. 'The black.' She killed Rakta-vīja. 7. Mukta-ke*s*ī. 'With dishevelled hair.' Again defeats the Asuras. 8. Tārā. 'Star.' She killed *S*umbha. 9. Chhinna-mastakā. 'Decapitated,' the headless form in which she killed Ni*s*umbha. 10. Jagad-gaurī. 'World's fair one,' as lauded by the gods for her triumphs. The names which Devī obtains from her husband are :—Babhravī (Babhru), Bhagavatī, Ī*s*ānī, Ī*s*warī, Kālanjarī, Kapālinī, Kau*s*ikī, Kirātī, Mahe*s*warī, M*ri*dā, M*ri*dānī, Rud-rā*n*ī, *S*arvā*n*ī, *S*ivā, Tryambakī. From her origin she is called Adri-jā and Giri-jā, 'mountain-born;' Ku-jā, 'earth-born;' Daksha-jā, 'sprung from Daksha.' She is Kanyā, 'the virgin;' Kanyā-kumārī, 'the youthful virgin;' and Ambikā, 'the mother;' Avarā, 'the youngest;' Anantā and Nityā, 'the ever-lasting;' Āryā, 'the revered;' Vijayā, 'victorious;' *Ri*ddhi, 'the rich;' Satī, 'virtuous;' Dakshi*n*ā, 'right-handed;' Pingā, 'tawny, dark;' Karburī, 'spotted;' Bhramarī, 'the bee;' Ko*t*arī, 'the naked;' Kar*n*a-motī, 'pearl-eared;' Padma-lānch-hanā, 'distinguished by a lotus;' Sarva-mangalā, 'always auspicious;' *S*ākam-bharī, 'nourisher of herbs;' *S*iva-dūtī, '*S*iva's messenger;' Sinha-rathī, 'riding on a lion.' As addicted to austerities she is Apar*n*ā and Kātyāyanī. As Bhūta-nāyakī she is chief or leader of the goblins, and as Ga*n*a-nāyakī, the leader of the Ga*n*as. She is Kāmākshī, 'wanton-eyed;' and Kāmākhyā, 'called by the name of Kāma, desire.' Other names, most of them applicable to her terrible forms, are Bhadra-kālī, Bhīma-devī, Chāmu*nd*ā, Mahā-kālī, Mahāmārī, Mahāsurī,

Mātangī, Rajasī, 'the fierce;' and Rakta-dantī, 'red or bloody toothed.'

DEVĪ BHĀGAVATA PURĀ*N*A. A *S*aiva Purā*n*a, which is by some placed among the eighteen Purā*n*as instead of the *S*rī Bhāgavata, which is devoted to Vish*n*u. This is devoted to the worship of the *S*aktis.

DEVĪ MĀHĀTMYA. 'The greatness of Devī.' A poem of 700 verses, which celebrates the triumphs of Devī over various Asuras. It is the text-book of the worshippers of Devī, and is read daily in her temples. It is an episode of the Mārka*nd*eya Purā*n*a, and is also called Cha*nd*ipā*t*ha.

DHANA-DA. 'Giver of wealth.' Kuvera, the god of riches.

DHANAN-JAYA. 'Conqueror of riches.' A title of Arjuna and of several others.

DHANANJAYA VIJAYA. 'Victories of Dhananjaya' (Arjuna). A drama in one act on the exploits of Arjuna when in the service of the Rāja Virā*t*a.

DHĀNA-PATI. 'Lord of wealth.' Kuvera.

DHANE*S*WARA. 'Lord of wealth,' *i.e.*, Kuvera.

DHANUR-VEDA. The science of archery, the military art.

DHANWANTARI. 1. Name of a Vedic deity to whom offerings at twilight were made in the north-east quarter. 2. The physician of the gods, who was produced at the churning of the ocean. He was a teacher of medical science, and the Āyur-veda is attributed to him. In another birth he was son of Dīrghatamas, and his "nature was exempt from human infirmities, and in every existence he had been master of universal knowledge." He is called also Sudhā-pā*n*i, 'carrying nectar in his hands,' and Am*ri*ta, 'the immortal.' Other physicians seem to have had the name applied to them, as Bhela, Divo-dāsa, and Pālakāpya. 3. A celebrated physician, who was one of "the nine gems" of the court of Vikrama. *See* Nava-ratna.

DHARA*N*Ī. The earth. The wife of Para*s*u-rāma.

DHARMA, DHARMA-RĀJA. 'Justice.' A name of Yama, the judge of the dead.

DHARMA. An ancient sage, sometimes classed among the Prajāpatis. He married thirteen (or ten) of the daughters of Daksha, and had a numerous progeny; but all his children "are manifestly allegorical, being personifications of intelligences and virtues and religious rites, and being therefore appropriately wedded to the probable authors of the Hindu code of religion and morals, or the equally allegorical representation of that code, Dharma, moral and religious duty."—*Wilson.*

DHARMA-PUTRA. 'Son of Dharma.' A name of Yudhi-sh*t*hira.

DHARMĀRA*N*YA. A sacred grove. 1. A forest in Madhyadesa into which Dharma retired. 2. A city mentioned in the Rāmāya*n*a as founded by Amūrta-rajas, son of Ku*s*a.

DHARMA-RĀJA. 1. Yama, king of the dead. 2. A title of Yudhi-sh*t*hira, who was mythically a son of Yama.

DHARMA-*S*ĀSTRA. A law-book or code of laws. This term includes the whole body of Hindu law, but it is more especially applicable to the laws of Manu, Yājnawalkya, and other inspired sages who first recorded the Sm*r*iti or "recollections" of what they had received from a divine source. These works are generally in three parts:—(1.) Āchāra, rules of conduct and practice; (2.) Vyavahāra, judicature; (3.) Prāya*s*chitta, penance.

The inspired lawgivers are spoken of as being eighteen in number, but the names of forty-two old authorities are mentioned. Manu and Yājnawalkya stand apart by themselves at the head of these writers. After them the eighteen other inspired sages are recognised as the great authorities on law, and the works ascribed to them are still extant, either wholly or partially, or in an abridged form:—(1.) Atri; (2.) Vish*n*u; (3.) Hārīta; (4.) U*s*anas; (5.) Angiras; (6.) Yama; (7.) Āpastamba; (8.) Samvarta; (9.) Kātyāyana; (10.) B*r*ihaspati; (11.) Parā*s*ara; (12.) Vyāsa; (13, 14.) *S*ankha and Likhita, whose joint treatise is frequently quoted; (15.) Daksha; (16.) Gotama; (17.) *S*ātātapa; (18.) Vasish*t*ha. But there are others who are more frequently cited than many of these, as Nārada, Bh*r*igu, Marīchi, Ka*s*yapa, Vi*s*wamitra, and Baudhāyana. Other names that are met with are Pulastya, Gārgya, Pai*t*hīnasi, Sumantu, Lokākshi, Kuthumi, and Dhaumya. The writings of some of these lawgivers have appeared in different forms, and are referred to with the descriptive epithets of V*r*iddha, 'old;' B*r*ihat, 'great;' and Laghu, 'light or small.'

A general collection of the Sm*r*itis or Dharma-*s*āstras has been printed in Calcutta under the title of Dharma-*s*āstra-sangraha, by Jīvānanda.

DHARMA-SĀVARNI. The eleventh Manu. *See* Manu.

DHARMA-SŪTRAS. The Sāmayāchārika Sūtras are so called because they had among them maxims of a legal nature.

DHARMA-VYĀDHA. 'The pious huntsman.' This man is represented in the Mahā-bhārata as living by selling the flesh of boars and buffaloes, and yet as being learned in the Vedas and in all the knowledge of a Brāhman. This is accounted for by his having been a Brāhman in a former birth, and cursed to this vile occupation for having wounded a Brāhman when hunting.

DHĀT*RI*. 'Maker, creator.' In the later hymns of the *Rig*-veda, Dhāt*ri* is a deity of no very defined powers and functions, but he is described as operating in the production of life and the preservation of health. He promotes generation, brings about matrimony, presides over domestic life, cures diseases, heals broken bones, &c. He is said to "have formed the sun, moon, sky, earth, air, and heaven *as before.*" He appears also as one of the Ādityas, and this character he still retains. In the later mythology he is identified with Prajāpati or Brahmā the creator; and in this sense of "maker" the term is used as an epithet of Vish*n*u and K*r*ish*n*a. Sometimes he is a son of Brahmā.

DHAUMYA. 1. The younger brother of Devala and family priest of the Pā*nd*avas. There are several others of the same name. 2. Author of a work on law.

DHENUKA. A demon killed by Bala-rāma. K*r*ish*n*a and Bala-rāma, as boys, picked some fruit in a grove belonging to Dhenuka, when he took the form of an ass, and running to the spot began to kick Bala-rāma. The young hero seized him by the heels, whirled him round till he was dead, and cast his carcase on to the top of a palm-tree. Several of his companions who ran to his assistance were treated in the same way, so that "the trees were laden with dead asses."

DH*RI*SHTA-DYUMNA. Brother of Draupadī, and commander-in-chief of the Pā*nd*ava armies. He killed, somewhat unfairly in combat, Dro*n*a, who had beheaded his father, and he in his turn was killed by Dro*n*a's son, A*s*watthāman, who stamped him to death with his feet as he lay asleep.

DH*RI*SHTA-KETU. 1. A son of Dh*r*ishta-dyumna. 2. A son of *S*isu-pāla, king of Chedi, and an ally of the Pā*nd*avas. 3. A king of the Kekayas, also an ally of the Pā*nd*avas. 4. Son of Satyadh*ri*ti. 5. Son of N*ri*ga.

DH*RI*TA-RĀSH*T*RA. 1. The eldest son of Vichitra-vīrya or Vyāsa, and brother of Pā*nd*u. His mother was Ambikā. He married Gāndhārī, and by her had a hundred sons, the eldest of whom was Dur-yodhana. Dh*ri*ta-rāsh*t*ra was blind, and Pā*nd*u was affected with a disease supposed, from his name, "the pale," to be a leprous affection. The two brothers in turn renounced the throne, and the great war recorded in the Mahā-bhārata was fought between their sons, one party being called Kauravas, from an ancestor, Kuru, and the other Pā*nd*avas, from their father Pā*nd*u. Dh*ri*ta-rāsh*t*ra and his wife were burned in a forest fire. (*See* Mahā-bhārata.) 2. An enormous serpent of many heads and immense strength.

DHRUVA. The polar star. According to the Vish*n*u Purā*na*; the sons of Manu Swāyam-bhuva were Priya-vrata and Uttānapāda. The latter had two wives; the favourite, Suruchi, was proud and haughty; the second, Sunīti or Sūn*ri*tā, was humble and gentle. Suruchi had a son named Uttama, and Sunīti gave birth to Dhruva. While quite a child Dhruva was contemptuously treated by Suruchi, and she told him that her own son Uttama would alone succeed to the throne. Dhruva and his mother submitted, and he declared that he wished for no other honours than such as his own actions should acquire. He was a Kshatriya, but he joined a society of *Ri*shis, and becoming a *Ri*shi himself, he went through a rigid course of austerities, notwithstanding the efforts of Indra to distract him. At the end he obtained the favour of Vish*n*u, who raised him to the skies as the pole-star. He has the patronymic Auttānapādi, and he is called Grahādhāra, 'the stay or pivot of the planets.'

DHŪMA-VAR*N*A. 'Smoke coloured.' A king of the serpents. A legend in the Hari-van*s*a relates that Yadu, the founder of the Yādava family, went for a trip of pleasure on the sea, where he was carried off by Dhūma-var*n*a to the capital of the serpents. Dhūma-var*n*a married his five daughters to him, and from them sprang seven distinct families of people.

DHUNDHU. An Asura who harassed the sage Uttanka in his devotions. The demon hid himself beneath a sea of sand, but was dug out and killed by King Kuvalayāśwa and his 21,000 sons, who were undeterred by the flames which checked their progress, and were all killed but three. This legend probably originated from a volcano or some similar phenomenon. From this exploit Kuvalayāswa got the name of Dhundhu-māra, 'slayer of Dhundhu.'

DHUNDHU-MĀRA. *See* Dhundhu and Kuvalayāswa.

DHŪR-JAṬI. 'Having heavy matted locks.' A name of Rudra or Śiva.

DHŪRTA-NARTAKA. 'The rogue actors.' A farce in two parts by Sāma Rāja Dīkshita. "The chief object of this piece is the ridicule of the Śaiva ascetics."

DHŪRTA-SAMĀGAMA. 'Assemblage of rogues.' A comedy by Śekhara or Jyotir Īswara. "It is somewhat indelicate, but not devoid of humour." It has been translated into French by Schoebel.

DIG-AMBARA. 'Clothed with space.' A naked mendicant. A title of Śiva.

DIG-GAJAS. The elephants who protect the eight points of the compass:—(1.) Airāvata; (2.) Puṇḍarīka; (3.) Vāmana; (4.) Kumuda; (5.) Anjana; (6.) Pushpa-danta; (7.) Sarva-bhauma; (8.) Su-pratīka.

DIG-VIJAYA. 'Conquest of the regions (of the world).' 1. A part of the Mahā-bhārata which commemorates the conquests effected by the four younger Pāṇḍava princes, and in virtue of which Yudhi-shṭhira maintained his claim to universal sovereignty. 2. A work by Śankarāchārya in support of the Vedānta philosophy, generally distinguished as Śankara Dig-vijaya.

DIK-PĀLA. 'Supporters of the regions.' The supporters of the eight points of the compass. *See* Dig-gaja.

DILĪPA. Son of Anśumat and father of Bhagīratha. He was of the Solar race and ancestor of Rāma. On one occasion he failed to pay due respect to Surabhi, the 'cow of fortune,' and she passed a curse upon him that he should have no offspring until he and his wife Su-dakshiṇā had carefully tended Surabhi's daughter Nandinī. They obediently waited on this calf Nandinī, and Dilīpa once offered his own life to save hers from the lion of Śiva. In due time the curse was removed, and a son, Raghu, was born to them. This story is told in the Raghu-vansa. There was another prince of the name. *See* Khatwānga.

DĪRGHA-SRAVAS. Son of Dīrgha-tamas, and therefore a *Ri*shi, but as in a time of famine he took to trade for a livelihood, the *Rig*-veda calls him "the merchant."

DĪRGHA-TAMAS, DĪRGHA-TAPAS. 'Long darkness.' A son of Kāsī-rāja, according to the Mahā-bhārata; of Uchāthya, according to the *Rig*-veda; and of Utathya and Mamatā in the Purā*n*as. His appellations of Auchathya and Māmateya favour the latter parentage. He was born blind, but is said to have obtained sight by worshipping Agni (*R. V.* iii. 128). He was father of Kakshīvat and Dhanwantari; and he is said (in the *V. P.*) to have had five children by Su-desh*n*ā, wife of Bali, viz., the countries Anga, Banga, Kalinga, Pu*nd*ra, and Suhma.

DITI. A goddess or personification in the Vedas who is associated with Aditi, and seems to be intended as an antithesis or as a complement to her.

In the Rāmāya*n*a and in the Purā*n*as she is daughter of Daksha, wife of Kasyapa, and mother of the Daityas. The Vish*n*u Purā*n*a relates that having lost her children, she begged of Kasyapa a son of irresistible prowess, who should destroy Indra. The boon was granted, but with this condition: "If, with thoughts wholly pious and person entirely pure, you carefully carry the babe in your womb for a hundred years." She assiduously observed the condition; but Indra knew what was preparing for him. So he went to Diti and attended upon her with the utmost humility, watching his opportunity. In the last year of the century, Diti retired one night to rest without washing her feet. Indra then with his thunderbolt divided the embryo in her womb into seven portions. Thus mutilated, the child cried bitterly, and Indra being unable to pacify it, became angry, and divided each of the seven portions into seven, thus forming the swift-moving deities called Maruts, from the words, 'Mā-rodī*h*,' 'Weep not,' which Indra used to quiet them.

DIVO-DĀSA. 1. A pious liberal king mentioned in the *Rig*-veda, for whom it is said that Indra demolished a hundred stone cities, meaning perhaps the mythological aerial cities of the Asuras. 2. A Brāhman who was the twin-brother of Ahalyā. He is represented in the Veda as a "very liberal sacrificer," and as being delivered by the gods from the oppressor *S*ambara. He is also called Atithi-gwa, 'he to whom guests should go.' 3. A king of Kā*s*ī, son of Bhīma-ratha and father of Pratardana. He was attacked by the sons of King Vīta-havya and all his sons were slain. His son Pratardana (q.v.) was born to him through a sacrifice performed by Bharadwāja. He was celebrated as a physician and was called Dhanwantari.

DRAUPADĪ. Daughter of Drupada, king of Panchāla, and wife of the five Pā*nd*u princes. Draupadī was a damsel of dark complexion but of great beauty, "as radiant and graceful as if she had descended from the city of the gods." Her hand was sought by many princes, and so her father determined to hold a swayam-vara and allow her to exercise her own choice in the selection of a husband. The swayam-vara was proclaimed, and princes assembled from all parts to contend in the lists for the hand of the princess; for although in such contests the lady was entitled to exercise her swayam-vara or own choice, it generally followed that the champion of the arena became her husband. Most astonishing feats of arms were performed, but Arjuna outshone all by his marvellous use of the bow, and he became the selected bridegroom. When the five brothers returned to the house where their mother, Kuntī, was staying, they told her that they had made a great acquisition, and she told them to share it among them. These words raised a great difficulty, for if they could not be adroitly evaded they must be obeyed. The sage Vyāsa settled the matter by saying, "The destiny of Draupadī has already been declared by the gods; let her become the wife of all the brethren." So she became their common wife, and it was arranged that she should stay successively two days in the house of each, and that no one of them but the master of the house should enter it while she was there. Arjuna was her favourite, and she showed her jealousy when he married Su-bhadrā. In the great gambling match which the eldest brother, Yudhi-sh*th*ira, played at Hastinā-pura against his cousins, the Kauvaras, he lost his all—his kingdom, his brothers, himself, and their wife Draupadī. So she became a slave, and Dur-yodhana called her to come and sweep the room. She refused, and then Duh-*s*āsana dragged her by the hair into the pavilion before all the chieftains, and tauntingly told her that she was a slave girl, and had no right to complain of being touched by men. He also abused her and tore off her veil and dress, while Dur-yodhana invited her to sit on his thigh. *Krishna* took compassion upon her, and restored her garments as fast as they were torn. She called vehemently upon her husbands to save her, but they were restrained by Yudhi-sh*t*hira. Bhīma was in a rage of passion; he was prevented from action; but he vowed in loud words that he would drink the blood of Duh-*s*āsana and smash the thigh of Dur-yodhana in retaliation of these outrages, which vows he eventually fulfilled. Draupadī vowed that her hair should remain dishevelled until Bhīma should tie it up with hands dripping with the blood of Duh-*s*āsana. The result of the gambling match was that the Pā*nd*avas, with Draupadī, went into exile for twelve years, and were to dwell quite incognito during another year. The period of thirteen years being successfully completed, they were at liberty to return. Twelve years of exile were passed in the jungle, and in the course of this period Jayad-ratha, king of Sindhu, came to the house of the Pā*nd*avas while they were out hunting. He was courteously received by Draupadī, and was fascinated by her charms. He tried to induce her to elope with him, and when he was scornfully repulsed, he dragged her to his chariot and drove off with her. When the Pā*nd*avas returned and heard of the rape, they pursued Jayad-ratha, and pressed him so close that he put down Draupadī, and endeavoured to escape alone. Bhīma resolved to overtake and punish him; and although Yudhi-sh*t*hira pleaded that Jayad-ratha was a kinsman, and ought not to be killed, Draupadī called aloud for vengeance, so Bhīma and Arjuna continued the pursuit. Bhīma dragged Jayad-ratha from his car, kicked and beat him till he was senseless, but spared his life. He cut off all Jayad-ratha's hair except five locks, and made him publicly acknowledge that he was a slave. Draupadī's revenge was then slaked, and Jayad-ratha was released at her intercession. In the thirteenth year, in which her husbands and she were to live undiscovered, they entered the service of the king of Virā*t*a, and she, without acknowledging any connection with them, became a waiting-maid to the queen. She stipulated that she should not be required to wash feet or to eat food left by others, and she quieted the jealous fears which her beauty excited in the queen's mind by representing that she was guarded by five Gandharvas, who would prevent any improper advances. She lived a quiet life for a while, but her beauty excited the passions of Kīchaka, the queen's brother, who was commander-in-chief, and the leading man in the kingdom. His importunities and insults greatly annoyed her, but she met with no protection from the queen, and was rebuked for her complaints and petulance by Yudhi-sh*th*ira. Her spirit of revenge was roused, and she appealed as usual to Bhīma, whose fiery passions she well knew how to kindle. She complained of her menial position, of the insults she had received, of the indifference of her husbands, and of the base offices they were content to occupy. Bhīma promised revenge. An assignation was made with Kīchaka which Bhīma kept, and he so mangled the unfortunate gallant that all his flesh and bones were rolled into a ball, and no one could discover the manner of his death. The murder was attributed to Draupadī's Gandharvas, and she was condemned to be burnt on Kīchaka's funeral pile. Then Bhīma disguised himself, and tearing up a tree for a club, went to her rescue. He was supposed to be the Gandharva, and every one fled before him. He released Draupadī, and they returned to the city by different ways. After the term of exile was over, and the Pā*nd*avas and she were at liberty to return, she was more ambitious than her husbands, and complained to K*ri*sh*n*a of the humility and want of resolution shown by Yudhi-sh*th*ira. She had five sons, one by each husband—Prati-vindhya, son of Yudhi-sh*th*ira; *S*ruta-soma, son of Bhīma; *S*ruta-kīrtti, son of Arjuna; *S*atānīka, son of Nakula; and *S*ruta-karman, son of Saha-deva. She with these five sons was present in camp on the eighteenth and last night of the great battle, while her victorious husbands were in the camp of the defeated enemy. A*s*watthāman with two companions entered the camp of the Pā*nd*avas, cut down these five youths, and all whom they found. Draupadī called for vengeance upon A*s*watthāman. Yudhi-sh*th*ira endeavoured to moderate her anger, but she appealed to Bhīma. Arjuna pursued A*s*watthāman, and overtook him, but he spared his life after taking from him a celebrated jewel which he wore as an amulet. Arjuna gave this jewel to Bhīma for presentation to Draupadī. On receiving it she was consoled, and presented the jewel to Yudhi-sh*th*ira as the head of the family. When her husbands retired from the world and went on their journey towards the Himālayas and Indra's heaven, she accompanied them, and was the first to fall on the journey. *See* Mahā-bhārata.

Draupadī's real name was K*ri*sh*n*ā. She was called Draupadī and Yājna-senī, from her father; Pārshatī, from her grandfather P*ri*shata; Pānchālī, from her country; Sairindhrī, 'the maid-servant' of the queen of Virā*t*a; Panchamī, 'having five husbands;' and Nita-yauvanī, 'the ever-young.'

DRĀVI*D*A. The country in which the Tamil language is spoken, extending from Madras to Cape Comorin. According to Manu, the people of this country were originally Kshatriyas, but sank to the condition of *S*ūdras from the extinction of sacred rites and the absence of Brāhmans. As applied to the classification of Brāhmans it has a much wider application, embracing Gujarāt, Mahā-rāsh*t*ra, and all the south.

D*R*ISHADWATĪ. A common female name. 1. The wife of King Divo-dāsa. 2. A river forming one of the boundaries of Brahmāvarta, perhaps the Kāgar before its junction with the Sarsuti.

DRO*N*A. 'A bucket.' A Brāhman so named from his having been generated by his father, Bharadwāja, in a bucket. He married K*ri*pā, half-sister of Bhīshma, and by her was father of A*s*watthāman. He was āchārya, or teacher of the military art, both to the Kaurava and Pā*nd*ava princes, and so he was called Dro*n*āchārya. He had been slighted by Drupada, king of Panchāla, and became his enemy. Through the instrumentality of the Pā*nd*avas he made Drupada prisoner, and took from him half of his kingdom; but he spared his life and gave him back the other half of his country But the old animosity rankled, and ended in the death of both. In the great war Dro*n*a sided with the Kauravas, and after the death of Bhīshma he became their commander-in-chief. On the fourth day of his command he killed Drupada, and in his turn he was unfairly slain in combat by Dh*ri*sh*t*a-dyumna, who had sworn to avenge his father's death. In the midst of this combat Dro*n*a was told that his son was dead, which so unnerved him that he laid down his arms and his opponent decapitated him. But Dro*n*a was a Brāhman and an Āchārya, and the crime of killing him was enormous, so it is glossed over by the statement that Dro*n*a "transported himself to heaven in a glittering state like the sun, and Dh*ri*sh*t*a-dyumna decapitated merely his lifeless body." Drona was also called Kūta-ja. The common meaning of Kūta is 'mountain-top,' but one of its many other meanings is 'water-jar.' His patronymic is Bhāradwāja.

DRUHYU. Son of Yayāti, by Sarmishthā, daughter of the Daitya king Vrisha-parvan. He refused to exchange his youth for the curse of decrepitude passed upon his father, and in consequence Yayāti cursed him that his posterity should not possess dominion. His father gave him a part of his kingdom, but his descendants became "princes of the lawless barbarians of the north."

DRUPADA. King of Panchāla and son of Prishata. Also called Yajna-sena. He was schoolfellow of Drona, the preceptor of the Kaurava and Pāndava princes, and he mortally offended his former friend by repudiating his acquaintance. Drona, in payment of his services as preceptor, required his pupils to make Drupada prisoner. The Kauravas attacked him and failed, but the Pāndavas took Drupada captive and occupied his territory. Drona spared his life and restored the southern half of his kingdom to him. Drupada returned home burning for revenge, and, to procure it, he prevailed upon two Brāhmans to perform a sacrifice, by the efficacy of which he obtained two children, a son and a daughter, who were called "the altar-born," because they came forth from the sacrificial fire. These children were named Dhrishta-dyumna and Krishnā, but the latter is better known by her patronymic Draupadī. After she had chosen Arjuna for her husband at her swayam-vara, and she had become, with Drupada's consent, the wife of the five Pāndavas, he naturally became the ally of his sons-in-law. He took an active part in the great battle, and on the fourteenth day he was killed and beheaded by Drona, who on the following day was killed by Dhrishta-dyumna, the son whom Drupada had obtained for wreaking his vengeance on Drona. Besides the two children mentioned, Drupada had a younger son named Sikhandin and a daughter Sikhandinī.

DUH-SALĀ. The only daughter of Dhrita-rāshtra and wife of Jayad-ratha.

DUH-SĀSANA. 'Hard to rule.' One of the hundred sons of Dhrita-rāshtra. When the Pāndavas lost their wife Draupadī in gambling with Dur-yodhana, Duh-sāsana dragged her forward by the hair and otherwise ill-used her. For this outrage Bhīma vowed he would drink his blood, a vow which he afterwards performed on the sixteenth day of the great battle.

DUR-GA. A commentator on the Nirukta.

DUR-GĀ 'Inaccessible.' The wife of *S*iva. *See* Devī.

DUR-MUKHA. 'Bad face.' A name of one of Dh*ri*ta-rāsh*t*ra's sons. Also of one of Rāma's monkey allies, and of several others.

DUR-VĀSAS. 'Ill-clothed.' A sage, the son of Atri and Anasūyā, but, according to some authorities, he was a son or emanation of *S*iva. He was noted for his irascible temper, and many fell under his curse. It was he who cursed *S*akuntalā for keeping him waiting at the door, and so caused the separation between her and King Dushyanta. But it was he who blessed Kuntī, so that she became a mother by the Sun. In the Vish*n*u Purā*n*a he is represented as cursing Indra for treating with disrespect a garland which the sage presented to him. The curse was that "his sovereignty over the three worlds should be subverted," and under it Indra and the gods grew weak and were overpowered by the Asuras. In their extremity they resorted to Vish*n*u, who directed them to churn the ocean of milk for the production of the Am*ri*ta (water of life) and other precious things. In the Mahā-bhārata it is stated that on one occasion K*ri*sh*n*a entertained him hospitably, but omitted to wipe the fragments of food from the foot of the sage. At this the latter grew angry and foretold how K*ri*sh*n*a should be killed. The Vish*n*u Purā*n*a states that K*ri*sh*n*a fell according to "the imprecation of Dur-vāsas," and in the same work Dur-vāsas is made to describe himself as one "whose nature is stranger to remorse."

DUR-VĀSASA PURĀ*N*A. One of the eighteen Upa Purā*n*as. *See* Purā*n*a.

DUR-YODHANA. 'Hard to conquer.' The eldest son of King Dh*ri*ta-rāsh*t*ra, and leader of the Kaurava princes in the great war of the Mahā-bhārata. His birth was somewhat marvellous. (*See* Gāndhārī.) Upon the death of his brother Pā*nd*u, Dh*ri*ta-rāsh*t*ra took his five sons, the Pā*nd*ava princes, to his own court, and had them educated with his hundred sons. Bickerings and jealousies soon sprang up between the cousins, and Dur-yodhana took a special dislike to Bhīma on account of his skill in the use of the club. Dur-yodhana had learnt the use of this weapon under Bala-rāma, and was jealous of any rival. He poisoned Bhīma and threw his body into the Ganges, but Bhīma sank to the regions of the Nāgas, where he was restored to health and vigour. When Dh*ri*ta-rāsh*t*ra proposed to make Yudhi-sh*t*hira heir-apparent, Dur-yodhana strongly remonstrated, and the result was that the Pā*nd*avas went into exile. Even then his animosity pursued them, and he laid a plot to burn them in their house, from which they escaped and retaliated upon his emissaries. After the return of the Pā*nd*avas from exile, and their establishment at Indra-prastha, his anger was further excited by Yudhi-sh*t*hira's performance of the Rāja-sūya sacrifice. He prevailed on his father to invite the Pā*nd*avas to Hastinā-pura to a gambling match, in which, with the help of his confederate *S*akuni, he won from Yudhi-sh*t*hira everything he possessed, even to the freedom of himself, his brothers, and his wife Draupadī. Dur-yodhana exultingly sent for Draupadī to act as a slave and sweep the room. When she refused to come, his brother, Du*h*-*s*āsana, dragged her in by the hair of her head, and Dur-yodhana insulted her by inviting her to, sit upon his knee. This drew from Bhīma a vow that he would one day smash Dur-yodhana's thigh. Dh*ri*ta-rash*t*ra interfered, and the result of the gambling was that the Pā*nd*avas again went into exile, and were to remain absent thirteen years. While the Pā*nd*avas were living in the forest, Dur-yodhana went out for the purpose of gratifying his hatred with a sight of their poverty. He was attacked and made prisoner by the Gandharvas, probably hill people, and was rescued by the Pā*nd*avas. This incident greatly mortified him. The exile of the Pā*nd*avas drew to a close. War was inevitable, and both parties prepared for the struggle. Dur-yodhana sought the aid of K*ri*sh*n*a, but made the great mistake of accepting K*ri*sh*n*a's army in preference to his personal attendance. He accompanied his army to the field, and on the eighteenth day of the battle, after his party had been utterly defeated, he fled and hid himself in a lake, for he was said to possess the power of remaining under water. He was discovered, and with great difficulty, by taunts and sarcasms, was induced to come out. It was agreed that he and Bhīma should fight it out with clubs. The contest was long and furious, and Dur-yodhana was getting the best of it, when Bhīma remembered his vow, and, although it was unfair to strike below the waist, he gave his antagonist such a violent blow on the thigh that the bone was smashed and Dur-yodhana fell. Then Bhīma kicked him on the head and triumphed over him. Left wounded and alone on the field, he was visited by Aswatthāman, son of Drona, and two other warriors, the only survivors of his army. He thirsted for revenge, and directed them to slay all the Pāndavas, and especially to bring him the head of Bhīma. These men entered the camp of the enemy, and killed the five youthful sons of the Pāndavas. The version of the Mahā-bhārata used by Wheeler adds that these warriors brought the heads of the five youths to Dur-yodhana, representing them to be the heads of the five brothers. Dur-yodhana was unable in the twilight to distinguish the features, but he exulted greatly, and desired that Bhīma's head might be placed in his hands. With dying energy he pressed it with all his might, and when he found that it crushed, he knew that it was not the head of Bhīma. Having discovered the deception that had been played upon him, with a redeeming touch of humanity he reproached Aswatthāman for his horrid deed in slaying the harmless youths, saying, with his last breath, "My enmity was against the Pāndavas, not against these innocents." Dur-yodhana was called also Su-yodhana, 'good fighter.'

DŪSHANA. A Rākshasa who fought as one of the generals of Rāvana, and was killed by Rāma. He was generally associated with Rāvana's brother, Khara.

DUSHMANTA, DUSHYANTA. A valiant king of the Lunar race, and descended from Puru. He was husband of Sakuntalā, by whom he had a son, Bharata. The loves of Dushyanta and Sakuntalā, her separation from him, and her restoration through the discovery of his token-ring in the belly of a fish, form the plot of Kāli-dāsa's celebrated play Sakuntalā.

DŪTĀNGADA. 'The ambassador Angada.' A short play founded on the mission of Angada to demand from Rāvana the restoration of Sītā. It is attributed to a poet named Subhata.

DWAIPĀYANA. *See* Vyāsa.

DWĀPARA YUGA. The third age of the world, extending to 864,000 years. *See* Yuga.

DWĀRAKĀ, DWĀRAVATĪ. 'The city of gates.' Krishna's capital, in Gujarat, which is said to have been submerged by the ocean seven days after his death. It is one of the seven sacred cities. Also called Abdhi-nagarī.

DWIJARSHIS. (Dwija-rishis.) *See* Brahmarshis.

DWĪPA. An insular continent. The Dwīpas stretch out from the mountain Meru as their common centre, like the leaves of a lotus, and are separated from each other by distinct circumambient oceans. They are generally given as seven in number:—1. Jambu, 2. Plaksha or Go-medaka, 3. *S*ālmala, 4. Ku*s*a, 5. Krauncha, 6. *S*āka, 7. Pushkara; and the seas which surround them are—1. Lava*n*a, salt water; 2. Ikshu, sugar-cane juice; 3. Surā, wine; 4. Sarpis or Gh*ri*ta, clarified butter; 5. Dadhi, curds; 6. Dugdha or Kshīra, milk; 7. Jala, fresh water. In the Mahā-bhārata four Dwīpas are named:—1. Bhadrā*s*wa, 2. Ketu-māla, 3. Jambu-dwīpa, 4. Uttara Kuru. Jambu-dwīpa has nine varshas or subdivisions:—1. Bhārata, 2. Kim-purusha, Kin-nara, 3. Hari-varsha, 4. Ilā-v*ri*ta, which contains Meru; 5. Ramyaka, 6. Hira*n*-maya, 7. Uttara Kuru, 8. Bhadrā*s*wa, 9. Ketu-māla. According to the Vish*n*u Purā*n*a, Bhārata-varsha or India is divided into nine Dwīpas or portions:—1. Indra-dwīpa, 2. Ka*s*erumat, 3. Tāmra-var*n*a, 4. Gabhastimat, 5. Nāga-dwīpa, 6. Saumya, 7. Gāndharva, 8. Vāru*n*a; 9. is generally left without a name in the books, but Bhāskara Āchārya calls it Kumāraka.

DWIVIDA. 1. An Asura in the form of a great ape, who was an implacable foe of the gods. He stole Bala-rāma's ploughshare weapon and derided him. This was the beginning of a terrific fight, in which Dwivida was felled to the earth, and "the crest of the mountain on which he fell was splintered into a hundred pieces by the weight of his body, as if the Thunderer had shivered it with his thunderbolt." 2. A monkey ally of Rāma.

DYAUS. The sky, heaven. In the Vedas he is a masculine deity, and is called occasionally Dyaus-pit*ri*, 'heavenly father,' the earth being regarded as the mother. He is father of Ushas, the dawn. *Cf.* Ζεύς, Deus, Jovis, Ju-piter. Dyāvā-p*ri*thivī, 'heaven and earth,' are represented as the universal parents, not only of men but of gods; but in other places they are spoken of as having been themselves created; and then, again, there are speculations as to their origin and priority. In one hymn it is asked, "Which of these two was the first and which the last? How have they been produced? Who knows?" The *S*atapatha Brāhma*n*a declares in favour of the earth, saying, "This earth is the first of created beings."

EKA-CHAKRĀ. A city in the country of the Kīchakas, where, by advice of Vyāsa, the Pa*nd*avas dwelt for a time during their exile. General Cunningham has identified it with the modern Ara or Arrah.

EKA-DANSH*T*RA, EKA-DANTA. 'Having one tusk.' A name of Ga*n*e*s*a.

EKALAVYA. Grandson of Deva-*s*ravas, the brother of Vasudeva. He was brother of *S*atru-ghna. He was exposed in infancy, and was brought up among the Nishādas, of whom he became king. He assisted in a night attack upon Dwārakā, and was eventually killed by K*ri*sh*n*a, who hurled a rock at him.

EKĀMRA, EKĀMRA KĀNANA. A forest in Utkala or Orissa, which was the favourite haunt of *S*iva, and became a great seat of his worship as the city of Bhuvane*s*wara, where some very fine temples sacred to him still remain. They have been described by Bābū Rājendra Lāla in his great work on Orissa.

EKA-PĀDA. 'One-footed.' A fabulous race of men spoken of in the Purā*n*as.

EKA-PAR*N*Ā, EKA-PĀ*T*ALĀ. These, with their sister Apar*n*ā, were, according to the Hari-van*s*a, daughters of Himavat and Menā. They performed austerities surpassing the powers of gods and Dānavas, and alarmed both worlds. Eka-par*n*ā took only one leaf for food, and Eka-pā*t*alā only one pā*t*alā (Bignonia). Apar*n*ā took no sustenance at all and lived a-par*n*a, 'without a leaf.' Her mother being distressed at her abstinence, exclaimed in her anxiety, "U-mā"—"O don't." Through this she became manifest as the lovely goddess Umā, the wife of *S*iva.

EKĀSH*T*AKĀ. A deity mentioned in the Atharva-veda as having practised austere devotion, and being the daughter of Prajāpati and mother of Indra and Soma.

EMŪSHA. In the Brāhma*n*a, a boar which raised up the earth, represented as black and with a hundred arms. This is probably the germ of the Varāha or boar incarnation. *See* Avatāra.

GADA. A younger brother of K*ri*sh*n*a.

GĀDHI, GĀTHIN. A king of the Ku*s*ika race, and father of Vi*s*wāmitra. He was son of Ku*s*āmba, or, according to the Vish*n*u Purā*n*a, he was Indra, who took upon himself that form.

GĀLAVA. A pupil of Vi*s*wāmitra. It is related in the Mahā-bhārata that at the conclusion of his studies he importuned his master to say what present he should make him. Viswāmitra was annoyed, and told him to bring 800 white horses, each having one black ear. In his perplexity Gālava applied to Garuda, who took him to King Yayāti at Pratishthāna. The king was unable to provide the horses, but he gave to Gālava his daughter Mādhavī. Gālava gave her in marriage successively to Haryaswa, king of Ayodhyā, Divo-dāsa, king of Kāsī, and Usīnara, king of Bhoja, receiving from each of them 200 of the horses he was in quest of, upon the birth of a son to each from Mādhavī. Notwithstanding her triple marriage and maternity, Mādhavī, by a special boon, remained a virgin. Gālava presented her and the horses to Viswāmitra. The sage accepted them, and had a son by Mādhavī, who was named Ashtaka. When Viswāmitra retired to the woods, he resigned his hermitage and his horses to Ashtaka, and Gālava having taken Mādhavī back to her father, himself retired to the forest as his preceptor had done. The horses were first obtained by the Brāhman *Richīka* from the god Varuna. They were originally 1000 in number, but his descendants sold 600 of them, and gave the rest away to Brāhmans.

According to the Hari-vansa, Gālava was son of Viswāmitra, and that sage in a time of great distress tied a cord round his waist and offered him for sale. Prince Satyavrata (q.v.) gave him liberty and restored him to his father. From his having been bound with a cord (*gala*) he was called Gālava.

There was a teacher of the White Yajur-veda named Gālava, and also an old grammarian named by Pānini.

GANA-DEVATAS. 'Troops of deities.' Deities who generally appear, or are spoken of, in classes. Nine such classes are mentioned:—(1.) Ādityas; (2.) Viswas or Viswe-devas; (3.) Vasus; (4.) Tushitas; (5.) Ābhāswaras; (6.) Anilas; (7.) Mahārājikas; (8.) Sādhyas; (9.) Rudras. These inferior deities are attendant upon *S*iva, and under the command of Ganesa. They dwell on Gana-parvata, *i.e.*, Kailāsa.

GANA-PATI. *See* Gaensa.

GĀNAPATYA. A small sect who worship Gana-pati or Ganesa as their chief deity.

GANAS. *See* Gana-devatas.

GANDAKĪ. The river Gandak (vulg. Gunduk), in Oude.

GANDHA-MĀDANA. 'Intoxicating with fragrance.' 1. A

mountain and forest in Ilāvrita, the central region of the world, which contains the mountain Meru. The authorities are not agreed as to its relative position with Meru. 2. A general of the monkey allies of Rāma. He was killed by Rāvana's son Indra-jit, but was restored to life by the medicinal herbs brought by Hanumān from Mount Kailāsa.

GANDHĀRA, GĀNDHĀRA. A country and city on the west bank of the Indus about Attock. Mahomedan geographers call it Kandahār, but it must not be confounded with the modern town of that name. It is the Gandaritis of the ancients, and its people are the Gandarii of Herodotus. The Vāyu Purāna says it was famous for its breed of horses.

GĀNDHĀRĪ. Princess of Gandhāra. The daughter of Subala, king of Gandhāra, wife of Dhrita-rāshtra, and mother of his hundred sons. Her husband was blind, so she always wore a bandage over her eyes to be like him. Her husband and she, in their old age, both perished in a forest fire. She is also called by the patronymics Saubalī and Saubaleyī. She is said to have owed her hundred sons to the blessing of Vyāsa, who, in acknowledgment of her kind hospitality, offered her a boon. She asked for a hundred sons. Then she became pregnant, and continued so for two years, at the end of which time she was delivered of a lump of flesh. Vyāsa took the shapeless mass and divided it into 101 pieces, which he placed in as many jars. In due time Dur-yodhana was produced, but with such accompanying fearful portents that Dhrita-rāshtra was besought, though in vain, to abandon him. A month afterwards ninety-nine other sons came forth, and an only daughter, Duh-salā.

GANDHARVA. The 'heavenly Gandharva' of the Veda was a deity who knew and revealed the secrets of heaven and divine truths in general. He is thought by Goldstücker to have been a personification of the fire of the sun. The Gandharvas generally had their dwelling in the sky or atmosphere, and one of their offices was to prepare the heavenly soma juice for the gods. They had a great partiality for women, and had a mystic power over them. The Atharva-veda speaks of "the 6333 Gandharvas." The Gandharvas of later times are similar in character; they have charge of the soma, are skilled in medicine, regulate the asterisms, and are fond of women. Those of Indra's heaven are generally intended by the term, and they are singers and musicians who attend the banquets of the gods. The Purāṇas give contradictory accounts of the origin of the Gandharvas. The Vishṇu Purāṇa says, in one place, that they were born from Brahmā, "imbibing melody. Drinking of the goddess of speech (*gām dhayantah*), they were born, and thence their appellation." Later on it says that they were the offspring of Kaśyapa and his wife Arishṭā. The Hari-vanśa states that they sprang from Brahmā's nose, and also that they were descended from Muni, another of Kaśyapa's wives. Chitra-ratha was chief of the Gandharvas; and the Apsarases were their wives or mistresses. The "cities of the Gandharvas" are often referred to as being very splendid. The Vishṇu Purāṇa has a legend of the Gandharvas fighting with the Nāgas in the infernal regions, whose dominions they seized and whose treasures they plundered. The Nāga chiefs appealed to Vishṇu for relief, and he promised to appear in the person of Purukutsa to help them. Thereupon the Nāgas sent their sister Narmadā (the Nerbudda river) to this Purukutsa, and she conducted him to the regions below, where he destroyed the Gandharvas. They are sometimes called Gātus and Pulakas. In the Mahā-bhārata, apparently, a race of people dwelling in the hills and wilds is so called.

GANDHARVA-LOKA. *See* Loka.

GĀNDHARVA-VEDA. The science of music and song, which is considered to include the drama and dancing. It is an appendix of the Sāma-veda, and its invention is ascribed to the Muni Bharata.

GĀNDINĪ. 1. Daughter of Kāśī-rāja; she had been twelve years in her mother's womb when her father desired her to come forth. The child told her father to present to the Brāhmans a cow every day for three years, and at the end of that time she would be born. This was done, and the child, on being born, received the name of Gāndinī, 'cow daily.' She continued the gift as long as she lived. She was wife of Śwa-phalka and mother of Akrūra. 2. The Gangā or Ganges.

GĀṆḌĪVA. The bow of Arjuna, said to have been given by Soma to Varuṇa, by Varuṇa to Agni, and by Agni to Arjuna.

GAṆESA (Gaṇa + Īsa), GAṆA-PATI. Lord of the Gaṇas or troops of inferior deities, especially those attendant upon Śiva. Son of Śiva and Pārvatī, or of Pārvatī only. One legend represents that he sprang from the scurf of Pārvatī's body. He is the god of wisdom and remover of obstacles; hence he is invariably propitiated at the beginning of any important undertaking, and is invoked at the commencement of books. He is said to have written down the Mahā-bhārata from the dictation of Vyāsa. He is represented as a short fat man of a yellow colour, with a protuberant belly, four hands, and the head of an elephant, which has only one tusk. In one hand he holds a shell, in another a discus, in the third a club or goad, and in the fourth a water-lily. Sometimes he is depicted riding upon a rat or attended by one; hence his appellation Akhu ratha. His temples are very numerous in the Dakhin. There is a variety of legends accounting for his elephant head. One is that his mother Pārvatī, proud of her offspring, asked *S*ani (Saturn) to look at him, forgetful of the effects of *S*ani's glance. *S*ani looked and the child's head was burnt to ashes. Brahmā told Pārvatī in her distress to replace the head with the first she could find, and that was an elephant's. Another story is that Pārvatī went to her bath and told her son to keep the door. *S*iva wished to enter and was opposed, so he cut off Ga*n*esa's head. To pacify Pārvatī he replaced it with an elephant's, the first that came to hand. Another version is that his mother formed him so to suit her own fancy, and a further explanation is that *S*iva slew Āditya the sun, but restored him to life again. For this violence Ka*s*yapa doomed *S*iva's son to lose his head; and when he did lose it, the head of Indra's elephant was used to replace it. The loss of one tusk is accounted for by a legend which represents Para*s*u-rāma as coming to Kailāsa on a visit to *S*iva. The god was asleep and Ga*n*esa opposed the entrance of the visitor to the inner apartments. A wrangle ensued, which ended in a fight. "Ga*n*esa had at first the advantage, seizing Para*s*u-rāma with his trunk and giving him a twirl that left him sick and senseless. On recovering, Para*s*u-rāma threw his axe at Ga*n*esa, who, recognising it as his father's weapon (*S*iva having given it to Para*s*u-rāma), received it with all humility on one of his tusks, which it immediately severed; hence Ga*n*esa has but one tusk, and is known by the name of Eka-danta or Eka-dansh*t*ra (the single-tusked). These legends are narrated at length in the Brahma Vaivartta Purā*n*a.

Ga*n*esa is also called Gajānana, Gaja-vadana, and Kari-mukha, 'elephant-faced;' Heramba;' 'boastful;' Lamba-kar*n*a, 'long-eared;' Lambodara, 'pendant-bellied;' Dwi-deha, 'double-bodied;' Vighnesa, Vighna-hārī, 'remover of obstacles.' A peculiar appellation is Dwai-mātura, 'having two mothers,' in allusion, it is said, to his birth from the scurf of Pārvatī's body.

GA*N*E*S*A-GĪTĀ. The Bhagavad-gītā, but with the name of Ga*n*e*s*a substituted for that of K*r*ish*n*a It is used by the Gāṇapatyas or worshippers of Ga*n*esa.

GA*N*E*S*A PURĀ*N*A. An Upa Purā*n*a having especial reference to the glory and greatness of Ga*n*esa.

GANGĀ. The sacred river Ganges. It is said to be mentioned only twice in the *R*ig-vedā. The Purā*n*as represent the Viyad-gangā, or heavenly Ganges, to flow from the toe of Vish*n*u, and to have been brought down from heaven, by the prayers of the saint Bhagīratha, to purify the ashes of the sixty thousand sons of King Sagara, who had been burnt by the angry glance of the sage Kapila. From this earthly parent the river is called Bhāgīrathī. Gangā was angry at being brought down from heaven, and *S*iva, to save the earth from the shock of her fall, caught the river on his brow, and checked its course with his matted locks. From this action he is called Gangā-dhara, 'upholder of the Ganges.' The river descended from *S*iva's brow in several streams, four according to some, and ten according to others, but the number generally accepted is seven, being the Sapta-sindhava, the seven sindhus or rivers. The Ganges proper is one of the number. The descent of the Ganges disturbed the sage Jahnu as he was performing a sacrifice, and in his anger he drank up the waters, but he relented and allowed the river to flow from his ear, hence the Ganges has the name of Jāhnavī. Personified as a goddess, Gangā is the eldest daughter of Himavat and Menā, and her sister was Umā. She became the wife of King *S*āntanu and bore a son, Bhīshma; who is also known by the metronymic Gāngeya. Being also, in a peculiar way, the mother of Kārtikeya (q.v.), she is called Kumāra-sū. Gold, according to the Mahā-bhārata, was borne by the goddess Gangā to Agni, by whom she had been impregnated. Other names and titles of the Ganges are Bhadra-somā, Gāndinī, Kirātī, Deva-bhūti, 'produced in heaven;' Hara-sekharā, 'crest of *S*iva;' Khāpagā, 'flowing from heaven;' Mandākinī, 'gently flowing;' Tri-patha-gā or Tri-srotā*h*, 'triple flowing,' running in heaven, earth, and hell.

GANGĀ-DHARA. A name of *S*iva. *See* Gangā.

GANGĀ-DWĀRA. The gate of the Ganges. The opening in the Himālaya mountains through which the river descends into the plains, now known as Hardwār.

GANGĀ-SĀGARA. The mouth of the Ganges, a holy bathing-place sacred to Vish*n*u.

GĀNGEYA. 1. A name of Bhīshma, from his reputed mother, the river goddess Gangā. 2. Also of Kārttikeya.

GARGA. An ancient sage, and one of the oldest writers on astronomy. He was a son of Vitatha. The Vish*n*u Purā*n*a says, "From Garga sprang *S*ina (or *S*ini); from them were descended the Gārgyas and *S*ainyas, Brāhmans of Kshatriya race." The statement of the Bhāgavata is, "From Garga sprang *S*ina; from them Gārgya, who from a Kshatriya became a Brāhman." There were many Gargas; one was a priest of K*ri*sh*n*a and the Yādavas.

GĀRGAS, GĀRGYAS. Descendants of Garga, who, "although Kshatriyas by birth, became Brāhmans and great *R*ishis."

GĀRGYA, GĀRGYA BĀLĀKI. Son of Bālāki. He was a Brāhman, renowned as a teacher and as a grammarian, who dealt especially with etymology, and was well read in the Veda, but still submitted to receive instruction from the Kshatriya Ajāta-*s*atru.

GARU*D*A. A mythical bird or vulture, half-man, half-bird, on which Vish*n*u rides. He is the king of birds, and descended from Ka*s*yapa and Vinatā, one of the daughters of Daksha. He is the great enemy of serpents, having inherited his hatred from his mother, who had quarrelled with her co-wife and superior, Kadru, the mother of serpents. His lustre was so brilliant that soon after his birth the gods mistook him for Agni and worshipped him. He is represented as having the head, wings, talons, and beak of an eagle, and the body and limbs of a man. His face is white, his wings red, and his body golden. He had a son named Sampāti, and his wife was Unnati or Vināyakā. According to the Mahā-bhārata, his parents gave him liberty to devour bad men, but he was not to touch Brāhmans. Once, however, he swallowed a Brāhman and his wife, but the Brāhman so burnt his throat that he was glad to disgorge them both.

Grau*d*a is said to have stolen the Am*ri*ta from the gods in order to purchase with it the freedom of his mother from Kadru. Indra discovered the theft and fought a fierce battle with Garuda. The Amrita was recovered, but Indra was worsted in the fight, and his thunderbolt was smashed.

Garuda has many names and epithets. From his parents he is called Kāsyapi and Vainateya. He is the Suparna and the Garutmān, or chief of birds. He is also called Dakshāya, Sālmalin, Tārkshya, and Vināyaka, and among his epithets are the following:—Sitānana, 'white faced;' Rakta-paksha, 'red winged;' Sweta-rohita, 'the white and red;' Suvarna-kāya, 'golden bodied;' Gaganeswara, 'lord of the sky;' Khageswara, 'king of birds;' Nāgāntaka, and Pannaga-nāsana, 'destroyer of serpents;' Sarpārāti, 'enemy of serpents;' Taraswin, 'the swift;' Rasāyana, 'who moves like quicksilver;' Kāma-chārin, 'who goes where he will;' Kāmāyus, 'who lives at pleasure;' Chirād, 'eating long;' Vishnu-ratha, 'vehicle of Vishnu;' Amritāharana and Sudhā-hara, 'stealer of the Amrita;' Surendra-jit, 'vanquisher of Indra;' Vajra-jit, 'subduer of the thunderbolt,' &c.

GARUDA PURĀNA. The description given of this Purāna is, "That which Vishnu recited in the Gāruda Kalpa, relating chiefly to the birth of Garuda from Vinatā, is called the Garuda Purāna, and in it there are read 19,000 stanzas." The works bearing this name which were examined by Wilson did not correspond in any respect with this description, and he considered it doubtful if a genuine Garuda Purāna is in existence.

GĀTHĀ. A song, a verse. A religious verse, but one not taken from the Vedas. Verses interspersed in the Sanskrit Buddhist work called Lalita-vistara, which are composed in a dialect between the Sanskrit and the Prākrit, and have given their name to this the Gāthā dialect. The Zend hymns of the Zoroastrians are also called Gāthās.

GĀTU. A singer, a Gandharva.

GAUDA, GAURA. The ancient name of Central Bengal; also the name of the capital of the country, the ruins of which city are still visible. The great northern nation of Brāhmans. *See* Brāhman.

GAUPĀYANAS. Sons or descendants of Gopa. Four Rishis, who were the authors of four remarkable hymns in the Rig-veda. One of them, named Su-bandhu, was killed and miraculously brought to life again. The hymns have been translated by Max Müller in the *Journal R. A. S.*, vol. ii. 1866.

GAURĪ. The 'yellow' or 'brilliant,' a name of the consort of *S*iva. (*See* Devī.) Varu*n*a's wife also is called Gaurī.

GAUTAMA. 1. A name of the sage *S*aradwat, as son of Gotama. He was husband of Ahalyā, who was seduced by Indra. This seduction has been explained mythologically as signifying the carrying away of night by the morning sun, Indra being the sun, and Ahalyā being explained as meaning night. 2. Author of a Dharma-*s*āstra, which has been edited by Stenzler. 3. A name common to many men.

GAUTAMES*A*. 'Lord of Gautama.' Name of one of the twelve great Lingas. *See* Linga.

GAUTAMĪ. 1. An epithet of Durgā. 2. Name of a fierce Rākshasī or female demon.

GAYĀ. A city in Bihār. It is one of the seven sacred cities, and is still a place of pilgrimage, though its glory has departed.

GĀYATRĪ. A most sacred verse of the *Ri*g-veda, which it is the duty of every Brāhman to repeat mentally in his morning and evening devotions. It is addressed to the sun as Savit*ri*, the generator, and so it is called also Sāvit*rī*. Personified as a goddess, Sāvit*rī* is the wife of Brahmā, mother of the four Vedas, and also of the twice-born or three superior castes. Colebrooke's translation of the Gāyatrī is "Earth, sky, heaven. Let us meditate on (these, and on) the most excellent light and power of that generous, sportive, and resplendent sun, (praying that) it may guide our intellects." Wilson's version is, in his translation of the *Ri*g-veda, "We meditate on that desirable light of the divine Savit*ri* who influences our pious rites." In the Vish*n*u Purā*n*a he had before given a somewhat different version, "We meditate on that excellent light of the divine sun: may he illuminate our minds." A later version by Benfey is, "May we receive the glorious brightness of this, the generator, of the god who shall prosper our works."

Wilson observes of it: "The commentators admit some variety of interpretation; but it probably meant, in its original use, a simple invocation of the sun to shed a benignant influence upon the customary offices of worship; and it is still employed by the unphilosophical Hindus with merely that signification. Later notions, and especially those of the Vedānta, have operated to attach to the text an import it did not at first possess, and have converted it into a mystical propitiation of the spiritual origin and essence of existence, or Brahma." It is considered so holy that copyists often refrain from transcribing it.

The name given to *S*ata-rūpā (q.v.), Brahmā's female half, daughter, and consort, as "the declarer of sacred knowledge." It is also applied to the consort of *S*iva in the Hari-van*s*a.

GHA*T*A-KARPARA. A poet, who was one of the "nine gems" of the court of Vikramāditya. There is a short artificial poem, descriptive of the rainy season, bearing this name, which has been translated into German by Dursch. The words mean 'potsherds,' and form probably an assumed literary name.

GHA*T*OTKACHA. A son of Bhīma by the Rākshasī Hi*d*imbā. He was killed in the great battle by Kar*n*a with the fatal lance that warrior had obtained from Indra.

GHOSHĀ. It is said in the Veda that the A*s*wins "bestowed a husband upon Ghoshā growing old," and the explanatory legend is that she was a daughter of Kakshīvat, but being a leper, was incapable of marriage. When she was advanced in years the A*s*wins gave her health, youth, and beauty, so that she obtained a husband.

GH*RI*TĀCHĪ. An Apsaras or celestial nymph. She had many amours with great sages and mortal men. She was mother of ten sons by Raudrā*s*wa or Kū*s*a-nābha, a descendant of Puru, and the Brahma Vaivartta Purā*n*a attributes the origin of some of the mixed castes to her issue by the sage Vi*s*wa-karman. The Hari-van*s*a asserts that she had ten daughters as well as ten sons by Raudrā*s*wa. Another legend represents her as mother by Ku*s*a-nābha of a hundred daughters, whom Vāyu wished to accompany him to the sky. They refused, and in his rage he cursed them to become deformed; but they recovered their natural shape and beauty, and were married to Brahma-datta, king of Kāmpila.

GIRI-JĀ. 'Mountain born.' A name of Pārvatī or Devī. *See* Devī.

GIRI-VRAJA. A royal city in Magadha, identified with Rāja-g*ri*ha in Bihar.

GĪTĀ. The Bhagavad-gītā (q.v.).

GĪTĀ-GOVINDA. A lyrical poem by Jaya-deva on the early life of K*ri*sh*n*a as Govinda the cowherd. It is an erotic work, and sings the loves of K*r*ish*n*a with Rādhā, and other of the cowherd damsels, but a mystical interpretation has been put upon it. The poems are supposed to have been written about the twelfth or thirteenth century. There are some translations in the *Asiatic Researches* by Sir W. Jones, and a small volume of translations has been lately published by Mr. Edwin Arnold. There is also an edition of the text, with a Latin translation and notes, by Lassen, and there are some others.

GOBHILA. An ancient writer of the Sūtra period. He was author of some G*r*ihya Sūtras, and of some Sūtras on grammar. The G*r*ihya Sūtras have been published in the *Bibliotheca Indica.*

GO-KAR*N*A. 'Cow's ear.' A place of pilgrimage sacred to *S*iva, on the west coast, near Mangalore.

GO-KULA. A pastoral district on the Yamunā, about Mathurā, where K*r*ish*n*a passed his boyhood with the cowherds.

GO-LOKA. 'The place of cows.' K*r*ish*n*a's heaven; a modern addition to the original series of seven Lokas.

GO-MANTA. A great mountain in the Western Ghāts. According to the Hari-vansa it was the scene of a defeat of Jarā-sandha by K*r*ish*n*a.

GO-MATĪ. The Gūmtī river in Oude; but there are others which bore the name. One fell into the Sindhu or Indus.

GO-PĀLA, GO-VINDA. 'Cow-keeper.' A name of the youthful K*r*ish*n*a, who lived among the cowherds in V*r*indāvana.

GOPĀLA-TĀPANI. An Upanishad in honour of K*r*ish*n*a. Printed in the *Bibliotheca Indica.*

GO-PATHA BRĀHMA*N*A. The Brāhma*n*a of the Atharva or fourth Veda. It has been published by Rājendra Lāla in the *Bibliotheca Indica.*

GOPATI-*RI*SHABHA. 'Chief of herdsmen.' 1. A title of *S*iva. 2. A demon mentioned in the Mahā-bhārata as slain by K*r*ish*n*a.

GOPĪS. The cowherd damsels and wives with whom K*r*ish*n*a sported in his youth.

GOTAMA. The founder of the Nyāya school of philosophy. He is called also *S*atānanda, and is author of a Dharma-*s*āstra or law-book, which has been edited by Stenzler. He is frequently called Gautama.

GO-VARDHANA. A mountain in V*ri*ndāvana, which K*ri*sh*na* induced the cowherds and cowherdesses to worship instead of Indra. This enraged the god, who sent a deluge of rain to wash away the mountain and all the people of the country, but K*ri*sh*na* held up the mountain on his little finger for seven days to shelter the people of V*ri*ndāvana. Indra retired baffled, and afterwards did homage to K*ri*sh*na*.

GOVARDHANA-DHARA. 'Upholder of Govardhana.' A title of K*ri*sh*na*.

GO-VINDA. 'Cow-keeper.' A name of K*ri*sh*n*a.

GRAHA. 'Seizing.' 1. The power that seizes and obscures the sun and moon, causing eclipses; the ascending node, Rāhu. 2. Evil spirits with which people, especially children, are possessed, and which cause sickness and death. They are supposed to be amenable to medicine and exorcism.

G*RI*HA-STHA. 'Householder.' A Brāhman in the second stage of his religious life. *See* Brāhman.

G*RI*HYA SŪTRAS. Rules for the conduct of domestic rites and the personal sacraments, extending from the birth to the marriage of a man. (*See* Sūtra.) The G*ri*hya Sūtras of Ā*s*walāyana have been printed in the *Bibliotheca Indica.*

G*RI*TSA-MADA. The reputed *Ri*shi of many hymns in the second Ma*nd*ala of the *Ri*g-veda. According to the Vish*n*u Purā*n*a he was a Kshatriya and son of *S*una-hotra, being descended from Purūravas of the Lunar race. From him sprang *S*aunaka, the eminent sage versed in the *Ri*g-veda "who originated the system of four castes." The Vāyu Purā*n*a makes *S*unaka to be the son of G*ri*tsa-mada, and *S*aunaka the son of *S*unaka: this seems probable. "It is related of him by Sāya*n*a that he was first a member of the family of Angiras, being the son of *S*una-hotra. He was carried off by the Asuras whilst performing a sacrifice, but was rescued by Indra, under whose authority he was henceforth designated as G*ri*tsa-mada, the son of *S*unaka or *S*aunaka of the race of Bh*ri*gu. Thus the Anukrama*n*ikā says of him: He who was an Āngirasa, the son of *S*una-hotra, became *S*aunaka of the race of Bh*ri*gu." According to the Mahā-bhārata, he was son of Vīta-havya, a king of the Haihayas, a Kshatriya, who became a Brāhman. (*See* Vīta-havya.) The Mahā-bhārata alludes to a legend of his having assumed the semblance of Indra, and so enabled that deity to escape from the Asuras, who were lying in wait to destroy him. There are several versions of the story, but they all agree that after Indra had escaped G*ri*tsa-mada saved himself by reciting a hymn in which he showed that Indra was a different person.

GU*D*Ā-KE*S*A. 'Whose hair is in tufts.' An epithet of Arjuna.

GUHA. 'Secret.' 1. A name of the god of war. (*See* Kārttikeya.) 2. A king of the Nishādas or Bhīls, who was a friend of Rāma. 3. A people near Kalinga, who possibly got their name from him.

GUHYAKAS. 'Hidden beings.' Inferior divinities attendant upon Kuvera, and guardians of his hidden treasures.

GUPTAS. A dynasty of kings who reigned in Magadha. The period of their ascendancy has been a subject of great contention, and cannot be said to be settled.

GURJJARA. The country of Gujarat.

HAIHAYA. This name is supposed to be derived from *haya*, 'a horse.' 1. A prince of the Lunar race, and great-grandson of Yadu. 2. A race or tribe of people to whom a Scythian origin has been ascribed. The Vishnu Purā*n*a represents them as descendants of Haihaya of the Yadu race, but they are generally associated with borderers and outlying tribes. In the Vāyu and other Purā*n*as, five great divisions of the tribe are named : Tāla-janghas, Vīti-hotras, Avantis, Tu*nd*ikeras, and Jātas, or rather Su-jātas. They conquered Bāhu or Bāhuka, a descendant of King Hari*s*-chandra, and were in their turn conquered, along with many other barbarian tribes, by King Sagara, son of Bāhu. According to the Mahā-bhārata, they were descended from *S*ar-yāti, a son of Manu. They made incursions into the Doāb, and they took the city of Kā*s*ī (Benares), which had been fortified against them by King Divo-dāsa ; but the grandson of this king, Pratardana by name, destroyed the Haihayas, and re-established the kingdom of Kā*s*ī. Arjuna-Kārtavīrya, of a thousand arms, was king of the Haihayas, and he was defeated and had his arms cut off by Para*s*u-rāma.

The Vindhya mountains would seem to have been the home of these tribes ; and according to Colonel Todd, a tribe of Haihayas still exists "near the very top of the valley of Sohagpoor, in Bhagelkhand, aware of their ancient lineage, and, though few in number, still celebrated for their valour."

HALA-BHRIT. 'Bearing a plough.' Bala-rāma.

HALĀYUDHA. 'Who has a ploughshare for his weapon,' *i.e.*, Bala-rāma.

HANSA. 1. This, according to the Bhāgavata Purāna, was the name of the "one caste," when, in olden times, there was only "one Veda, one God, and one caste." 2. A name used in the Mahā-bhārata for Krishna. 3. A mountain range north of Meru.

HANSA. Hansa and Dimbhaka were two great warrior-brothers mentioned in the Mahā-bhārata as friends of Jarā-sandha. A certain king also named Hansa was killed by Bala-rāma. Hearing that "Hansa was killed," Dimbhaka, unable to live without him, committed suicide, and when Hansa heard of this he drowned himself in the Yamunā.

HANUMĀN, HANUMAT, HANŪMAT. A celebrated monkey chief. He was son of Pavana, 'the wind,' by Anjanā, wife of a monkey named Kesarī. He was able to fly, and is a conspicuous figure in the Rāmāyana. He and the other monkeys who assisted Rāma in his war against Rāvana were of divine origin, and their powers were superhuman. Hanumān jumped from India to Ceylon in one bound; he tore up trees, carried away the Himālayas, seized the clouds, and performed many other wonderful exploits. (*See* Surasā.) His form is "as vast as a mountain and as tall as a gigantic tower. His complexion is yellow and glowing like molten gold. His face is as red as the brightest ruby; while his enormous tail spreads out to an interminable length. He stands on a lofty rock and roars like thunder. He leaps into the air, and flies among the clouds with a rushing noise, whilst the ocean waves are roaring and splashing below." In one of his fights with Rāvana and the Rākshasas, they greased his tail and set it on fire, but to their own great injury, for with it he burnt down their capital city, Lankā. This exploit obtained for him the name Lankā-dāhī. His services to Rāma were great and many. He acted as his spy, and fought most valiantly. He flew to the Himālayas, from whence he brought medicinal herbs with which he restored the wounded, and he killed the monster Kāla-nemi, and thousands of Gandharvas who assailed him. He accompanied Rāma on his return to Ayodhyā, and there he received from him the reward of perpetual life and youth. The exploits of Hanumān are favourite topics among Hindus from childhood to age, and paintings of them are common. He is called Marut-putra, and he has the patronymics Ānili, Māruti, &c., and the metronymic Ānjaneya. He is also Yoga-chara, from his power in magic or in the healing art, and Rajata-dyuti, 'the brilliant.' Among his other accomplishments, Hanumat was a grammarian; and the Rāmāyana says, "The chief of monkeys is perfect; no one equals him in the sāstras, in learning, and in ascertaining the sense of the scriptures [or in moving at will]. In all sciences, in the rules of austerity, he rivals the preceptor of the gods. . . . It is well known that Hanumat was the ninth author of grammar."—*Muir*, iv. 490.

HANUMĀN-NĀTAKA. A long drama by various hands upon the adventures of the monkey chief Hanumān. This drama is fabled to have been composed by Hanumān, and inscribed by him on rocks. Vālmīki, the author of the Rāmāyana, saw it and feared that it would throw his own poem into the shade. He complained to the author, who told him to cast the verses into the sea. He did so, and they remained concealed there for ages. Portions were discovered and brought to King Bhoja, who directed Dāmodara Misra to arrange them and fill up the lacunæ. He did so, and the result was this drama. "It is probable," says Wilson, "that the fragments of an ancient drama were connected in the manner described. Some of the ideas are poetical, and the sentiments just and forcible; the language is generally very harmonious, but the work itself is, after all, a most disjointed and nondescript composition, and the patchwork is very glaringly and clumsily put together." It is a work of the tenth or eleventh century. It has been printed in India.

HARA. A name of Siva.

HARI. A name which commonly designates Vishnu, but it is exceptionally used for other gods.

HARI-DWĀRA. 'The gate of Hari.' The modern Hardwār. The place where the Ganges finally breaks through the mountains into the plains of Hindustan. It is a great place of pilgrimage.

HARI-HARA. A combination of the names of Vishnu and Siva, and representing the union of the two deities in one, a combination which is differently accounted for.

HARIS-CHANDRA. Twenty-eighth king of the Solar race, and son of Tri-*s*anku. He was celebrated for his piety and justice. There are several legends about him. The Aitareya Brāhma*n*a tells the story of his purchasing *S*unа*h*-*s*ephas to be offered up as a vicarious sacrifice for his own son. (*See S*una*h*-*s*ephas.) The Mahā-bhārata relates that he was raised to the heaven of Indra for his performance of the Rāja-sūya sacrifice and for his unbounded liberality. The Mārka*nd*eya Purā*n*a expands the story at considerable length. One day while Haris-chandra was hunting he heard female lamentations, which proceeded "from the Sciences, who were being mastered by the austerely fervid sage Vi*s*wāmitra, and were crying out in alarm at his superiority." Hari*s*-chandra, as defender of the distressed, went to the rescue, but Vi*s*wāmitra was so provoked by his interference that the Sciences instantly perished, and Hari*s*-chandra was reduced to a state of abject helplessness. Vi*s*wāmitra demanded the sacrificial gift due to him as a Brāhman, and the king offered him whatever he might choose to ask, "gold, his own son, wife, body, life, kingdom, good fortune," whatever was dearest. Vi*s*wāmitra stripped him of wealth and kingdom, leaving him nothing but a garment of bark and his wife and son. In a state of destitution he left his kingdom, and Vi*s*wāmitra struck *S*aibyā, the queen, with his staff to hasten her reluctant departure. To escape from his oppressor he proceeded to the holy city of Benares, but the relentless sage was waiting for him and demanded the completion of the gift. With bitter grief wife and child were sold, and there remained only himself. Dharma, the god of justice, appeared in the form of a hideous and offensive Cha*nd*āla, and offered to buy him. Notwithstanding the exile's repugnance and horror, Vi*s*wāmitra insisted upon the sale, and Hari*s*-chandra was carried off "bound, beaten, confused, and afflicted," to the abode of the Cha*nd*āla. He was sent by his master to steal grave-clothes from a cemetery. In this horrid place and degrading work he spent twelve months. His wife then came to the cemetery to perform the obsequies of her son, who had died from the bite of a serpent. They recognised each other, and Hari*s*-chandra and his wife resolved to die upon the funeral pyre of their son, though he hesitated to take away his own life without the consent of his master. After all was prepared, he gave himself up to meditation on Vish*n*u. The gods then arrived, headed by Dharma and accompanied by Vi*s*wāmitra. Dharma entreated him to refrain from his intention, and Indra informed him "that he, his wife, and son, had conquered heaven by their good works." Hari*s*-chandra declared that he could not go to heaven without the permission of his master the Cha*nd*āla. Dharma then revealed himself. When this difficulty was removed, Hari*s*-chandra objected to go to heaven without his faithful subjects. "This request was granted by Indra, and after Vi*s*wāmitra had inaugurated Rohitā*s*wa, the king's son, to be his successor, Hari*s*-chandra, his friends, and followers, all ascended in company to heaven." There he was induced by the sage Nārada to boast of his merits, and this led to his expulsion from heaven. As he was falling he repented of his fault and was forgiven. His downward course was arrested, and he and his followers dwell in an aerial city, which, according to popular belief, is still visible occasionally in mid-air.

HARITA, HĀRĪTA. 1. A son of Yuvanā*s*wa of the Solar race, descended from Ikshwāku. From him descended the Hārita Angirasas. In the Linga Purā*n*a it is said, "The son of Yuvanā*s*wa was Harita, of whom the Hāritas were sons. They were, on the side of Angiras, twice-born men (Brāhmans) of Kshatriya lineage;" or according to the Vāyu, "they were the sons of Angiras, twice-born men (Brāhmans), of Kshatriya race," possibly meaning that they were sons raised up to Harita by Angiras. According to some he was a son of Chyavana. 2. Author of a Dharma-*s*āstra or law-book.

HĀRITAS, HĀRITA-ĀNGIRASES. *See* Harita.

HARITS, HARITAS. 'Green.' In the *Ri*g-veda the horses, or rather mares, of the sun, seven or ten in number, and typical of his rays. "The prototype of the Grecian Charites."—*Max Müller.*

HARI-VANSA. The genealogy of Hari or Vish*n*u, a long poem of 16,374 verses. It purports to be a part of the Mahābhārata, but it is of much later date, and "may more accurately be ranked with the Paura*n*ik compilations of least authenticity and latest date." It is in three parts; the first is introductory, and gives particulars of the creation and of the patriarchal and regal dynasties; the second contains the life and adventures of K*r*ish*n*a; and the last and the third treats of the future of the world and the corruptions of the Kali age. It contains many indications of its having been written in the south of India.

HARSHAṆA. A deity who presides over the *S*rāddha offerings.

HARYAS*W*A. A grandson of the Kuvalayā*s*wa who killed the demon Dhundhu. The country of Panchāla is said to have been named from his five (*pancha*) sons. There were several others of this name.

HARYAS*W*AS. Five thousand sons of the patriarch Daksha, begotten by him for the purpose of peopling the earth. The sage Nārada dissuaded them from producing offspring, and they "dispersed themselves through the regions and have not returned."

HASTINĀ-PURA. The capital city of the Kauravas, for which the great war of the Mahā-bhārata was waged. It was founded by Hastin, son of the first Bharata, and hence, as some say, its name; but the Mahā-bhārata and the Vish*n*u Purā*n*a call it the "elephant city," from *hastin*, an elephant. The ruins are traceable near an old bed of the Ganges, about 57 miles N.E. of Delhi, and local tradition has preserved the name. It is said to have been washed away by the Ganges.

HĀSYĀR*N*AVA. 'Ocean of laughter.' A modern comic piece in two acts, by a Pa*nd*it named Jagadīsa. "It is a severe but grossly indelicate satire upon the licentiousness of Brāhmans assuming the character of religious mendicants."—*Wilson.*

HAVIR-BHUJ, HAVISH-MATA. Pit*r*is or Manes of the Kshatriyas, and inhabitants of the solar sphere. *See* Pit*r*is.

HAYA-GRĪVA. 'Horse-necked.' According to one legend, a Daitya who stole the Veda as it slipped out of the mouth of Brahmā while he was sleeping at the end of a kalpa, and was killed by Vish*n*u in the Fish Avatāra. According to another, Vish*n*u himself, who assumed this form to recover the Veda, which had been carried off by two Daityas.

HAYA-*S*IRAS, HAYA-*S*ĪṚSHA. 'Horse-head.' In the Mahā-bhārata it is recorded that the sage Aurva (q.v.) "cast the fire of his anger into the sea," and that it there "became the great Haya-*s*iras, known to those acquainted with the Veda, which vomits forth that fire and drinks up the waters." A form of Vish*n*u.

In the Bhāgavata Purā*n*a Brahmā is represented as saying, "In my sacrifice Bhagavat himself was Haya-*s*īrsha, the male of the sacrifice, whose colour is that of gold, of whom the Vedas and the sacrifices are the substance and the gods the soul; when he respired, charming words came forth from his nostrils."

HEMA-CHANDRA. Author of a good Sansk*ri*t vocabulary, printed under the superintendence of Colebrooke.

HEMĀDRI. 'The golden mountain,' *i.e.*, Meru.

HEMA-KŪ*T*A. 'Golden peak.' A chain of mountains represented as lying north of the Himālayas, between them and Mount Meru.

HI*D*IMBA (mas.), HI*D*IMBĀ (fem.). A powerful Asura, who had yellow eyes and a horrible aspect. He was a cannibal, and dwelt in the forest to which the Pa*nd*avas retired after the burning of their house. He had a sister named Hi*d*imbā, whom he sent to lure the Pā*nd*avas to him; but on meeting with Bhīma, she fell in love with him, and offered to carry him away to safety on her back. Bhīma refused, and while they were parleying, Hi*d*imba came up, and a terrible fight ensued, in which Bhīma killed the monster. Hi*d*imbā was at first much terrified and fled, but she returned and claimed Bhīma for her husband. By his mother's desire Bhīma married her, and by her had a son named Gha*t*otkacha.

HIMĀCHALA, HIMĀDRI. The Himālaya mountains.

HIMAVAT. The personification of the Himālaya mountains, husband of Menā or Menakā, and father of Umā and Gangā.

HIRA*N*YA-GARBHA. 'Golden egg' or 'golden womb.' In the *Ri*g-veda Hira*n*ya-garbha "is said to have arisen in the beginning, the one lord of all beings, who upholds heaven and earth, who gives life and breath, whose command even the gods obey, who is the god over all gods, and the one animating principle of their being." According to Manu, Hira*n*ya-garbha was Brahmā, the first male, formed by the undiscernible eternal First Cause in a golden egg resplendent as the sun. "Having continued a year in the egg, Brahmā divided it into two parts by his mere thought, and with these two shells he formed the heavens and the earth; and in the middle he placed the sky, the eight regions, and the eternal abode of the waters." *See* Brahmā.

HIRA*N*YĀKSHA. 'Golden eye.' A Daitya who dragged the earth to the depths of the ocean. He was twin-brother of Hira*n*yakasipu, and was killed by Vish*n*u in the Boar incarnation.

HIRAṆYA-KASIPU. 'Golden dress.' A Daitya who, according to the Mahā-bhārata and the Purāṇas, obtained from Siva the sovereignty of the three worlds for a million of years, and persecuted his son Prahlāda for worshipping Vishṇu. He was slain by Vishṇu in the Nara-sinha, or man-lion incarnation. He and Hiraṇyāksha were twin-brothers and chiefs of the Daityas.

HITOPADESA. 'Good advice.' The well-known collection of ethical tales and fables compiled from the larger and older work called Pancha-tantra. It has been often printed, and there are several translations; among them is an edition by Johnson of text, vocabulary, and translation.

HOTṚI. A priest who recites the prayers from the Ṛig-veda.

HṚISHĪKESA. A name of Kṛishṇa or Vishṇu.

HŪṆAS. According to Wilson, "the White Huns or Indo-Scythians, who were established in the Panjāb and along the Indus at the commencement of our era, as we know from Arrian, Strabo, and Ptolemy, confirmed by recent discoveries of their coins," and since still further confirmed by inscriptions and additional coins. Dr. Fitzedward Hall says, "I am not prepared to deny that the ancient Hindus, when they spoke of the Hūṇas, intended the Huns. In the Middle Ages, however, it is certain that a race called Hūṇa was understood by the learned of India to form a division of the Kshatriyas."—*V. P.* ii. 134.

HŪN-DESA. The country round Lake Mānasarovara.

HUSHKA HUVISHKA. A Tushkara or Turki king, whose name is mentioned in the Rāja Taranginī as Hushka, which has been found in inscriptions as Huvishka, and upon the corrupt Greek coins as Oerki. He is supposed to have reigned just at the commencement of the Christian era. *See* Kanishka.

IḌĀ. In the Ṛig-veda Iḍā is primarily food, refreshment, or a libation of milk; thence a stream of praise, personified as the goddess of speech. She is called the instructress of Manu, and frequent passages ascribe to her the first institution of the rules of performing sacrifices. According to Sāyaṇa, she is the goddess presiding over the earth. A legend in the Satapatha Brāhmaṇa represents her as springing from a sacrifice which Manu performed for the purpose of obtaining offspring. She was claimed by Mitra-Varuṇa, but remained faithful to him who had produced her. Manu lived with her, and praying and fasting to obtain offspring, he begat upon her the race of Manu. In the Purā*n*as she is daughter of the Manu Vaivaswata, wife of Budha (Mercury), and mother of Purūravas. The Manu Vaivaswata, before he had sons, instituted a sacrifice to Mitra and Varu*n*a for the purpose of obtaining one; but the officiating priest mismanaged the performance, and the result was the birth of a daughter, I*d*ā or Ilā. Through the favour of the two deities her sex was changed, and she became a man, Su-dyumna. Under the malediction of *S*iva, Su-dyumna was again turned into a woman, and, as Ilā, married Budha or Mercury. After she had given birth to Purūravas, she, under the favour of Vish*n*u, once more became Su-dyumna, and was the father of three sons. According to another version of the legend, the Manu's eldest son was named Ila. He having trespassed on a grove sacred to Pārvatī, was changed into a female, Ilā. Upon the supplications and prayers of Ilā's friends, *S*iva and his consort conceded that the offender should be a male one month and a female another. There are other variations in the story which is apparently ancient.

I*D*ĀVI*D*Ā. Daughter of T*rin*abindu and the Apsaras Alambushā. There are different statements in the Purānas as regards her. She is represented to be the wife of Vi*s*ravas and mother of Kuvera, or the wife of Pulastya and mother of Vi*s*ravas.

IKSHWĀKU. Son of the Manu Vaivaswat, who was son of Vivaswat, the sun. "He was born from the nostril of the Manu as he happened to sneeze." Ikshwāku was founder of the Solar race of kings, and reigned in Ayodhyā at the beginning of the second Yuga or age. He had a hundred sons, of whom the eldest was Vikukshi. Another son, named Nimi, founded the Mithilā dynasty. According to Max Müller the name is mentioned once, and only once, in the *Ri*g-veda. Respecting this he adds: "I take it, not as the name of a king, but as the name of a people, probably the people who inhabited Bhājeratha, the country washed by the northern Gangā or Bhāgīrathī." Others place the Ikshwākus in the north-west.

ILA, ILĀ. *See* I*d*ā.

ILĀVILĀ. *See* I*d*āvi*d*ā.

ILVALA. *See* Vātāpi.

INDRA. The god of the firmament, the personified atmosphere. In the Vedas he stands in the first rank among the gods, but he is not uncreate, and is represented as having a father and mother: "a vigorous god begot him; a heroic female brought him forth." He is described as being of a ruddy or golden colour, and as having arms of enormous length; "but his forms are endless, and he can assume any shape at will." He rides in a bright golden car, drawn by two tawny or ruddy horses with flowing manes and tails. His weapon is the thunderbolt, which he carries in his right hand; he also uses arrows, a great hook, and a net, in which he is said to entangle his foes. The soma juice is his especial delight; he takes enormous draughts of it, and, stimulated by its exhilarating qualities, he goes forth to war against his foes, and to perform his other duties. As deity of the atmosphere, he governs the weather and dispenses the rain; he sends forth his lightnings and thunder, and he is continually at war with V*ri*tra or Ahi, the demon of drought and inclement weather, whom he overcomes with his thunderbolts, and compels to pour down the rain. Strabo describes the Indians as worshipping Jupiter Pluvius, no doubt meaning Indra, and he has also been compared to Jupiter Tonans. One myth is that of his discovering and rescuing the cows of the priests or of the gods, which had been stolen by an Asura named Pa*n*i or Vala, whom he killed, and he is hence called Vala-bhid. He is frequently represented as destroying the "stone-built cities" of the Asuras or atmospheric demons, and of the Dasyus or aborigines of India. In his warfare he is sometimes represented as escorted by troops of Maruts, and attended by his comrade Vish*n*u. More hymns are addressed to Indra than to any other deity in the Vedas, with the exception of Agni. For he was reverenced in his beneficent character as the bestower of rain and the cause of fertility, and he was feared as the awful ruler of the storm and director of the lightning and thunder. In many places of the *Ri*g-veda the highest divine functions and attributes are ascribed to him. There was a triad of gods—Agni, Vāyu, and Sūrya—which held a pre-eminence above the rest, and Indra frequently took the place of Vāyu. In some parts of the Veda, as Dr. Muir remarks, the ideas expressed of Indra are grand and lofty; at other times he is treated with familiarity, and his devotion to the soma juice is dilated upon, though nothing debasing is perceived in his sensuality. Indra is mentioned as having a wife, and the name of Indrāṇī or Aindrī is invoked among the goddesses. In the *S*atapatha Brāhmaṇa she is called Indra's beloved wife.

In the later mythology Indra has fallen into the second rank. He is inferior to the triad, but he is the chief of all the other gods. He is the regent of the atmosphere and of the east quarter of the compass, and he reigns over Swarga, the heaven of the gods and of beatified spirits, which is a region of great magnificence and splendour. He retains many of his Vedic characteristics, and some of them are intensified. He sends the lightning and hurls the thunderbolt, and the rainbow is his bow. He is frequently at war with the Asuras, of whom he lives in constant dread, and by whom he is often worsted. But he slew the demon Vṛitra, who, being regarded as a Brāhman, Indra had to conceal himself and make sacrifice until his guilt was purged away. His continued love for the soma juice is shown by a legend in the Mahā-bhārata, which represents him as being compelled by the sage Chyavana to allow the A*s*wins to partake of the soma libations, and his sensuality has now developed into an extreme lasciviousness. Many instances are recorded of his incontinence and adultery, and his example is frequently referred to as an excuse in cases of gallantry, as by King Nahusha when he tried to obtain Indra's wife while the latter was hiding in fear for having killed the Brāhman in the person of the demon Vṛitra. According to the Mahā-bhārata he seduced, or endeavoured to seduce, Ahalyā, the wife of the sage Gautama, and that sage's curse impressed upon him a thousand marks resembling the female organ, so he was called Sa-yoni; but these marks were afterwards changed to eyes, and he is hence called Netra-yoni, and Sahasrāksha 'the thousand-eyed.' In the Rāmāyaṇa it is related that Rāvaṇa, the Rākshasa king of Lankā or Ceylon, warred against Indra in his own heaven, and that Indra was defeated and carried off to Lankā by Rāvaṇa's son Megha-nāda, who for this exploit received the title of Indra-jit (q.v.), 'conqueror of Indra.' Brahmā and the gods had to sue for the release of Indra, and to purchase it with the boon of immortality to the victor. Brahmā then told the humiliated god that his defeat was a punishment for the seduction of Ahalyā. The Taittirīya Brāhmaṇa states that he chose Indrāṇī to be his wife in preference to other goddesses because of her voluptuous attractions, and later authorities say that he ravished her, and slew her father, the Daitya Puloman, to escape his curse. Mythologically he was father of Arjuna (q.v.), and for him he cheated Karna of his divine coat of mail, but gave Kārna in recompense a javelin of deadly effect. His libertine character is also shown by his frequently sending celestial nymphs to excite the passions of holy men, and to beguile them from the potent penances which he dreaded.

In the Purānas many stories are told of him, and he appears especially in rivalry with Krishna. He incurred the wrath of the choleric sage Dur-vāsas by slighting a garland of flowers which that sage presented to him, and so brought upon himself the curse that his whole dominion should be whelmed in ruin. He was utterly defeated by the Daityas, or rather by their ally, Raja, son of Āyus, and grandson of Purūravas, and he was reduced to such a forlorn condition that he, "the god of a hundred sacrifices," was compelled to beg for a little sacrificial butter. Puffed up by their victory, his conquerors neglected their duties, and so they became the easy prey of Indra, who recovered his dominion. The Bhāgavata Purāna represents him as having killed a Brāhman, and of being haunted by that crime, personified as a Chāndālī.

Indra had been an object of worship among the pastoral people of Vraja, but Krishna persuaded them to cease this worship. Indra was greatly enraged at this, and sent a deluge of rain to overwhelm them; but Krishna lifted up the mountain Govardhana on his finger to shelter them, and so held it for seven days, till Indra was baffled and rendered homage to Krishna. Again, when Krishna went to visit Swarga, and was about to carry off the Pārijāta tree, Indra resented its removal, and a fierce fight ensued, in which Indra was worsted, and the tree was carried off. Among the deeds of Indra recorded in the Purānas is that of the destruction of the offspring of Diti in her womb, and the production therefrom of the Maruts (*see* Diti); and there is a story of his cutting off the wings of the mountains with his thunderbolts, because they were refractory and troublesome. Indra is represented as a fair man riding on a white horse or an elephant, and bearing the vajra or thunderbolt in his hand. His son is named Jayanta. Indra is not the object of direct worship, but he receives incidental adoration, and there is a festival kept in his honour called *S*akra-dhwajot-thāna, 'the raising of the standard of Indra.'

Indra's names are many, as Mahendra, *S*akra, Maghavān, *R*ibhuksha, Vāsava, Arha, Datteya. His epithets or titles also are numerous. He is V*ri*tra-han, 'the destroyer of V*ri*tra;' Vajra-pā*n*i, 'of the thunderbolt hand;' Megha-vāhana, 'borne upon the clouds;' Pāka-*s*āsana, 'the subduer of Pāka;' *S*ata-kratu, 'of a hundred sacrifices;' Deva-pati and Surā-dhipa, 'chief of the gods;' Divas-pati, 'ruler of the atmosphere;' Marutwān, 'lord of the winds;' Swarga-pati, 'lord of paradise;' Jish*n*u, 'leader of the celestial host;' Puran-dara, 'destroyer of cities;' Ulūka, 'the owl;' Ugra-dhanwan, 'of the terrible bow,' and many others. The heaven of Indra is Swarga; its capital is Amarāvatī; his palace, Vaija-yanta; his garden, Nandana, Kandasāra, or Pārushya; his elephant is Airāvata; his horse, Uchchai*h*-*s*ravas; his chariot, Vimāna; his charioteer, Mātali; his bow, the rainbow, *S*akra-dhanus; and his sword, Paran-ja.

INDRA-DYUMNA. Son of Su-mati and grandson of Bharata. There were several of the name, among them a king of Avantī, by whom the temple of Vish*n*u was built, and the image of Jagan-nātha was set up in Orissa.

INDRA-JIT. Megha-nāda, son of Rāva*n*a. When Rāva*n*a went against Indra's forces in Swarga, his son Megha-nāda accompanied him, and fought most valiantly. Indra himself was obliged to interfere, when Megha-nāda, availing himself of the magical power of becoming invisible, which he had obtained from *S*iva, bound Indra and carried him off to Lankā. The gods, headed by Brahmā, went thither to obtain the release of Indra, and Brahmā gave to Megha-nāda the name Indra-jit, 'conqueror of Indra.' Still the victor refused to release his prisoner for anything less than the boon of immortality. Brahmā refused, but Indra-jit persisted in his demand and achieved his object. One version of the Rāmāya*n*a states that Indra-jit was killed and had his head cut off by Lakshma*n*a, who surprised him while he was engaged in a sacrifice.

INDRA-KĪLA. The mountain Mandara.

INDRA-LOKA. Indra's heaven, Swarga. *See* Loka.

INDRĀ*N*Ī. Wife of Indra, and mother of Jayanta and Jayantī. She is also called *S*achī and Aindrī. She is mentioned a few times in the *Rig*-veda, and is said to be the most fortunate of females, "for her husband shall never die of old age." The Taittirīya Brāhmana states that Indra chose her for his wife from a number of competing goddesses, because she surpassed them all in voluptuous attractions. In the Rāmāyana and Purānas she appears as the daughter of the Daitya Puloman, from whom she has the patronymic Paulomī. She was ravished by Indra, who killed her father to escape his curse. According to the Mahā-bhārata, King Nahusha became enamoured of her, and she escaped from him with difficulty. Indrānī has never been held in very high esteem as a goddess.

INDRA-PRAMATI. An early teacher of the *Rig*-veda, who received one Sanhitā direct from Paila.

INDRA-PRASTHA. The capital city of the Pāndu princes. The name is still known, and is used for a part of the city of Delhi.

INDRA-SENA (mas.), INDRA-SENĀ (fem.). Names of the son and daughter of Nala and Damayantī.

INDU. The moon. *See* Soma.

INDU-MATĪ. Sister of Bhoja, king of Vidarbha, who chose Prince Aja for her husband at her swayam-vara. She was killed by Nārada's garland falling upon her while asleep in an arbour.

INDU-MANI. The moon gem. *See* Chandra-kānta.

IRĀVAT. A son of Arjuna by his Nāga wife Ulupī.

IRĀVATĪ. The river Rāvī or Hydraotes.

ĪSA. 'Lord.' A title of Siva. Name of a Upanishad (q.v.) which has been translated by Dr. Roer in the *Bibliotheca Indica*.

ĪSĀNA. A name of Siva or Rudra, or of one of his manifestations. (*See* Rudra.) He is guardian of the north-east quarter.

ISHTI-PASAS. 'Stealers of offerings.' Rākshasas and other enemies of the gods, who steal the oblations.

ĪSWARA. 'Lord.' A title given to Siva.

ISWARA KRISHNA. Author of the philosophical treatise called Sānkhya Kārika.

ITIHĀSAS. Legendary poems. Heroic history. "Stories like those of Urvasī and Purūravas." The term is especially applied to the Mahā-bhārata.

JĀBĀLI, JĀVĀLI. A Brāhman who was priest of King

Dasa-ratha, and held sceptical philosophical opinions. He is represented in the Rāmāyana as enforcing his views upon Rāma, who decidedly repudiated them. Thereupon he asserted that his atheistical arguments had been used only for a purpose, and that he was really imbued with sentiments of piety and religion. He is said to have been a logician, so probably he belonged to the Nyāya school.

JAGAD-DHĀTRĪ (DHĀTĀ). 'Sustainer of the world.' An epithet given to both Saraswatī and Durgā.

JAGAN-MĀTRI (MĀTĀ). 'Mother of the world.' One of the names of Siva's wife. *See* Devī.

JAGAN-NĀTHA. 'Lord of the world.' A particular form of Vishnu, or rather of Krishna. He is worshipped in Bengal and other parts of India, but Puri, near the town of Cuttack, in Orissa, is the great seat of his worship, and multitudes of pilgrims resort thither from all parts, especially to the two great festivals of the Snāna-yātra and Ratha-yātra, in the months of Jyaishtha and Āshādha. The first of these is when the image is bathed, and in the second, or car festival, the image is brought out upon a car with the images of his brother Bala-rāma and sister Su-bhadrā, and is drawn by the devotees. The legend of the origin of Jagan-nātha is peculiar. Krishna was killed by a hunter, and his body was left to rot under a tree, but some pious persons found the bones and placed them in a box. A devout king named Indra-dyumna was directed by Vishnu to form an image of Jagan-nātha and to place the bones of Krishna inside it. Viswa-karma, the architect of the gods, undertook to make the image, on condition of being left quite undisturbed till the work was complete. After fifteen days the king was impatient and went to Viswa-karma, who was angry, and left off work before he had made either hands or feet, so that the image has only stumps. Indra-dyumna prayed to Brahmā, who promised to make the image famous, and he did so by giving to it eyes and a soul, and by acting as high priest at its consecration.

JĀHNAVĪ. The Ganges. *See* Jahnu.

JAHNU. A sage descended from Purūravas. He was disturbed in his devotions by the passage of the river Gangā, and consequently drank up its waters. He afterwards relented, and allowed the stream to issue from his ear, hence Gangā is called Jāhnavī, daughter of Jahnu. *See* Gangā.

JAIMINI. A celebrated sage, a disciple of Vyāsa. He is said to have received the Sāma-veda from his master, and to have been its publisher or teacher. He was also the founder of the Pūrva-mīmānsā philosophy. The text of Jaimini is printed in the *Bibliotheca Indica.*

JAIMINĪYA-NYĀYA-MĀLA-VISTARA. A work on philosophy by Mādhava. It has been edited by Goldstücker and Cowell.

JĀJALI. A Brāhman mentioned in the Mahā-bhārata as having by ascetism acquired a supernatural power of locomotion, of which he was so proud that he deemed himself perfect in virtue and superior to all men. A voice from the sky told him that he was inferior to Tulādhāra, a Vai*s*ya and a trader. He went to this Tulādhāra and learnt wisdom from him.

JALA-RŪPA. The fish or the Makara on the banner of Kāma.

JALA-*S*ĀYIN. 'Sleeping on the waters.' An appellation of Vish*n*u, as he is supposed to sleep upon his serpent couch on the waters during the rainy season, or during the submersion of the world.

JAMAD-AGNI. A Brāhman and a descendant of Bh*r*igu. He was the son of *R*ichīka and Satya-vatī, and was the father of five sons, the youngest and most renowned of whom was Para*s*u-rāma. Jamad-agni's mother, Satya-vatī, was daughter of King Gādhi, a Kshatriya. The Vish*n*u Purā*n*a relates that when Satya-vati was pregnant, her Brāhman husband, *R*ichīka, prepared a mess for her to eat for the purpose of securing that her son should be born with the qualities of a Brāhman. He also gave another mess to her mother that she might bear a son with the character of a warrior. The women changed the messes, and so Jamad-agni, the son of *R*ichīka, was born as a warrior-Brāhman, and Vi*s*wāmitra, son of the Kshatriya Gādhi, was born as a priest. The Mahā-bhārata relates that Jamad-agni engaged deeply in study and "obtained entire possession of the Vedas." He went to King Re*n*u or Prasena-jit of the Solar race and demanded of him his daughter Re*n*ukā. The king gave her to him, and he retired with her to his hermitage, where the princess shared in his ascetic life. She bore him five sons, Ruma*n*wat, Sushena, Vasu, Vi*s*wāvasu, and Para*s*u-rāma, and she was exact in the performance of all her duties. One day she went out to bathe and beheld a loving pair sporting and dallying in the water. Their pleasure made her feel envious, so she was "defiled by unworthy thoughts, and returned wetted but not purified by the stream." Her husband beheld her "fallen from perfection and shorn of the lustre of her sanctity." So he reproved her and was exceeding wroth. His sons came into the hermitage in the order of their birth, and he commanded each of them in succession to kill his mother. Influenced by natural affection, four of them held their peace and did nothing. Their father cursed them and they became idiots bereft of all understanding. When Parasu-rāma entered, he obeyed his father's order and struck off his mother's head with his axe. The deed assuaged the father's anger, and he desired his son to make a request. Parasu-rāma begged that his mother might be restored to life in purity, and that his brothers might regain their natural condition. All this the father granted.

The mighty Kārta-vīrya, king of the Haihayas, who had a thousand arms, paid a visit to the hermitage of Jamad-agni. The sage and his sons were out, but his wife treated her guest with all proper respect. Unmindful of the hospitality he had received, Kārta-vīrya threw down the trees round the hermitage, and carried of the calf of the sacred cow, Surabhi, which Jamad-agni had acquired by penance. Parasu-rāma returned and discovered what had happened, he then pursued Kārta-vīrya, cut off his thousand arms with arrows, and killed him. The sons of Kārta-vīrya went in revenge to the hermitage of Jamad-agni, and in the absence of Parasu-rāma slew the pious sage without pity. When Parasu-rāma found the lifeless body of his father, he laid it on a funeral pile, and vowed that he would extirpate the whole Kshatriya race. He slew all the sons of Kārta-vīrya, and "thrice seven times" he cleared the earth of the Kshatriya caste.

JĀMADAGNYA. The patronymic of Parasu-rāma.

JĀMBAVAT. King of the bears. A celebrated gem called Syamantaka had been given by the Sun to Satrā-jit. He, fearing that K*ri*sh*n*a would take it from him, gave it to his brother, Prasena. One property of this jewel was to protect its wearer when good, to ruin him when bad. Prasena was wicked and was killed by a lion, which was carrying off the gem in its mouth, when he was encountered and slain by Jāmbavat. After Prasena's disappearance, K*ri*sh*n*a was suspected of having killed him for the sake of the jewel. K*ri*sh*n*a with a large party tracked the steps of Prasena, till it was ascertained that he had been killed by a lion, and that the lion had been killed by a bear. K*ri*sh*n*a then tracked the bear, Jāmbavat, into his cavern, and a great fight ensued between them. After waiting outside seven or eight days, K*ri*sh*n*a's followers went home and performed his funeral ceremonies. On the twenty-first day of the fight, Jāmbavat submitted to his adversary, gave up the gem, and presented to him his daughter, Jāmbavatī, as an offering suitable to a guest. Jāmbavat with his army of bears aided Rāma in his invasion of Lankā, and always acted the part of a sage counsellor.

JĀMBAVATĪ. Daughter of Jāmbavat, king of the bears, wife of K*ri*sh*n*a, and mother of *S*āmba.

JAMBHA. Name of several demons. Of one who fought against the gods and was slain by Indra, who for this deed was called Jambha-bhedin. Also of one who fought against Arjuna and was killed by K*ri*sh*n*a.

JAMBU-DWĪPA. One of the seven islands or continents of which the world is made up. The great mountain, Meru, stands in its centre, and Bhārata-varsha or India is its best part. Its varshas or divisions are nine in number :—(1.) Bhārata, south of the Himālayas and southernmost of all. (2.) Kim-purusha. (3.) Hari-varsha. (4.) Ilā-v*ri*ta, containing Meru. (5.) Ramyaka. (6.) Hira*n*-maya. (7.) Uttara-Kuru, each to the north of the preceding one. (8.) Bhadrā*s*wa and (9.) Ketu-māla lie respectively to the east and west of Ilā-v*ri*ta, the central region.

JAMBU-MĀLI. A Rākshasa general of Rāva*n*a. He was killed by Hanumān.

JANAKA. 1. King of Mithilā, of the Solar race. When Nimi, his predecessor, died without leaving a successor, the sages subjected the body of Nimi to attrition, and produced from it a prince "who was called Janaka, from being born without a progenitor." He was the first Janaka, and twenty generations earlier than Janaka the father of Sītā.

2. King of Videha and father of Sītā, remarkable for his great knowledge and good works and sanctity. He is called *S*īra-dhwaja, 'he of the plough banner,' because his daughter Sītā sprang up ready formed from the furrow when he was

ploughing the ground and preparing for a sacrifice to obtain offspring. The sage Yājnawalkya was his priest and adviser. The Brāhma*n*as relate that he "refused to submit to the hierarchical pretensions of the Brāhmans, and asserted his right of performing sacrifices without the intervention of priests." He succeeded in his contention, for it is said that through his pure and righteous life he became a Brāhman and one of the Rājarshis. He and his priest Yājnawalkya are thought to have prepared the way for Buddha.

JĀNAKĪ. A patronymic of Sītā (q.v.).

JANA-LOKA. *See* Loka.

JANAMEJAYA. A great king, who was son of Parikshit, and great-grandson of Arjuna. It was to this king that the Mahā-bhārata was recited by Vai*s*ampāyana, and the king listened to it in expiation of the sin of killing a Brāhman. His father, Parikshit, died from the bite of a serpent, and Janemajaya is said to have performed a great sacrifice of serpents (Nāgas) and to have conquered the Nāga people of Taksha-*s*ilā. Hence he is called Sarpa-sattrin, 'serpent-sacrificer.' There were several others of the same name.

JANĀRDDANA. 'The adored of mankind.' A name of K*ri*sh*n*a, but other derivations are offered, as 'extirpator of the wicked,' by Sankarāchārya.

JANA-STHĀNA. A place in the Da*nd*aka forest where Rāma sojourned for a while in his exile.

JARAS. 'Old age.' The hunter who unwittingly killed K*ri*sh*n*a.

JARĀ-SANDHA. Son of B*ri*had-ratha, and king of Magadha. B*ri*had-ratha had two wives, who after being long barren brought forth two halves of a boy. These abortions were regarded with horror and thrown away. A female man-eating demon named Jarā picked them up and put them together to carry them off. On their coming in contact a boy was formed, who cried out so lustily that he brought out the king and his two queens. The Rākshasī explained what had happened, resigned the child, and retired. The father gave the boy the name of Jarā-sandha, because he had been put together by Jarā. Future greatness was prophesied for the boy, and he became an ardent worshipper of *S*iva. Through the favour of this god he prevailed over many kings, and he especially fought against

Krishna, who had killed Kansa, the husband of two of Jarā-sandha's daughters. He besieged Mathurā, and attacked Krishna eighteen times, and was as often defeated; but Krishna was so weakened that he retired to Dwārakā. Jarā-sandha had many kings in captivity, and when Krishna returned from Dwārakā, he, with Bhīma and Arjuna, went to Jarā-sandha's capital for the purpose of slaying their enemy and liberating the kings. Jarā-sandha refused to release the kings, and accepted the alternative of a combat, in which he was killed by Bhīma.

JARAT-KĀRU. An ancient sage who married a sister of the great serpent Vāsukī, and was father of the sage Āstīka.

JARITĀ. A certain female bird of the species called Śārngikā, whose story is told in the Mahā-bhārata. The saint Manda-pāla, who returned from the shades because he had no son, assumed the form of a male bird, and by her had four sons. He then abandoned her. In the conflagration of the Khāndava forest she showed great devotion in the protection of her children, and they were eventually saved through the influence of Manda-pāla over the god of fire. Their names were Jaritāri, Sārisrikta, Stamba-mitra, and Drona. They were "interpreters of the Vedas;" and there are hymns of the *Rig*-veda bearing the names of the second and third.

JATĀSURA. A Rākshasa who disguised himself as a Brāhman and carried off Yudhi-shthira, Saha-deva, Nakula, and Draupadī. He was overtaken and killed by Bhīma.

JĀTA-VEDAS. A Vedic epithet for fire. "The meaning is explained in five ways:—(1.) Knowing all created beings; (2.) Possessing all creatures or everything existent; (3.) Known by created beings; (4.) Possessing vedas, riches; (5.) Possessing vedas, wisdom. Other derivations and explanations are found in the Brāhmanas, but the exact sense of the word seems to have been very early lost, and of the five explanations given, only the first two would seem to be admissible for the Vedic texts. In one passage a form, Jāta-veda, seems to occur."—*Williams.* This form of the term, and the statement of Manu that the Vedas were milked out from fire, air, and the sun, may perhaps justify the explanation, 'producer of the Vedas.'

JATĀYU, JATĀYUS. According to the Rāmāyana, a bird who was son of Vishnu's bird Garuda, and king of the vultures. Others say he was a son of Aruna. He became an ally of

Rāma's, and he fought furiously against Rāva*n*a to prevent the carrying away of Sītā. Rāva*n*a overpowered him and left him mortally wounded. Rāma found him in time to hear his dying words, and to learn what had become of Sītā. Rāma and Laksmma*n*a performed his funeral rites to "secure his soul in the enjoyments of heaven," whither he ascended in a chariot of fire. In the Purā*n*as he is the friend of Dasa-ratha. When that king went to the ecliptic to recover Sītā from *S*ani (Saturn), his carriage was consumed by a glance from the eye of the latter, but Ja*t*āyu caught the falling king and saved him. The Pādma Purā*n*a says Da*s*a-ratha assailed Saturn because of a dearth, and when he and his car were hurled from heaven, Ja*t*āyu caught him.

JA*T*ILĀ. A daughter of Gotama, who is mentioned in the Mahā-bhārata as a virtuous woman and the wife of seven husbands.

JAYA-DEVA. A poet, author of the Gītā-govinda (q.v.).

JAYAD-RATHA. A prince of the Lunar race, son of B*ri*hanmanas. He was king of Sindhu, and was "indifferently termed Rāja of the Sindhus or Saindhavas, and Rāja of the Sauvīras, or sometimes in concert Sindhu-sauvīras," the Saindhavas and Sauvīras both being tribes living along the Indus. Jayad-ratha married Du*h*-salā, daughter of Dh*ri*ta-rāsh*t*ra, and was an ally of the Kauravas. When the Pā*n*davas were in exile he called at their forest abode while they were out hunting and Draupadī was at home alone. He had with him six brothers and a large retinue, but the resources of the Pā*n*davas were equal to the occasion, and Draupadī was able to supply five hundred deer with accompaniments for breakfast. This is explained by the statement that Yudhi-sh*t*hira, having worshipped the sun, obtained from that luminary an inexhaustible cauldron which was to supply all and every viand that might be required by the Pā*n*davas in their exile. Jayad-ratha was captivated by the charms of Draupadī, and tried to induce her to elope with him. When he was indignantly repulsed he carried her off by force. On the return of the Pā*n*davas they pursued the ravisher, defeated his forces, and made him prisoner. His life was spared by command of Yudhi-sh*t*hira, but Bhīma kicked and beat him terribly, cut off his hair, and made him go before the assembled Pā*n*davas and acknowledge himself to be their slave. At the intercession of Draupadī he was allowed to depart. He was killed, after a desperate conflict, by Arjuna on the fourteenth day of the great battle.

JAYANTA. Son of Indra, also called Jaya.

JAYANTĪ. Daughter of Indra. She is called also Jayanī, Deva-senā, and Tāvīshī.

JĪMŪTA. A great wrestler, who was overcome and killed by Bhīma at the court of Virā*t*a.

JĪMŪTA-VĀHANA. 'Whose vehicle is the clouds.' A title of Indra. A name borne by several persons, and among them by the author of the Dāya-bhāga.

JISH*N*U. A name of Arjuna.

JUSHKA. A Turushka or Turki king, who ruled in Kashmīr and in Northern India. *See* Kanishka.

JWĀLĀ-MUKHĪ. 'Mouth of fire.' A volcano. A celebrated place of pilgrimage in the Lower Himālayas, north of the Panjāb, where fire issues from the ground. According to the legend, it is the fire which Satī, the wife of *S*iva, created, and in which she burnt herself.

JYĀMAGHA. A king of the Lunar race, proverbial as "most eminent among husbands submissive to their wives." *S*aibyā, his wife, was barren, but he was afraid to take another wife till, having overcome an enemy and driven him from his country, the daughter of the vanquished king became his captive. She was beautiful, and Jyāmagha desired to marry her. He took her in his chariot and carried her to his palace to ask the assent of his queen. When *S*aibyā saw the maiden, she was filled with jealousy, and angrily demanded who the "light-hearted damsel" was. The king was disconcerted, and humbly replied, "She is the young bride of the future son whom thou shalt bring forth." It had ceased to be with *S*aibyā after the manner of women, but still she bore a son who was named Vidarbha, and married the captive princess.

JYOTISHA. Astronomy. One of the Vedāngas. The object of this Vedānga is to fix the most auspicious days and seasons for the performance of sacrifices. There has been little discovered that is ancient on this subject; only one "short tract, consisting of thirty-six verses, in a comparatively modern style, to which scholars cannot assign an earlier date than 300 years B.C."

KA. The interrogative pronoun "who?" This word has

been raised to the position of a deity. In the words of Max Müller, "The authors of the Brāhmanas had so completely broken with the past, that, forgetful of the poetical character of the hymns (of the Veda) and the yearning of the poets after the unknown god, they exalted the interrogative pronoun itself into a deity, and acknowledged a god Ka or Who? In the Taittirīya Brāhmana, in the Kaushītaki Brāhmana, in the Tāndya Brāhmana, and in the *S*atapatha Brāhmana, wherever interrogative verses occur, the author states that Ka is Prajāpati, or the lord of creatures. Nor did they stop here. Some of the hymns in which the interrogative pronoun occurred were called Kadvat, *i.e.*, having *kad* or *quid*. But soon a new adjective was formed, and not only the hymns but the sacrifice also offered to the god were called Kāya or Who-ish. . . . At the time of Pānini, this word had acquired such legitimacy as to call for a separate rule explaining its formation. The commentator here explains Ka by Brahman. After this we can hardly wonder that in the later Sanskrit literature of the Purānas Ka appears as a recognised god, as a supreme god, with a genealogy of his own, perhaps even with a wife; and that in the laws of Manu one of the recognised forms of marriage, generally known by the name of the Prajāpati marriage, occurs under the monstrous title of Kāya." The Mahā-bhārata identifies Ka with Daksha, and the Bhāgavata Purāna applies the term to Kasyapa, no doubt in consequence of their great generative powers and similarity to Prajāpati.

KABANDHA. 1. A disciple of Su-mantu, the earliest teacher of the Atharva-veda. 2. A monstrous Rākshasa slain by Rāma. He is said to have been a son of the goddess *S*rī. He is described as "covered with hair, vast as a mountain, without head or neck, having a mouth armed with immense teeth in the middle of his belly, arms a league long, and one enormous eye in his breast." He was originally a Gandharva, and his hideous deformity arose, according to one account, from a quarrel with Indra, whom he challenged, and who struck him with his thunderbolt, and drove his head and thighs into his body. According to another statement, his deformity arose from the curse of a sage. When mortally wounded, he requested Rāma to burn his body, and when that was done he came out of the fire in his real shape as a Gandharva, and counselled Rāma as to the conduct of the war against Rāvaṇa. He was also called Danu.

KACHA. A son of Bṛihaspati. According to the Mahābhārata he became a disciple of Śukra or Uśanas, the priest of the Asuras, with the object of obtaining from him the mystic power of restoring the dead to life, a charm which Śukra alone possessed. To prevent this the Asuras killed Kacha again and again, but on both occasions he was restored to life by the sage at the intercession of Devayānī, his daughter, who had fallen in love with Kacha. They killed him a third time, burnt his body, and mixed his ashes with Śukra's wine, but Devayānī again implored her father to bring back the young man. Unable to resist his daughter's importunity, Śukra once more performed the charm, and to his surprise heard the voice of Kacha come out from his own belly. To save his own life, Śukra taught his pupil the great charm. He then allowed himself to be ripped open, and Kacha, upon coming out, performed the charm, and restored his master to life. This incident is said to have caused Śukra to prohibit the use of wine to Brāhmans. Kacha resisted the proposals of Devayānī, and refused to make her his wife. She then cursed him, that the charms he had learnt from her father should be powerless, and he in return condemned her to be sought by no Brāhman, and to become the wife of a Kshatriya.

KĀDAMBARĪ. A daughter of Chitra-ratha and Madirā. Her name has been given to a well-known prose work, a kind of novel, written by Vāṇa or Bāṇa-bhaṭṭa, in the seventh century. The work has been printed at Bombay.

KADRŪ. A daughter of Daksha, and one of the thirteen that were married to Kaśyapa. She was mother of "a thousand powerful many-headed serpents, the chief amongst whom were Śesha, Vāsuki, . . . and many other fierce and venomous serpents." The Vishṇu Purāṇa, from which this is taken, names twelve, the Vāyu Purāṇa forty. Her offspring bear the metronymic Kādraveya.

KAHOḌA. A learned Brāhman, father of Ashṭāvakra. He with many others was overcome in argument at the court of Janaka by a Buddhist sage, and as a penalty was thrown into the river. Some years afterwards he was recovered by his son, who overcame the supposed Buddhist sage, and thus brought about a restoration. *See* Ashṭāvakra.

KAIKASĪ. Daughter of the Rākshasa Su-mālī and his wife Ketu-matī, wife of Vi*s*ravas and mother of Rāva*n*a.—*Muir*, iv. 487, 488.

KAIKEYA. Name of a country and of its king. He was father-in-law of K*r*ish*n*a, and his five sons were allies of the Pā*n*d*avas. His real name appears to have been Dh*r*ish*t*a-ketu.

KAIKEYAS, KEKAYAS. The people of Kaikeya, one of the chief nations in the war of the Mahā-bhārata. The Rāmāya*n*a places them in the west, beyond the Saraswatī and Byās.

KAIKEYĪ. A princess of Kaikeya, wife of King Da*s*a-ratha, and mother of Bharata, his third son. She carefully tended Da*s*a-ratha when he was wounded in battle, and in gratitude he promised to grant any two requests she might make. Urged by the malignant counsels of Mantharā, a female attendant, she made use of this promise to procure the exile of Rāma, and to promote the advancement of her own son, Bharata, to his place. *See* Da*s*a-ratha, Rāma.

KAILĀSA. A mountain in the Himālayas, north of the Mānasa lake. *S*iva's paradise is said to be on Mount Kailāsa, so also is Kuvera's abode. It is called also Ga*n*a-parvata and Rajatādri, 'silver mountain.'

KAI*T*ABHA. Kai*t*abha and Madhu were two horrible demons, who, according to the Mahā-bhārata and the Purā*n*as, sprang from the ear of Vish*n*u while he was asleep at the end of a kalpa, and were about to kill Brahmā, who was lying on the lotus springing from Vish*n*u's navel. Vish*n*u killed them, and hence he obtained the names of Kai*t*abha-jit and Madhu-sūdana. The Mārka*n*d*eya Purā*n*a attributes the death of Kai*t*abha to Umā, and she bears the title of Kai*t*abhā. The Hari-van*s*a states that the earth received its name of Medinī from the marrow (*medas*) of these demons. In one passage it says that their bodies, being thrown into the sea, produced an immense quantity of marrow or fat, which Nārāya*n*a used in forming the earth. In another place it says that the *medas* quite covered the earth, and so gave it the name of Medinī. This is another of the many etymological inventions.

KAKSHĪVAT, KAKSHĪVĀN. A Vedic sage, particularly connected with the worship of the A*s*wins. He was the son of Dīrgha-tamas and U*s*ij (q.v.), and is author of several hymns in the *Rig*-veda. He was also called Pajriya, because he was of the race of Pajra. In one of his hymns he lauds the liberality of King Swanaya. The following legend, in explanation, is given by the commentator Sāyana and the Nītī-manjara:—Kakshīvat, having finished his course of study, took leave of his preceptor and departed homewards. As he journeyed night came on, and he fell asleep by the roadside. In the morning he was aroused by Rāja Swanaya, who, being pleased with his appearance, treated him cordially and took him home. After ascertaining his worthiness, he married him to his ten daughters, presenting him at the same time with a hundred *nishkas* of gold, a hundred horses, a hundred bulls, a thousand and sixty cows, and eleven chariots, one for each of his ten wives, and one for himself, each drawn by four horses. With these he returned home to his father, and recited the hymn in praise of the munificence of Swanaya.

KAKUDMIN. A name of Raivata (q.v.).

KAKUT-STHA. *See* Puranjaya.

KĀLA. 'Time.' A name of Yama, the judge of the dead. In the Atharva-veda Time is addressed as the source and ruler of all things. "It is he who drew forth the worlds and encompassed them. Being their father, he became their son. There is no other power superior to him." The Vishnu, Bhāgavata, and Padma Purānas state that Brahmā existed in the form of Time, "but the Purānas do not generally recognise Time as an element of the first cause."

KĀLAKĀ. A wife of Kasyapa. According to the Rāmāyana and Mahā-bhārata she was a daughter of Daksha, but the Vishnu Purāna states that she and her sister Pulomā were daughters of the Dānava Vaiswanara, "who were both married to Kasyapa, and bore him 60,000 distinguished Dānavas, called Paulomas and Kālakanjas, who were powerful, ferocious, and cruel." The Mahā-bhārata states that she obtained from the deity, in reward for her severe devotion and penance, the privilege of bringing forth children without pain. The giants or Dānavas were called after her Kālakeyas.

KĀLAKANJAS, KĀLAKEYAS. Sons of Kasyapa by his wife Kālakā. There were many thousands of them, and they were "distinguished Dānavas, who were powerful, ferocious, and cruel."

KĀLA-MUKHAS. 'Black faces.' People who sprang from men and Rākshasa females.

KALĀNAS. (Kalyā*n*a.) A Brāhman who yielded to the inducements of Alexander the Great and left his native country to accompany the court of the conqueror. He afterwards repented of what he had done and burnt himself at Pasargada.

KĀLA-NEMI. 1. In the Rāmāya*n*a a Rākshasa, uncle of Rāva*n*a. At the solicitation of Rāva*n*a, and with the promise of half his kingdom, he endeavoured to kill Hanumān. Assuming the form of a hermit-devotee, he went to the Gandha-mādana mountain, and when Hanumān proceeded thither in search of medicinal herbs, the disguised Rākshasa invited him to his hermitage and offered him food. Hanumān refused, but went to bathe in a neighbouring pond. Upon his placing his foot in the water it was seized by a crocodile, but he dragged the creature out and killed it. From the dead body there arose a lovely Apsaras, who had been cursed by Daksha to live as a crocodile till she should be released by Hanumān. She told her deliverer to be beware of Kāla-nemi; so Hanumān went back to that deceiver, told him that he knew him, and, taking him by the feet, sent him whirling through the air to Lankā, where he fell before the throne of Rāva*n*a in the council-room. 2. In the Purā*n*as a great Asura, son of Virochana, the grandson of Hira*n*ya-ka*s*ipu. He was killed by Vish*n*u, but was said to live again in Kan*s*a and in Kāliya.

KĀLA-YAVANA. (Lit. 'Black Yavana,' Yavana meaning a Greek or foreigner.) A Yavana or foreign king who led an army of barbarians to Mathurā against K*ri*sh*n*a. That hero lured him into the cave of the mighty Muchukunda, who being disturbed from sleep by a kick from Kāla-yavana, cast a fiery glance upon him and reduced him to ashes. This legend appears to indicate an invasion from the Himālayas. According to the Vish*n*u Purā*n*a and Hari-van*s*a, Kāla-yavana was the son of a Brāhman named Garga, who had an especial spite against the Yādavas, and was begotten by him on the wife of a childless Yavana king.

KALHANA PANDIT. Author of the Rāja Tarangi*n*ī, a history of Kashmīr. He is supposed to have lived about 1148 A.D.

KALI. The Kali-yuga, personified as the spirit of evil. In playing dice Kali is the ace, and so is a personification of ill luck.

KĀLĪ. 'The black.' In Vedic days this name was associated with Agni (fire), who had seven flickering tongues of flame for devouring oblations of butter. Of these seven, Kālī was the black or terrific tongue. This meaning of the word is now lost, but it has developed into the goddess Kālī, the fierce and bloody consort of *S*iva. *See* Devī.

KĀLI-DĀSA. The greatest poet and dramatist of India. He was one of "the nine gems" that adorned the court of King Vikramāditya at Ujjayinī. Wilson inclines to the belief that this was the Vikramāditya whose era begins in 56 B.C., but Dr. Bhāu Dājī argues in favour of Harsha Vikramāditya who lived in the middle of the sixth century, so the date of Kāli-dāsa is unsettled. Williams thinks that Kāli-dāsa wrote about the beginning of the third century. Lassen places him half a century earlier. Some believe that there was more than one poet who bore this name as an honorary title. Kāli-dāsa was author of the dramas *S*akuntalā and Vikramorva*s*ī, and a third drama Mālavikāgnimitra is attributed to him. *S*akuntalā was translated by Sir W. Jones, and first brought Sansk*rit* literature to the notice of Europe. Wilson has translated Vikramorva*s*ī, and given a sketch of Mālavikāgnimitra. The following poems are ascribed to Kāli-dāsa :—Raghu-van*s*a, Kumāra-sambhava, Megha-dūta, *Ri*tu-sanhāra, Nalodaya, but his authorship of all these, especially of the last, may well be doubted. He was also author of the *S*ruta-bodha, a work on prosody. The merits of Kāli-dāsa as a poet are well attested by his great popularity in India, as well as by the great favour with which *S*akuntalā was received in Europe, and the praise it elicited from Goethe :—

"Willst du die Blüthe des frühen, die Früchte des späteren Jahres,
Willst du, was reizt und entzückt, willst du, was sättigt und nährt,
Willst du den Himmel, die Erde, mit einem Namen begreifen,
Nenn' ich *S*akuntalā dich, und so ist Alles gesagt."

"Wouldst thou the young year's blossoms and the fruits of its decline,
And all by which the soul is charmed, enraptured, feasted, fed?
Wouldst thou the earth and heaven itself in one sole name combine?
I name thee, O *S*akuntalā! and all at once is said."

Lassen in his *Indische Alterthumskunde* says, "Kāli-dāsa may be considered as the brightest star in the firmament of Hindu artificial poetry. He deserves this praise on account of the mastery with which he wields the language, and on account of the consummate tact with which he imparts to it a more simple or more artificial form, according to the requirements of the subjects treated by him, without falling into the artificial diction of later poets or over-stepping the limits of good taste; on account of the variety of his creations, his ingenious conceptions, and his happy choice of subjects; and not less on account of the complete manner in which he attains his poetical ends, the beauty of his narrative, the delicacy of his sentiment, and the fertility of his imagination." Many of his works have been translated, and there is a French translation of the whole by Fauche.

KĀLIKĀ. The goddess Kālī.

KĀLIKĀ PURĀNA. One of the eighteen Upa Purāṇas. "It contains about 9000 stanzas in 98 chapters, and is the only work of the series dedicated to recommend the worship of the bride of Śiva, in one or other of her manifold forms as Giri-jā, Devī, Bhadra-kālī, Kālī, Mahā-māyā. It belongs, therefore, to the Śākta modification of Hindu belief, or the worship of the female powers of the deities. The influence of this worship shows itself in the very first pages of the work, which relate the incestuous passion of Brahmā for his daughter, Sandhyā, in a strain that has nothing analogous to it in the Vāyu, Linga, or Śiva Purāṇas. The marriage of Śiva and Pārvatī is a subject early described, with the sacrifice of Daksha and the death of Satī. And this work is authority for Śiva's carrying the dead body about the world, and the origin of the Pīṭha-sthānas, or places where the different members of it were scattered, and where Lingas were consequently erected. A legend follows of the births of Bhairava and Vetāla, whose devotion to the different forms of Devī furnishes occasion to describe, in great detail, the rites and formulæ of which her worship consists, including the chapters on sanguinary sacrifices translated in the *Asiatic Researches* (vol. v.). Another peculiarity in this work is afforded by very prolix descriptions of a number of rivers and mountains at Kāmarūpa Tīrtha, in Assam, and rendered holy ground by the celebrated temple of Durgā in that country, as Kāmākshī or Kāmākshyā. It is a singular and yet uninvestigated circumstance, that Assam, or at least the north-east of Bengal, seems to have been, in a great degree, the source from which the Tāntrika and *S*ākta corruptions of the religion of the Vedas and Purā*n*as proceeded."—*Wilson.*

KĀLINDĪ. A name of the river Yamunā, as daughter of Kalinda (the sun).

KALINGA. The country along the Coromandel coast, north of Madras. The Calingæ proximi mari of Pliny. The Purā*n*as absurdly make it one of the sons of Bali.

KĀLIYA. A serpent king who had five heads, and dwelt in a deep pool of the Yamunā, with numerous attendant serpents. His mouths vomited fire and smoke, and he laid waste all the country round. K*ri*sh*n*a, while yet a child, jumped into his pool, when he was quickly laced and entwined in the coils of the snakes. His companions and friends were horrified, but Bala-rāma called upon him to exercise his divine power. He did so, and the serpents were soon overcome. Placing his foot on the middle head of Kāliya, he compelled him and his followers to implore mercy. He spared them, but bade Kāliya and his followers to free the earth from their presence, and to remove to the ocean. The Asura Kāla-nemi is said to have been animate in him.

KALI YUGA. The fourth or present age of the world, which is to endure for 432,000 years. It commenced in 3102 B.C. *See* Yuga.

KALKĪ, KALKIN. 'The white horse.' Vish*n*u's tenth incarnation, which is yet to come. *See* Avatāra.

KALMĀSHA-PĀDA. A king of the Solar race, son of Su-dāsa (hence he is called Saudāsa), and a descendant of Ikshwāku. His legend, as told in the Mahā-bhārata, relates that while hunting in the forest he encountered *S*aktri, the eldest son of Vasish*th*a, and as this sage refused to get out of his way, he struck him with his whip. The incensed sage cursed him to become a cannibal. This curse was heard by Viswāmitra, the rival of Vasish*th*a, and he so contrived that the body of the king became possessed by a man-eating Rākshasa. In this condition he caused human flesh to be served up to a Brāhman named Mitrasaha, who discovered what it was, and intensified the curse of *S*aktri by a new imprecation. One of Kalmāsha-pada's first victims was *S*aktri himself, and all the hundred sons of Vasish*th*a fell a prey to his disordered appetite. After remaining twelve years in this state, he was restored to his natural condition by Vasish*t*ha. The Vish*n*u Purā*n*a tells the story differently. The king went out to hunt and found two destructive tigers. He killed one of them, but as it expired it was changed into a Rākshasa. The other tiger disappeared threatening vengeance. Kalmāsha-pāda celebrated a sacrifice at which Vasish*t*ha officiated. When it was over and Vasish*t*ha went out, the Rākshasa assumed his appearance, and proposed that food should be served. Then the Rākshasa transformed himself into a cook, and, preparing human flesh, he served it to Vasish*t*ha on his return. The indignant sage cursed the king that henceforth his appetite should be excited only by similar food. A wrangle ensued, and Vasish*t*ha having found out the truth, limited the duration of his curse to twelve years. The angry king took water in his hands to pronounce, in his turn, a curse upon Vasish*t*ha, but was dissuaded from his purpose by his wife, Madayantī. "Unwilling to cast the water on the ground, lest it should wither up the grain, and equally reluctant to throw it up into the air, lest it should blast the clouds and dry up their contents, he threw it upon his own feet," and they were so scalded by it that they became black and white, and so gained for him the name of Kalmāsha-pāda, 'spotted feet.' Every day for twelve years, at the sixth watch of the day, he gave way to his cannibal appetite, "and devoured multitudes of men." On one occasion he devoured a Brāhman in the midst of his connubial happiness, and the Brāhman's wife passed upon him a curse that he should die whenever he associated with his wife. At the expiration of Vasish*t*ha's curse, the king returned home, but, mindful of the Brāhma*n*ī's imprecation, he abstained from conjugal intercourse. By the interposition of Vasish*t*ha, his wife, Madayantī, became pregnant, and bore a child in her womb for seven years, when she performed the Cæsarean operation with a sharp stone, and a child came forth who was called A*s*maka (from A*s*man, 'a stone').

KALPA. A day and night of Brahmā, 4,320,000,000 years. *See* Yuga.

KALPA, KALPA SŪTRAS. Ceremonial; one of the Vedāngas. A ceremonial directory or rubric expressed in the form of Sūtras, short technical rules.

KĀMA, KĀMA-DEVA. The god of love. Eros, Cupid. In the *Ri*g-veda (x. 129) desire is said to have been the first movement that arose in the One after it had come into life through the power of fervour or abstraction. "Desire first arose in It, which was the primal germ of mind; (and which) sages, searching with their intellect, have discovered in their heart to be the bond which connects entity with non-entity." "It is well known," observes Dr. Muir, "that Greek mythology connected Eros, the god of love, with the creation of the universe somewhat in the same way." "This Kāma or desire, not of sexual enjoyment, but of good in general, is celebrated in a curious hymn of the Atharva-veda," which exalts Kāma into a supreme God and Creator: "Kāma was born the first. Him neither gods, nor fathers, nor men have equalled. Thou art superior to these and for ever great." In another part of the same Veda Kāma appears to be first desire, then the power which gratifies the desire. Kāma is also in the same Veda often identified with Agni, and when "distinguished from each other, Kāma may be looked upon as a superior form of the other deity." According to the Taittirīya Brāhma*n*a, he is the son of Dharma, the god of justice, by *S*raddhā, the goddess of faith; but according to the Hari-van*s*a he is son of Lakshmī. Another account represents him as springing from the heart of Brahmā. A fourth view is that he was born from water, wherefore he is called Irā-ja, 'the water-born;' a fifth is that he is Ātma-bhū, 'self-existent,' and therefore he is called, like other of the gods, A-ja, 'unborn,' or An-anya-ja, 'born of no other.' In the Purā*n*as his wife is Rati or Revā, the goddess of desire He inspired *S*iva with amorous thoughts of Pārvatī while he was engaged in penitential devotion, and for this offence the angry god reduced him to ashes by fire from his central eye. *S*iva afterwards relented and allowed Kāma to be born again as Pradyumna, son of K*ri*sh*n*a and Rukmi*n*ī or Māyā, 'delusion.' He has a son named Aniruddha, and a daughter, T*ri*shā. He is lord of the Apsarases or heavenly nymphs. He is armed with a bow and arrows: the bow is of sugar-cane, the bowstring a line of bees, and each arrow is tipped with a distinct flower. He is usually represented as a handsome youth riding on a parrot and attended by nymphs, one of whom bears his banner displaying the Makara, or a fish on a red ground.

The mysterious origin of Kāma and the universal operation of the passion he inspires have accumulated upon him a great variety of names and epithets. Among his names are Ishma, Kanjana and Kinkira, Mada, Rama or Ramaṇa, and Smara. As produced in the mind or heart he is Bhava-ja and Mano-ja. As Pradyumna, son of Kṛishṇa, he is Kārshṇī, and as son of Lakshmī he is Māyī or Māyā-suta and Śrī-nandana. As reduced to ashes by Śiva he is An-anga, 'the bodiless.' He is Abhi-rūpa, 'the beautiful;' Darpaka and Dīpaka, 'the inflamer;' Gadayitnu, Gṛidhu, and Gṛitsa, 'lustful or sharp;' Kamana and Kharu, 'desirous;' Kandarpa, 'the inflamer of Brahmā;' Kantu, 'the happy;' Kalākeli, 'the gay or wanton;' Māra, 'destroyer;' Māyī, 'deluder;' Madhu-dīpa, 'the lamp of honey or of spring;' Muhira, 'the bewilderer;' Murmura, 'the crackling fire;' Rāga-vṛinta, 'the stalk of passion;' Rūpāstra, 'the weapon of beauty;' Rata-nārīcha, 'the voluptuary;' Śamāntaka, 'destroyer of peace;' Sansāra-guru, 'teacher of the world;' Smara, 'remembrance;' Śṛingāra-yoni, 'source of love;' Titha, 'fire;' Vāma, 'the handsome.' From his bow and arrows he is called Kusumāyudha, 'armed with flowers;' Pushpa-dhanus, 'whose bow is flowers;' and Pushpa-sara, 'whose arrows are flowers.' From his banner he is known as Makara-ketu; and from the flower he carries in his hand he is Pushpa-ketana.

KĀMA-DHENU. The cow which grants desires, belonging to the sage Vasishṭha. She was produced at the churning of the ocean. Among the examples of her supernatural powers was the creation of a host of warriors who aided Vasishṭha against Kārta-vīrya. She is called also Kāma-duh, Śavalā, and Surabhi.

KĀMĀKSHĪ. A form of Devī worshipped at Kāmarūpa-tīrtha in Assam. *See* Kālikā Purāṇa.

KĀMANDAKI. Author of a work known by his name on "The Elements of Polity." The text has been printed in the *Bibliotheca Indica* by Rājendra Lāla Mittra.

KĀMARŪPA. The north-eastern part of Bengal and the western portion of Assam. The name still survives as Kāmrūp.

KĀMBOJAS. A race or tribe always associated with the tribes living to the north-west, and famous for their horses. They were among the races conquered by King Sagara.

KĀMPILYA. The city of King Drupada in the country of the Pānchālas, where the swayam-vara of Draupadī was held.

It corresponds with the Kāmpila of modern times, situated in the Doāb on the old Ganges, between Badāūn and Farrukhābād.

KĀMYAKA. The forest in which the Pā*n*davas passed their exile on the banks of the Saraswatī.

KA*N*ĀDA. The sage who founded the Vai*s*eshika school of philosophy. *See* Darsana.

KĀNCHĪ. One of the seven sacred cities, *hodie* Conjeveram.

KANDARPA. The Hindu Cupid. *See* Kāma.

KĀ*ND*ARSHI. A *R*ishi who teaches one particular Kā*nd*a or part of the Vedas.

KA*ND*U. A sage who was beguiled from long and severe austerities by Pramlochā, a nymph sent from heaven by Indra for this purpose. He lived with her some hundreds of years, which seemed to him only as a day, but he at length repudiated her and "went to the region of Vish*n*u." Pramlochā gave birth, in an extraordinary manner, to his daughter Māri*sh*ā (q.v.).

KANISHKA. "Hushka, Jushka, Kanishka." These are the names recorded in the Rāja Tarangi*n*ī of three great Turushka, that is Turk or Tatar, kings, who were of the Buddhist religion. It may, perhaps, be taken for granted that Hushka and Jushka come in their natural succession, for the names might be transposed without detriment to the metre; but the short syllable of the name Kanishka is required where it stands by the rules of prosody, so that the position of the name in the verse is not decisive of his place in the succession of kings. Nothing is known of Jushka beyond the simple recital of his name as above quoted, but the names of Kanishka and Hushka (or Huvishka) have been found in inscriptions and upon coins, showing that their dominions were of considerable extent in Northern India, and that they were, as the Rāja Tarangi*n*ī represents, great supporters of the Buddhist religion. The name of Kanishka has been found in inscriptions at Mathurā, Manikyāla, Bhāwalpur, and Zeda, while his name appears on the corrupt Greek coins as Kanerki. Huvishka's name has been found at Mathurā and on a metal vase from Wardak in Afghanistan; on the coins his name is represented as Oerki. Kanishka preceded Huvishka, and it is certain that their reigns covered a period of fifty-one years, and probably more. The time at which they reigned seems to have been just before the Christian era. A Roman coin of the date 33 B.C. was found in the tope of Manikyāla, which was built by Kanishka.

KANSA. A tyrannical king of Mathurā, son of Ugra-sena and cousin of Devakī the mother of Krishna; so he was the cousin, not the uncle, of Krishna, as he is often called. He married two daughters of Jarā-sandha, king of Magadha. He deposed his father. It was foretold that a son born of Devakī should kill him, so he endeavoured to destroy all her children. But Bala-rāma, her seventh son, was smuggled away to Gokula, and was brought up by Rohinī. When Krishna the eighth was born his parents fled with him. The tyrant then gave orders for a general massacre of all vigorous male infants. Kansa became the great persecutor of Krishna, but was eventually killed by him. Kansa is also called Kalānkura, 'crane.' He is looked upon as an Asura, and is in some way identified with the Asura Kāla-nemi.

KANSA-BADHA. A drama in seven acts upon the destruction of Kansa by Krishna. The author is called Krishna Kavi, and the play was probably written about two centuries ago. It is weak as a drama, but "the language is in general good, although highly elaborate."—*Wilson.*

KĀNWA. *See* Satapatha Brāhmana.

KANWA. Name of a *Rishi* to whom some hymns of the *Rig*-veda are ascribed; he is sometimes counted as one of the seven great *Rishis*. The sage who brought up Sakuntalā as his daughter. There are several others of the same name.

KĀNWAS. The descendants or followers of Kanwa.

KANYĀ-KUBJA. The modern form of the name is Kanauj or Kinnauj, spelt in a variety of ways. 1. An ancient city of Hindustan on the Kālī-nadi, an affluent of the Ganges, and lying a little to the west of the latter. It was once the capital of a powerful dynasty. It was known to classical geographers as "Canogyza." The name means "humpbacked damsel," and refers to a legend relating to the hundred daughters of King Kusa-nābha, who were all made crooked by Vāyu for refusing to comply with his licentious desires. 2. A great national division of the Brāhman caste. *See* Brāhman.

KANYĀ-KUMĀRĪ. 'The virgin-damsel.' A name of Durgā. Her worship extended to the southernmost extremity of India in the days of Pliny, and 'Kumārī' still appears in the name Cape Comorin.

KAPARDIN. 'Wearing the kaparda,' a peculiar braid or knot of hair. This epithet is applied to *S*iva, to one of the Rudras, and some others.

KAPI-DHWAJA. An epithet of Arjuna, because he bore an ape (*kapi*) on his standard (*dhwaja*).

KAPILA. A celebrated sage, the founder of the Sānkhya philosophy. The Hari-van*s*a makes him the son of Vitatha. He is sometimes identified with Vish*n*u and sometimes with Agni. He is said to have destroyed the hundred thousand sons of King Sagara with a glance. *See* Sagara.

KAPILA, KAPILA-VASTU. A town on the river Rohi*n*ī, an affluent of the Rāptī, which was the capital of *S*uddhodana, the father of Gotama Buddha.

KAPILA PURĀ*N*A. *See* Purā*n*a.

KAPI*S*Ā. Mother of the Pi*s*āchas, who bear the metronymic Kāpi*s*eya.

KARĀLĪ. 'Dreadful, terrible.' In Vedic times one of the seven tongues of Agni (fire), but in later days a name of the terrible consort of *S*iva. *See* Devī.

KARDAMA. According to the Mahā-bhārata and Rāmāya*n*a, he is one of the Prajāpatis who sprang from Brahmā. According to other authorities, he, or another sage of the same name, was a son of Daksha or a son of Pulaha.

KARMA-MĪMĀNSĀ. The Pūrva-mīmānsā. *See* Darsana.

KARMA-MĪMĀNSĀ-SŪTRA. A work on the Vedānta philosophy, ascribed to Jaimini.

KAR*N*A. Son of P*ri*thā or Kuntī by Sūrya, the sun, before her marriage to Pā*nd*u. Kar*n*a was thus half-brother of the Pā*nd*avas, but this relationship was not known to them till after his death. Kuntī, on one occasion, paid such attention to the sage Dur-vāsas, that he gave her a charm by virtue of which she might have a child by any god she preferred to invoke. She chose the sun, and the result was Kar*n*a, who was born equipped with arms and armour. Afraid of censure and disgrace, Kuntī exposed the child on the banks of the Yamunā, where it was found by Nandana or Adhiratha, the sūta or charioteer of Dh*ri*ta-rāsh*t*ra. The charioteer and his wife, Rādhā, brought him up as their own, and the child passed as such. When he grew up, Indra disguised himself as a Brāhman, and cajoled him out of his divine cuirass. He gave him in return great strength and a javelin charged with certain death to whomsoever it was hurled against. Karna became king of Anga or Bengal. Some authorities represent his foster-father as having been ruler of that country, but others say that Karna was made king of Anga by Dur-yodhana, in order to qualify him to fight in the passage of arms at the swayam-vara of Draupadī. This princess haughtily rejected him, saying, "I wed not with the base-born." Karna knew that he was half-brother of the Pāndavas, but he took the side of their cousins, the Kauravas, and he had especial rivalry and animosity against Arjuna, whom he vowed to kill. In the great battle he killed Ghatotkacha, the son of Bhīma, with Indra's javelin. Afterwards there was a terrific combat between him and Arjuna, in which the latter was nearly overpowered, but he killed Karna with a crescent-shaped arrow. After Karna's death his relationship to the Pāndavas became known to them, and they showed their regret for his loss by great kindness to his widows, children, and dependants. From his father, Vikarttana (the sun), Karna was called Vaikarttana; from his foster-parents, Vāsu-sena; from his foster-father's profession, Ādhirathi and Sūta; and from his foster-mother, Rādheya. He was also called Anga-rāja, 'king of Anga;' Champādhipa, 'king of Champā;' and Kānīna, 'the bastard.'

KARNA-PRĀVARANAS. Men whose ears served them for coverings. They are mentioned in the Mahā-bhārata, Rāmāyana, and other works.

KARNĀTA, KARNĀTAKA. The country where the Canarese language is spoken, in the central districts of the Peninsula, including Mysore. The name "Carnatic" is derived from this.

KĀRTA-VĪRYA. Son of Krita-vīrya, king of the Haihayas. This is his patronymic, by which he is best known; his real name was Arjuna. "Having worshipped a portion of the divine being called Dattātreya, sprung from the race of Atri, he sought and obtained these boons, viz., a thousand arms and a golden chariot that went wheresoever he willed it to go; the power of restraining wrong by justice; the conquest of the earth and the disposition to rule it righteously; invincibility by enemies, and death at the hands of a man renowned over the whole world. By him this earth was perfectly governed," and of him it is said:—"No other king shall ever equal Kārta-vīrya in regard to sacrifices, liberality, austerities, courtesy, and self-restraint." "Thus he ruled for 85,000 years with unbroken health, prosperity, strength, and valour."—*V.P.* He visited the hermitage of Jamad-agni, and was received by that sage's wife with all respect; but he made an ill return for her hospitality, and carried off by violence "the calf of the milch-cow of the sacred oblation." For this outrage Parasu-rāma cut off his thousand arms and killed him. In another place a different character is given to him, and more in accordance with his behaviour at Jamad-agni's hut. "He oppressed both men and gods," so that the latter appealed to Vish*n*u for succour. That god then came down to the earth as Para*s*u-rāma for the especial purpose of killing him. Kārta-vīrya was the contemporary of Rāva*n*a, and when that demon monarch came "in the course of his campaign of conquest to Mahishmatī (the capital of Kārta-vīrya), he was captured without difficulty, and was confined like a wild beast in a corner of his city." The statement of the Vāyu Purā*n*a is that Kārta-vīrya invaded Lankā, and there took Rāva*n*a prisoner.

KĀRTTIKEYA. The god of war and the planet Mars, also called Skanda. He is said in the Mahā-bhārata and Rāmāya*n*a to be the son of *S*iva or Rudra, and to have been produced without the intervention of a woman. *S*iva cast his seed into fire, and it was afterwards received by the Ganges: Kārtti-keya was the result; hence he is called Agni-bhū and Gangā-ja. He was fostered by the Pleiades (K*ri*ttikā), and hence he has six heads and the name Kārttikeya. His paternity is sometimes assigned to Agni (fire); Gangā (the Ganges) and Pārvatī are variously represented to be his mother. He was born for the purpose of destroying Tāraka, a Daitya whose austerities had made him formidable to the gods. He is represented riding on a peacock called Paravā*n*i, holding a bow in one hand and an arrow in the other. His wife is Kaumārī or Senā. He has many titles: as a warrior he is called Mahā-sena, Senā-pati; Siddha-sena, 'leader of the Siddhas;' and Yudha-ranga; also Kumāra, the boy; Guha, 'the mysterious one;' *S*akti-dhara, 'spear-holder;' and in the south he is called Su-brahma*n*ya. He is Gangā-putra, 'son of the Ganges;' *S*ara-bhū, 'born in the thicket;' Tāraka-jit, 'vanquisher of Tāraka;' Dwāda*s*a-kara and Dwāda*s*āksha, 'twelve-handed' and 'twelve-eyed;' *Ri*ju-kāya, 'straight-bodied.' *See* Krauncha.

KĀRUSHAS. A people of Mālwa, inhabiting the back of the Vindhya mountains. They are said to be descended from Karusha, one of the sons of the Manu Vaivaswata.

KĀŚĪ. Benares.

KĀŚĪ KHAṆḌA. A long poem, forming a part of the Skanda Purāṇa. It gives a very minute description of the temples of Śiva in and around Benares, and is presumably anterior to the Mahomedan conquest. *See* Skanda Purāṇa.

KAŚYAPA. A Vedic sage to whom some hymns are attributed. All authorities agree in assigning to him a large part in the work of creation. According to the Mahā-bhārata, the Rāmāyaṇa, and the Purāṇas, he was the son of Marīchi, the son of Brahmā, and he was father of Vivaswat, the father of Manu, the progenitor of mankind. The Śatapatha Brāhmaṇa gives a different and not very intelligible account of his origin thus:—"Having assumed the form of a tortoise, Prajāpati created offspring. That which he created he made (*akarot*); hence the word *kūrma* (tortoise). Kaśyapa means tortoise; hence men say, 'All creatures are descendants of Kaśyapa.' This tortoise is the same as Āditya." The Atharva-veda says, "The self-born Kaśyapa sprang from Time," and Time is often identical with Vishṇu. The Mahā-bhārata and later authorities agree in representing that Kaśyapa married Aditi and twelve other daughters of Daksha. Upon Aditi he begat the Ādityas, headed by Indra, and also Vivaswat, and "to Vivaswat was born the wise and mighty Manu." The Rāmāyaṇa and Vishṇu Purāṇa also state that "Vishṇu was born as a dwarf, the son of Aditi and Kaśyapa." By his other twelve wives he had a numerous and very diversified offspring: demons, nāgas, reptiles, birds, and all kinds of living things. He was thus the father of all, and as such is sometimes called Prajāpati. He is one of the seven great Ṛishis, and he appears as the priest of Paraśu-rāma and Rāma-chandra.

KĀ-TANTRA. A Sanskṛit grammar by Sarva-varman. Edited by Eggeling for the *Bibliotheca Indica*.

KAṬA-PRŪ. 'Worm.' A class of beings similar to or identical with the Vidyā-dharas.

KATHA. Name of a Upanishad (q.v.). It has been translated by Dr. Roer in the *Bibliotheca Indica*.

KĀṬHAKA. A school or recension of the Yajur-veda,

occupying a position between the Black and the White. It is supposed to be lost.

KATHĀRNAVA. 'Sea of stories.' A compilation of miscellaneous stories in four books; the first two are the originals of the Hindī Baitāl Pachīsī and Singhāsan Battīsī.

KATHĀ-SARIT-SĀGARA. 'The ocean of the rivers of stories.' A collection of popular stories by Soma-deva-bhatta of Kashmīr, made about the beginning of the twelfth century A.D. It is drawn from a larger work called Brihat-kathā. Thet ext has been printed and in part translated by Brockhaus.

KĀTYĀYANA. An ancient writer of great celebrity, who came after Pānini, whose grammar he completed and corrected in what he called Vārttikas, 'supplementary rules and annotations.' He is generally identified with Vararuchi, the author of the Prākrita Prakāsa. Max Müller places him in the second half of the fourth century B.C.; Goldstücker in the first half of the second century B.C.; Weber about twenty-five years B.C. Besides his additions to Pānini's Grammar, he was the author of the Srauta-sūtras which bear his name, and of the Yajur-veda Prātisākhya. His Sūtras have been edited by Weber. A story in the Kathā-sarit-sagara makes him the incarnation of a demigod named Pushpa-danta. A Kātyāyana was author also of a Dharma-sāstra.

KĀTYĀYANĪ. A name of Durgā. *See* Devī.

KAUMĀRA. The creation of the Kumāras (q.v.).

KAUMODAKĪ. The mace of Krishna, presented to him by Agni when engaged with him in fighting against Indra and burning the Khāndava forest.

KAUNDINYA. An ancient sage and grammarian. He offended Siva, but was saved from that god's wrath by Vishnu: he was hence called Vishnu-gupta, 'saved by Vishnu.'

KAUNTEYA. Son of Kuntī. A metronymic applicable to Yudhi-shthira, Bhīma, and Arjuna, but commonly applied to Arjuna.

KAURAVAS. Descendants of Kuru. A patronymic especially applied to the sons of Dhrita-rāshtra. *See* Mahā-bhārata.

KAUSALYA (mas.), KAUSALYĀ (fem.). Belonging to the Kosala nation. There are several women known by this name. The wife of Puru and mother of Janamejaya. The wife of Dasa-ratha and mother of Rāma. (*See* Dasa-ratha.) The mother of Dhrita-rāshtra and the mother of Pāndu both were known by this name, being daughters of a king of Kāsī.

KAUSĀMBĪ. The capital of Vatsa, near the junction of the Ganges and Jumna. An inscription found at Karra on the Ganges mentions that place as being situated in Kausāmbī-mandala, the circle of Kausāmbī; but General Cunningham identifies the place with the village of Kosam, said to be still called Kosambi-nagar on the Jumna, about thirty miles above Allahabad. It is the scene of the drama Ratnāvalī.

KAUSHĪTAKĪ. 1. A sākhā of the Rig-veda. 2. (Kaushītaki) the name of a Brāhmana, an Āranyaka, and a Upanishad. (*See* those terms.) The Brāhmana has been published with a translation by Professor Cowell in the *Bibliotheca Indica.*

KAUSIKA. A devotee mentioned in the Mahā-bhārata as having gone to a hell of torment for having pointed out to robbers a road by which they pursued and killed some persons who fled from them.

KAUSIKAS. Descendants of Kusika (q.v.). In one of the hymns of the Rig the epithet is given to Indra.

KAUSIKĪ. The river Kosī in Bihār, but there were more rivers than one bearing this name. Satyavatī, mother of Jamad-agni is said to have been changed into a river of this name.

KAUSTUBHA. A celebrated jewel obtained at the churning of the ocean, and worn by Vishnu or Krishna on his bosom.

KAUTILYA. Another name of Chānakya, the minister of Chandra-gupta. *See* Chānakya.

KAUTSA. A rationalistic philosopher, who lived before the days of Yāska the author of the Nirukta. He regarded "the Veda as devoid of meaning, and the Brāhmanas as false interpretations." Yāska replied to his objections.

KAUTUKA-SARVASWA. A modern farce, in two acts, by a Pandit named Gopī-nātha. "It is a satire upon princes who addict themselves to idleness and sensuality, and fail to patronise the Brāhmans."—*Wilson.*

KAVASHA, KAVASHA-AILŪSHA. Son of Ilūsha by a slave girl. He was author of several hymns in the tenth book of the Rig-veda. The Aitareya Brāhmana relates that the Rishis were performing a sacrifice on the banks of the Saraswatī, and that Kavasha was with them; but they drove him from among them because he was the son of a slave, and therefore unworthy to drink the water of the Saraswatī. When he was alone in the desert, a prayer was revealed to him by which he prevailed over the Saraswatī, and its waters came and surrounded him. The *R*ishis saw this, and knowing that it was by the special favour of the gods, they admitted him to their society.

KAVI-RĀJA. Author of a poem of studied ambiguity called Rāghava-Pā*nd*aviyam (q.v.).

KĀVYA-DAR*S*A. 'Mirror of poetry.' A work on the Ars Poetica by *S*rī Da*nd*ī. It has been printed in the *Bibliotheca Indica*.

KĀVYA-PRAKĀ*S*A. A work on poetry and rhetoric by Mamma*t*a Bha*tt*a of Kashmīr. It has been printed at Calcutta.

KAVYAS, KĀVYAS. A class of Pit*ri*s; according to some they are the Manes of men of the third caste.

KĀYAVYA. The son of a Kshatriya by a Nishāda female, who is related in the Mahā-bhārata to have risen by virtue, knowledge, and devotion from the state of a Dasyu to perfection.

KEDĀRE*S*A, KEDĀRA-NĀTHA. A name of *S*iva. Name of one of the twelve great Lingas. It is a shapeless mass of stone at Kedāra-nātha in the Himālayas. *See* Linga.

KEKAYA. *See* Kaikeya.

KELI-KILA. A demigod attendant upon *S*iva.

KENA, KENOPANISHAD. Name of a Upanishad (q.v.) translated by Dr. Roer for the *Bibliotheca Indica*.

KERAKAS. One-footed men who live in forests, according to the Mahā-bhārata.

KERALA. The country of Malabar proper on the western coast.

KE*S*AVA. 'Having much or fine hair.' A name of Vish*n*u or K*ri*sh*n*a.

KE*S*Ī, KE*S*IN. In the Mahā-bhārata, a demon who fought with and was defeated by Indra. In the Purā*n*as, a Daitya who took the form of a horse and attacked K*ri*sh*n*a, but was killed by that hero's thrusting his arm into his jaws and rending him asunder.

KE*S*INĪ. Wife of Vi*s*ravas and mother of Rāva*n*a; also called Kaikasī.

KE*S*I-DHWAJA. Son of K*ri*ta-dhwaja. Ke*s*i-dhwaja "was endowed with spiritual knowledge," and he had a cousin, Khā*n*-*d*ikya, who "was diligent in the way of works and was renowned for religious rites." There was contention and hostilities between them, and Khāndikya was driven from his dominions. But they subsequently became useful to each other and friendly. Khāndikya by his practical religion enabled Kesi-dhwaja to make atonement for the killing of a cow, and Kesi-dhwaja initiated Khāndikya in the mysteries of spiritual meditation (*yoga*).

KETU. The descending node in astronomy, represented by a dragon's tail; also a comet or meteor, and the ninth of the planets. He is said to be a Dānava, and son of Viprachitti and Sinhikā. He is also called A-kacha, 'hairless;' Aslesha-bhava, 'cut off;' Munda, 'bald.' *See* Rāhu.

KHĀNDAVA, KHĀNDAVA-PRASTHA. A forest and country on the banks of the Yamunā, which the Pāndavas received as their moiety when Dhrita-rāshtra divided his kingdom. In it they built the city of Indra-prastha and made it their capital. The forest was consumed with fire by the god Agni assisted by Krishna and Arjuna.

KHĀNDIKYA. *See* Kesi-dhwaja.

KHARA. A man-eating Rākshasa, the younger brother of Rāvana. He was killed by Rāma-chandra.

KHARVA. A dwarf. *See* Vālakhilya.

KHASĀ. A daughter of Daksha, wife of Kasyapa, and mother of the Yakshas and Rākshasas, called after her Khasātmajas.

KHĀSAS, KHASĀKAS, KHASĪKAS. An outlying or border people classed with the Sakas and other northern tribes. Professor Wilson thought that traces of them might be sought among the barbarous tribes on the north-east of Bengal, the Khasiyas.

KHATWĀNGA (also called Dilīpa). 1. A prince of the Solar race. In a battle between the gods and the demons he rendered great assistance to the former, who desired him to ask a boon. He begged that he might know the duration of his life, and the answer was, "Only an hour." He hastened to the world of mortals, and by earnest prayer he became united with the supreme being, Vishnu. "Like unto Khatwānga will there be no one upon earth, who, having come from heaven and dwelt an hour amongst men, became united with the three worlds by his liberality and knowledge of truth."—*V. P.* 2. A club; the club of Siva; it is also called Khinkhira and Pānsula.

KĪCHAKA. Brother-in-law of the king of Virā*t*a, who was commander of the forces and general director of the affairs of the kingdom. He made love to Draupadī, and was slain by Bhīma, who rolled his bones and flesh into a ball, so that no one could tell how he was killed.

KĪKATA. A country inhabited by people who were not Āryans; it is identified with Magadha or South Bihār.

KILATĀKULI. (Kilata + Akuli.) Two priests of the Asuras, who, according to the *S*atapatha Brāhma*n*a, exercised a special influence between Manu and an "Asura-slaying voice."

KIM-PURUSHA. 'What man?' An indescribable man; one of a low type, partaking of the nature and appearance of animals. In later times it is synonymous with Kin-nara. Name of a region between Himavat and Hema-kū*t*a. (*See* Jambu-dwīpa.) Also of a king of the latter region.

KIN-NARAS. 'What men?' Mythical beings with the form of a man and the head of a horse. They are celestial choristers and musicians, dwelling in the paradise of Kuvera on Kailāsa. They sprang from the toe of Brahmā with the Yakshas, but according to others, they are sons of Ka*s*yapa. They are also called A*s*wa-mukhas Turanga-vaktras, 'horse-faced,' and Mayus.

KIRĀTĀRJUNĪYA. A poem descriptive of the combat between *S*iva in the guise of a Kirāta or mountaineer and the Pā*nd*u prince Arjuna. The story is first told in the Mahābhārata, and has been worked up in this artificial poem of eighteen cantos by Bhāravi. Part of it has been translated into German by Schütz. There are several editions of the text. *See* Arjuna.

KIRĀTAS. Foresters and mountaineers living in the mountains east of Hindustan. (There is a tribe in the Central Himālayas called Kirāntis.) They are described in the Rāmāya*n*a as "islanders, who eat raw fish, live in the waters, and are men-tigers" (men below and tigers above, according to the commentator). Their females are described as "gold-coloured and pleasant to behold," and as having "sharp-pointed hair-knots." They are perhaps the Cirrhadæ placed on the Coromandel coast by classic writers.

KIRĪTIN. 'Crowned with a diadem.' A title of Indra and also of Arjuna.

KIRMĪRA. A monster Rākshasa, brother of Vaka. He opposed the entrance of the Pa*nd*avas into the Kāmyaka forest, and threatened that he would eat Bhīma. A furious combat ensued, in which Bhīma and he hurled large trees at each other, but the demon was at length strangled and had all his bones broken by Bhīma.

KISHKINDHYA. A country in the peninsula, thought to be in the Mysore, which was taken by Rāma from the monkey king Bālī, and given back to his brother Su-grīva, the friend and ally of Rāma. The capital city was Kishkindhyā.

KOHALA. An ancient sage, to whom the invention of the drama is attributed; also a writer on music.

KOSALA. A country on the *S*arayu river, having Ayodhyā for its capital. The name is variously applied to other countries in the east, and in the south, and in the Vindhya mountains. It probably widened with the dominions of its rulers, and part of Birar is called Dakshi*n*a-Kosala, the Southern Kosala.

KO*T*AVĪ, KO*T*ARĪ, KO*TT*AVĪ. 'A naked woman.' A mystical goddess, the tutelary deity of the Daityas, and mother of Bā*n*a the demon. The name is sometimes applied to Durgā.

KRAMA-PĀ*T*HA. *See* Pā*t*ha.

KRATU. One of the Prajāpatis, and sometimes reckoned among the great *R*ishis and mind-born sons of Brahmā. (*See R*ishi.) The Vish*n*u Purā*n*a says that his wife Samnati brought forth the 60,000 Vālikhilyas, pigmy sages no bigger than a joint of the thumb.

KRAUNCHA. 1. A pass situated somewhere in the Himālayas, said to have been opened by Para*s*u-rāma with his arrows to make a passage from Kailāsa to the southwards. The Vāyu Purā*n*a attributes the splitting of the mountain to Kārttikeya. Indra and Kārttikeya had a dispute about their respective powers, and agreed to decide it by running a race round the mountain. They disagreed as to the result, and therefore appealed to the mountain, who untruly decided in favour of Indra. "Kārttikeya hurled his lance at the mountain and pierced at once it and the demon Mahisha." 2. A confederate of the demon Tāraka, against whom Kārttikeya led the gods and triumphed. 3. One of the seven Dwīpas. *See* Dwīpa.

KRAVYĀD. 'A flesh-eater.' A Rākshasa or any carnivorous animal. In the Veda, Agni is in one place called a Kravyād of terrible power. Fire is also a Kravyād in consuming bodies on the funeral pile. *See* Agni.

K*RI*PA. Son of the sage *S*aradwat, and the adopted son of King *S*āntanu. He became one of the privy council at Hastinā-pura, and was one of the three surviving Kuru warriors who made the murderous night attack upon the camp of the Pā*nd*avas. He was also called Gautama and *S*āradwata. *See* K*ri*pā and Mahā-bhārata.

K*RI*PĀ, K*RI*PĪ. Wife of Dro*n*a and mother of A*s*watthāman. The sage *S*aradwat or Gotama so alarmed Indra by his austerities that the god sent a nymph to tempt him. Though she was unsuccessful, two children were found born to the sage in a tuft of grass. King *S*āntanu found them and brought them up out of compassion (*kripā*), whence their names, K*ri*pa and K*ri*pā. The children passed as *S*āntanu's own. Dro*n*a was a Brāhman and *S*āntanu a Kshatriya: the myth makes K*ri*pī a Brāhma*n*ī, and so accounts for her being the wife of Dro*n*a. The Vish*n*u Purā*n*a represents them as children of Satya-dh*ri*ti, grandson of *S*aradwat by the nymph Urva*s*ī, and as being exposed in a clump of long grass.

K*RI*SH*N*A. 'Black.' This name occurs in the *Ri*g-veda, but without any relation to the great deity of later times. The earliest mention of K*ri*sh*n*a, the son of Devakī, is in the Chhāndogya Upanishad, where he appears as a scholar. There was a *Ri*shi of the name who was a son of Vi*s*waka. There was also a great Asura so named, who with 10,000 followers committed fearful devastation, until he was defeated and skinned by Indra. In another Vedic hymn, 50,000 K*ri*sh*n*as are said to have been slain, and it is added in another that his pregnant wives were slain with him that he might leave no posterity. This is supposed to have reference to the Rākshasas or to the dark-coloured aborigines of India.

The modern deity K*ri*sh*n*a is the most celebrated hero of Indian mythology, and the most popular of all the deities. He is said to be the eighth Avatāra or incarnation of Vish*n*u, or rather a direct manifestation of Vish*n*u himself. This hero, around whom a vast mass of legend and fable has been gathered, probably lived in the Epic age, when the Hindus had not advanced far beyond their early settlements in the north-west. He appears prominently in the Mahā-bhārata, where his character is invested with a certain degree of mysticism. Additions and interpolations have raised him to divinity, and it is in the character of the "Divine One" that he delivered the celebrated song, Bhagavad-gītā, a production of comparatively late date, now held to be part of the great epic. In this work he distinctly declares himself to be the Supreme Being. He says:—"All this universe has been created by me; all things exist in me;" and Arjuna addresses him as "the supreme universal spirit, the supreme dwelling, the eternal person, divine, prior to the gods, unborn, omnipresent." The divine character of K*ri*sh*na* having thus been established, it was still further developed in the Hari-van*s*a, a later addition to the Mahā-bhārata; and in the Purā*n*as, especially in the Bhāgavata Purā*n*a, it attained full expansion. There the story of the life of K*ri*sh*na*, from his earliest days, is related with minute details, and it is upon this portion of his life that the popular mind delights to dwell. The mischievous pranks of the child, the follies of the boy, and the amours of the youth, are the subjects of boundless wonder and delight. All these stories, as told in the Bhāgavata Purā*n*a, have been made accessible and popular by the Hindī translation known by the name Prem Sāgar, 'ocean of love,' and by other versions. Much of the story of the early days of K*ri*sh*na* is thus of comparatively modern invention, while the incidents of his relations with the Pā*nd*ava princes are among the most ancient.

K*ri*sh*na* was of the Yādava race, being descended from Yadu, one of the sons of Yayāti. The Yādavas of old were a pastoral race, and dwelt on the river Yamunā (Jumna), in V*ri*ndāvana, on the western side, and in Gokula on the other. In those days, Kan*s*a, Rāja of the Bhojas, having deposed his father, Ugrasena, ruled in the city of Mathurā, near V*ri*ndāvana. Ugrasena had a brother named Devaka, and Devaka had a daughter named Devakī, who married Vasu-deva, son of *S*ūra, also a descendant of Yadu. The history of K*ri*sh*na*'s birth, as given in the Mahā-bhārata and followed by the Vish*n*u Purā*n*a, is that Vish*n*u plucked out two of his own hairs, one white, the other black. These two hairs entered the wombs of Rohi*n*ī and Devakī; the white hair became Balarāma and the black (*krishna*) hair (*kesa*) became K*ri*sh*na* or Kesava.

His reputed father, Vasu-deva, was brother of Kuntī, the wife of Pā*n*d*u, and so K*r*ish*n*a was cousin of the three elder Pā*n*d*ava princes.

The Mahā-bhārata gives two summaries of his exploits, of which the following are abridgments :—"While K*r*ish*n*a was growing up as a high-souled boy in the tribe of cowherds, the force of his arms was rendered famous by him in the three worlds." He slew the king of the Hayas (horses), dwelling in the woods of the Yamunā. He slew the direful Dānava, who bore the form of a bull. He also slew Pralambha, Naraka, Jambha, and Pītha, the great Asura, and Muru. He overthrew and slew Kan*s*a, who was supported by Jarā-sandha. With the help of Bala-rāma he defeated and destroyed Su-nāman, brother of Kan*s*a and king of the *S*ūrasenas. He carried off the daughter of the king of the Gāndhāras at a swayam-vara, and princes were yoked to his car. He secured the death of Jarā-sandha and slew *S*i*s*u-pāla. He overthrew Saubha, the self-supporting or flying city of the Daityas, on the shore of the ocean. He conquered the Angas and Bangas, and numerous other tribes. Entering the ocean filled with marine monsters, he overcame Varu*n*a. In Pātāla he slew Panchajana, and obtained the divine shell Pānchajanya. With Arjuna he propitiated Agni in the Khā*n*d*ava forest, and obtained the fiery weapon the discus. Mounted on Garu*d*a, he alarmed Amarāvatī, the city of Indra, and brought away the Pārijāta tree from thence.

In another passage, Arjuna rehearses some of K*r*ish*n*a's exploits. He destroyed the Bhoja kings in battle, and carried off Rukmi*n*ī for his bride. He destroyed the Gāndhāras, vanquished the sons of Nagnajit, and released King Su-dar*s*ana, whom they had bound. He slew Pā*n*d*ya with the fragment of a door, and crushed the Kalingas in Dantakūra. Through him the burnt city of Benares was restored. He killed Ekalavya, king of the Nishādas, and the demon Jambha. With the aid of Bala-rāma he killed Su-nāman, the wicked son of Ugrasena, and restored the kingdom to the latter. He conquered the flying city of Saubha and the king of the *S*ālwas, and there he obtained the fiery weapon *S*ata-ghnī. Naraka, son of the earth, had carried off the beautiful jewelled earrings of Aditi to Prāg-jyotisha, the impregnable castle of the Asuras. The gods, headed by Indra, were unable to prevail against Naraka, so they appointed K*r*ish*n*a to slay him. Accordingly he killed

Muru and the Rākshasa Ogha; and finally he slew Naraka and brought back the earrings.

It further appears in different parts of the Mahā-bhārata that K*ri*sh*n*a, prince of Dwārakā, was present at the swayam-vara of Draupadī, and gave his judgment that she had been fairly won by Arjuna. While the Pā*n*d*a*vas were reigning at Indra-prastha, he paid them a visit, and went out hunting with them in the Khā*n*d*a*va forest. There he and Arjuna allied themselves with Agni, who was desirous of burning the Khā*n*d*a*va forest, but was prevented by Indra. Agni having secured the help of K*ri*sh*n*a and Arjuna, he gave the former the celebrated chakra (discus) Vajra-nābha, and the club Kaumodakī. Then Indra was defeated and Agni burnt the forest. Arjuna afterwards visited K*ri*sh*n*a at Dwārakā, and was received with great demonstrations of joy. Arjuna, with the connivance of K*ri*sh*n*a, eloped with Su-bhadrā, K*ri*sh*n*a's sister, much to the annoyance of Bala-rāma, her elder brother. When Yudhi-sh*t*hira was desirous of performing the Rāja-sūya sacrifice, K*ri*sh*n*a told him that he must first conquer Jarā-sandha, king of Magadha. Jarā-sandha was attacked and slain, and K*ri*sh*n*a was thus revenged upon the enemy who had forced him to leave Mathurā and emigrate to Dwārakā. K*ri*sh*n*a attended the Rāja-sūya sacrifice performed by Yudhi-sh*t*hira, and there he met *S*isu-pāla, whose betrothed wife he had carried off. *S*isu-pāla reviled him and acted very violently, so K*ri*sh*n*a cast his discus and cut off his enemy's head. He was present at the gambling match between Yudhi-sh*t*hira and the Kauravas. When Draupadī had been staked and lost, she was dragged into the public hall by Du*h*-*s*āsana, who tore off her clothes, but K*ri*sh*n*a pitied her, and renewed her clothes as fast as they were torn away. After the close of the exile of the Pā*n*d*a*vas, K*ri*sh*n*a was present, and took part in the council which preceded the great war, and strongly advised a peaceful settlement. Then he returned to Dwārakā. Thither Arjuna and Dur-yodhana followed him with the object of enlisting his services in the coming war, but he refused to take any active part because he was related to both parties. He gave them the choice of his personal attendance or of the use of his army. Arjuna, who had arrived first, and therefore had the first choice, asked for K*ri*sh*n*a himself, and Dur-yodhana joyfully accepted the army. K*ri*sh*n*a then became the charioteer of Arjuna. After this, at the request of the Pāndavas, he went in splendid state to Hastinā-pura as a mediator, but his efforts were unavailing, and he returned. Preparations for action were then made and the forces drawn out. On the eve of the battle, while acting as Arjuna's charioteer, he is represented as relating to Arjuna the Bhagavad-gītā or divine song. He rendered valuable services to Arjuna throughout the battle, but on two occasions he suggested unfair dealing. He prompted the lie by which Yudhi-shthira broke down the prowess of Drona, and he suggested the foul blow by which Bhīma shattered the thigh of Dur-yodhana. He afterwards went to Hastinā-pura with the conquerors, and he also attended their Aswa-medha sacrifice. On returning to Dwārakā he issued a proclamation forbidding the use of wine. Portents and fearful signs appeared, and a general feeling of alarm spread among all in Dwārakā. Krishna gave directions that the inhabitants should go out to Prabhāsa on the sea-shore and endeavour to propitiate the deity. He gave permission also that wine might be drunk for one day. A drunken brawl followed, in which his son Pradyumna was killed in his presence, and nearly all the chiefs of the Yādavas were slain. Bala-rāma went out from the fray and died peacefully under a tree, and Krishna himself was killed unintentionally by a hunter named Jaras, who shot him with an arrow, mistaking him at a distance for a deer. Arjuna proceeded to Dwārakā and performed the obsequies of Krishna. A few days afterwards the city was swallowed up by the sea. Five of Krishna's widows were subsequently burnt upon a funeral pile in the plain of Kuru-kshetra.

"Among the texts of the Mahā-bhārata," says Dr. Muir, "there are some in which Krishna is distinctly subordinated to Mahā-deva (Siva), of whom he is exhibited as a worshipper, and from whom, as well as from his wife Umā, he is stated to have received a variety of boons. Even in these passages, however, a superhuman character is ascribed to Krishna."

The popular history of Krishna, especially of his childhood and youth, is given in the Purānas, and is the subject of many a story. The Bhāgavata Purāna is the great authority, and from that the following account is condensed:—

The sage Nārada had foretold to Kansa that a son of Devakī, his brother's daughter, should destroy him and overthrow his kingdom. To obviate this danger, Kansa kept his cousin Devakī confined in his own palace, and six children that she bore he caused to be put to death. She conceived a seventh time, but the child was an incarnation of Vishnu, and was miraculously preserved by being transferred from the womb of Devakī to that of Rohinī, who was Vasu-deva's second wife. This child was Bala-rāma. Devakī again conceived, and her eighth child was born at midnight with a very dark skin, whence he was called Krishna. He had a peculiar curl of hair, called srī-vatsa, upon his breast. The gods interposed to preserve the life of this divinely begotten child. The guards of the palace were overpowered with sleep, and bolts and barriers were removed. Vasu-deva took up the child and escaped with him from Mathurā. He repaired to the bank of the Yamunā (Jumna), and, crossing the river, went to the house of Nanda, a cowherd, whose wife, Yasodā, had on that very night been delivered of a female child. Vasu-deva secretly changed the infants, and carried back the daughter of Yasodā to his wife Devakī. Kansa discovered that he had been cheated, and in his wrath he ordered that every male infant that gave signs of vigour should be put to death. Vasu-deva and Devakī, being no longer dangerous, were set at liberty. Nanda, alarmed by the order for the massacre, took the young child and removed with Yasodā and with Rohinī and Bala-rāma to Gokula. Here Krishna was brought up, and wandered about in company of his elder brother Bala-rāma. They played many pranks and passed many practical jokes; but they exhibited such marvellous strength and such godlike powers that they soon became famous. Kansa was continually forming schemes for the death of Krishna. The female demon Pūtanā assumed a lovely form, and tried to kill him by suckling him, but the child sucked away her life. Another demon tried to drive a cart over him, but he dashed the cart to pieces. A demon named Trinávartta took the form of a whirlwind and flew off with him, but the child brought the demon to the ground with such violence that he died. One day Krishna broke the vessels of milk and curds and ate the butter, which made Yasodā angry. She fastened a rope round his body, and tied him to a large bowl, but he dragged the bowl away till it caught between two trees and uprooted them. From this feat he got the name of Dāmodara (rope-belly). He had a terrible conflict with the great serpent Kāliya, who lived in the Yamunā, and he compelled him to go away. On one occasion, when the *gopīs* or milkmaids were bathing, he took away all their clothes and climbed up a tree, and there he remained till the damsels came to him naked to recover them. He persuaded Nanda and the cowherds to give up the worship of Indra, and to worship the mountain Govardhana, which sheltered them and their cattle. Incensed at the loss of his offerings, Indra poured down a heavy rain, which would have deluged them, but K*r*ish*n*a lifted up the mountain Govardhana, and held it upon his finger as a shelter for seven days and nights, till Indra felt that he was foiled. From this feat he obtained the name of Govardhana-dhara and Tungīsa. As he had protected the kine, Indra expressed his satisfaction, and gave him the title of Upendra. He was now approaching manhood, and was very handsome. The *gopīs* were all enamoured of him, and he dispensed his favours very freely. He married seven or eight of them, but his first and favourite wife was Rādhā. At this period of his life he is represented with flowing hair and with a flute in his hand. One of his favourite pastimes was a round dance, called Ma*nd*ala-n*r*itya or Rāsa-ma*nd*ala, in which he and Rādhā formed the centre whilst the *gopīs* danced round them. But his happiness was interrupted by the machinations of Kan*s*a, who sent formidable demons to destroy him—Arish*t*a in the form of a bull, and Ke*s*in in the form of a horse. These attempts having failed, Kan*s*a sent his messenger, Akrūra, to invite K*r*ish*n*a and Balarāma to Mathurā to attend some games, and he formed several plans for their destruction. They accepted the invitation, and went to Mathurā. Near the city they found Kan*s*a's washerman engaged in his calling. They threw down some of his clothes, and he addressed them insolently, upon which they killed him, and took such clothes as they liked. In his progress he met Kubjā, a crooked damsel, who gave him some unguent, and he repaid her gift by making her straight. In the games he killed Chā*n*ūra, the king's boxer. Afterwards he killed Kan*s*a himself, and replaced Ugrasena on the throne. He remained in Mathurā and studied the science of arms under Sāndīpani. He went down to the infernal regions and brought back his six brothers, whom Kan*s*a had killed, and these, having tasted the milk of their mother, ascended to heaven. During this period he killed a demon named Panchajana, who had attacked the son of his teacher. This demon lived in the sea in the form of a conch-shell, and Krishna afterwards used this shell, called Pāncha-janya, as a trumpet. Kansa's two wives were daughters of Jarā-sandha, king of Magadha. This king assembled his forces and marched against Mathurā to chastise Krishna, but he was defeated. He renewed his attacks eighteen times, and was as often defeated. A new enemy then threatened Krishna, a Yavana or foreigner named Kāla-yavana, and Krishna had been so weakened that he knew he must succumb either to him or to his old enemy the king of Magadha, so he and all his people migrated to the coast of Guzerat, where he built and fortified the city of Dwārakā. [The Mahā-bhārata makes no mention of this foreign king, and says that Krishna retired before the eighteenth attack of Jarā-sandha. The foreign king would, therefore, seem to be an invention of the Purānas for saving Krishna's reputation.]

After his settlement at Dwārakā, Krishna carried off and married Rukminī, daughter of the Rāja of Vidarbha, and the betrothed of Sisu-pāla. An incident now occurred which brought him two more wives. A Yādava chief named Satrājit had a beautiful gem called Syamantaka, which Krishna wished to possess. Satrājit, for the sake of security, gave the gem into the charge of his brother Prasena, and Prasena was killed in the forest by a lion, who carried off the jewel in his mouth. This lion was killed by Jāmbavat, the king of the bears. Satrājit suspected Krishna of taking the jewel, and he, to clear himself, went out into the forest, ascertained the manner of Prasena's death, fought with Jāmbavat, and recovered the jewel. Krishna then married Jāmbavatī, the daughter of Jāmbavat, and Satya-bhāmā, the daughter of Satrājit. But the number of his wives was practically unlimited, for he had 16,000 and a hundred or so besides, and he had 180,000 sons. By Rukminī he had a son Pradyumna and a daughter Chārumatī. His son by Jāmbavatī was Sāmba, and by Satya-bhāmā he had ten sons. Indra came to visit Krishna at Dwārakā, and implored him to suppress the evil deeds of the demon Naraka. Krishna accordingly went to the city of Naraka, killed the demon Muru, who guarded the city, and then destroyed Naraka himself. Krishna next went to pay a visit to Indra in Swarga, taking with him his wife

Satya-bhāmā. At her request he requited the hospitality shown him by carrying off the famed Pārijāta tree, which was produced at the churning of the ocean. The tree belonged to *S*achī, wife of Indra, and she complained to her husband. Indra drew out his forces and tried to recover it, but was defeated by K*r*ish*n*a. Pradyumna, son of K*r*ish*n*a, had a son named Aniruddha, with whom a female Daitya, Ushā, daughter of Bā*n*a, fell in love. She induced a companion to carry off the young man, and K*r*ish*n*a, Bala-rāma, and Pradyumna went to rescue him. Bā*n*a, with the whole Daitya host, and assisted by *S*iva and Skanda, the god of war, encountered them. K*r*ish*n*a, "with the weapon of yawning, set *S*iva agape," and so overpowered him. Skanda was wounded. Bā*n*a maintained a fierce combat with K*r*ish*n*a, and was severely wounded, but K*r*ish*n*a spared his life at the intercession of *S*iva, and Aniruddha was released.

There was a man named Pau*nd*raka, who was a Vāsu-deva, or descendant of one Vasu-deva. Upon the strength of the identity of this name with that of Vasu-deva, the father of K*r*ish*n*a, this man Pau*nd*raka assumed the insignia and title of K*r*ish*n*a, and he had the king of Kā*s*ī or Benares for an ally. K*r*ish*n*a slew Pau*n*-*d*raka, and he hurled his flaming discus at Benares and destroyed that city. Such are the principal incidents of the life of K*r*ish*n*a as given in the Hari-van*s*a, the Purā*n*as, and the Prem Sāgar.

Similarity in the sound of the name, and some incidents in the life of K*r*ish*n*a, have led some to believe that the legend of K*r*ish*n*a had its origin in the life of Christ, but this is not the general opinion.

K*r*ish*n*a has many appellations derived from his family relations, his exploits, and personal characteristics; and there are many which apply both to the full deity, Vishnu, and his incarnation, K*r*ish*n*a.

K*RI*SH*N*Ā. The personal name of Draupadī.

K*RI*SHNA DWAIPĀYANA. *See* Vyāsa.

K*RI*TĀNTA. A name of Yama, the god of death.

K*RI*TA-VARMAN. A Kuru warrior, one of the last surviving three who made the murderous night attack upon the camp of the Pā*nd*avas. (*See* Mahā-bhārata.) He was killed in a drunken brawl at Dwārakā. He was also called Bhoja.

K*RI*TA-VĪRYA. Son of Dhanaka and father of the Arjuna who is better know by his patronymic Kārta-vīrya.

Krita-vīrya was a great patron of the Bhrigus, and according to the Purānas, "he ruled over the whole earth with might and justice, and offered 10,000 sacrifices. Of him this verse is still recited, 'The kings of the earth will assuredly never pursue his steps in sacrifice, in munificence, in devotion, in courtesy, and in self-control.'"

KRITA YUGA. The first age of the world, a period of 1,728,000 years. *See* Yuga.

KRITTIKĀS. The Pleiades. The six nurses of Kārttikeya, the god of war. They were daughters of a king according to one legend, wives of Rishis according to another.

KRIYĀ-YOGA-SĀRA. A portion of the Padma Purāna treating of rites and ceremonies. *See* Padma Purāna.

KRODHA, KRODHA-VASĀ. One of the many daughters of Daksha and sister-wives of Kasyapa. She was the mother "of all sharp-toothed monsters, whether on the earth, amongst the birds, or in the waters, that were devourers of flesh."

KSHANADĀ-CHARA. 'Night walkers.' Ghosts of evil character, goblins, Rākshasas.

KSHAPANAKA. An author who was one of "the nine gems" at the court of Vikramāditya. *See* Nava-ratna.

KSHATRIYA. The second or regal and warrior caste. *See* Varna.

KSHATTRI. A name by which Vidura was familiarly called. The term, as explained in Manu, means the son of a Sūdra father and Brāhman mother, but Vidura's father was a Brāhman and his mother a slave girl.

KSHEMAKA. Son of Nira-mitra or Nimi, and the last prince of the Lunar race. There is a memorial verse quoted in the Vishnu Purāna which say, "The race which gave origin to Brāhmans and Kshatriyas, and which was purified by regal sages, terminated with Kshemaka in the Kali age."

KSHEMA-VRIDDHI. A general of the Sālwas who had a command in the army which attacked Dwārakā, and was defeated by Krishna's son, Sāmba.

KULA-PARVATAS. 'Family mountains.' A series or system of seven chains of mountains in Southern India. They are Mahendra, Malaya, Sahya, Suktimat, Riksha (for which Gandha-mādana is sometimes substituted), Vindhya and Pāripātra. Mahendra is the Orissa chain; Malaya, the hills of Malabar proper, the south part of the Western Ghāts; Sahya, the northern parts of the Western Ghāts; *S*uktimat is doubtful; *Ri*ksha, the mountains of Gondwāna; Vindhya is here applied to the eastern division of the Vindhya mountains; and Pāripātra, or Pāriyātra as it is frequently written, applies to the northern and western portions of the same range. The classification seems to have been known to Ptolemy, for he specifies seven ranges of mountains, but his names are not in accord.

KULIKA. One of the eight serpent kings, described as of a dusky brown colour and having a half-moon on his head.

KULINDAS. A people living in the north-west.

KULLŪKA-BHA*TT*A. The famous commentator on Manu, whose gloss was used by Sir W. Jones in making the translation of Manu.

KUMĀRA. A name of Skanda, god of war. In the Brāhma*n*as the term is applied to Agni.

KUMĀRAS. Mind-born sons of Brahmā, who, declining to create progeny, remained ever boys and ever pure and innocent. There were four of them, Sanat-kumāra, Sananda, Sanaka, and Sanātana; a fifth, *Ri*bhu, is sometimes added. *See* Vish*n*u Purā*n*a.

KUMĀRA-SAMBHAVA. 'The birth of the war god (Kumāra).' A poem by Kāli-dāsa. The complete work consists of sixteen cantos, but only seven are usually given, and these have been translated into Latin by Stenzler. Parts have been rendered into English verse by Griffiths. There are several editions of the text.

KUMĀRĪ. 'The damsel.' An epithet of *S*ītā, also of Durgā. Cape Comorin.

KUMĀRILA-BHA*TT*A, KUMĀRILA-SWĀMĪ. A celebrated teacher of the Mīmānsā philosophy and opponent of the Buddhists, whom he is said to have extirpated by argument and by force. He was prior to *S*ankarāchārya, in whose presence he is recorded to have burnt himself.

KUMBHA-KAR*N*A. Son of Vi*s*ravas by his Rākshasa wife Ke*s*inī, and full brother of Rāva*n*a. A monster who, under the curse of Brahmā (or, as otherwise represented, as a boon), slept for six months at a time and remained awake for only a single day. When Rāva*n*a was hard pressed by Rāma he sent to arouse Kumbha-kar*n*a. This was effected with great difficulty,

After drinking 2000 jars of liquor he went to consult with his brother, and then took the field against the monkey army. He beat down Su-grīva, the monkey chief, with a large stone, and carried him a prisoner into the city of Lankā. When he returned to the battle he encountered Rāma, and after a stout fight he was defeated, and Rāma cut off his head.

KUMUDA. 'A lotus.' A Naga or serpent king whose sister, Kumudvatī, married Kusa, son of Rāma.

KUMUDVATĪ. A Nāga or serpent princess whose marriage to Kusa, son of Rāma, is described in the Raghu-vansa.

KU*ND*INA-PURA. The capital of Vidarbha. It survives as the modern Kundapur, situated about 40 miles east of Amarāvatī, in Birar.

KUNTALA. A country in the Dakhin, about Adoni; the Dakhin.

KUNTĪ (also called P*ri*thā and Pārsh*n*ī). 1. Daughter of the Yādava prince *S*ūra, king of the *S*ūrasenas, whose capital was Mathurā on the Yamunā. She was sister of Vasu-deva, and was given by her father to his childless cousin Kunti-bhoja, by whom she was brought up. In her maidenhood she showed such respectful devotion to the sage Dur-vāsas, that he gave her a charm by means of which she might have a child by any god she pleased to invoke. She called upon the sun, and by him had a son named Kar*n*a, but without any detriment to her virginity; still, to keep the affair secret, the child was exposed on the banks of the Yamunā. Subsequently she married Pā*nd*u, whom she chose at a swayam-vara, and bore three sons, Yudhish*th*ira, Bhīma, and Arjuna, who were called Pā*nd*avas although they were said to be the sons of the gods Dharma, Vāyu, and Indra respectively. This may have happened, as is stated, from the potency of the old charm, but if so, it is strange that Mādrī, the second wife of Pā*nd*u, should have enjoyed the same privilege, and have borne twin children to the A*s*wins. This difficulty, however, is got over by a statement that Kuntī imparted to her the charm. Kuntī was a discreet and devoted mother, and although rather jealous of Mādrī, she was a kind mother to her children after Mādrī was burnt on her husband's pyre. After the end of the great war she retired into the forest with Dh*ri*tarāsh*t*ra and his wife Gāndhārī, and there they all perished in a forest fire. 2. Name of a people and country in Upper India.

KUNTI-BHOJA. King of the people called Kuntis. The adoptive father of Kuntī.

KŪRMA-AVATĀR. The tortoise incarnation. *See* Avatāra.

KŪRMA PURĀ*N*A. "That in which Janārdana (Vish*n*u), in the form of a tortoise, in the regions under the earth, explained the objects of life—duty, wealth, pleasure, and liberation,—in communication with Indra-dyumna and the *R*ishis in the proximity of *S*akra, which refers to the Lakshmī Kalpa, and contains 17,000 stanzas, is the Kūrma Purā*n*a." The account which the Purā*n*a gives of itself and its actual contents do not agree with this description. "The name being that of an Avatāra of Vish*n*u, might lead us to expect a Vaish*n*ava work; but it is always and correctly classed with the *S*aiva Purā*n*as, the greater portion of it inculcating the worship of *S*iva and Durgā. The date of this Purā*n*a cannot be very remote."—*Wilson.*

KURU. A prince of the Lunar race, son of Samvara*n*a by Tapatī, a daughter of the sun. He ruled in the north-west of India over the country about Delhi. A people called Kurus, and dwelling about Kuru-kshetra in that part of India, are connected with him. He was ancestor both of Dh*r*ita-rāsh*t*ra and Pā*nd*u, but the patronymic Kaurava is generally applied to the sons of the former.

KURU-JĀNGALA. A forest country in the upper part of the Doāb.

KURU-KSHETRA. 'The field of the Kurus.' A plain near Delhi where the great battle between the Kauravas and Pa*nd*avas was fought. It lies south-east of Thānesar, not far from Pānipat, the scene of many battles in later days.

KU*S*A. One of the twin sons of Rāma and Sītā. After the death of Rāma, his two sons Kusa and Lava became kings of the Southern and Northern Kosalas, and Ku*s*a built Ku*s*a-sthalī or Ku*s*āvatī in the Vindhyas, and made it his capital. *See* Rāma.

KU*S*A-DHWAJA. A brother of Janaka, king of Mithilā, and consequently uncle of Sītā. His two daughters, Mā*nd*avī and *S*ruta-kīrtti, were married to Bharata and *S*atru-ghna, the sons of Janaka. Some make him king of Sānkā*s*yā, and others king of Kā*s*ī, and there are differences also as to his genealogy.

KU*S*ĀMBA. Son of Ku*s*a and a descendant of Purūravas. He engaged in devout penance to obtain a son equal to Indra, and that god was so alarmed at his austerities, that he himself became incarnate as Gādhi, son of Kusāmba.

KU*S*A-STHALĪ. 1. A city identical with or standing on the same spot as Dwārakā. It was built by Raivata, and was the capital of his kingdom called Ānarta. When Raivata went on a visit to the region of Brahmā, his city was destroyed by Pu*n*ya-janas, *i.e.*, Yakshas or Rākshasas. 2. A city built by Ku*s*a, son of Rāma, on the brow of the Vindhyas. It was the capital of Southern Kosalā. Also called Ku*s*ā-vatī.

KU*S*Ā-VATĪ. The capital of Southern Kosala, built upon the Vindhyas by Ku*s*a, son of Rāma.

KUSHMĀ*N**D*AS. 'Gourds.' A class of demigods or demons in the service of *S*iva.

KU*S*IKA. A king who, according to some, was the father of Vi*s*wāmitra, or, according to others, the first of the race of Ku*s*ikas from whom Gādhi, the father of Vi*s*wāmitra descended.

KUSUMA-PURA. 'The city of flowers.' Pā*t*ali-putra or Patna.

KUSUMĀYUDHA. A name of Kāma, or Cupid as the bearer of the bow (*āyudha*) of flowers (*kusuma*).

KUTSA. A Vedic *R*ishi and author of hymns. He is represented as being persecuted by Indra, but on one occasion he was defended by that god against the demon *S*ush*n*a. It is said that Indra took him to his palace, and that they were so much alike that *S*achī or Pushpotka*t*ā, Indra's wife, did not know which was her husband.

KUVALĀ*S*WA, KUVALAYĀ*S*WA. A prince of the Solar race, who, according to the Vish*n*u Purā*n*a, had 21,000 sons, but the Hari-van*s*a numbers them only as 100. Attended by his sons he attacked the great Asura, Dhundhu, who lived in a sea of sand, and harassed the devotions of the pious sage Uttanka. They unearthed the demon and slew him, from which exploit Kuvalā*s*wa got the title of Dhundhu-māra, slayer of Dhundhu; but all his sons except three perished by the fiery breath of the monster.

KUVALAYĀPĪ*D*A. An immense elephant, or a demon in elephantine form, belonging to Kan*s*a, and employed by him to trample the boys K*r*ish*n*a and Bala-rāma to death. The attempt failed and the elephant was killed.

KUVERA. In the Vedas, a chief of the evil beings or spirits

living in the shades: a sort of Pluto, and called by his patronymic Vaisravana. Later he is Pluto in another sense, as god of wealth and chief of the Yakshas and Guhyakas. He was son of Visravas by Idāvidā, but he is sometimes called son of Pulastya, who was father of Visravas. This is explained by the Mahā-bhārata, according to which Kuvera was son of Pulastya, but that sage being offended with Kuvera for his adulation of Brahmā, "reproduced the half of himself in the form of Visravas," and had Rāvana and other children. (*See* Visravas.) Kuvera's city is Alakā (also called Prabhā, Vasu-dharā, and Vasu-sthalī) in the Himālayas, and his garden Chaitra-ratha on Mandara, one of the spurs of Mount Meru, where he is waited upon by the Kinnaras. Some authorities place his abode on Mount Kailāsa in a palace built by Viswa-karma. He was half-brother of Rāvana, and, according to the Rāmāyana and Mahā-bhārata, he once had possession of the city of Lankā in Ceylon, which was also built by Viswa-karma, and from which he was expelled by Rāvana. The same authority states that he performed austerities for thousands of years, and obtained the boon from Brahmā that he should be immortal, one of the guardian deities of the world, and the god of wealth. So he is regent of the north, and the keeper of gold and silver, jewels and pearls, and all the treasures of the earth, besides nine particular Nidhis, or treasures, the nature of which is not well understood. Brahmā also gave him the great self-moving aerial car Pushpaka (q.v.). His wife is Yakshī, Chārvī, or Kauverī, daughter of the Dānava Mura. His sons are Mani-grīva or Varna-kavi and Nala-kubara or Mayu-rāja, and his daughter Mīnākshī (fish-eyed). He is represented as a white man deformed in body, and having three legs and only eight teeth. His body is covered with ornaments. He receives no worship. The name Ku-vera, as also the variant Ku-tanu, signifies 'vile body,' referring to his ugliness. He is also called Dhana-pati, 'lord of wealth;' Ichchhā-vasu, 'who has wealth at will;' Yaksha-rāja, 'chief of the Yakshas;' Mayu-rāja, 'king of the Kinnaras;' Rākshasendra, 'chief of the Rākshasas;' Ratna-garbha, 'belly of jewels;' Rāja-rāja, 'king of kings;' and Nara-rāja, 'king of men' (in allusion to the power of riches). From his parentage he is called Vaisravana, Paulastya, and Aidavida or Ailavila. As an especial friend of Siva he is called Isa-sakhi, &c.

LAGHU-KAUMUDĪ. A modern and very much simplified edition of Pāṇini's Grammar by Varada Rāja. It has been edited and translated by Dr. Ballantyne.

LAKSHMAṆA. 1. Son of King Daśa-ratha by his wife Su-mitrā. He was the twin brother of Śatru-ghna, and the half-brother and especial friend of Rāma-chandra. Under the peculiar circumstances of his birth, one-eighth part of the divinity of Vishṇu became manifest in him. (*See* Daśa-ratha.) But according to the Adhyātma Rāmāyaṇa, he was an incarnation of Śesha. When Rāma left his father's court to go to the hermitage of Viśwāmitra, Lakshmaṇa accompanied him, and afterwards attended him in his exile and in all his wanderings. He was also very attached to Rāma's wife Sītā, which gave rise to the reproach that the two brothers were husbands of one wife. On one occasion, indeed, Sītā reproached Lakshmaṇa that he did not hasten to rescue Rāma from danger, because he wished to obtain herself. His own wife was Ūrmilā, the sister of Sītā, and he had two sons, Angada and Chandra-ketu. While Rāma and Lakshmaṇa were living in the wilderness, a Rākshasī named Śūrpa-nakhā, sister of Rāvaṇa, fell in love with Rāma and made advances to him. He jestingly referred her to Lakshmaṇa, who in like manner sent her back to Rāma. When she was again repulsed she attacked Sītā, whom Rāma was obliged to defend. Rāma then called upon Lakshmaṇa to disfigure the Rākshasī, and accordingly he cut off her nose and ears. The mutilated female called upon her brother to avenge her, and a fierce war ensued. When Sītā was carried off by Rāvaṇa, Lakshmaṇa accompanied Rāma in his search, and he ably and bravely supported him in his war against Rāvaṇa. Rāma's earthly career was drawing to a close, and Time was sent to inform him that he must elect whether to stay longer on earth, or to return to the place from whence he had come. While they were in conference, the irascible sage Dur-vāśas came and demanded to see Rāma instantly, threatening him with the most direful curses if any delay were allowed to occur. To save his brother Rāma from the threatened curse, but aware of the consequences that would ensue to himself from breaking in upon Rāma's interview with Time, he went in and brought Rāma out. Lakshmaṇa knowing his fate, retired to the river Śarayū and resigned himself. The gods then showered down flowers upon him and conveyed him bodily to heaven. 2. A son of Duryodhana, killed by Abhimanyu.

LAKSHMĪ. The word occurs in the *Rig*-veda with the sense of good fortune, and in the Atharva-veda the idea has become personified in females both of a lucky and unlucky character. The Taittirīya Sanhitā, as explained by the commentator, makes Lakshmī and *S*rī to be two wives of Āditya, and the *S*atapatha Brāhma*n*a describes *S*rī as issuing forth from Prajāpati.

Lakshmī or *S*rī in later times is the goddess of fortune, wife of Vish*n*u, and mother of Kāma. The origin ascribed to her by the Rāmāya*n*a is the one commonly received. According to this legend she sprang, like Aphrodite, from the froth of the ocean, in full beauty with a lotus in her hand, when it was churned by the gods and the Asuras. Another legend represents her as floating on the flower of a lotus at the creation. With reference to this origin, one of her names is Kshīrābdhi-tanayā, 'daughter of the sea of milk.' From her connection with the lotus she is called Padmā. According to the Purā*n*as, she was the daughter of Bh*ri*gu and Khyāti. The Vish*n*u Purā*n*a says, "Her first birth was the daughter of Bh*ri*gu by Khyāti. It was at a subsequent period that she was produced from the sea at the churning of the ocean. . . . When Hari was born as a dwarf, Lakshmī appeared from a lotus (as Padmā or Kamalā). When he was born as Rāma of the race of Bh*ri*gu (or Para*s*u-rāma), she was Dhara*n*ī. When he was Rāghava (Rāma-chandra), she was Sītā. And when he was K*ri*sh*n*a she became Rukmi*n*ī. In the other descents of Vish*n*u she is his associate." One version of the Rāmāya*n*a also affirms that "Lakshmī, the mistress of the worlds, was born by her own will, in a beautiful field opened up by the plough," and received from Janaka the name of Sītā.

Lakshmī is said to have four arms, but she is the type of beauty, and is generally depicted as having only two. In one hand she holds a lotus. "She has no temples, but being goddess of abundance and fortune, she continues to be assiduously courted, and is not likely to fall into neglect." Other names of Lakshmī are Hīrā, Indirā, Jaladhi-jā, 'ocean born;' Chanchalā or Lolā, 'the fickle,' as goddess of fortune; Loka-mātā, 'mother of the world.'

LALITA-VISTARA. A work in Sanskrit verse on the life and doctrines of Buddha. It has been printed in the *Bibliotheca Indica.*

LĀNGALĪ. 'Armed with a ploughshare.' Bala-rāma.

LANKĀ. 1. The island of Ceylon or its capital city. The city is described in the Rāmāya*n*a as of vast extent and of great magnificence, with seven broad moats and seven stupendous walls of stone and metal. It is said to have been built of gold by Vi*s*wa-karma for the residence of Kuvera, from whom it was taken by Rāva*n*ā. The Bhāgavata Purā*n*a represents that the island was originally the summit of Mount Meru, which was broken off by the god of the wind and hurled into the sea. 2. Name of one of the *S*ākinīs or evil spirits attendant on *S*iva and Devī.

LĀ*T*A. A country comprising Kandesh and part of Guzerat about the Mhye river. It is also called Lār, and is the Λαρικη of Ptolemy.

LĀ*T*YĀYANA. Author of a Sūtra work. It has been printed in the *Bibliotheca Indica.*

LAVA. One of the twin sons of Rāma and Sītā. He reigned at *S*rāvastī. *See* Rāma.

LAVA*N*A. A Rākshasa, son of Madhu by Kumbhīnasī, the sister of Rāva*n*a and daughter of Vi*s*ravas. He inherited from his father an invincible trident which had been presented to him by *S*iva. He was surprised without his weapon and killed by *S*atru-ghna. Lava*n*a was king of Mathurā and *S*atru-ghna succeeded him.

LIKHITA. Author of a Dharma-*s*āstra or code of law.

LĪLĀVATĪ. 'Charming.' The fanciful title of that chapter of Bhāskara's Siddhānta-*s*iroma*n*i which treats of arithmetic and geometry. It has been translated by Colebrooke and Dr. Taylor, and the text has been printed.

LINGA, LINGAM. The male organ. The phallus. The symbol under which *S*iva is universally worshipped. It is of comparatively modern introduction and is unknown to the Vedas, but it receives distinct notice in the Mahā-bhārata. "The emblem—a plain column of stone, or sometimes a cone of plastic mud—suggests no offensive ideas. The people call it *S*iva or Mahā-deva, and there's an end." In the *S*iva Purā*n*a, and in the Nandi Upa-purā*n*a, *S*iva is made to say, "I am omnipresent, but I am especially in twelve forms and places." These are the twelve great Lingas, which are as follow :—

1. *Soma-nātha.* 'Lord of the moon.' At Somnāth Pattan, a city which still remains in Guzerat. This was the celebrated "idol" destroyed by Mahmūd of Ghaznī.

2. *Mallikārjuna* or *Srī-saila.* 'The mountain of *Srī.*' On a mountain near the river Krishnā.

3. *Mahā-kāla, Mahā-kāleswara.* At Ujjain. Upon the capture of Ujjain in the reign of Altamsh, 1231 A.D., this deity of stone was carried to Delhi and there broken up.

4. *Omkāra.* This is also said to have been at Ujjain, but it is probably the shrine of Mahādeva at Omkāra Māndhāttā, on the Narmadā.

5. *Amareswara.* 'God of gods.' This is also placed at Ujjain.

6. *Vaidya-nātha.* 'Lord of physicians.' At Deogarh in Bengal. The temple is still in being, and is a celebrated place of pilgrimage.

7. *Rāmesa* or *Rāmeswara.* 'Lord of Rāma.' On the island of Ramisseram, between the continent and Ceylon. This Lingam, whose name signifies 'Rāma's lord,' is fabled to have been set up by Rāma. The temple is still in tolerable repair, and is one of the most magnificent in India.

8. *Bhīma Sankara.* In *Dākinī.* This is in all probability the same with Bhīmeswara, a Lingam worshipped at Dracharam, in the Rājamahendrī (Rajamundry) district, and there venerated as one of the twelve.

9. *Visweswara.* 'Lord of all.' At Benares. It has been for many centuries the chief object of worship at Benares. Also called Jyotir-lingam.

10. *Tryambaka, Tryaksha.* 'Tri-ocular.' On the banks of the Gomatī.

11. *Gautamesa.* 'Lord of Gautama.'

12. *Kedāresa, Kedāra-nātha.* In the Himālaya. The deity is represented as a shapeless mass of rock.

Nāga-nātha or Nāga-nāthesa and Vāmeswara are other names, probably of No. 6 and No. 11.

LINGA PURĀNA. "Where Maheswara (Siva), present in the Agni Linga, explained (the objects of life), virtue, wealth, pleasure, and final liberation, at the end of the Agni Kalpa, that Purāna, consisting of 11,000 stanzas, was called the Linga by

Brahmā himself." The work conforms accurately enough to this description. "Although the Linga holds a prominent place in this Purāna, the spirit of the worship is as little influenced by the character of the type as can well be imagined. There is nothing like the phallic orgies of antiquity: it is all mystical and spiritual. The work has preserved, apparently, some *S*aiva legends of an early date, but the greater part is ritual and mysticism of comparatively recent introduction."—*Wilson.* It is not likely that this Purāna is earlier than the eighth or ninth century. This Purāna has been lithographed in Bombay.

LOHA-MUKHAS. 'Iron-faced men.' Described in the Mahā-bhārata as swift, one-footed, undecaying, strong men-eaters.

LOKA. A world, a division of the universe. In general the tri-loka or three worlds are heaven, earth, and hell. Another classification enumerates seven, exclusive of the infernal regions, also seven in number which are classed under Pātāla. The upper worlds are :—(1.) Bhur-loka, the earth. (2.) Bhuvar-loka, the space between the earth and the sun, the region of the Munis, Siddhas, &c. (3.) Swar-loka, the heaven of Indra, between the sun and the polar star. (4.) Mahar-loka, the usual abode of Bh*ri*gu and other saints, who are supposed to be coexistent with Brahmā. During the conflagration of these lower worlds the saints ascend to the next, or (5.) Jana-loka, which is described as the abode of Brahmā's sons, Sanaka, Sānanda, and Sanat-kumāra. Above this is the (6.) Tapar-loka, where the deities called Vairāgīs reside. (7.) Satya-loka or Brahmā-loka, is the abode of Brahmā, and translation to this world exempts beings from further birth. The first three worlds are destroyed at the end of each kalpa, or day of Brahmā; the last three at the end of his life, or of a hundred of his years; the fourth loka is equally permanent, but is uninhabitable from heat at the time the first three are burning. Another enumeration calls the seven worlds earth, sky, heaven, middle region, place of birth, mansion of the blest, and abode of truth; placing the sons of Brahmā in the sixth division, and stating the fifth, or Jana-loka, to be that where animals destroyed in the general conflagration are born again. The Sānkhya and Vedānta schools of philosophy recognise eight lokas or regions of material existence :—(1.) Brahmā-loka, the world of the superior deities; (2.) Pit*ri*-loka, that of the Pit*ri*s, *R*ishis, and Prajāpatis; (3.)

Soma-loka, of the moon and planets; (4.) Indra-loka, of the inferior deities; (5.) Gandharva-loka, of heavenly spirits; (6.) Rākshasa-loka, of the Rākshasas; (7.) Yaksha-loka, of the Yakshas; (8.) Piśācha-loka, of the Piśāchas or imps and fiends.

LOKĀLOKA. 'A world and no world,' A fabulous belt of mountains bounding the outermost of the seven seas and dividing the visible world from the regions of darkness. It is "ten thousand yojanas in breadth, and as many in height, and beyond it perpetual darkness invests the mountains all around, which darkness is again encompassed by the shell of an egg." It is called also Chakra-vā*d*a or Chakra-vāla.

LOKA-PĀLAS. Supporters or guardians of the world. The guardian deities who preside over the eight points of the compass, *i.e.*, the four cardinal and four intermediate points of the compass:—(1.) Indra, east; (2.) Agni, south-east; (3.) Yama, south; (4.) Sūrya, south-west; (5.) Varu*n*a, west; (6.) Vāyu, north-west; (7.) Kuvera, north; (8.) Soma, north-east. Nir*ri*ti is by some substituted for No. 4, and P*ri*thivī or *S*iva, especially in his form Īśāna, for No. 8. Each of these guardian deities has an elephant who takes part in the defence and protection of the quarter, and these eight elephants are themselves called Loka-pālas:—(1.) Indra's elephant at the east is Airāvata. He is also called Abhra-mātanga, 'elephant of the clouds;' Arka-sodara, 'brother of the sun;' Nāga-malla, 'the fighting elephant;' Sadā-dāna, 'always in rut;' Madāmbara, 'covered with ichor.' His wife's name is Abhramu. (2.) Agni's elephant at the south-east is Pu*n*ḍarīka and his female Kapilā. (3.) Yama's at the south is Vāmana and his female Pingalā. (4.) Sūrya's at the south-west is Kumuda and his female is Anupamā. (5.) Varu*n*a's at the west is Anjana, whose female is Anjanavatī. (6.) Vāyu's at the north-west is Pushpa-danta, whose female is *S*ubha-dantī. (7.) Kuvera's at the north is Sārva-bhauma; and (8.) Soma's elephant at the north-east is Su-pratīka. The two other females are Anjanā and Tāmra-kar*n*ī, whose spouses are doubtful. Anjanāvatī is sometimes assigned to Su-pratīka. In the Rāmāya*n*a (1.) Indra's eastern elephant is called Virūpāksha; (2.) Varu*n*a's elephant at the west, Saumanasa; (3.) Yama's at the south is Mahā-padma, and (4.) Kuvera's at the north is Hima-pā*n*ḍara.

LOMA-HARSHA*N*A (or Roma-harsha*n*a). A bard or panegyrist who first gave forth the Purā*n*as.

LOMA-PĀDA (or Roma-pāda). A king of Anga, chiefly remarkable for his connection with *Ri*shya-*sri*nga (q.v.).

LOPĀMUDRĀ. A girl whom the sage Agastya formed from the most graceful parts of different animals and secretly introduced into the palace of the king of Vidarbha, where the child was believed to be the daughter of the king. Agastya had made this girl with the object of having a wife after his own heart, and when she was marriageable he demanded her hand. The king was loath to consent, but was obliged to yield, and she became the wife of Agastya. Her name is explained as signifying that the animals suffered loss (*lopa*) by her engrossing their distinctive beauties (*mudrā*), as the eyes of the deer, &c. She is also called Kaushītakī and Vara-pradā. A hymn in the *Ri*g-veda is attributed to her.

MADA. 'Intoxication.' Described in the Mahā-bhārata as "a fearful open-mouthed monster, created by the sage Chyavana, having teeth and grinders of portentous length, and jaws one of which enclosed the earth and the other the sky," who got Indra and the other gods into his jaws "like fishes in the mouth of a sea monster."

MADAYANTĪ. Wife of King Saudāsa or Kalmāsha-pada. She was allowed to consort with the sage Vasish*th*a. According to some this was a meritorious act on the king's part and a favour to Vasish*th*a; according to others it was for the sake of obtaining progeny. *See* Kalmāsha-pāda.

MĀDHAVA. A name of K*ri*sh*n*a or Vish*n*u.

MĀDHAVA, MĀDHAVĀCHĀRYA. A celebrated scholar and religious teacher. He was a native of Tuluva, and became prime minister of Vīra Bukka Rāya, king of the great Hindu state of Vijaya-nagara, who lived in the fourteenth century. He was brother of Sāya*n*a, the author of the great commentary on the Veda, in which work Mādhava himself is believed to have shared. Wilson observes, "Both the brothers are celebrated as scholars, and many important works are attributed to them; not only scholia on the Sanhitās and Brāhma*n*as of the Vedas, but original works on grammar and law; the fact no doubt being, that they availed themselves of those means which their situation and influence secured them, and employed the most learned Brāhmans they could attract to Vijaya-nagara upon the works which bear their names, and to which they contributed their own labour and learning; their works were therefore compiled under peculiar advantages, and are deservedly held in the highest estimation." Among the works of Mādhava are the Sarva-darsana-sangraha and the Sankshepa *S*ankara-vijaya. Mādhava was a worshipper of Vish*n*u, and as a religious philosopher he held the doctrine of *dwaita* or dualism, according to which the supreme soul of the universe and the human soul are distinct. Thus he was opposed to the teaching of *S*ankarācharya, who was a follower of *S*iva, and upheld the Vedānta doctrine of *a-dwaita*, "no duality," according to which God and soul, spirit and matter, are all one.

MĀDHAVĪ. A name of Lakshmī.

MADHU. 1. A demon slain by K*r*ish*n*a. (*See* Kai*t*abha.) 2. Another, or the same demon, said to have been killed by *S*atru-ghna.

MADHU-CHHANDAS. A son of Viswāmitra, who had fifty sons older and fifty younger than this one; but they are spoken of as "a hundred sons." He is the reputed author of some hymns of the *Ri*g-veda.

MADHU-KA*S*Ā. Described in the Atharva-veda as "the brilliant grand-daughter of the Maruts, the mother of the Ādityas, the daughter of the Vasus, the life of creatures, and the centre of immortality." She "sprang from the sky, the earth, the air, the sea, fire, and wind;" and it is added, "all creatures, worshipping her who dwells in immortality, rejoice in their hearts."

MADHURĀNIRUDDHA. A drama in eight acts by *S*ayani Chandra *S*ekhara. It is quite a modern work. "The subject is the secret loves of Ūshā, daughter of the Asura Bā*n*a and Aniruddha, grandson of K*r*ish*n*a. The piece abounds too much with description to be a good play; the style has considerable merit."—*Wilson.*

MADHU-SŪDANA. 'Slayer of Madhu.' A name of K*r*ish*n*a.

MADHYA-DE*S*A. The middle country, described by Manu as "the tract situated between the Himavat and the Vindhya ranges to the east of Vinā*s*ana and to the west of Prayāga (Allahabad)." Another authority makes it the Doab.

MĀDHYANDINA. A Vedic school, a subdivision of the Vājasaneyī school, and connected with the *S*atapatha Brāhma*n*a. It had also its own system of astronomy, and obtained its name from making noon (*madhya-dina*) the starting-point of the planetary movements.

MADIRĀ. A name of Vāruṇī, wife of Varuṇa, and goddess of wine.

MADRA. Name of a country and people to the north-west of Hindustan. Its capital was Sakala, and the territory extended from the Biyās to the Chināb, or, according to others, as far as the Jhilam.

MĀDRĪ. A sister of the king of the Madras, and second wife of Pāṇḍu, to whom she bore twin-sons, Nakula and Sahadeva; but the Aświns are alleged to have been their real father. She became a satī on the funeral pile of her husband.

MAGADHA. The country of South Bihar, where the Pāli language was spoken.

MĀGHA. A poet, son of Dattaka, and author of one of the great artificial poems called, from its subject, Śiśupāla-badha, or, from its author, Māgha-kāvya.

MAGHAVAT, MAGHAVĀN. A name of Indra.

MAHĀ-BALI. A title of the dwarf Bali, whose city is called Mahā-bali-pura, which name is applied to the Tamil "Māmallai-pura," or Seven Pagodas near Madras. *See* Bali.

MAHĀ-BHĀRATA. 'The great (war of the) Bhāratas.' The great epic poem of the Hindus, probably the longest in the world. It is divided into eighteen *parvas* or books, and contains about 220,000 lines. The poem has been subjected to much modification and has received numerous comparatively modern additions, but many of its legends and stories are of Vedic character and of great antiquity. They seem to have long existed in a scattered state, and to have been brought together at different times. Upon them have been founded many of the poems and dramas of later days, and among them is the story of Rāma, upon which the Rāmāyaṇa itself may have been based. According to Hindu authorities, they were finally arranged and reduced to writing by a Brāhman or Brāhmans. There is a good deal of mystery about this, for the poem is attributed to a divine source. The reputed author was Kṛishṇa Dwaipāyana, the Vyāsa, or arranger, of the Vedas. He is said to have taught the poem to his pupil Vaiśampāyana, who afterwards recited it at a festival to King Janamejaya. The leading subject of the poem is the great war between the Kauravas and Pāṇḍavas, who were descendants, through Bhārata, from Puru, the great ancestor of one branch of the Lunar race. The object of the great struggle was the kingdom whose capital was Hastinā-pura (elephant city), the ruins of which are traceable fifty-seven miles north-east of Delhi, on an old bed of the Ganges.

K*ri*sh*n*a Dwaipāyana Vyāsa is not only the author of the poem, but the source from whom the chief actors sprung. He was the son of the *Ri*shi Parāsara by a nymph named Satyavatī, who, although she had given birth to a son, remained a virgin. There was a king, a descendant of Bhārata, named *S*āntanu, who had a son called *S*āntavana, better known as Bhīshma. In his old age *S*āntanu wished to marry again, but the hereditary rights of Bhīshma were an obstacle to his obtaining a desirable match. To gratify his father's desire, Bhīshma divested himself of all rights of succession, and *S*āntanu then married Satyavatī. She bore him two sons, the elder of whom, Chitrāngada, succeeded to the throne, but was soon killed in battle by a Gandharva king who bore the same name. Vichitra-vīrya, the younger, succeeded, but died childless, leaving two widows, named Ambikā and Ambālikā, daughters of a king of Kāsī. Satyavatī then called on K*ri*sh*n*a Dwaipāyana Vyāsa to fulfil the law, and raise up seed to his half-brother. Vyāsa had lived the life of an anchorite in the woods, and his severe austerities had made him terrible in appearance. The two widows were so frightened at him that the elder one closed her eyes, and so gave birth to a blind son, who received the name of Dh*ri*ta-rāsh*t*ra; and the younger turned so pale that her son was called Pā*nd*u, 'the pale.' Satyavatī wished for a child without blemish, but the elder widow shrank from a second association with Vyāsa, and made a slave girl take her place. From this girl was born a son who was named Vidura. These children were brought up by their uncle Bhīshma, who acted as regent. When they became of age, Dh*ri*ta-rāsh*t*ra was deemed incapable of reigning in consequence of his blindness, and Pā*nd*u came to the throne. The name Pā*nd*u has suggested a suspicion of leprosy, and either through that, or in consequence of a curse, as the poem states, he retired to the forest, and Dh*ri*ta-rāsh*t*ra then became king.

Pā*nd*u had two wives, Kuntī or P*ri*thā, daughter of *S*ūra, king of the *S*ūra-senas, and Mādrī, sister of the king of the Madras; but either through disease or the curse passed upon him, he did not consort with his wives. He retired into solitude in the Himālaya mountains, and there he died; his wives, who accompanied him having borne him five sons. The paternity of these children is attributed to different gods, but Pā*nd*u acknowledged them, and they received the patronymic of Pā*nd*ava. Kuntī was the mother of the three elder sons, and Mādrī of the two younger. Yudhi-sh*th*ira (firm in fight), the eldest, was son of Dharma, the judge of the dead, and is considered a pattern of manly firmness, justice, and integrity. Bhīma or Bhīma-sena (the terrible), the second, was son of Vāyu, the god of the wind. He was noted for his strength, daring, and brute courage; but he was coarse, choleric, and given to vaunting. He was such a great eater that he was called V*ri*kodara, 'wolf's belly.' Arjuna (the bright or silvery), the third, was son of Indra, the god of the sky. He is the most prominent character, if not the hero, of the poem. He was brave as the bravest, high-minded, generous, tender-hearted, and chivalric in his notions of honour. Nakula and Saha-deva, the fourth and fifth sons, were the twin children of Mādrī by the A*s*winī Kumāras, the twin sons of Sūrya, the sun. They were brave, spirited, and amiable, but they do not occupy such prominent positions as their elder brothers.

Dh*ri*ta-rāsh*t*ra, who reigned at Hastinā-pura, was blind. By his wife Gāndhārī he had a hundred sons, and one daughter named Du*h*-salā. This numerous offspring was owing to a blessing from Vyāsa, and was produced in a marvellous way. (*See* Gāndhārī.) From their ancestor Kuru these princes were known as the Kauravas. The eldest of them, Dur-yodhana (hard to subdue), was their leader, and was a bold, crafty, malicious man, an embodiment of all that is bad in a prince. While the Pā*nd*u princes were yet children, they, on the death of their father, were brought to Dh*ri*ta-rāsh*t*ra, and presented to him as his nephews. He took charge of them, showed them great kindness, and had them educated with his own sons. Differences and dislikes soon arose, and the juvenile emulation and rivalry of the princes ripened into bitter hatred on the part of the Kauravas. This broke into an open flame when Dh*ri*ta-rāsh*t*ra nominated Yudhi-sh*th*ira as his Yuva-rāja or heir-apparent. The jealousy and the opposition of his sons to this act was so great that Dh*ri*ta-rāsh*t*ra sent the Pā*nd*avas away to Vāra*n*āvata, where they dwelt in retirement. While they were living there Dur-yodhana plotted to destroy his cousins by setting fire to their house, which he had caused to be made very combustible All the five brothers were for a time supposed to have perished in the fire, but they had received timely warning from Vidura, and they escaped to the forest, where they dressed and lived in disguise as Brāhmans upon alms.

While the Pā*nd*avas were living in the forest they heard that Draupada, king of the Pānchālas, had proclaimed a swayam-vara, at which his daughter Draupadī was to select her husband from among the princely and warlike suitors. They went there, still disguised as Brāhmans. Arjuna bent the mighty bow which had defied the strength of the Kauravas and all other competitors, and the Pā*nd*avas were victorious over every opponent. They threw off their disguise, and Draupadī was won by Arjuna. The brothers then conducted Draupadī to their home. On their arrival they told their mother Kuntī that they had made a great acquisition, and she unwittingly directed them to share it among them. The mother's command could not be evaded, and Vyāsa confirmed her direction; so Draupadī became the wife in common of the five brothers, and it was arranged that she should dwell for two days in the house of each of the five brothers in succession. This marriage has been justified by a piece of special pleading, which contends that the five princes were all portions of one deity, and therefore only one distinct person, to whom a woman might lawfully be married.

This public appearance made known the existence of the Pā*nd*avas. Their uncle Dh*r*itā-rāsh*t*ra recalled them to his court and divided his kingdom between his own sons and them. His sons received Hastinā-pura, and the chief city given to his nephews was Indra-prastha on the river Yamunā, close to the modern Delhi, where the name still survives. The close proximity of Hastinā-pura and Indra-prastha shows that the territory of Dh*r*ita-rāsh*t*ra must have been of very moderate extent. The reign of Yudhi-sh*th*ira was a pattern of justice and wisdom. Having conquered many countries, he announced his intention of performing the Rāja-sūya sacrifice, thus setting up a claim to universal dominion, or at least to be a king over kings. This excited still more the hatred and envy of the sons of Dh*r*ita-rāsh*t*ra, who induced their father to invite the Pā*nd*avas to Hastinā-pura. The Kauravas had laid their plot, and insidiously prevailed upon Yudhi-sh*th*ira to gamble. His opponent was *S*akuni, uncle of the Kaurava princes, a great gambler and a cheat. Yudhi-sh*th*ira lost his all: his wealth, his palace, his kingdom, his brothers, himself, and, last of all, their wife. Draupadī was brought into the assembly as a slave, and when she rushed out she was dragged back again by her hair by Du*h*-śāsana, an insult for which Bhīma vowed to drink his blood. Dur-yodhana also insulted her by seating her upon his thigh, and Bhīma vowed that he would smash that thigh. Both these vows he afterwards performed. Through the interference and commands of Dh*ri*ta-rāsh*t*ra the possessions of Yudhi-sh*th*ira were restored to him. But he was once more tempted to play, upon the condition that if he lost he and his brothers should pass twelve years in the forest, and should remain incognito during the thirteenth year. He was again the loser, and retired with his brothers and wife into exile. In the thirteenth year they entered the service of the king of Virā*t*a in disguise—Yudhi-sh*th*ira as a Brāhman skilful as a gamester; Bhīma as a cook; Arjuna as a eunuch and teacher of music and dancing; Nakula as a horse-trainer; and Saha-deva as a herdsman. Draupadī also took service as attendant and needlewoman of the queen, Su-desh*n*ā. The five princes each assumed two names, one for use among themselves and one for public use. Yudhi-sh*th*ira was Jaya in private, Kanka in public; Bhīma was Jayanta and Ballava; Arjuna was Vijaya and B*ri*han-nala; Nakula was Jaya-sena and Granthika; Saha-deva was Jayad-bala and Arish*t*a-nemi, a Vai*s*ya. The beauty of Draupadī attracted Kīchaka, brother of the queen, and the chief man in the kingdom. He endeavoured to seduce her, and Bhīma killed him. The relatives of Kīchaka were about to burn Draupadī on his funeral pile, but Bhīma appeared as a wild Gandharva and rescued her. The brothers grew in favour, and rendered great assistance to the king in repelling the attacks of the king of Trigartta and the Kauravas. The time of exile being expired, the princes made themselves known, and Abhimanyu, son of Arjuna, received Uttara, the king's daughter, in marriage.

The Pā*nd*avas now determined to attempt the recovery of their kingdom. The king of Virā*t*a became their firm ally, and preparations for the war began. Allies were sought on all sides. K*ri*sh*n*a and Bala-rāma, being relatives of both parties, were reluctant to fight. K*ri*sh*n*a conceded to Arjuna and Dur-yodhana the choice of himself unarmed or of a large army. Arjuna chose K*ri*sh*n*a and Dur-yodhana joyfully accepted the army. K*ri*sh*n*a agreed to act as charioteer of his especial friend Arjuna. It was in this capacity that he is represented to have spoken the divine song Bhagavad-gītā, when the rival armies were drawn up for battle at Kuru-kshetra, a plain north of Delhi. Many battles follow. The army of Dur-yodhana is commanded in succession by his great-uncle Bhīshma, Dro*n*a his military preceptor, Kar*n*a, king of Anga, and *S*alya, king of Madra and brother of Mādrī. Bhīshma was wounded by Arjuna, but survived for a time. All the others fell in succession, and at length only three of the Kuru warriors—K*ri*pa, A*s*watthāman, and K*ri*ta-varma—were left alive with Dur-yodhana. Bhīma and Dur-yodhana fought in single combat with maces, and Dur-yodhana had his thigh broken and was mortally wounded. The three surviving Kauravas fell by night upon the camp of the Pā*nd*avas and destroyed five children of the Pā*nd*avas, and all the army except the five brothers themselves. These five boys were sons of Draupadī, one by each of the five brothers. Yudhi-sh*t*hira's son was Prativindhya, Bhīma's was *S*ruta-soma, Arjuna's was *S*ruta-kīrtti, Nakula's was *S*atānīka, and Saha-deva's was *S*ruta-karman. Yudhi-sh*t*hira and his brothers then went to Hastinā-pura, and after a reconciliation with Dh*ri*ta-rash*t*ra, Yudhi-sh*t*hira was crowned there. But he was greatly depressed and troubled at the loss of kindred and friends. Soon after he was seated on the throne, the A*s*wa-medha sacrifice was performed with great ceremony, and the Pā*nd*avas lived in peace and prosperity.

The old blind king Dhrita-rāsh*t*ra could not forget or forgive the loss of his sons, and mourned especially for Dur-yodhana. Bitter reproaches and taunts passed between him and Bhīma; at length he, with his wife Gāndhārī, with Kuntī, mother of the Pā*nd*avas, and with some of his ministers, retired to a hermitage in the woods, where, after two years' residence, they perished in a forest fire. Deep sorrow and remorse seized upon the Pā*nd*avas, and after a while Yudhi-sh*t*hira abdicated his throne and departed with his brothers to the Himālayas, in order to reach the heaven of Indra on Mount Meru. A dog followed them from Hastinā-pura. The story of this journey is full of grandeur and tenderness, and has been most effectively rendered into English by Professor Goldstücker. Sins and moral defects now prove fatal to the pilgrims. First fell Draupadī: "too great was her love for Arjuna." Next Saha-deva: "he esteemed none equal to himself." Then Nakula: "ever was the thought in his heart, There is none equal in beauty to me." Arjuna's turn came next: "In one day I could destroy all my enemies." "Such was Arjuna's boast, and he falls, for he fulfilled it not." When Bhīma fell he inquired the reason of his fall, and he was told, "When thou gazedst on thy foe, thou hast cursed him with thy breath; therefore thou fallest to-day." Yudhi-sh*th*ira went on alone with the dog until he reached the gate of heaven. He was invited by Indra to enter, but he refused unless his brothers and Draupadī were also received. "Not even into thy heaven would I enter if they were not there." He is assured that they are already there, and is again told to enter "wearing his body of flesh." He again refuses unless, in the words of Pope, "admitted to that equal sky, his faithful dog shall bear him company." Indra expostulates in vain. "Never, come weal or come woe, will I abandon yon faithful dog." He is at length admitted, but to his dismay he finds there Dur-yodhana and his enemies, but not his brothers or Draupadī. He refuses to remain in heaven without them, and is conducted to the jaws of hell, where he beholds terrific sights and hears wailings of grief and anguish. He recoils, but well-known voices implore him to remain and assuage their sufferings. He triumphs in this crowning trial, and resolves to share the fate of his friends in hell rather than abide with their foes in heaven. Having endured this supreme test, the whole scene is shown to be the effect of *māyā* or illusion, and he and his brothers and friends dwell with Indra in full content of heart for ever.

Such is the leading story of the Mahā-bhārata, which no doubt had a basis of fact in the old Hindu traditions. Different poets of different ages have added to it and embellished it by the powers of their imagination. Great additions have been made in later times. The Bhagavad-gītā and the episode of Nala, with some others, are the productions of later writers; the Hari-van*s*a, which affects to be a part of the Mahā-bhārata, is of still later date, and besides these, it cannot be doubted that numerous interpolations, from single verses to long passages, have been made to uphold and further the religious opinions of sects and individuals. To use the words of Max Müller, "The epic character of the story has throughout been changed and almost obliterated by the didactic tendencies of the latest editors, who were clearly Brāhmans brought up in the strict school of the laws of Manu."

The date of the Mahā-bhārata is very uncertain, and is at best a matter of conjecture and deduction. As a compiled work it is generally considered to be about a century later in date than the Rāmāyana, though there can be no doubt that the general thread of the story, and the incidents directly connected with it, belong to a period of time anterior to the story and scenes of that epic. The fact that the scene of the Mahā-bhārata is in Upper India, while that of the Rāmāyana is in the Dakhin and Ceylon, is of itself sufficient to raise a strong presumption in favour of the superior antiquity of the former. Weber shows that the Mahā-bhārata was known to Dion Chrysostom in the second half of the first century A.D.; and as Megasthenes, who was in India about 315 B.C., says nothing about the epic, Weber's hypothesis is that the date of the Mahā-bhārata is between the two. Professor Williams believes that "the earliest or pre-brahmanical composition of both epics took place at a period not later than the fifth century B.C.," but that "the first orderly completion of the two poems in their Brahmanised form may have taken place in the case of the Rāmāyana about the beginning of the third century B.C., and in the case of the Mahā-bhārata still later." Lassen thinks that three distinct arrangements of the Mahā-bhārata are distinctly traceable. The varied contents of the Mahā-bhārata and their disjointed arrangement afford some warrant for these opinions, and although the Rāmāyana is a compact, continuous, and complete poem, the professed work of one author, there are several recensions extant which differ considerably from each other. Taking a wide interval, but none too wide for a matter of such great uncertainty, the two poems may be considered as having assumed a complete form at some period in the six centuries preceding the Christian era, and that the Rāmāyana had the priority. The complete text of the Mahā-bhārata has been twice printed in India, and a complete translation in French by Fauche has been interrupted by his death. But M. Fauche's translations are not in much repute. This particular one, says Weber, "can only pass for a translation in a very qualified sense." Many episodes and portions of the poem have been printed and translated. The following is a short epitome of the eighteen books of the Mahā-bhārata:—

1. *Ādi-parva*, 'Introductory book.' Describes the genealogy of the two families, the birth and nurture of Dhrita-rāshtra and Pāndu, their marriages, the births of the hundred sons of the former and the five of the latter, the enmity and rivalry between

the young princes of the two branches, and the winning of Draupadī at the swayam-vara.

2. *Sabhā-parva*, 'Assembly book.' The assembly of the princes at Hastinā-pura when Yudhi-shthira lost his kingdom and the Pāndavas had to retire into exile.

3. *Vana-parva*, 'Forest chapter.' The life of the Pāndavas in the Kāmyaka forest. This book is one of the longest and contains many episodes: among them the story of Nala, and an outline of the story of the Rāmāyana.

4. *Virāta-parva*, 'Virāta chapter.' Adventures of the Pāndavas in the thirteenth year of their exile, while they were in the service of King Virāta.

5. *Udyoga-parva*, 'Effort book.' The preparations of both sides for war.

6. *Bhīshma-parva*, 'Book of Bhīshma.' The battles fought while Bhīshma commanded the Kaurava army.

7. *Drona-parva*, 'The Book of Drona.' Drona's command of the Kaurava army.

8. *Karna-parva*, 'Book of Karna.' Karna's command and his death at the hands of Arjuna.

9. *Salya-parva*, 'Book of Salya.' Salya's command, in which Dur-yodhana is mortally wounded and only three Kauravas are left alive.

10. *Sauptika-parva*, 'Nocturnal book.' The night attack of the three surviving Kauravas on the Pāndava camp.

11. *Strī-parva*, 'Book of the women.' The lamentations of Queen Gāndhārī and the women over the slain.

12. *Sānti-parva*, 'Book of consolation.' A long and diffuse didactic discourse by Bhīshma on the morals and duties of kings, intended to assuage the grief of Yudhi-shthira.

13. *Anusāsana-parva*, 'Book of precepts.' A continuation of Bhīshma's discourses and his death.

14. *Aswa-medhika-parva*, 'Book of the Aswa-medha.' Yudhi-shthira's performance of the horse sacrifice.

15. *Āsrama-parva*, 'Book of the hermitage.' The retirement of Dhrita-rashtra, Gāndhārī, and Kuntī to a hermitage in the woods, and their death in a forest fire.

16. *Mausala-parva*, 'Book of the clubs.' The death of Krishna and Bala-rāma, the submersion of Dwārakā by the sea, and the mutual destruction of the Yādavas in a fight with clubs (*musala*) of miraculous origin.

17. *Mahā-prasthānika-parva*, 'Book of the great journey.' Yudhi-sh*t*hira's abdication of the throne, and his departure with his brothers towards the Himālayas on their way to Indra's heaven on Mount Meru.

18. *Swargārohana-parva*, 'Book of the ascent to heaven.' Entrance into heaven of Yudhi-sh*t*hira and his brothers, and of their wife Draupadī.

The Hari-va*n*sa (q.v.), detailing the genealogy, birth, and life of K*r*ish*n*a at great length, is a supplement of much later date.

GENEALOGY OF THE KAURAVAS AND PA*N*DAVAS.

Atri, the *R*ishi.
Soma (Chandra or Indu), the Moon.
Budha.
Āyu.
Nahusha.
Devayānī + Yayāti + Sarmish*t*hā.

Yādavas.
Yadu (and another son).
V*r*ish*n*i.
Devarāta.
Andhaka.
***S*ūra.**
Vasudeva. Kuntī.
K*r*ish*n*a. Bala-rāma.
(Line extinct.)

Puru (and two other sons).
Pauravas.
Dushyanta + *S*akuntalā.
Bharata.
Hastin.
Kuru.
Gangā + *S*āntanu + Satyavatī.
Bhīshma. Chitrāngada. Vichitra-vīrya.
Vyāsa + the two widows of Vichitra-vīrya.
Ambikā. Ambālikā.
Dh*r*ita-rāsh*t*ra + Gāndhārī.
Dur-yodhana and 99 other sons.
Kuntī + Pā*n*du + Mādrī.
Kar*n*a. Yudhi-sh*t*hira. Bhīma. Arjuna. Nakula. Saha-deva.
Abhimanyu.
Parikshit.
Janamejaya.

(*See* Chandra-vansa for the intervening and following names.)

MAHĀ-BHĀSHYA. A commentary by Patanjali on the Grammar of Pāṇini, in answer to the criticisms of Kātyāyana. A fine photo-lithographed edition has been produced, under the superintendence of Professor Goldstücker, at the expense of the Indian Government. The work has received a long notice in Weber's *Indische Studien*, vol. xiii., and has been the subject of much discussion in the *Indian Antiquary*. Other editions have appeared in India.

MAHĀ-BHOJA. *See* Bhoja.

MAHĀ-DEVA. 'The great god.' A name of *S*iva. One of the Rudras.

MAHĀ-DEVĪ. 'The great goddess.' A name of Devī, the wife of *S*iva. *See* Devī.

MAHĀ-KĀLA. 'Great Time.' 1. A name of *S*iva in his destructive character. (*See S*iva.) 2. One of the twelve great Lingas. (*See* Linga.) 3. In the caves of Elephanta this form of *S*iva is represented with eight arms. In one hand he holds a human figure; in another, a sword or sacrificial axe; in a third, a basin of blood; in a fourth, the sacrificial bell; with two he is drawing behind him the veil which extinguishes the sun; and two are broken off. 4. Chief of the Ga*n*as or attendants on *S*iva.

MAHĀ-KĀVYAS. 'Great poems.' Six are classified under this title:—(1.) Raghu-van*s*a; (2) Kumāra-sambhava; (3.) Megha-dūta; (4.) Kirātārjunīya; (5.) *S*i*s*upāla-badha; (6.) Naishadha-charitra.

MAHĀ-MĀYĀ. *See* Māyā.

MAHĀ-NĀ*T*AKA. 'The great drama.' The Hanumān-nā*t*aka (q.v.).

MAHĀ-PADMA NANDA. The last of the Nanda dynasty. *See* Chandra-gupta.

MAHĀ-PRALAYA. A total dissolution of the universe at the end of a kalpa, when the seven lokas and their inhabitants, men, saints, gods, and Brahmā himself, are annihilated. Called also Jahānaka, Kshiti, and Sanhāra.

MAHĀ-PURĀ*N*AS. 'The great Purā*n*as.' The Vishnu and the Bhāgavata, the two great Purā*n*as of the Vaishnavas.

MAHĀ-PURUSHA. 'The great or supreme male;' the supreme spirit. A name of Vish*n*u.

MAHĀRĀJIKAS. A Ga*n*a or class of inferior deities, 236 or 220 in number.

MAHAR. *See* Vyāh*ri*ti.

MAHĀ-RĀSH*T*RA. The land of the Mahrattas.

MAHAR-LOKA. *See* Loka.

MAHARSHIS (Mahā-*ri*shis). 'Great *Ri*shis.' The great *Ri*shis or Prajāpatis. *See Ri*shi.

MAHĀ-SENA. 'The great captain.' A name of Kārtikeya, god of war.

MAHAT. The great intellect produced at the creation. *See* Vish*n*u Purā*n*a, i. 29.

MĀHĀTMYA. 'Magnanimity.' A legend of a shrine or other holy place.

MAHĀ-VĪRA CHARITA. 'The exploits of the great hero (Rāma).' A drama by Bhava-bhūti, translated into English by Pickford. There are several editions of the text. "The situations and sentiments of this drama are of a stirring and martial description, and the language is adapted with singular felicity to the subject from which it springs."—*Wilson.*

MAHĀ-YOGĪ. 'The great ascetic.' A name of *S*iva.

MAHĀ-YUGA. A great Yuga or age, consisting of 4,320,000 years. *See* Yuga.

MAHENDRA. A name of Indra. One of the seven mountain ranges of India; the hills which run from Gondwāna to Orissa and the Northern Circars. *See* Kula-parvatas.

MAHE*S*WARA. A name of *S*iva.

MĀHE*S*WARA PURĀ*N*A. *See* Purā*n*a.

MAHISHA, MAHISHĀSURA. 1. The great Asura or demon killed by Skanda in the Mahā-bhārata. (*See* Krauncha.) 2. Also a demon killed by Cha*n*dā or Durgā.

MAHISHMATĪ, MĀHISHMATĪ. The capital of Kārtavīrya, king of the Tālajanghas, who had a thousand arms. It has been identified by Colonel Tod with the village of Chuli Mahe*s*war, which, according to him, is still called "the village of the thousand-armed."

MAHODAYA. A name of the city of Kanauj.

MAHORAGA (Mahā + uraga). 'Great serpent.' The serpent *S*esha, or any other great serpent.

MAINĀKA. A mountain stated in the Mahā-bhārata to be north of Kailāsa; so called as being the son of Himavat and Menakā. When, as the poets sing, Indra clipped the wings of the mountains, this is said to have been the only one which escaped.

This mountain, according to some, stands in Central India, and, according to others, near the extremity of the Peninsula.

MAITREYA. A *R*ishi, son of Kusarava, and disciple of Parāsara. He is one of the interlocutors in the Vish*n*u and Bhāgavata Purā*n*as.

MAITREYĪ. Wife of the *R*ishi Yājnawalkya, who was indoctrinated by her husband in the mysteries of religion and philosophy.

MAITRI, MAITRĀYA*N*I. An Upanishad of the Black Yajur-veda. It has been edited and translated by Professor Cowell for the *Bibliotheca Indica.*

MĀKANDĪ. A city on the Ganges, the capital of Southern Panchāla.

MAKARA. A huge sea animal, which has been taken to be the crocodile, the shark, the dolphin, &c., but is probably a fabulous animal. It represents the sign Capricornus in the Hindu zodiac, and is depicted with the head and forelegs of an antelope and the body and tail of a fish. It is the vehicle of Varu*n*a, the god of the ocean, and its figure is borne on the banner of Kāma-deva, god of love. It is also called Ka*n*/aka, Asita-dansh*t*ra, 'black teeth,' and Jala-rūpa, 'water form.'

MĀKĀRAS. The five *m*'s. *See* Tantra.

MAKHAVAT. A name of Indra.

MĀLATĪ-MĀDHAVA (Mālatī and Mādhava). A drama by Bhava-bhūti, translated by Wilson. "This drama," says the translator, "offers nothing to offend the most fastidious delicacy, and may be compared in this respect advantageously with many of the dramas of modern Europe which treat of the passion (of love) that constitutes its subject."

MĀLAVA. The country of Mālwa.

MĀLAVIKĀGNIMITRA (Mālavika and Agnimitra). A drama ascribed to Kāli-dāsa, and although inferior to his other productions, it is probably his work. The text, with a translation, has been published by Tullberg. There is a German translation by Weber, an English one by Tawney, and a French one by Foucaux. The text has been printed at Bombay and Calcutta.

MALAYA. The country of Malabar proper; the mountains bordering Malabar. *See* Kula-parvatas.

MALINA-MUKHA. 'Black faced.' Rākshasas and other demons, represented as having black faces.

MĀLINĪ. 'Surrounded with a garland (*māla*)' of Champa trees. A name of the city of Champā.

MALLIKĀRJUNA. A name of *S*iva. One of the twelve great Lingas. *See* Linga.

MALLINĀTHA. A poet, and author of commentaries of great repute on several of the great poems, as the Raghu-vansa, Megha-dūta, *S*isupāla-badha, &c.

MĀNASA. 'The intellectual.' A name of the supreme being. Thus defined in the Mahā-bhārata: "The primeval god, without beginning or dissolution, indivisible, undecaying, and immortal, who is known and called by great *R*ishis Mānasa."

MĀNASA, MĀNASA-SAROVARA. The lake Mānasa in the Himālayas. In the Vāyu Purā*n*a it is stated that when the ocean fell from heaven upon Mount Meru, it ran four times round the mountain, then it divided into four rivers which ran down the mountain and formed four great lakes, Aru*n*oda on the east, Sitoda on the west, Mahā-bhadra on the north, and Mānasa on the south. According to the mythological account, the river Ganges flows out of it, but in reality no river issues from this lake, though the river Satlej flows from another and larger lake called Rāva*n*a-hrāda, which lies close to the west of Mānasa.

MANASĀ, MANASĀ-DEVĪ. Sister of the serpent king *S*esha, and wife of the sage Jarat-kāru. She is also called Jagad-gaurī, Nityā (eternal), and Padmāvatī. She had special power in counteracting the venom of serpents, and was hence called Visha-harā.

MĀNASĀ-PUTRAS. 'Mind (born) sons.' The seven or ten mind-born sons of Brahmā. *See* Prajāpati.

MANAS-TĀLA. The lion on which Devī rides.

MĀNAVA DHARMA-*S*ĀSTRA. The code of Manu. *See* Manu Sanhitā.

MĀNAVA KALPA-SŪTRA. Manu's work on Vaidik rites. Part of it has been published in facsimile by Goldstücker.

MĀNAVA PURĀ*N*A. *See* Purā*n*a.

MĀNAVĪ. The wife of Manu. Also called Manāyī.

MANDA-KAR*N*I. A sage who dwelt in the Da*nd*aka forest, and is said in the Rāmāya*n*a to have formed a lake which was known by his name. His austerities alarmed the gods, and Indra sent five Apsarases to beguile him from his penance of "standing in a pool and feeding on nothing but air for 10,000 years." They succeeded, and became his wives, and inhabited a house concealed in the lake, which, from them, was called Panchāpsaras.

MANDĀKINĪ. The heavenly Ganges. The Ganges. An arm of the Ganges which flows through Kedāra-nātha. A river near the mountain Chitra-kūta (q.v.) in Bundelkhand. It was near the abode of Rāma and Sītā, and is mentioned both in the Rāmāyana and Mahā-bhārata. It would seem to be the modern Pisuni.

MANDALA. 'A circle, orb.' A circuit or territorial division, as Chola-mandala, *i.e.*, Coromandel. According to one arrangement, the Sanhitā of the *Rig*-veda is divided into ten Mandalas.

MANDALA-NRITYA. A circular dance. The dance of the Gopīs round Krishna and Rādhā.

MANDA-PĀLA. A childless saint, who, according to the Mahā-bhārata, after long perseverance in devotion and asceticism, died and went to the abode of Yama. His desires being still unsatisfied, he inquired the cause, and was told that all his devotions had failed because he had no son, no *putra* (*put*, 'hell,' *tra*, 'drawer'), to save him from hell. He then assumed the form of a species of bird called Sārngikā, and by a female of that species, who was called Jaritā, he had four sons.

MANDARA. The great mountain which the gods used for the churning of the ocean. It is supposed to be the mountain so named in Bhāgalpur, which is held sacred. *See* Kūrma-avatāra, under Avatāra.

MĀNDAVĪ. Daughter of Kusa-dhwaja, cousin of Sītā, and wife of Rāma's brother Bharata.

MANDEHAS. A class of terrific Rākshasas, who were hostile to the sun and endeavoured to devour him.

MĀNDHĀTRI. A king, son of Yuvanāswa, of the race of Ikshwāku, and author of a hymn in the *Rig*-veda. The Harivansa and some of the Purānas make Māndhātri to have been born in a natural way from his mother Gaurī, but the Vishnu and Bhāgavata Purānas tell an extraordinary story about his birth, which is probably based upon a forced derivation of his name. Yuvanāswa had no son, which grieved him much. Some holy sages near whom he lived instituted a religious rite to procure progeny for him. One night they placed a consecrated vessel of water upon an altar as part of their ceremony, and the water became endowed with prolific energy. Yuvanāswa woke up in the night thirsty, and finding the water, he drank it. So he conceived, and in due time a child came forth from his right side. The sages then asked who would suckle the child, whereupon Indra appeared, gave his finger for the child to suck, and said, "He shall suck me," *mām ayam dhāsyati.* These words were contracted, and the boy was named Māndhātri. When he grew up he had three sons and fifty daughters. An old sage named Saubhari came to Māndhātri and asked that one might be given him to wife. Unwilling to give one to so old and emaciated a man, but yet afraid to refuse, the king temporised, but at length yielded to the sage's request that the matter might be left to the choice of the girls. Saubhari then assumed a handsome form, and there was such a contention for him that he had to marry the whole fifty, and he provided for them a row of crystal palaces in a most beautiful garden.

MANDODARĪ. Rāvana's favourite wife and the mother of Indra-jit.

MĀNDUKEYA. A teacher of the *Rig*-veda, who derived his knowledge from his father, Indra-pramati.

MĀNDUKYA. Name of an Upanishad translated by Dr. Roer in the *Bibliotheca Indica.*

MANGALA. The planet Mars, identified with Kārtikeya, the god of war. He was son of Siva and the Earth, and as son of the Earth is called Angāraka, Bhauma, Bhūmi-putra, Mahīsuta. He is also called Siva-gharma-ja, 'born of the sweat of Siva;' Gaganolmuka, 'the torch of the sky;' Lohita, 'the red;' Navārchi, 'the nine-rayed;' Chara, 'the spy;' *Rin*āntaka, 'ender of debts, patron of debtors.' *See* Kārtikeya.

MANI-BHADRA. The chief of the Yakshas and guardian of travellers.

MANIMAT. A Rākshasa slain by Bhīma.

MANI-PURA. A city on the sea-coast of Kalinga, where Babhru-vāhana, the son of Arjuna, dwelt. Wheeler identifies it with the modern Munnipur or Muneepore, east of Bengal; but this is very questionable.

MANMATHA. A name of Kāma, god of love.

MANTHARĀ. An ugly deformed slave, nurse of Queen Kaikeyī, who stirred up her mistress's jealousy against Rāma-chandra, and led her to persuade King Dasa-rathā to banish Rāma from court. *S*atru-ghna beat her and threatened to kill her, but she was saved by his brother Bharata.

MANTRA. That portion of the Veda which consists of hymns, as distinct from the Brāhma*n*as. *See* Veda.

MANU. (From the root *man*, to think.) 'The man.' This name belongs to fourteen mythological progenitors of mankind and rulers of the earth, each of whom holds sway for the period called a Manwantara (*manu-antara*), the age of a Manu, *i.e.*, a period of no less than 4,320,000 years. The first of these Manus was Swāyam-bhuva, who sprang from Swayam-bhū, the self-existent. The self-existent, as identified with Brahmā the creator, divided himself into two persons, male and female. From this pair was produced the male Virāj, and from him sprang the Manu Swāyam-bhuva. As the acting creator, this Manu produced the ten Prajāpatis or progenitors of mankind, called also Maharshis (*mahā-rishis*). According to another account, this Manu sprang from the incestuous intercourse of Brahmā with his daughter and wife, *S*ata-rūpā. Brahmā created himself Manu, "born of and identical with his original self, and the female portion of himself he constituted *S*ata-rūpā," whom Manu took to wife. The law-book commonly known as Manu is ascribed to this Manu, and so also is a Sūtra work on ritual bearing the same name. The Manu of the present age is the seventh, named Vaivaswata, 'sun-born,' who was the son of Vivaswat, the sun, and he is a Kshatriya by race. He is also called Satya-vrata. There are various legends about his having been saved from a great flood by Vish*n*u or Brahmā. The names of the fourteen Manus are—(1.) Swāyam-bhuva, (2.) Swārochisha, (3.) Auttami, (4.) Tāmasa, (5.) Raivata, (6.) Chākshusha, (7.) Vaivaswata or Satya-vrata, (8.) Sāvar*n*a, (9.) Daksha-sāvar*n*a, (10.) Brahma-sāvar*n*a, (11.) Dharma-sāvar*n*a, (12.) Sāvar*n*a or Rudra-sāvar*n*a, (13.) Rauchya, (14.) Bhautya.

The sons of Manu Vaivaswata were—Ikshwāku, Nabhaga or N*ri*ga, Dh*ri*sh*t*a, *S*aryāti, Narishyanta, Prān*s*u, Nābhāganedish*t*a or Nābhānedish*t*a, Karūsha, and P*ri*shadhra. But there is some variety in the names.

With the seventh Manu, Vaivaswata, is connected the very curious and interesting legend of the deluge. The first account of this is found in the *S*atapatha Brāhma*n*a, of which the following is a summary :—One morning, in the water which was brought to Manu for washing his hands, he caught a fish which spake, and said, "Take care of me and I will preserve thee." Manu asked, "From what wilt thou preserve me?" The fish answered, "A flood will carry away all living beings; I will save thee from that." The fish desired Manu to keep him alive in an earthen vessel, to remove him to a dyke as he grew larger, and eventually to the ocean, "so that he might be beyond the risk of destruction." The fish grew rapidly, and again addressed Manu, saying, "After so many years the deluge will take place; then construct a ship and pay me homage, and when the waters rise, go into the ship and I will rescue thee." Manu did as he was desired, he built the ship, conveyed the fish to the ocean, and did him homage. The flood rose, and Manu fastened the cable of the ship to the fish's horn. Thus he passed over the northern mountain (the Himālaya, as the commentator explains). The fish then desired Manu to fasten the ship to a tree, and to go down with the subsiding waters. He did so, and found that the flood had swept away all living creatures. He alone was left. Desirous of offspring, he offered sacrifice and engaged in devotion. A woman was produced, who came to Manu and declared herself his daughter. "With her he lived, worshipping and toiling in arduous religious rites, desirous of offspring. With her he begat the offspring which is the offspring of Manu."

The story, as told in the Mahā-bhārata, represents Manu as engaged in devotion by the side of a river, and the fish craving his protection from the bigger fish. Manu placed the fish in a glass vase, but it grew larger and larger till the ocean alone could contain it. Then it warned Manu of the coming flood, and directed him to build a ship and to embark with the seven *Ri*shis. He did so, and fastened his ship to the horn of the fish. Then, according to the rendering of Professor Williams—

"Along the ocean in that stately ship was borne the lord of men, and through
Its dancing, tumbling billows and its roaring waters; and the bark,
Tossed to and fro by violent winds, reeled on the surface of the deep,
Staggering and trembling like a drunken woman: land was seen no more,

Nor far horizon, nor the space between ; for everywhere around
Spread the wild waste of waters, reeking atmosphere, and boundless sky.
And now, when all the world was deluged, nought appeared above the waves
But Manu and the seven sages, and the fish that drew the bark.
Unwearied thus for years on years that fish pulled on the ship across
The heaped-up waters, till at length it bore the vessel to the peak
Of Himavān ; then, softly smiling, thus the fish addressed the sage :
'Haste now to bind thy ship to this high crag. Know me, the lord of all,
The great creator Brahmā, mightier than all might, omnipotent.
By me, in fish-like shape, have you been saved in dire emergency.
From Manu all creation, gods, Asuras, men, must be produced ;
By him the world must be created, that which moves and moveth not.'"

The commentators on this legend of the Mahā-bhārata give a metaphysical turn to the legend, and endeavour to illustrate it by philosophical and allegorical interpretations. The same story is reproduced with variations in the Matsya, Bhāgavata, and Agni Purānas, and Muir has given translations of the passages in vol. i. of his *Sanskrit Texts.*

In the Rāmāyana mention is made of a female Manu, and it appears that the word is sometimes used for "the wife of Manu."

MANU-SANHITĀ. The well-known law-book, the Code of Manu, or Institutes of Manu. It is attributed to the first Manu, Swāyam-bhuva, who existed nearly thirty millions of years ago, but it bears the marks of being the production of more than one mind. This is the first and chief of the works classified as Smriti, and is a collection or digest of current laws and creeds rather than a planned systematic code. It is the foundation of Hindu law, and is held in the highest reverence. The work belongs to a period later than that of the Vedas, when the Brāhmans had obtained the ascendancy, but its deities are those of the Vedic rather than the Epic or Purānic age. It is apparently anterior to the philosophical schools. The fifth century B.C. is supposed to be about the time when it was composed, but the rules and precepts it contains had probably existed as traditions long before. It is commonly called the Code of Manu, and was current among the Mānavas, a class or school of Brāhmans who were followers of the Black Yajur-veda; but it deals with many subjects besides law, and is a most important record of old Hindu society. It is said to have consisted originally of 100,000 verses, arranged in twenty-four chapters; that Nārada shortened the work to 12,000 verses; and that Sumati made a second abridgment, reducing it to 4000, but only 2685 are extant. It is evident that there was more than one redaction of the laws of the Mānavas, for a B*ri*han or V*ri*han Manu, 'great Manu,' and V*ri*ddha Manu, 'old Manu,' are often referred to. Sir W. Jones's translation, edited by Haughton, is excellent, and is the basis of all others in French, German, &c. The text has often been printed.

MANWANTARA (Manu-antara). The life or period of a Manu, 4,320,000 years.

MĀRĪCHA. A Rākshasa, son of Tārakā. According to the Rāmāya*n*a he interfered with a sacrifice which was being performed by Vi*s*wāmitra, but was encountered by Rāma, who discharged a weapon at him, which drove him one hundred yojanas out to sea. He was afterwards the minister of Rāva*n*a, and accompanied him to the hermitage where Rāma and Sītā were dwelling. There, to inveigle Rāma, he assumed the shape of a golden deer, which Rāma pursued and killed. On receiving his death-wound he resumed a Rākshasa form and spake, and Rāma discovered whom he had killed. In the meanwhile Rāva*n*a had carried off Sītā.

MARĪCHI. Chief of the Maruts. Name of one of the Prajāpatis. (*See* Prajāpati.) He is sometimes represented as springing direct from Brahmā. He was father of Ka*s*yapa, and one of the seven great *Ri*shis. *See Ri*shi.

MĀRISHĀ. Daughter of the sage Ka*nd*u, and wife of the Prachetasas, but from the mode of her birth she is called "the nursling of the trees, and daughter of the wind and the moon." She was mother of Daksha. Her mother was a celestial nymph named Pramlochā, who beguiled the sage Ka*nd*u from his devotions and lived with him for a long time. When the sage awoke from his voluptuous delusion, he drove her from his presence. "She, passing through the air, wiped the perspiration from her with the leaves of the trees," and "the child she had conceived by the *Ri*shi came forth from the pores of her skin in drops of perspiration. The trees received the living dews, and the winds collected them into one mass. Soma matured this by his rays, and gradually it increased in size till the exhalations that had rested on the tree-tops became the lovely girl named Mārishā."—*Vishnu Purāna.* According to the same authority Mārishā had been in a former birth the childless widow of a king. Her devotion to Vish*n*u gained his favour, and he desired her to ask a boon. She bewailed her childless state, and prayed that in succeeding births she might have "honourable husbands and a son equal to a patriarch." She received the promise that she should be of marvellous birth, should be very beautiful, and should have ten husbands of mighty prowess, and a son whose posterity should fill the universe. This legend is no doubt an addition of later date, invented to account for the marvellous origin of Mārishā.

MĀRKA*ND*EYA. A sage, the son of M*ri*ka*nd*a, and reputed author of the Mārka*nd*eya Purā*n*a. He was remarkable for his austerities and great age, and is called Dīrghāyus, 'the long-lived.'

MĀRKA*ND*EYA PURĀ*N*A. "That Purā*n*a in which, commencing with the story of the birds that were acquainted with right and wrong, everything is narrated fully by Mārka*nd*eya as it was explained by holy sages in reply to the question of the Muni, is called the Mārka*nd*eya, containing 9000 verses." This Purā*n*a is narrated in the first place by Mārka*nd*eya, and in the second by certain fabulous birds profoundly versed in the Vedas, who relate their knowledge in answer to the questions of the sage Jaimini. "It has a character different from all the other Purā*n*as. It has nothing of a sectarial spirit, little of a religious tone; rarely inserting prayers and invocations to any deity, and such as are inserted are brief and moderate. It deals little in precepts, ceremonial or moral. Its leading feature is narrative, and it presents an uninterrupted succession of legends, most of which, when ancient, are embellished with new circumstances, and, when new, partake so far of the spirit of the old, that they are disinterested creations of the imagination, having no particular motive, being designed to recommend no special doctrine or observance. Whether they are derived from any other source, or whether they are original inventions, it is not possible to ascertain. They are most probably, for the greater part at least, original;

and the whole has been narrated in the compiler's own manner, a manner superior to that of the Purāṇas in general, with exception of the Bhāgavata." The popular Durgā Māhātmya or Chaṇḍipāṭha is an episode of this Purāṇa. In the absence of any guide to a positive conclusion as to the date, it may conjecturally be placed in the ninth or tenth century. Professor Banerjea places it in the eighth century. This Purāṇa has been published in the *Bibliotheca Indica*, and translated by the Rev. Professor K. M. Banerjea.

MĀRTTĀNDA. In the Vedas the sun or sun god.

MARTYA-MUKHA. 'Human-faced.' Any being in which the figures of a man and animal are combined.

MARUTS. The storm gods, who hold a very prominent place in the Vedas, and are represented as friends and allies of Indra. Various origins are assigned to them. They are sons of Rudra, sons and brothers of Indra, sons of the ocean, sons of heaven, sons of earth. They are armed with lightnings and thunderbolts, and "ride on the whirlwind and direct the storm." The number of them is said in one place to be thrice sixty, and in another only twenty-seven. In the Rāmāyaṇa they are represented to have their origin in an unborn son of Diti, whom Indra dashed into forty-nine pieces with his thunderbolt, and in compassion converted into Maruts. This is also the story told in the Purāṇas, and they are said to have obtained their name from the words *mā rodīh*, 'weep not,' which Indra addressed to them. A scholiast on the Veda says, that after their birth from Diti, as above told, Śiva and Pārvatī beheld them in great affliction, and the latter asked Śiva to transform the lumps of flesh into boys; he accordingly made them boys of like form, like age, and similarly accoutred, and gave them to Pārvatī as her sons, whence they are called the sons of Rudra. Other legends are, that Pārvatī, hearing the lamentations of Diti, entreated Śiva to give forms to the shapeless births, telling them not to weep (*mā rodīh*); and another, that he actually begot them in the form of a bull on Pṛithivī, the earth, as a cow. (*See* Diti.) All these legends have manifestly been invented to explain those passages of the Vedas which make the Maruts the sons of Rudra. The world of the Maruts, called Māruta, is the appointed heaven of Vaiśyas. 2. The god of the wind, and regent of the north-west quarter.

MARUTTA. 1. A descendant of Manu Vaivaswata. He was a Chakravartī, or universal monarch, and performed a celebrated sacrifice. "Never," says the Vish*n*u Purā*n*a, "was beheld on earth a sacrifice equal to the sacrifice of Marutta. All the implements and utensils were made of gold. Indra was intoxicated with the libations of soma juice, and the Brāhmans were enraptured with the magnificent donations they received. The winds of heaven encompassed the rite as guards, and the assembled gods attended to behold it." According to the Vāyu Purā*n*a, Marutta was taken to heaven with his kindred and friends by Samvarta, the officiating priest at this sacrifice. But the Marka*nd*eya Purā*n*a says he was killed after he had laid down his crown and retired to the woods. 2. A king of the Solar race, who was killed by Vapushmat, and fearfully avenged by his son Dama (q.v.).

MĀTALI. Charioteer of Indra.

MATANGA. 'An elephant.' A man who was brought up as a Brāhman but was the son of a Cha*nd*āla. His story, as told in the Mahā-bhārata, relates that he was mercilessly goading an ass's foal which he was driving. The mother ass, seeing this, tells her foal that she could expect no better, for her driver was no Brāhman but a Cha*nd*āla. Matanga, addressing the ass as "most intelligent," begged to know how this was, and was informed that his mother when intoxicated had received the embraces of a low-born barber, and that he, the offspring, was a Cha*nd*āla and no Brāhman. In order to obtain elevation to the position of a Brāhman, he went through such a course of austerities as alarmed the gods. Indra refused to admit him. He persevered again for a hundred years, but still Indra persistently refused such an impossible request, and advised him to seek some other boon. Nothing daunted, he went on a thousand years longer, with the same result. Though dejected he did not despair, but proceeded to balance himself on his great toe. He continued to do this for a hundred years, when he was reduced to mere skin and bone, and was on the point of falling. Indra went to support him, but inexorably refused his request, and, when further importuned, "gave him the power of moving about like a bird, and changing his shape at will, and of being honoured and renowned." In the Rāmāya*n*a, Rāma and Sītā visited the hermitage of Matanga near *R*ishya-mūka mountain.

MĀTARI-SWAN. An aerial being who is represented in the *Rig*-veda as bringing down or producing Agni (fire) for the Bhrigus. By some supposed to be the wind.

MATHURĀ. An ancient and celebrated city on the right bank of the Yamunā, surviving in the modern Muttra. It was the birthplace of Krishna and one of the seven sacred cities. The Vishnu Purāna states that it was originally called Madhu or Madhu-vana, from the demon Madhu, who reigned there, but that when Lavana, his son and successor, was killed by Satrughna, the conqueror set up his own rule there and built a city which he called Madhurā or Mathurā.

MĀTRIS. 'Mothers' The divine mothers. These appear to have been originally the female energies of the great gods, as Brahmānī of Brahmā, Maheswarī of Siva, Vaishnavī of Vishnu, Indrāni or Aindrī of Indra, &c. The number of them was seven or eight or sixteen, but in the later mythology they have increased out of number. They are connected with the Tantra worship, and are represented as worshipping Siva and attending upon his son Kārtikeya.

MATSYA. 'A fish.' 1. The Fish Incarnation. (*See* Avatāra.) 2. Name of a country. Wilson says, "Dinajpoor, Rungpoor, and Cooch Behar;" but there was more than one country of this name, and one would appear to have been situated in Northern India. Manu places Matsya in Brahmarshi. According to the Mahā-bhārata, King Virāta's capital was called Matsya, his people also were called Matsyas, and he himself was styled Matsya. General Cunningham finds it in the neighbourhood of Jaypur, and says that the town of Virāt or Bairāt, 105 miles south of Delhi, was its capital.

MATSYA PURĀNA. This Purāna is so called from its contents having been narrated to Manu by Vishnu in the form of a fish (*matsya*). It consists of between 14,000 and 15,000 stanzas. This work "is a miscellaneous compilation, but includes in its contents the elements of a genuine Purāna. At the same time, it is of too mixed a character to be considered as a genuine work of the Paurānik class. Many of its chapters are the same as parts of the Vishnu and Padma Purānas. It has also drawn largely from the Mahā-bhārata. "Although a Saiva work, it is not exclusively so, and it has no such sectarial absurdities as the Kūrma and Linga."

MAUNEYAS. A class of Gandharvas, sons of Kasyapa, who dwelt beneath the earth, and were sixty millions in number. They overpowered the Nāgas, and compelled them to flee to Vishnu for assistance, and he sent Purukutsa against them, who destroyed them.

MAURYA. The dynasty founded by Chandra-gupta at Pātali-putra (Patna) in Magadha. According to the Vishnu Purāna, the Maurya kings were ten in number and reigned 137 years. Their names were—(1.) Chandra-gupta, (2.) Bindu-sāra, (3.) Asoka-vardhana, (4.) Su-yasas, (5.) Dasa-ratha, (6.) Sangata, (7.) *S*āli-sūka, (8.) Soma-sarman, (9.) *S*asa-dharman, (10.) B*ri*-had-ratha. The names vary in other Purānas. *See* Chandra-gupta.

MAYA. A Daitya who was the architect and artificer of the Asuras, as Viswa-karma was the artificer of the Suras or gods. He was son of Viprachitti and father of Vajra-kāmā and Mando-darī, wife of Rāvana. He dwelt in the Deva-giri mountains not very far from Delhi, and his chief works were in the neighbourhood of that city, where he worked for men as well as Daityas. The Mahā-bhārata speaks of a palace he built for the Pāndavas. In the Hari-vansa he appears frequently both as victor and vanquished in contests with the gods.

MĀYĀ. 'Illusion, deception.' 1. Illusion personified as a female form of celestial origin, created for the purpose of beguiling some individual. Sometimes identified with Durgā as the source of spells, or as a personification of the unreality of worldly things. In this character she is called Māyā-devī or Mahā-māyā. 2. A name of Gayā, one of the seven sacred cities.

MĀYĀ-DEVĪ, MĀYĀ-VATĪ. Wife of the demon *S*ambara. She brought up Pradyumna, the son of K*ri*sh*na*, and subsequently married him. Pradyumna is represented as being a revived embodiment of Kāma, the god of love; and in accordance with this legend Māyā-vatī is identified with his wife Rati, the Hindu Venus. *See* Māyā.

MĀYU. 'Bleater, bellower.' The Kinnaras are called Māyus.

MEDHĀTITHI. Name of a Kānwa who was a Vedic *R*ishi. There is a legend in one of the Upanishads that he was carried up to heaven by Indra in the form of a ram, because the god had been pleased with his austerities. *Cf.* Ganymede.

MEDINĪ. The earth. *See* Kai*t*abha.

MEDINĪ, MEDINĪ-KOSHA. A well-known Sanskrit vocabulary. There are printed editions.

MEGHA-DŪTA. 'Cloud messenger.' A celebrated poem by Kāli-dāsa, in which a banished Yaksha implores a cloud to convey tidings of him to his wife. It has been translated into English verse by Wilson, and there are versions in French and German. The text has been printed with a vocabulary by Johnson.

MEGHA-NĀDA. A son of Rāvana. *See* Indra-jit.

MEKALA. Name of a mountain from which the Narmadā river is said to rise, and from which it is called Mekalā and Mekala-kanyā, 'daughter of Mekala.' There was a people of this name, who probably lived in the vicinity of this mountain. Their kings were also called Mekalas, and there appears to have been a city Mekalā.

MENĀ, MENAKĀ. 1. In the *Rig*-veda, a daughter of Vrishan-aswa. A Brāhmana tells a strange story of Indra having assumed the form of Menā and then fallen in love with her. In the Purānas, wife of Himavat and mother of Umā and Gangā, and of a son named Maināka. 2. An Apsaras sent to seduce the sage Viswāmitra from his devotions, and succeeding in this object, she became the mother of the nymph Sakuntalā.

MERU. A fabulous mountain in the navel or centre of the earth, on which is situated Swarga, the heaven of Indra, containing the cities of the gods and the habitations of celestial spirits. The Olympus of the Hindus. Regarded as a terrestrial object, it would seem to be some mountain north of the Himālayas. It is also Su-meru, Hemādri, 'golden mountain;' Ratnasānu, 'jewel peak;' Karnikāchala, 'lotus mountain;' and Amarādri and Deva-parvata, 'mountain of the gods.'

MERU-SĀVARNAS. The ninth, tenth, eleventh, and twelfth Manus, said to be the "mind-engendered sons of a daughter of Daksha by himself and the three gods Brahmā, Dharma, and Rudra, to whom he presented her on Mount Meru." The signification of the appellation Meru is obvious; that of Sāvarna or Sāvarni signifies that they were all of one caste (*varna*).

MĪMĀNSĀ. A school of philosophy. *See* Darsana.

MĪMĀNSĀ-DARSANA. A work on the Mīmānsā philosophy. Printed in the *Bibliotheca Indica*.

MÎMÂNSÂ-VÂRTTIKA. A work on the Mîmânsâ philosophy by Kumârila Bhaṭṭa.

MINJIKA (mas.) and MINJIKÂ (fem.). Two beings who, according to the Mahâ-bhârata, sprang from the seed of Rudra, which was spilt upon a mountain. They are to be worshipped by those who desire the welfare of children.

MITÂKSHARÂ. A commentary by Vijnâneswara on the Smriti or text-book of Yâjnawalkya. The authority of this book is admitted all over India, with the exception of Bengal proper. The portion on inheritance has been translated by Colebrooke, and into French by Orianne. The text has been printed in India.

MITHILÂ. A city, the capital of Videha or North Bihâr, which corresponds to the modern Tirhut and Puraniya, between the Gandakî and Kosî rivers. It has given its name to one of the five northern nations of Brâhmans (*see* Brâhman), and to a school of law. It was the country of King Janaka, and the name of his capital, Janaka-pura, still survives in "Janakpoor," on the northern frontier.

MITRA. Probably connected with the Persian Mithra. A form of the sun. In the Vedas he is generally associated with Varuna, he being the ruler of the day and Varuna the ruler of the night. They together uphold and rule the earth and sky, guard the world, encourage religion, and chastise sin. He is one of the Âdityas or sons of Aditi.

MITRA-SAHA. A king called also Kalmâsha-pâda (q.v.).

MLECHHAS. Foreigners, barbarians, people not of Âryan race.

MOHA-MUDGARA. 'Hammers for ignorance.' A poem in explanation of the Vedânta philosophy. It has been printed and translated by Nève.

MRICHCHHAKATÎ. 'The toy-cart.' A drama in ten acts by King Sûdraka, supposed to be the oldest Sanskrit drama extant, and to have been written in the first or second century A.D. The country over which Sûdraka reigned is not known. This play, says Wilson, its translator, "is a curious and interesting picture of national manners . . . free from all exterior influence or adulteration. It is a portrait purely Indian. It represents a state of society sufficiently advanced in civilisation to be luxurious and corrupt, and is certainly very far from offering a flattering similitude, although not without some attractive features." Williams observes, "The dexterity with which the plot is arranged, the ingenuity with which the incidents are connected, the skill with which the characters are delineated and contrasted, the boldness and felicity of the diction, are scarcely unworthy of our own great dramatists." There are translations in French and several editions of the text.

MRIGĀNKA-LEKHĀ. A play in four acts, written by Viswa-nātha at Benares. The piece takes its name from the heroine, a princess of Kāmarūpa. It is a comparatively modern work.

MRITYU. 'Death.' A name of Yama, the god of the dead.

MUCHUKUNDA. In the Purānas, son of Māndhātri, and called 'king of men.' He rendered assistance to the gods in their wars with the Asuras or demons, and he asked and obtained as a reward the boon of a long uninterrupted sleep. Whosoever disturbed him was to be burnt to ashes by fire issuing from his body. Kāla-yavana was lured into his cave by Krishna and woke the sleeper, who cast a fiery glance upon the intruder which destroyed him. Muchukunda then paid laud and honour to Krishna, who gave him power to go to whatever celestial region he wished, and to enjoy all heavenly pleasures. Muchukunda left his cave and went to Gandhamādana to perform penance. The Mahā-bhārata says he was reproved by Kuvera for trusting to his priest more than to his own prowess for success in war, but he replied that the religious aid of Brāhmans was as necessary as the warlike powers of Kshatriyas.

MUDGALA. A Vedic Rishi from whom the Maudgalya Brāhmans sprang. There were several other Brāhmans named Mudgala. A sage of this name is recorded in the Mahā-bhārata to have "lived a life of poverty, piety, and self-restraint, offering hospitality to thousands of Brāhmans, according to his humble means, with the grain which he gleaned like a pigeon, and which (like the widow of Zarephath's oil) never underwent diminution, or rather increased again, when it was required." The choleric sage Dur-vāsas went to test the patience of Mudgala, and six times devoured all the food which his host possessed without ruffling his temper. Dur-vāsas in his admiration declared that Mudgala would go bodily to heaven, and the messenger of the gods arrived with his heavenly car. The sage, before accepting the invitation, desired to be informed of the joys and ills of heaven. After hearing a full explanation, he found that the enjoyments of heaven must come to a close, so he declared that he "had no desire for heaven, and would seek only that eternal abode where there is no sorrow, nor distress, nor change." He dismissed the messenger of the gods, and began to practise ascetic virtues, becoming indifferent to praise and blame, regarding clods, gold, stones, and gold as alike. Pure knowledge led to fixed contemplation; and that again imparted strength and complete comprehension, whereby he obtained supreme eternal perfection in the nature of quietude (*nirvāna*).

MUDRĀ-RĀKSHASA. 'The signet of the minister.' A drama by Viśākha-datta. This play has an historical interest, for Chandra-gupta, the Sandracottus of Greek writers, is a leading character in it. The date of its production is apparently the eleventh or twelfth century A.D. It is one of the dramas translated by Wilson, who says, "The author was not a poet of the sphere of Bhava-bhūti or Kāli-dāsa. His imagination rises not to their level, and there is scarcely a brilliant or beautiful thought in the play. As some equivalent for the want of imagination, he has a vigorous perception of character and a manly strain of sentiment, that are inferior only to elevated conception and delicate feeling. He is the Massinger of the Hindus. The language of the original partakes of the general character of the play; it is rarely beautiful or delicate, but always vigorous, and occasionally splendid."

MUGDHA-BODHA. A standard Grammar by Vopadeva, written towards the end of the thirteenth century. It has been edited by Böhtlingk, and there are several Indian editions.

MŪKA. A Dānava, son of Upasunda. He assumed the form of a wild boar in order to kill Arjuna, but was himself killed by Śiva in his form of the Kirāta or mountaineer.

MUKHĀGNI. 'Fiery-faced.' Spirits or goblins with faces of fire, perhaps meteors.

MUṆḌA. 'Bald.' An appellation of Ketu. Name of a demon slain by Durgā.

MUṆḌAKA. Name of a Upanishad (q.v.) translated by

Dr. Roer in the *Bibliotheca Indica* and by Rammohun Roy. There are several editions of the text.

MUNI. "A holy sage, a pious and learned person, endowed with more or less of a divine nature, or having attained to it by rigid abstraction and mortification. The title is applied to the *R*ishis, and to a great number of persons distinguished for their writings considered as inspired, as Pā*n*ini, Vyāsa." Their superhuman powers over gods and men have been often displayed in blessings, but more frequently in curses.

MURA, MURU. A great demon who had seven thousand sons. He was an ally of the demon Naraka, who ruled over Prāg-jyotisha, and assisted him in the defence of that city against K*r*ish*n*a. He placed in the environs of the city "nooses the edges of which were as sharp as razors," but K*r*ish*n*a cut them to pieces with his discus, slew Muru, "and burnt his seven thousand sons like moths with the flame of the edge of his discus."

MURĀRI. 'The foe of Mura.' An appellation of K*r*ish*n*a.

MURĀRĪ MI*S*RA. Author of the drama Murāri Nā*t*aka or Anargha Rāghava (q.v.).

MUSALA. The pestle-shaped club carried by Bala-rāma. It was named Saunanda.

MUSALA - DHARA, MUSALĀYUDHA, MUSALIN. 'Armed with a pestle.' An appellation of Bala-rāma.

MUSH*T*IKA. A celebrated boxer in the service of Kansa, who directed him to kill K*r*ish*n*a or Bala-rāma in a public encounter, but Bala-rāma overthrew him and killed him.

NĀBHĀGADISH*T*A, NĀBHĀGANEDISH*T*HA, NĀBHĀNEDISH*T*HA. A son of Manu, who, while he was living as a Brahmachārī, was deprived of his inheritance, by his father according to the Yajur-veda, by his brothers according to the Aitareya Brāhma*n*a. He subsequently acquired wealth by imparting spiritual knowledge.

NACHIKETAS. The story of Nachiketas is told in the Taittirīya Brāhma*n*a and Kathā Upanishad. Vāja-*s*ravasa or Aru*n*i, the father of Nachiketas, desirous of attaining heaven, performed great sacrifices, and was profuse in his gifts to the priests. The son told him that he had not given all, for that he, his son, was left, and said, "To whom shall I be given?" On repeating the question, the father angrily replied, "To death." So the son departed to the abodes of death, and, after staying there three nights, Yama was constrained to offer him a boon. He prayed to see his father again and be reconciled. This boon was granted and another offered. All kinds of blessings were proposed, but the youth refused to be contented with anything but a true knowledge of the soul. Yama then proceeded to instruct him. The story has been done into verse by Muir (*Texts*, vol. v. p. 329).

NĀGA. A snake, especially the cobra-capella. A mythical semi-divine being, having a human face with the tail of a serpent, and the expanded neck of the cobra. The race of Nāgas is said to be a thousand in number, and to have sprung from Kadru, the wife of Ka*s*yapa, for the purpose of peopling Pātāla, or the regions below the earth, where they reign in great splendour. From the name of their mother they are called Kādraveyas. Their mother is sometimes called Su-rasā. This dominion was taken from them by the Gandharvas, but they recovered it through their sister, the Narmadā river, who induced Vish*n*u to send Pratardana to their assistance. Their females were handsome, and some of them intermarried with men, as Ulupī with Arjuna.

The Nāgas, or a people bearing the same name, are historical, and have left many traces behind them. There were mountains so called, and Nāga-dwīpa was one of the seven divisions of Bhārata-varsha. Kings of this race reigned at Mathurā, Padmāvatī, &c., and the name survives in the modern Nāgpur. There are various speculations as to who and what they were, but it seems clear they were a race distinct from the Hindus. The mythological accounts are probably based upon the historical, but they have been mixed up together and confused. The favourite theory is that they were a Scythic race, and probably obtained their name from worshipping serpents or holding them in awe and reverence.

NĀGA-LOKA. Pātāla, the residence of the Nāgas.

NĀGA-NANDANA. A Buddhist drama in five acts by *S*rī Harsha Deva. It has been translated by Boyd. The text has been printed.

NAGARA. A city. There are seven sacred cities which confer eternal happiness—(1.) Ayodhyā, (2.) Mathurā, (3.) Māyā (Gaya), (4.) Kā*s*ī (Benares), (5.) Kānchī (Conjeveram), (6.) Avanti or Avantikā (Ujjayinī), (7.) Dwārakā or Dwārāvatī.

NAHUSHA. Son of Āyus the eldest son of Purūravas, and

father of Yayāti. This king is mentioned by Manu as having come into conflict with the Brāhmans, and his story is repeated several times with variations in different parts of the Mahā-bhārata as well as in the Purā*n*as, the aim and object of it evidently being to exhibit the retribution awaiting any man who derogates from the power of Brāhmans and the respect due to them. "By sacrifices, austere fervour, sacred study, self-restraint, and valour, Nahusha acquired the undisturbed sovereignty of the three worlds. . . . Through want of virtuous humility the great king Nahusha was utterly ruined."—*Manu.* One version of the story says that he aspired to the possession of Indrā*n*ī, wife of Indra, when that god had concealed himself for having killed a Brāhman. A thousand great *R*ishis bore the car of Nahusha through the air, and on one occasion he touched with his foot the great Agastya, who was carrying him The sage in his anger cried out, "Fall, thou serpent," and Nahusha fell from his glorious car and became a serpent. Agastya, at the supplication of Nahusha, put a limit to the curse; and according to one version, the doomed man was released from it by the instrumentality of Yudhi-sh*th*ira, when he threw off "his huge reptile form, became clothed in a celestial body, and ascended to heaven."

NAIKASHEYAS. Carnivorous imps descended from Ni-kashā, mother of Rāva*n*a. They are called also Nikashātmajas.

NAIMISHA, NAIMISHĀRA*N*YA. A forest (*ara*n*ya*) near the Gomatī (Gūmtī) river, in which the Mahā-bhārata was rehearsed by Sauti to the assembled *R*ishis.

NAIR*R*ITA. Belonging to the south-west quarter; the regent of that quarter. An imp, goblin, or Rākshasa.

NAISHADHA-CHARITA, NAISHADHĪYA. A poem on the life of Nala, king of Nishadha, by *S*rī Harsha, a great sceptical philosopher who lived in the eleventh or twelfth century A.D. It is one of the six Mahā-kāvyas. There are several printed editions.

NAKSHATRAS. Mansions of the moon, lunar asterisms. At first they were twenty-seven in number, but they were increased to twenty-eight. They are said to be daughters of Daksha who were married to the moon. *See* Daksha.

NAKULA. The fourth of the Pā*n*du princes. He was the twin son of Mādrī, the second wife of Pā*n*du, but mythologically he was son of the Aswins, or more specifically of the Aswin

Nāsatya. He was taught the art of training and managing horses by Droṇa, and when he entered the service of the king of Virāṭa he was master of the horse. He had a son named Nir-amitra by his wife Kareṇu-matī, a princess of Chedi. *See* Mahā-bhārata.

NALA. 1. King of Nishadha and husband of Damayantī. The story of Nala and Damayantī is one of the episodes of the Mahā-bhārata, and is well known from having been translated into Latin by Bopp and into English verse by Dean Milman. Damayantī was the only daughter of Bhīma, king of Vidarbha (Birar), and was very lovely and accomplished. Nala was brave and handsome, virtuous, and learned in the Vedas, skilled in arms and in the management of horses, but addicted to the vice of gambling. They loved each other upon the mere fame of their respective virtues and beauty, and Damayantī pined for the presence of her unknown lover. Bhīma determined that his daughter should hold a swayam-vara. Rājas flocked to it in crowds, and among them Nala. Four gods, Indra, Agni, Varuṇa, and Yama, also attended. Nala met them on the way, and reverently promised to do their will. They bade him enter the palace and inform Damayantī that they would present themselves among the candidates, and that she must choose one of them. Nala reluctantly performed his task, but his presence perfected his conquest, and the maiden announced her resolve to pay due homage to the gods, but to choose him for her lord. Each of the four gods assumed the form of Nala, but the lover's eye distinguished the real one, and she made her choice. They married and lived for some time in great happiness, a son and a daughter, named Indrasena and Indrasenā, being born to them. Kali, a personification of the Kali or iron age, arrived too late for the swayam-vara. He resolved to be revenged, and he employed his peculiar powers to ruin Nala through his love of gambling. At his instigation, Pushkara, Nala's younger brother, proposed a game of dice. Kali charmed the dice, and Nala went on losing; but he was infatuated; the entreaties of friends and ministers, wife and children, were of no avail; he went on till he had lost his all, even to his clothes. His rival Pushkara became king, and proclaimed that no one was to give food or shelter to Nala, so the ruined monarch wandered forth into the forest with his wife, and suffered great privations. Some birds flew away with his only garment. He resolved to abandon his wife in the hope that she would return to her father's court, so he divided her sole remaining garment while she slept and left her. Thus left alone, Damayantī wandered about in great distress. She did not go home, but she at length found service and protection with the princess of Chedi. Nala fell in with the king of serpents, who was under a curse from which Nala was to deliver him. The serpent bit Nala, and told him that the poison should work upon him till the evil spirit was gone out of him, and that he should then be restored to all he loved. Through the effects of the bite he was transformed into a misshapen dwarf. In this form he entered the service of *Ri*tupar*n*a, king of Ayodhyā, as a trainer of horses and an accomplished cook, under the name of Bāhuka. Damayantī was discovered and conducted to her father's home, where she found her children. Great search was made for Nala, but in vain, for no one knew him in his altered form. One Brāhman, however, suspected him, and informed Damayantī. She resolved to test his feelings by announcing her intention of holding a second swayam-vara. King *Ri*tupar*n*a determined to attend, and took Nala with him as driver of his chariot. *Ri*tupar*n*a was skilled in numbers and the rules of chances. On their journey he gave a wonderful proof of this, and he instructed Nala in the science. When Nala had acquired this knowledge the evil spirit went out of him, but still he retained his deformity. Damayantī half penetrated his disguise, and was at length convinced that he was her husband by the flavour of a dish which he had cooked. They met, and, after some loving reproaches and the interference of the gods, they became reconciled, and Nala resumed his form. He again played with Pushkara, and staked his wife against the kingdom. Profiting by the knowledge he had obtained from *Ri*tupar*n*a, he won back all and again became king. Pushkara then humbled himself, and Nala not only forgave him, but sent him home to his own city enriched with many gifts. The text of this poem has been often printed, and there are translations in various languages.

2. A monkey chief, said to be a son of Viśwa-karma. According to the Rāmāya*n*a, he had the power of making stones float in water. He was in Rāma's army and built the bridge of

stone called Rāma-setu, or Nala-setu, from the continent to Ceylon, over which Rāma passed with his army.

NALA-KŪVARA. A son of Kuvera.

NALODAYA (Nala + udaya). 'The rise of Nala.' A poem describing the restoration to power of King Nala after he had lost his all. It is ascribed to a Kāli-dāsa, but the composition is very artificial, and the ascription to the great Kāli-dāsa may well be doubted. The text has been printed, and there is a metrical translation by Yates.

NALOPĀKHYĀNA. The story of Nala, an episode of the Mahā-bhārata. *See* Nala.

NAMUCHI. A demon slain by Indra with the foam of water. The legend of Namuchi first appears in the *Ri*g-veda, where it is said that Indra ground "the head of the slave Namuchi like a sounding and rolling cloud," but it is amplified by the commentator and also in the *S*atapatha Brāhma*n*a and Mahā-bhārata. When Indra conquered the Asuras there was one Namuchi who resisted so strongly that he overpowered Indra and held him. Namuchi offered to let Indra go on promise not to kill him by day or by night, with wet or with dry. Indra gave the promise and was released, but he cut off Namuchi's head at twilight, between day and night, and with foam of water, which was, according to the authorities, neither wet nor dry. The Mahā-bhārata adds that the dissevered head followed Indra calling out "O wicked slayer of thy friend."

NANDA. 1. The cowherd by whom K*r*ish*n*a was brought up. 2. A king, or dynasty of kings, of Magadha, that reigned at Pā*t*ali-putra, and was overthrown by Chandra-gupta the Maurya about 315 B.C. *See* Chandra-gupta.

NANDANA. The grove of Indra, lying to the north of Meru.

NANDI. The bull of *S*iva. The Vāyu Purā*n*a makes him the son of Kasyapa and Surabhi. His image, of a milky white colour, is always conspicuous before the temples of *S*iva. He is the chamberlain of *S*iva, chief of his personal attendants (*ganas*), and carries a staff of office. He is guardian of all quadrupeds. He is also called *S*ālankāyana, and he has the appellations of Nādi-deha and Tā*nd*ava-tālika, because he accompanies with music the tā*nd*ava dance of his master.

NĀNDI-MUKHAS. A class of Pit*r*is or Manes, concerning whose character there is a good deal of uncertainty.

NANDINĪ. The cow of plenty belonging to the sage Vasish*th*a, said to have been born of Surabhi, the cow of plenty that was produced at the churning of the ocean.

NANDI-PURĀ*N*A. *See* Purā*n*a.

NANDĪ*S*A, NANDĪ*S*WARA. 'Lord of Nandi.' A title of *S*iva. It is related in the Rāmāya*n*a that Rāva*n*a went to the *S*ara-vana, the birthplace of Kārttikeya, and on his way through the mountains he beheld "a formidable, dark, tawny-coloured dwarf called Nandī*s*wara, who was a follower of Mahā-deva, or rather that deity himself in another body. This being desired Rāva*n*a to halt, as *S*iva was sporting in the mountain, and no one, not even a god, could pass. Rāva*n*a asked derisively who *S*iva was, and laughed contemptuously at Nandī*s*wara, who had the face of a monkey. Nandī*s*wara retorted that monkeys having the same shape as himself and of similar energy should be produced to destroy Rāva*n*a's race. In reply to this menace, Rāva*n*a threatened to pull up the mountain by its roots and let *S*iva know his own danger. So he threw his arms round the mountain and lifted it up, which made the hosts of *S*iva tremble and Pārvatī quake and cling to her husband. *S*iva then pressed down the mountain with his great toe, and crushed and held fast the arms of Rāva*n*a, who uttered a loud cry which shook all creation. Rāva*n*a's friends counselled him to propitiate *S*iva, and he did so for a thousand years with hymns and weeping. *S*iva then released him, and said that his name should be Rāva*n*a from the cry (*rāva*) which he had uttered. The origin of this story is sufficiently manifest, it has been built up on the name Rāva*n*a, to the glory of *S*iva, by a zealous partisan of that deity.

NARA. 'Man.' The original eternal man.

NĀRADA. A *Ri*shi to whom some hymns of the *Ri*g-veda are ascribed. He is one of the Prajāpatis, and also one of the seven great *Ri*shis. The various notices of him are somewhat inconsistent. The *Ri*g-veda describes him as "of the Ka*n*wa family." Another authority states that he sprang from the forehead of Brahmā, and the Vish*n*u Purā*n*a makes him a son of Ka*s*yapa and one of Daksha's daughters. The Mahā-bhārata and some Purā*n*as state that he frustrated the scheme which Daksha had formed for peopling the earth, and consequently incurred that patriarch's curse to enter again the womb of a woman and be born. Daksha, however, relented at the solicitation of Brahmā, and consented that Nārada should be born again of Brahmā and one of Daksha's daughters; he was hence called Brāhma and Deva-brahmā. In some respects he bears a resemblance to Orpheus. He is the inventor of the vīnā (lute), and was chief of the Gandharvas or heavenly musicians. He also went down to the infernal regions (Pātāla), and was delighted with what he saw there. In later times he is connected with the legend of Krishna. He warned Kansa of the imminent incarnation of Vishnu, and he afterwards became the friend and associate of Krishna.

The Nārada-pancha-rātra relates that Brahmā advised his son Nārada to marry, but Nārada censured his father as a false teacher, because devotion to Krishna was the only true means of felicity. Brahmā then cursed Nārada to lead a life of sensuality, in subjection to women, and Nārada retorted the curse, condemning Brahmā to lust after his own daughter, and to be an object unworthy of adoration. Nārada has the appellations, Kali-kāraka, 'strife-maker;' Kapi-vaktra, 'monkey-faced;' Pisuna, 'messenger or spy.'

Nārada was also one of the great writers upon law. His text-book, called "Nāradīya Dharma-sāstra," has been translated into English by Dr. Jolly.

NĀRADA PANCHA-RĀTRA. A ritualistic work of the Vaishnavas. It has been printed in the *Bibliotheca Indica.*

NĀRADA-PURĀNA, NĀRADĪYA-PURĀNA. "Where Nārada has described the duties which were observed in the Brihat Kalpa, that is called the Nāradīya, having 25,000 stanzas." But the only copy that Wilson analysed contained not more than 3000 stanzas. There is another work called the Brihan or Great Nāradīya, but this extends only to 3500 verses. These Purānas, says Wilson, bear "no conformity to the definition of a Purāna; both are sectarial and modern compilations, intended to support the doctrine of Bhakti or faith in Vishnu." They are modern compositions, possibly even of so late a date as the sixteenth or seventeenth century. One of them refers to the "killers of cows" and "contemners of the gods," meaning, no doubt, the Mohammadans, so that the passage would seem to have been written after India was in their hands.

NARAKA. Hell; a place of torture to which the souls of the wicked are sent. Manu enumerates twenty-one hells:—

Tāmisra, Andha-tāmisra, Mahā-raurava, Raurava, Naraka, Kāla-sūtra, Mahā-naraka, Sanjīvana, Mahā-vīchi, Tapana, Sampratāpana, Sanhāta, Sakākola, Ku*d*mala, Pūti-m*ri*ttika, Loha-*s*anku, *Ri*jisha, Panthāna, *S*ālmali, Asi-patra-vana, and Loha-dāraka. Other authorities vary greatly as to the numbers and names of the hells. *See* Vish*n*u Purā*n*a, ii. 214.

NARAKA. An Asura, son of the Earth. In the Mahābhārata and Vish*n*u Purā*n*a he is said to have carried off the ear-rings of Aditi to the impregnable castle of Prāg-jyotisha, but K*ri*sh*n*a, at the request of the gods, went there and killed him and recovered the jewels. In the Hari-van*s*a the legend differs. According to this, Naraka, king of Prāg-jyotisha, was an implacable enemy of the gods. He assumed the form of an elephant, and having carried off the daughter of Vi*s*wa-karma, he subjected her to violation. He seized the daughters of the Gandharvas, and of gods and of men, as well as the Apsarasas themselves, and had more than 16,000 women, for whom he built a splendid residence. He also appropriated to himself jewels, garments, and valuables of all sorts, and no Asura before him had ever been so horrible in his actions.

NARA-NĀRĀYA*N*A. Two ancient *Ri*shis, sons of Dharma and Ahinsa. The names are sometimes applied to K*ri*sh*n*a and to K*ri*sh*n*a and Arjuna. The Vāmana Purā*n*a has a legend about them which is alluded to in the drama of Vikramorva*s*ī. Their penances and austerities alarmed the gods, so Indra sent nymphs to inspire them with passion and disturb their devotions. Nārāya*n*a took a flower and placed it on his thigh. Immediately there sprung from it a beautiful nymph whose charms far excelled those of the celestial nymphs, and made them return to heaven filled with shame and vexation. Nārāya*n*a sent this nymph to Indra with them, and from her having been produced from the thigh (*uru*) of the sage, she was called Urva*s*ī.

NARASINHA-AVATĀRA. *See* Avatāra.

NARASINHA PURĀ*N*A. *See* Purā*n*a.

NARA-VISHWANA. 'A man-devourer;' a Rākshasa or other malignant being.

NĀRĀYA*N*A. 1. The son of Nara, the original man, and often identified or coupled with Nara. 2. The creator Brahmā, who, according to Manu, was so called because the waters (*nara*) were his first ayana or place of motion. The name is found for the first time in the *S*atapatha Brāhma*n*a. The name as commonly used applies to Vish*n*u, and is that under which he was first worshipped.

NARMADĀ. The Nerbudda river, which is esteemed holy. The personified river is variously represented as being daughter of a *Ri*shi named Mekala (from whom she is called Mekalā and Mekala-kanyā), as a daughter of the moon, as a 'mind-born daughter' of the Somapas, and as sister of the Nāgas. It was she who brought Purukutsa to the aid of the Nāgas against the Gandharvas, and the grateful snake-gods made her name a charm against the venom of snakes. According to the Vish*n*u Purā*n*a, she had a son by Purukutsa who was named Trasadasyu. The Matsya Purā*n*a gives Du*h*-saha as the name of her husband. The Hari-van*s*a is inconsistent with itself. In one place it makes her wife of Purukutsa and mother of Trasadasyu; in another it makes her the wife of Trasadasyu. She is also called Revā and Pūrvā-gangā, and, as a daughter of the moon, Indu-jā and Somodbhavā.

NĀSATYA. Name of one of the A*s*wins. It is also used in the plural for both of them.

NAVA-RATNA. The nine gems: pearl, ruby, topaz, diamond, emerald, lapis lazuli, coral, sapphire, and one not identified called Go-meda. The nine gems of the court of Vikrama, probably meaning Vikramāditya, whose era the Samvat begins in 56 B.C. A verse gives their names as Dhanwantari, Kshapa*n*aka, Amara Sinha, *S*anku, Vetāla-bha*tt*a, Gha*t*a-karpara, Kāli-dāsa, Varāha-mihira, Vararuchi. The date of Vikramāditya is by no means settled. Bhau Dājī endeavours to identify Vikrama with Harsha Vikramāditya, who lived in the middle of the sixth century.

NIDĀGHA. A Brāhman, son of Pulastya, who dwelt "at Vīra-nagara, a large handsome city on the banks of the Devikā river" (the Gogra). He was a disciple of the sage *Ri*bhu, and when *Ri*bhu went to visit his disciple, Nidāgha entertained him reverentially. *Ri*bhu instructed him in divine knowledge until he learned to "behold all things as the same with himself, and, perfect in holy knowledge, obtained final liberation."

NIDĀNA-SŪTRA. An old work upon the metres of the Vedas.

NIDHI. 'A treasure.' Nine treasures belonging to the god

Kuvera. Each of them is personified or has a guardian spirit, which is an object of worship among the Tāntrikas. The nature of these Nidhis is not clearly understood. See a note by Wilson on verse 534 of the Megha-dūta, Collected Works, iv. 379. Their names are Kachchhapa, Mukunda, Nanda (or Kunda), Kharba, Makara, Nīla, *S*ankha, Padma, and Mahā-padma. The Nidhis are called also Nidhāna, Nikara, and *S*evadhi.

NIDRĀ. 'Sleep.' Sometimes said to be a female form of Brahmā, at others to have been produced at the churning of the ocean.

NIGHA*NT*U, NIGHA*NT*UKA. A glossary, especially of synonyms and obsolete and obscure Vedic terms. There was at least one work of this kind before the days of Yāska. *See* Nirukta.

NIKASHĀ. A female demon, the mother of Rāva*n*a. The mother of the carnivorous imps called Pi*s*itā*s*anas, or by their metronymic Naikusheyas and Nikashātmajas.

NIKUMBHA. 1. A Rākshasa who fought against Rāma. He was son of Kumbha-kar*n*a. 2. An Asura who, according to the Hari-van*s*a, received the boon from Brahmā that he should die only by the hands of Vish*n*u. He was king of Sha*t*-pura and had great magical powers, so that he could multiply himself into many forms, though he commonly assumed only three. He carried off the daughters of Brahmā-datta, the friend of K*ri*sh*n*a, and that hero attacked him and killed him under different forms more than once, but he was eventually slain outright by K*ri*sh*n*a, and his city of Sha*t*-pura was given to Brahmā-datta.

NĪLA. 'Blue.' 1. A mythic range of mountains north of Meru. 2. A mountain range in Orissa. 3. A monkey ally of Rāma. 4. A Pa*nd*ava warrior killed by A*s*watthāman.

NĪLA-KAN*T*HA. 'Blue throat.' An epithet of *S*iva. *See* *S*iva.

NIMI. Son of Ikshwāku, and founder of the dynasty of Mithilā. He was cursed by the sage Vasish*t*ha to lose his corporeal form, and he retorted the imprecation upon the sage. Both abandoned the bodily condition. Vasish*t*ha was born again as the issue of Mitra and Varu*n*a, but "the corpse of Nimi was preserved from decay by being embalmed with fragrant oils and resins, and it remained as entire as if it were immortal." The gods were willing to restore him to bodily life, but Nimi declined, declaring that the separation of soul and body was so distressing that he would never resume a corporeal shape and become liable to it again. "To this desire the gods assented, and Nimi was placed by them in the eyes of all living creatures, in consequence of which their eyelids are ever opening and shutting."—*Vishnu Purāna.* A wink of the eye is called *nimisha*, and the legend was probably built upon the resemblance of the two words.

NIR*N*AYA-SINDHU. A work on religious ceremonies and law by Kamalākara. It has been printed at Bombay and Benares.

NIR*RI*TI. 'Death, decay.' Death personified as a goddess; sometimes regarded as the wife and sometimes as the daughter of A-dharma. One of the Rudras.

NIRUKTA. 'Etymology, glossary.' One of the Vedāngas. The Nirukta is devoted to the explanation of difficult Vedic words. The only work of the kind now known to us is that of Yāska, who was a predecessor of Pā*n*ini; but such works were no doubt numerous, and the names of seventeen writers of Niruktas are mentioned as having preceded Yāska. The Nirukta consists of three parts:—(1.) Naigha*nt*uka, a collection of synonymous words; (2.) Naigama, a collection of words peculiar to the Vedas; (3.) Daivata, words relating to deities and sacrifices. These are mere lists of words, and are of themselves of little value. They may have been compiled by Yāska himself, or he may have found them ready to his hand. The real Nirukta, the valuable portion of the work, is Yāska's commentary which follows. In this he explains the meaning of words, enters into etymological investigations, and quotes passages of the Vedas in illustration. These are valuable from their acknowledged antiquity, and as being the oldest known examples of a Vedic gloss. They also throw a light upon the scientific and religious condition of their times, but the extreme brevity of their style makes them obscure and difficult to understand. The text of the Nirukta has been published by Roth.

NISHĀDA. A mountain tribe dwelling in the Vindhya mountains, said to have been produced from the thigh of Ve*n*a; the Bhīls or foresters, and barbarians in general. (*See* Ve*n*a.) Any outcast, especially the offspring of a Brāhman father and *S*ūdra mother.

NISHADHA. 1. A mythic range of mountains lying south of Meru, but sometimes described as on the east. It is north of the Himālaya. 2. The country of Nala, probably the Bhīl country.

NISH*T*IGRĪ. In the *Rig*-veda, the mother of Indra.

NI*S*UMBHA. An Asura killed by Durgā. *See* *S*umbha.

NĪTI-MANJARĪ. A work on ethics by Dyā Dwiveda, exemplified by stories and legends with special reference to the Vedas. Some specimens are given in the *Indian Antiquary*, vol. v.

NĪTI-*S*ĀSTRAS. Works on morals and polity, consisting either of proverbs and wise maxims in verse, or of stories and fables inculcating some moral precept and illustrating its effects. These fables are generally in prose interspersed with pithy maxims in verse.

NIVĀTA-KAVACHAS. 'Clothed in impenetrable armour.' A class of Daityas descended from Prahlāda, "whose spirits were purified by rigid austerity." According to the Mahābhārata they were 30,000,000 in number, and dwelt in the depths of the sea. They were destroyed by Arjuna.

N*RI*-SINHA. The Nara-sinha or man-lion incarnation. *See* Avatāra.

N*RI*-SINHA PURĀ*N*A. *See* Purā*n*a.

N*RI*-SINHA TĀPANI. An Upanishad in which Vish*n*u is worshipped under his form N*ri*-sinha. Published with the commentary of *S*ankarāchārya in the *Bibliotheca Indica*.

NYĀYA. The logical school of philosophy. *See* Dar*s*ana.

NYĀYA-DAR*S*ANA, NYĀYA-SŪTRA-V*RI*TTI. Works of Gotama on the Nyāya philosophy. They have been printed.

O*D*RA. The country of Orissa A man of that country.

OM. A word of solemn invocation, affirmation, benediction, and consent, so sacred that when it is uttered no one must hear it. The word is used at the commencement of prayers and religious ceremonies, and is generally placed at the beginning of books. It is a compound of the three letters *a*, *u*, *m*, which are typical of the three Vedas; and it is declared in the Upanishads, where it first appears, to have a mystic power and to be worthy of the deepest meditation. In later times the monosyllable represents the Hindu triad or union of the three gods, *a* being Vish*n*u, *u* *S*iva, and *m* Brahmā. This monosyllable is called Udgītha.

OMKĀRA. The sacred monosyllable Om. Name of one of the twelve great lingas. *See* Linga.

OSHADHI-PRASTHA. 'The place of medicinal herbs.' A city in the Himālaya mentioned in the Kumāra-sambhava.

OSH*T*HA-KAR*N*AKAS. A people whose lips extended to their ears, mentioned in the Mahā-bhārata.

PADA. The Pada text of the Vedas, or of any other work, is one in which each word (*pada*) stands separate and distinct, not joined with the next according to the rules of *sandhi* (coalition). *See* Pa*t*ha.

PADMĀ, PADMĀVATĪ. A name of Lakshmī.

PADMĀVATĪ. Name of a city. It would seem, from the mention made of it in the drama Mālatī Mādhava, to lie in the Vindhya mountains.

PADMA-KALPA. The last expired kalpa or year of Brahmā.

PADMA-PURĀ*N*A, PĀDMA-PURĀ*N*A. This Purā*n*a generally stands second in the list of Purā*n*as, and is thus described:—"That which contains an account of the period when the world was a golden lotos (*padma*), and of all the occurrences of that time, is, therefore, called Padma by the wise. It contains 55,000 stanzas." The work is divided into five books or Kha*n*das:—"(1.) S*r*ish*t*i Kha*n*da, or section on creation; (2.) Bhūmi Kha*n*da, on the earth; (3.) Swarga Kha*n*da, on heaven; (4.) Pātāla Kha*n*da, on the regions below the earth; (5.) Uttara Kha*n*da, last or supplementary chapter. There is also current a sixth division, the Kriyā-yoga-sāra, a treatise on the practice of devotion." These denominations of the various divisions convey but an imperfect and partial notion of their heterogeneous contents, and it seems probable that the different sections are distinct works associated together under one title. There is no reason to consider any of them as older than the twelfth century. The tone of the whole Purā*n*a is strongly Vaish*n*ava; that of the last section especially so. In it *S*iva is represented as explaining to Pārvatī the nature and attributes of Vish*n*u, and in the end the two join in adoration of that deity. A few chapters have been printed and translated into Latin by Wollheim.

PAHLAVA. Name of a people. Manu places the Pahlavas among the northern nations, and perhaps the name is connected with the word Pahlavi, *i.e.*, Persian. They let their beards grow by command of King Sagara. According to Manu, they were

Kshatriyas who had become outcasts, but the Mahā-bhārata says they were created from the tail of Vasishṭha's cow of fortune; and the Rāmāyaṇa states that they sprang from her breath. They are also called Pahnavas.

PAIJAVANA. A name of the King Sudās, his patronymic as son of Pījavana.

PAILA. A learned man who was appointed in ancient days to collect the hymns of the *Ṛig*-veda. He arranged it in two parts, and must have been a coadjutor of Veda Vyāsa.

PĀKA-ŚĀSANA. A name of Indra, and of Arjuna as descended from Indra.

PĀLAKĀPYA. An ancient sage who wrote upon medicine, and is supposed to have been an incarnation of Dhanwantari.

PAMPĀ. A river which rises in the *Ṛ*ishyamūka mountain and falls into the Tungabhadra below Anagundi. Also a lake in the same locality.

PANCHA-CHŪḌĀ. A name of Rambhā.

PANCHAJANA. 1. Name of a demon who lived in the sea in the form of a conch-shell. He seized the son of Sāndīpani, under whom Kṛishṇa learnt the use of arms. Kṛishṇa rescued the boy, killed the demon, and afterwards used the conch-shell for a horn. 2. A name of Asamanjas (q.v.).

PĀNCHAJANYA. Kṛishṇa's conch, formed from the shell of the sea-demon Panchajana.

PANCHĀLA. Name of a country. From the Mahā-bhārata it would seem to have occupied the Lower Doab; Manu places it near Kanauj. It has sometimes been identified with the Panjāb, and with "a little territory in the more immediate neighbourhood of Hastināpur." Wilson says, "A country extending north and west from Delhi, from the foot of the Himālayas to the Chambal." It was divided into Northern and Southern Panchālas, and the Ganges separated them. Cunningham considers North Panchāla to be Rohilkhand, and South Panchāla the Gangetic Doab. The capital of the former was Ahi-chhatra, whose ruins are found near Rāmnagar, and of the latter Kāmpilya, identical with the modern Kāmpila, on the old Ganges between Badāūn and Farrukhābād.

PANCHA-LAKSHAṆA. The five distinguishing characteristics of a Purāṇa. *See* Purāṇa.

PĀNCHĀLĪ. Draupadī as princess of Panchāla.

PANCHĀNANA. 'Five-faced.' An epithet applied to *S*iva.

PANCHĀPSARAS. Name of a lake. *See* Manda-kar*n*i.

PANCHA-*S*IKHA. One of the earliest professors of the Sānkhya philosophy.

PANCHA-TANTRA. A famous collection of tales and fables in five (*pancha*) books (*tantra*). It was compiled by a Brāhman named Vish*n*u-*s*arman, about the end of the fifth century A.D., for the edification of the sons of a king, and was the original of the better-known Hitopadesa. This work has reappeared in very many languages both of the East and West, and has been the source of many familiar and widely known stories. It was translated into Pahlavi or old Persian by order of Naushīrvān in the sixth century A.D. In the ninth century it appeared in Arabic as Kalila o Damna, then, or before, it was translated into Hebrew, Syriac, Turkish, and Greek; and from these, versions were made into all the languages of Europe, and it became familiar in England as Pilpay's Fables (Fables of Bidpai). In modern Persia it is the basis of the Anwār-i Suhailī and Iyār-i Dānish. The latter has reappeared in Hindustani as the Khirad-afroz. The stories are popular throughout Hindustan, and have found their way into most of the languages and dialects. There are various editions of the text and several translations.

PANCHĀVATĪ. A place in the great southern forest near the sources of the Godāvarī, where Rāma passed a long period of his banishment. It has been proposed to identify it with the modern Nāsik, because Lakshma*n*a cut off Sūrpa-nakhā's nose (*nāsika*) at Panchāvatī.

PANCHAVIN*S*A. *See* Prau*d*ha Brāhma*n*a.

PANCHA-V*RI*KSHA. 'Five trees.' The five trees of Swarga, named Mandāra, Pārijātaka, Santāna, Kalpa-v*r*iksha, and Hari-chandana.

PANCHOPĀKHYĀNA. The Pancha-tantra.

PĀ*N*DAVAS. The descendants of Pā*n*du.

PĀ*N*DU. 'The pale.' Brother of Dh*r*ita-rāsh*t*ra, king of Hastinā-pura and father of the Pā*n*davas or Pa*n*du princes. *See* Mahā-bhārata.

PĀ*N*DYA. Pā*n*dya, Chola, and Chera were three kingdoms in the south of the Peninsula for some centuries before and after the

Christian era. Pāndya was well known to the Romans as the kingdom of King Pandion, who is said to have sent ambassadors on two different occasions to Augustus Cæsar. Its capital was Madura, the Southern Mathurā. Pāndya seems to have fallen under the ascendancy of the Chola kings in the seventh or eighth century.

PĀNINI. The celebrated grammarian, author of the work called Pāninīyam. This is the standard authority on Sanskrit grammar, and it is held in such respect and reverence that it is considered to have been written by inspiration. So in old times Pānini was placed among the *Ri*shis, and in more modern days he is represented to have received a large portion of his work by direct inspiration from the god *S*iva. It is also said that he was so dull a child that he was expelled from school, but the favour of *S*iva placed him foremost in knowledge. He was not the first grammarian, for he refers to the works of several who preceded him. The grammars which have been written since his time are numberless, but although some of them are of great excellence and much in use, Pānini still reigns supreme, and his rules are incontestable. "His work," says Professor Williams, "is perhaps the most original of all productions of the Hindu mind." The work is written in the form of Sūtras or aphorisms, of which it contains 3996, arranged in eight (*ashta*) chapters (*adhyāya*), from which the work is sometimes called Ashtādhyāyī. These aphorisms are exceedingly terse and complicated. Special training and study are required to reach their meaning. Colebrooke remarks, that "the endless pursuit of exceptions and limitations so disjoins the general precepts, that the reader cannot keep in view their intended connection and mutual relations. He wanders in an intricate maze, and the key of the labyrinth is continually slipping from his hand." But it has been well observed that there is a great difference between the European and Hindu ideas of a grammar. In Europe, grammar has hitherto been looked upon as only a means to an end, the medium through which a knowledge of language and literature is acquired. With the Pandit, grammar was a science; it was studied for its own sake, and investigated with the most minute criticism; hence, as Goldstücker says, "Pānini's work is indeed a kind of natural history of the Sanskrit language." Pānini was a native of *S*alātura, in the country of Gandhāra, west of the Indus, and so is known as *S*ālottarīya. He is described as a descendant of Pa*n*in and grandson of Devala. His mother's name was Dākshi, who probably belonged to the race of Daksha, and he bears the metronymic Dāksheya. He is also called Āhika. The time when he lived is uncertain, but it is supposed to have been about four centuries B.C. Goldstücker carries him back to the sixth century, but Weber is inclined to place him considerably later. Pā*n*ini's grammar has been printed by Böhtlingk, and also in India. *See* Goldstücker's *Pāninī, his Place in Literature.*"

PA*N*IS. 'Niggards.' In the *Ri*g-veda, "the senseless, false, evil-speaking, unbelieving, unpraising, unworshipping Pa*n*is were Dasyus or envious demons who used to steal cows and hide them in caverns." They are said to have stolen the cows recovered by *S*aramā (q.v.).

PANNAGA. A serpent, snake. *See* Nāga.

PĀPA-PURUSHA. 'Man of sin.' A personification of all wickedness in a human form, of which all the members are great sins. The head is brahmanicide, the arm cow-killing, the nose woman-murder, &c.

PĀRADAS. A barbarous people dwelling in the north-west. Manu says they were Kshatriyas degraded to be *S*ūdras.

PARAMARSHIS (Parama-*ri*shis). The great *Ri*shis. *See* *Ri*shi.

PARAMĀTMAN. The supreme soul of the universe.

PARAMESH*T*HIN. 'Who stands in the highest place.' A title applied to any superior god and to some distinguished mortals. A name used in the Vedas for a son or a creation of Prajāpati.

PARĀ*S*ARA. A Vedic *Ri*shi to whom some hymns of the *Ri*g-veda are attributed. He was a disciple of Kapila, and he received the Vish*n*u Purā*n*a from Pulastya and taught it to Maitreya. He was also a writer on Dharma-*s*āstra, and texts of his are often cited in books on law. Speculations as to his era differ widely, from 575 B.C. to 1391 B.C., and cannot be trusted. By an amour with Satyavatī he was father of K*ri*sh*n*a Dwaipāyana, the Vyāsa or arranger of the Vedas. According to the Nirukta, he was son of Vasish*t*ha, but the Mahā-bhārata and the Vish*n*u Purā*n*a make him the son of *S*aktri and grandson of Vasish*t*ha. The legend of his birth, as given in the Mahā-bhārata, is that King Kalmāsha-pāda met with *S*aktri in a narrow path, and desired him to get out of the way. The sage refused, and the Rāja struck him with his whip. Thereupon the sage cursed the Rāja so that he became a man-eating Rākshasa. In this state he ate up *S*aktri, whose wife, Ad*ris*yantī, afterwards gave birth to Parā*s*ara. When this child grew up and heard the particulars of his father's death, he instituted a sacrifice for the destruction of all the Rākshasas, but was dissuaded from its completion by Vasish*th*a and other sages. As he desisted, he scattered the remaining sacrificial fire upon the northern face of the Himālaya, where it still blazes forth at the phases of the moon, consuming Rākshasas, forests, and mountains.

PĀRĀ*S*ARA-PURĀ*N*A. *See* Purā*n*a.

PĀRA*S*IKAS. Pārsikas or Fārsikas, *i.e.*, Persians.

PARA*S*U-RĀMA. 'Rāma with the axe.' The first Rāma and the sixth Avatāra of Vish*n*u. He was a Brāhman, the fifth son of Jamad-agni and Re*n*ukā. By his father's side he descended from Bh*ri*gu, and was, *par excellence*, the Bhārgava; by his mother's side he belonged to the royal race of the Ku*s*ikas. He became manifest in the world at the beginning of the Tretā-yuga, for the purpose of repressing the tyranny of the Kshatriya or regal caste. His story is told in the Mahā-bhārata and in the Purā*n*as. He also appears in the Rāmāya*n*a, but chiefly as an opponent of Rāma-chandra. According to the Mahā-bhārata, he instructed Arjuna in the use of arms, and had a combat with Bhīshma, in which both suffered equally. He is also represented as being present at the great war council of the Kaurava princes. This Para*s*u-rāma, the sixth Avatāra of Vish*n*u, appeared in the world before Rāma or Rāma-chandra, the seventh Avatāra, but they were both living at the same time, and the elder incarnation showed some jealousy of the younger. The Mahā-bhārata represents Para*s*u-rāma as being struck senseless by Rāma-chandra, and the Rāmāya*n*a relates how Para*s*u-rāma, who was a follower of *S*iva, felt aggrieved by Rāma's breaking the bow of *S*iva, and challenged him to a trial of strength. This ended in his defeat, and in some way led to his being "excluded from a seat in the celestial world." In early life Para*s*u-rāma was under the protection of *S*iva, who instructed him in the use of arms, and gave him the *parasu*, or axe, from which he is named. The first act recorded of him by the Mahā-bhārata is that, by command of his father, he cut off the head of his mother, Re*n*ukā. She had incensed her husband by entertaining impure thoughts, and he called upon each of his sons in succession to kill her. Para*s*u-rāma alone obeyed, and his readiness so pleased his father that he told him to ask a boon. He begged that his mother might be restored pure to life, and, for himself, that he might be invincible in single combat and enjoy length of days. Para*s*u-rāma's hostility to the Kshatriyas evidently indicates a severe struggle for the supremacy between them and the Brāhmans. He is said to have cleared the earth of the Kshatriyas twenty-one times, and to have given the earth to the Brāhmans. The origin of his hostility to the Kshatriyas is thus related:—Kārta-vīrya, a Kshatriya, and king of the Haihayas, had a thousand arms. This king paid a visit to the hermitage of Jamad-agni in the absence of that sage, and was hospitably entertained by his wife, but when he departed he carried off a sacrificial calf belonging to their host. This act so enraged Para*s*u-rāma that he pursued Kārta-vīrya, cut off his thousand arms and killed him. In retaliation the sons of Kārta-vīrya killed Jamad-agni, and for that murder Para*s*u-rāma vowed vengeance against them and the whole Kshatriya race. "Thrice seven times did he clear the earth of the Kshatriya caste, and he filled with their blood the five large lakes of Samanta-panchaka." He then gave the earth to Ka*s*yapa, and retired to the Mahendra mountains, where he was visited by Arjuna. Tradition ascribes the origin of the country of Malabar to Para*s*u-rāma. According to one account he received it as a gift from Varu*n*a, and according to another he drove back the ocean and cut fissures in the Ghāts with blows of his axe. He is said to have brought Brāhmans into this country from the north, and to have bestowed the land upon them in expiation of the slaughter of the Kshatriyas. He bears the appellations Kha*nd*a-para*s*u, 'who strikes with the axe,' and Nyaksha, 'inferior.'

PARĀVASU. *See* Raibhya and Yava-krīta.

PĀRIJĀTA. The tree produced at the churning of the ocean, "and the delight of the nymphs of heaven, perfuming the world with its blossoms." It was kept in Indra's heaven, and was the pride of his wife *S*achī, but when K*r*ish*n*a visited Indra in Swarga, his wife Satya-bhāmā induced him to carry the tree away, which led to a great fight between the two gods and their adherents, in which Indra was defeated. The tree was taken to

Dwārakā and planted there, but after K*ri*sh*n*a's death it returned to Indra's heaven.

PARIKSHIT. Son of Abhimanyu by his wife Uttarā, grandson of Arjuna, and father of Janamejaya. He was killed by A*s*watthāman in the womb of his mother and was born dead, but he was brought to life by K*ri*sh*n*a, who blessed him and cursed A*s*watthāman. When Yudhi-sh*th*ira retired from the world, Parikshit succeeded him on the throne of Hastinā-pura. He died from the bite of a serpent, and the Bhāgavata Purā*n*a is represented as having been rehearsed to him in the interval between the bite and his death. Also written Parīkshit.

PĀRIPĀTRA. The northern part of the Vindhya range of mountains. According to the Hari-vansa, it was the scene of the combat between K*ri*sh*n*a and Indra, and its heights sank down under the pressure of K*ri*sh*n*a's feet. Also called Pāriyātra.

PARISHAD. A college or community of Brāhmans associated for the study of the Vedas.

PARI*S*ISH*T*A. A supplement or appendix. A series of works called Pari*s*ish*t*as belong to the Vedic period, but they are the last of the series, and indicate a transition state. They "supply information on theological or ceremonial points which had been passed over in the Sūtras, and they treat everything in a popular and superficial manner, as if the time was gone when students would spend ten or twenty years of their lives in fathoming the mysteries and mastering the intricacies of the Brāhma*n*a literature."—*Max Müller.*

PARIVRĀJAKA. A religious mendicant. A Brāhman in the fourth stage of his religious life. *See* Brāhman.

PARJANYA. 1. A Vedic deity, the rain-god or rain personified. Three hymns in the *Ri*g-veda are addressed to this deity, and one of them is very poetical and picturesque in describing rain and its effects. The name is sometimes combined with the word *vāta* (wind), *parjanya-vāta*, referring probably to the combined powers and effects of rain and wind. In later times he is regarded as the guardian deity of clouds and rain, and the name is applied to Indra. 2. One of the Ādityas.

PĀRSHADA. Any treatise on the Vedas produced in a Parishad or Vedic college.

PĀRTHA. A son of P*ri*thā or Kuntī. A title applicable to the three elder Pā*nd*avas, but especially used for Arjuna.

PĀRVATĪ. 'The mountaineer.' A name of the wife of *S*iva. *See* Devī.

PĀ*S*U-PATI. 'Lord of creatures.' A name of Rudra or of one of his manifestations. *See* Rudra.

PĀTĀLA. The infernal regions, inhabited by Nāgas (serpents), Daityas, Dānavas, Yakshas, and others. They are seven in number, and their names, according to the Vish*n*u Purā*n*a, are Atala, Vitala, Nitala, Gabhastimat, Mahātala, Sutala, and Pātāla, but these names vary in different authorities. The Padma Purā*n*a gives the names of the seven regions and their respective rulers as follow :—(1.) Atala, subject to Mahā-māya ; (2.) Vitala, ruled by a form of *S*iva called Hātakeswara ; (3.) Sutala, ruled by Bali ; (4.) Talātala, ruled by Māya ; (5.) Mahātala, where reside the great serpents ; (6.) Rasātala, where the Daityas and Dānavas dwell ; (7.) Pātāla, the lowermost, in which Vāsuki reigns over the chief Nāgas or snake-gods. In the *S*iva Purā*n*a there are eight : Pātāla, Tala, Atala, Vitala, Tāla, Vidhi-pātāla, *S*arkarā-bhūmi, and Vijaya. The sage Nārada paid a visit to these regions, and on his return to the skies gave a glowing account of them, declaring them to be far more delightful than Indra's heaven, and abounding with every kind of luxury and sensual gratification.

PĀ*T*ALI-PUTRA. The Palibothra of the Greek writers, and described by them as being situated at the confluence of the Errannaboas (the Sone river) with the Ganges. It was the capital of the Nandas, and of the Maurya dynasty, founded by Chandragupta, which succeeded them as rulers of Magadha. The city has been identified with the modern Patna ; for although the Sone does not now fall into the Ganges there, the modern town is smaller in extent than the ancient one, and there is good reason for believing that the rivers have changed their courses.

PĀTANJALA. The Yoga philosophy. *See* Dar*s*ana.

PATANJALI. The founder of the Yoga philosophy. (*See* Dar*s*ana.) The author of the Mahā-bhāshya, a celebrated commentary on the Grammar of Pā*n*ini, and a defence of that work against the criticisms of Kātyāyana. He is supposed to have written about 200 B.C. Rām K*ri*sh*n*a Gopāl Bha*nd*arkar, a late inquirer, says, "He probably wrote the third chapter of his Bhāshya between 144 and 142 B.C." Weber, however, makes his date to be 25 A.D. He is also called Gonardīya and Gonikāputra. A legend accounting for his name represents that he fell as a small snake from heaven into the palm of Pānini (*pata*, 'fallen;' *anjali*, 'palm').

PĀTHA. 'Reading.' There are three forms, called Pāthas, in which the Vedic text is read and written:—(1.) Sanhitā-pātha, the ordinary form, in which the words coalesce according to the rules of Sandhi; (2.) Pāda-pātha, in which each word stands separate and independent; (3.) Krama-pātha, in which each word is given twice, first joined with the word preceding and then with the word following.

PATTANA. 'City.' Several great places have been known as Pattan or 'the city.' Soma-nātha was Pattan; Anhalwāra is still known as Pattan, and there is also Patna.

PAULOMAS. Kasyapa by his wife Puloma had many thousand "distinguished Dānavas called Paulomas, who were powerful, ferocious, and cruel." They were killed by Arjuna.

PAUNDRA, PAUNDRAKA. Belonging to the country of Pundra. The conch-shell of Bhīshma.

PAUNDRAKA. A pretender who, on the strength of being a Vāsu-deva, or descendant of one named Vasu-deva, set himself up in opposition to Krishna, who was son of Vasu-deva, and assumed his style and insignia. He was supported by the king of Kāsī (Benares), but he was defeated and killed by Krishna, and Benares was burnt.

PAURAVAS. Descendants of Puru of the Lunar race. *See* Puru.

PAVANA. 'Wind.' The god of the wind. *See* Vāyu.

PHĀLGUNA. 1. A name of Arjuna. 2. Name of a month.

PINDĀRAKA. A watering-place on the coast of Gujarat, near Dwārakā, resorted to occasionally by Krishna. It still survives as a village, and is held in veneration. It is about twenty miles from the north-west extremity of the Peninsula.

PINGALA. 1. The great authority on the Chhandas or Prosody of the Vedas. He is supposed to have written about two centuries B.C. 2. Name of one of the serpent kings sometimes identified with the foregoing.

PIPPALĀDA. A school of the Atharva-veda, founded by a sage of that name.

PISĀCHAS (mas.), PISĀCHĪ (fem.). Fiends, evil spirits,

placed by the Vedas as lower than Rākshasas. The vilest and most malignant order of malevolent beings. Accounts differ as to their origin. The Brāhmana and the Mahā-bhārata say that they were created by Brahmā, together with the Asuras and Rākshasas, from the stray drops of water which fell apart from the drops out of which gods, men, gandharvas, &c., had been produced. According to Manu they sprang from the Prajāpatis. In the Purānas they are represented as the offspring of Kasyapa by his wife Krodhavasā, or Pisāchā, or Kapisā.

PISĀCHA-LOKA. *See* Loka.

PISITĀSANAS, PISITĀSINS. Carnivorous and cannibal imps descended from Nikashā.

PITĀ-MAHA. A paternal grandfather. A name of Brahmā as the great father of all.

PĪTĀMBARA. 'Clothed in yellow garments.' A name of Vishnu.

PĪTHA-STHĀNA. 'Seat,' or lit. 'place of a seat.' "Fifty-one places where, according to the Tantras, the limbs of Satī fell when scattered by her husband Siva, as he bore her dead body about and tore it to pieces after she had put an end to her existence at Daksha's sacrifice. This part of the legend seems to be an addition to the original fable, made by the Tantras, as it is not in the Purānas. (*See* Daksha.) It bears some analogy to the Egyptian fable of Isis and Osiris. At the Pītha-sthānas, however, of Jwāla-mukhi, Vindhya-vāsinī, Kālī-ghāt, and others, temples are erected to the different forms of Devī or Satī, not to the phallic emblem of Mahā-deva, which, if present, is there as an accessory, not as a principal; and the chief object of worship is a figure of the goddess—a circumstance in which there is an essential difference between the temples of Durgā and the shrines of Osiris."—*Wilson.*

PITRIS. Patres; the fathers; the Manes. This name is applied to three different classes of beings:—1. The Manes of departed forefathers, to whom *pindas* (balls of rice and flour) and water are offered at stated periods. 2. The ten Prajāpatis or mythical progenitors of the human race. 3. "According to a legend in the Hari-vansa and in the Vāyu Purāna, the first Pitris were the sons of the gods. The gods having offended Brahmā by neglecting to worship him, were cursed by him to become fools; but, upon their repentance, he directed them to apply to their sons for instruction. Being taught accordingly the rites of expiation and penance by their sons, they addressed them as fathers; whence the sons of the gods were the first Pit*r*is." The account given of the Pit*r*is is much the same in all the Purā*n*as. "They agree in distinguishing them into seven classes, three of which are without form, or composed of intellectual, not elementary substance, and assuming what forms they please; and four are corporeal. When the Purā*n*as come to the enumeration of the particular classes, they somewhat differ, and the accounts in all the works are singularly imperfect." The incorporeal Pit*r*is, according to one enumeration, are the Vairājas, Agnishwāttas, and Barhishads. The first of these seem also to be called Subhāswaras, Somasads, and Saumyas. The corporeal are the Su-kālas or Su-kālins, Āngirasas, Su-swadhas, and Somapas. The Sukālas are also called Mānasas; the Somapas are also called Ushmapas; the Āngirasas seem also to be called Havishmats, Havirbhūjas, and Upahutas; and the Su-swadhas are apparently the same as the Ājyapas and Kāvyas or Kavyas. The Vairājas are the Manes of great ascetics and anchorites, the Agnishwāttas are the Pit*r*is of the gods, the Barhishads of demons, the Somapas of Brāhmans, the Havishmats of Kshatriyas, the Ājyapas of Vai*s*yas, and the Su-kālins of the *S*ūdras; but one authority, the Hari-van*s*a, makes the Somapas belong to the *S*ūdras, and the Su-kālins to the Brāhmans, and there appears to be good reason for this. Other names are given by Dr. F. Hall from various authorities (Vish*n*u Purā*n*a, iii. 339): Ra*s*mipas, Phenapas, Sudhāvats, Gārhapatyas, Eka*s*ringas, Chaturvedas, and Kālas. Besides these there are the Vyāmas, 'fumes,' the Pit*r*is of the barbarians. The *R*ig-veda and Manu make two independent classes, the Agni-dagdhas and the Anagni-dagdhas, those 'who when alive kept up (or did not keep up) the household flame,' and presented (or did not present) oblations with fire. The Vish*n*u Purā*n*a makes the Barhishads identical with the former, and the Agnishwāttas with the latter. Yama, god of the dead, is king of the Pit*r*is, and Swadhā, 'oblation,' is sometimes said to be their mother, at others their wife.—*Wilson, Vishnu Purāna,* iii. 157, 339. *See* Manu, iii. 192.

PIT*R*I-LOKA. *See* Loka.

PIT*R*I-PAṬI. 'The lord of the Manes.' Yama, judge of the dead.

PIYADASI. *See* Asoka.

PRABHĀSA. A place of pilgrimage on the coast of Gujarat, near to Dwārakā, and also near to the temple of Soma-nātha.

PRABHĀVATĪ. Wife of Pradyumna (q.v.).

PRABODHA-CHANDRODAYA. 'The rise of the moon of knowledge.' A philosophical drama by K*ri*sh*n*a Mi*s*ra, who is supposed to have lived about the twelfth century. It has been translated into English by Dr. Taylor, and into German by Rosenkranz and by Hirzel.

PRACHA*ND*A-PĀ*ND*AVA. 'The incensed Pa*nd*avas.' A drama in two acts by Rāja *S*ekhara, the main incident in which is the outrage of Draupadī by the assembled Kaurava princes.

PRACHETAS. 1. One of the Prajāpatis. 2. An ancient sage and lawgiver. 3. The ten Prachetasas were sons of Prāchina-barhis and great-grandsons of P*ri*thu, and, according to the Vish*n*u Purā*n*a, they passed ten thousand years in the great ocean, deep in meditation upon Vish*n*u, and obtained from him the boon of becoming the progenitors of mankind. They took to wife Mārishā, daughter of Ka*nd*u, and Daksha was their son. *See* Daksha.

PRĀCHYAS. The people of the east; those east of the Ganges; the Prasii of the Greeks.

PRADHĀNA. Matter. Primary matter, or nature as opposed to spirit.

PRADYUMNA. A son of K*ri*sh*n*a by Rukmi*n*ī. When a child only six days old, he was stolen by the demon *S*ambara and thrown into the ocean. There he was swallowed by a fish, which was afterwards caught and carried to the house of *S*ambara. When the fish was opened, a beautiful child was discovered, and Māyā-devī or Māyā-vatī, the mistress of *S*ambara's household, took him under her care. The sage Nārada informed her who the child was, and she reared him carefully. When he grew up she fell in love with him, and informed him who he was and how he had been carried off by *S*ambara. He defied the demon to battle, and after a long conflict slew him. Then he flew through the air with Māyāvati, and alighted in the inner apartments of his father's palace. K*ri*sh*n*a presented him to his mother Rukmi*n*ī "with the virtuous Māyāvatī his wife," declaring her really to be the goddess Rati. Pradyumna also married Kakudmatī, the daughter of Rukmin, and had by her a son named Aniruddha.

Pradyumna was killed at Dwārakā in the presence of his father during a drunken brawl. Though Pradyumna passed as the son of K*ri*sh*n*a, he was, according to the legend, a revival or resuscitation of Kāma, the god of love, who was reduced to ashes by the fiery glance of *S*iva, and so the name Pradyumna is used for Kāma. (*See* Kāma.) The Vish*n*u Purā*n*a puts the following words into the mouth of Nārada when he presented Pradyumna to Rukmi*n*ī :—"When Manmatha (the deity of love) had perished, the goddess of beauty (Rati), desirous to secure his revival, assumed a delusive form, and by her charms fascinated the demon *S*ambara, and exhibited herself to him in various illusory enjoyments. This thy son is the descended Kāma; and this is (the goddess) Rati, his wife. There is no occasion for any uncertainty; this is thy daughter-in-law." In the Harivan*s*a he has a wife named Prabhāvatī, daughter of King Vajranābha. When he went to see her for the first time, he changed himself into a bee and lived in a garland of flowers which had been prepared for her. According to the Mahā-bhārata, he was Sanat-kumāra, the son of Brahmā.

PRADYUMNA-VIJAYA. 'Pradyumna victorious.' A drama in seven acts upon the victory of Pradyumna over the Daitya Vajra-nābha, written by *S*ankara Dīkshita about the middle of the last century. "The play is the work of a Pa*nd*it, not of a poet."—*Wilson.*

PRĀG-JYOTISHA. A city situated in the east, in Kāmarūpa on the borders of Assam. *See* Naraka.

PRAHLĀDA, PRAHRĀDA. A Daitya, son of Hira*n*ya-ka*s*ipu and father of Bali. Hira*n*ya-ka*s*ipu, in his wars with the gods, had wrested the sovereignty of heaven from Indra and dwelt there in luxury. His son Prahlāda, while yet a boy, became an ardent devotee of Vish*n*u, which so enraged his father that he ordered the boy to be killed; but not the weapons of the Daityas, the fangs of the serpents, the tusks of the celestial elephants, nor the flames of fire took any effect, and his father was constrained to send him back to his preceptor, where he continued so earnest in performing and promoting the worship of Vish*n*u that he eventually obtained final exemption from existence. According to some accounts, it was to avenge Prahlāda, as well as to vindicate his own insulted majesty, that Vish*n*u became incarnate as the Nara-sinha, 'man-lion,' and slew

Hira*n*ya-ka*s*ipu. After the death of his father, Prahlāda became king of the Daityas and dwelt in Pātāla; but, according to the Pādma Purā*n*a, he was raised to the rank of Indra for life, and finally united with Vish*n*u. The Pādma Purā*n*a carries the story farther back to a previous birth. In this previous existence Prahlāda was a Brāhman named Soma-*s*arman, fifth son of *S*iva-*s*arman. His four brothers died and obtained union with Vish*n*u, and he desired to follow them. To accomplish this he engaged in profound meditation, but he allowed himself to be disturbed by an alarm of the Daityas, and so was born again as one of them. He took the part of his race in the war between them and the gods, and was killed by the discus of Vish*n*u, after that he was again born as son of Hira*n*ya-ka*s*ipu.

PRAJĀ-PATI. 'Lord of creatures,' a progenitor, creator. In the Veda the term is applied to Indra, Savit*ri*, Soma, Hira*n*ya-garbha, and other deities. In Manu the term is applied to Brahmā as the active creator and supporter of the universe; so Brahmā is the Prajā-pati. It is also given to Manu Swāyambhuva himself, as the son of Brahmā and as the secondary creator of the ten *Ri*shis, or "mind-born sons" of Brahmā, from whom mankind has descended. It is to these ten sages, as fathers of the human race, that the name Prajā-pati most commonly is given. They are Marīchi, Atri, Angiras, Pulastya, Pulaha, Kratu, Vasish*t*ha, Prachetas or Daksha, Bh*ri*gu, and Nārada. According to some authorities the Prajā-patis are only seven in number, being identical with the seven great *Ri*shis. (*See Ri*shi.) The number and names of the Prajā-patis vary in different authorities: the Mahā-bhārata makes twenty-one.

PRAKĀ*S*AS. Messengers of Vish*n*u, also called Vish*n*u-dūtas.

PRĀK*RI*TA. The Prāk*ri*ts are provincial dialects of the Sansk*ri*t, exhibiting more or less deterioration from the original language; and they occupy an intermediate position between that language and the modern vernaculars of India, very similar to that of the Romance languages between the Latin and the modern languages of Europe. They resemble the European languages also in another respect: they have in them a small proportion of words which have not been affiliated on the original classical language, and are apparently remnants of a different tongue and an older race. The Prākrits are chiefly known from the dramas in which kings and Brāhmans speak Sanskrit, while characters of inferior position speak in different Prākrits. Sometimes these Prākrit passages are so very debased that it hardly seems possible for them to be specimens of really spoken vernaculars. Such passages may perhaps be comic exaggerations of provincial peculiarities. The Prākrits have received careful study, and the Prākrita-prakāsa, a Grammar by Vararuchi, translated by Professor Cowell, was probably written about the beginning of the Christian era. *See* Kātyāyana.

PRAKRITI. Nature; matter as opposed to spirit. The personified will of the Supreme in the creation, and the prototype of the female sex, identified with Māyā or illusion. The Sakti or female energy of any deity.

PRALAMBA. An Asura killed by Krishna, according to the Mahā-bhārata. His story as told in the Vishnu Purāna is, that he was an Asura and a dependant of Kansa. With the object of devouring the boys Krishna and Bala-rāma, he joined them and their playmates in jumping. Pralambā was beaten by his opponent Bala-rāma, and by the rules of the game had to carry the victor back on his shoulders to the starting-place. He took up Bala-rāma and then expanded his form, and was making off with his rider when Bala-rāma called upon Krishna for assistance. Krishna made a long speech, and ended by telling him to suspend awhile his mortal character and do what was right. Bala-rāma laughed, squeezed Pralamba with his knees, and beat him on the head with his fists till his eyes were knocked out and his brain forced through his skull, so that he fell to the ground and expired.

PRALAYA. A dissolution of the world at the end of a kalpa.

PRAMATHAS. A class of demi-gods or fiends attendant upon Siva.

PRAMLOCHĀ. A celestial nymph sent by Indra to beguile the sage Kandu from his devotion and austerities. She lived with him for some hundreds of years, which were but as a day to the sage. When he awoke from his delusion he drove the nymph from his presence. The child with which she was pregnant by him came forth from her body in drops of perspiration, which she left upon the leaves of the trees. These drops congealed and became eventually the lovely nymph Mārishā (q.v.).

PRĀ*N*A. 'Breath or life.' In the Atharva-veda it is personified and a hymn is addressed to it.

PRASANNA-RĀGHAVA. A drama by Jaya-deva in seven acts. It has been printed at Benares.

PRASENA. Son of Nighna and brother of Satrā-jit or Sattrājita. He was killed by a lion. *See* Syamantaka.

PRA*S*NA. Name of an Upanishad (q.v.).

PRASŪTI. A daughter of Manu and wife of Daksha.

PRATARDANA. Son of Divodāsa, king of Kāsī. The whole family of Divodāsa was slain by a king named Vīta-havya. The afflicted monarch through a sacrifice performed by Bh*ri*gu obtained a son, Pratardana, who became a mighty warrior, and avenged the family wrongs upon his father's foe. Vīta-havya then flew to the sage Bh*ri*gu for protection, and was by him raised to the dignity of a Brahmarshi.

PRĀTI*S*ĀKHYAS. Treatises on the phonetic laws of the language of the Vedas, dealing with the euphonic combination of letters and the peculiarities of their pronunciation as they prevailed in the different *S*ākhās or Vedic schools. These treatises are very ancient, but they are considerably later than the hymns, for the idiom of the hymns must have become obscure and obsolete before these treatises were necessary. Four such treatises are known :—

Rig-veda.—One which is considered to belong to the *S*ākhalā-sākhā of this Veda, and is ascribed to *S*aunaka. It has been edited and translated into German by Max Müller, and into French by M. Regnier.

Yajur-veda.—Taittirīya-prātisākhya, belonging to the Black Yajur, printed in the *Bibliotheca Indica* and also in the Journal of the American Oriental Society, with a translation by Professor Whitney.

Vājasaneyī-prātisākhya.—Belonging to the White Yajur. It is attributed to Kātyāyana, and has been edited and translated by Weber.

Atharva-veda.—The *S*aunakīya Chaturādhyāyika, *i.e.*, *S*aunaka's treatise in four chapters. Edited and translated into English by Whitney.

No Prātisākhya of the Sāma-veda has been discovered.

PRATI-SH*T*HĀNA. An ancient city, the capital of the early kings of the Lunar race; "it was situated on the eastern side of the confluence of the Ganges and Jumna," opposite to the modern Allāhābād. The capital of *S*ālivāhana on the Godāvarī, supposed to be the same as "Pattan" or "Pyetan."

PRAU*D*HA-BRĀHMA*N*A. One of the eight Brāhma*n*as of the Sāma-veda. It contains twenty-five sections, and is therefore also called Pancha-vin*s*a.

PRAYĀGA. The modern Allāhābād. The place where the Ganges, Jumna, and the fabled subterranean Saraswatī unite, called also Tri-ve*n*ī, 'the triple braid.' It has always been a celebrated place of pilgrimage.

PRETA. A ghost; an evil spirit animating a dead carcase, and haunting cemeteries and other places.

P*RI*SHADHRA. A son of Manu Vaivaswata, who, according to the Hari-van*s*a and the Purā*n*as, became a *S*ūdra because he killed the cow of his religious preceptor.

P*RI*SHATA. Drupada's father.

P*RIS*NI. In the Vedas and Purā*n*as, the earth, the mother of the Maruts. The name is used in the Vedas also for a cow. There were several females of this name, and one of them is said to have been a new birth of Devakī.

PRITHĀ. A name of Kuntī.

P*RI*THĪ, P*RI*THU, P*RI*THĪ - VAI*N*YA. P*ri*thī or P*ri*thī-vai*n*ya, *i.e.*, P*ri*thī, son of Ve*n*a, is mentioned in the *Ri*g-veda, and he is the declared *Ri*shi or author of one of the hymns. The Atharva-veda says, "She (Virāj) ascended: she came to men. Men called her to them, saying, 'Come, Irāvatī.' Manu Vaivaswata was her calf, and the earth her vessel. P*ri*thī-vai*n*ya milked her; he milked from her agriculture and grain. Men subsist on agriculture and grain." The *S*atapatha Brāhma*n*a refers to P*ri*thī as "first of men who was installed as a king." These early allusions receive a consistent form in the Purā*n*as, and we have the following legend:—P*ri*thī was son of Ve*n*a, son of Anga. He was called the first king, and from him the earth received her name P*ri*thivī. The Vish*n*u Purā*n*a says that the *Ri*shis "inaugurated Ve*n*a monarch of the earth," but he was wicked by nature and prohibited worship and sacrifice. Incensed at the decay of religion, pious sages beat Ve*n*a to death with blades of holy grass. In the absence of a king robbery and anarchy arose, and the Munis, after consultation, proceeded to rub the thigh of the dead king in order to produce a son. There came forth "a man like a charred log, with flat face and extremely short." This man became a Nishāda, and with him came out the sins of the departed king. The Brāhmans then rubbed the right arm of the corpse, "and from it sprang the majestic P*ri*thu, Ve*na*'s son, resplendent in body, glowing like the manifested Agni. . . . At his birth all creatures rejoiced, and through the birth of this virtuous son Ve*na*, delivered from the hell called Put, ascended to heaven." P*ri*thu then became invested with universal dominion. His subjects, who had suffered from famine, besought him for the edible plants which the earth withheld. In anger he seized his bow to compel her to yield the usual supply. She assumed the form of a cow and fled before him. Unable to escape, she implored him to spare her, and promised to restore all the needed fruits if a calf were given to her, through which she might be able to secrete milk. "He therefore, having made *S*wāyam-bhuva Manu the calf, milked the earth, and received the milk into his own hand for the benefit of mankind. Thence proceeded all kinds of corn and vegetables upon which people subsist now and perpetually. By granting life to the earth P*ri*thu was as her father, and she thence derived the patronymic appellation P*ri*thivī." This milking the earth has been made the subject of much allegory and symbolism. The Matsya Purā*n*a specifies a variety of milkers, gods, men, Nāgas, Asuras, &c., in the follow style:—"The *R*ishis milked the earth through B*ri*haspati; their calf was Soma, the Vedas were the vessel, and the milk was devotion." Other Purā*n*as agree with only slight deviations. "These mystifications," says Wilson, "are all, probably, subsequent modifications of the original simple allegory which typified the earth as a cow, who yielded to every class of beings the milk they desired, or the object of their wishes."

P*RI*THIVĪ. 'The broad.' The earth or wide world. In the Vedas the earth is personified as the mother of all beings, and is invoked together with the sky. According to the Vedas there are three earths corresponding to the three heavens, and our earth is called Bhūmi. Another name of the earth is Urvī, 'wide.' In the Vishnu Purā*n*a she is represented as receiving her name from a mythical person named P*ri*thu, who granted her life, and so was to her as a father. *See* above, P*ri*thī or P*ri*thu.

P*RI*THU. A king of the Solar race, a descendant of Ikshwāku. There are many P*ri*thus. *See* P*ri*thī.

PRIYA-DARSĪ. *See* Asoka.

PRIYAM-VADA. A Vidyā-dhara, son of the king of the Gandharvas.

PRIYA-VRATA. One of the two sons of Brahmā and Sata-rūpā; or, according to other statements, a son of Manu Swāyam-bhuva. "Priya-vrata being dissatisfied that only half the earth was illuminated at one time by the solar rays, followed the sun seven times round the earth in his own flaming car of equal velocity, like another celestial orb, resolved to turn night into day." He was stopped by Brahmā. "The ruts which were formed by the motion of his chariot wheels were the seven oceans. In this way the seven continents of the earth were made."—*Bhāgavata Purāna.* In the Vishnu Purāna his wife is stated to be Kāmyā, daughter of Kardama, by whom he had ten sons and two daughters. Three of the sons adopted a religious life, and Priya-vrata divided the seven continents among the others.

PULAHA. Name of one of the Prajā-patis and great *Ri*shis. His wife was Kshamā, and he had three sons, Kardama, Arvarīvat, and Sahishnu. A Gandharva (q.v.).

PULASTYA. One of the Prajā-patis or mind-born sons of Brahmā, and one of the great *Ri*shis. He was the medium through which some of the Purānas were communicated to man. He received the Vishnu Purāna from Brahmā and communicated it to Parāsara, who made it known to mankind. He was father of Visravas, the father of Kuvera and Rāvana, and all the Rākshasas are supposed to have sprung from him.

PULINDAS. Barbarians; barbarous tribes living in woods and mountains, especially in Central India; but there were some in the north and on the Indus.

PULOMAN. A Dānava and father of Sachī, wife of Indra. He was killed by Indra when he wished to curse that deity for having ravished his daughter.

PUNDARĪKĀKSHA. 'The lotus-eyed;' a name of Vishnu.

PUNDRA. A country corresponding "to Bengal proper, with part of South Bihār and the Jungle Mahals." A fabulous city between the Hima-vat and Hema-kūta.

PUNYA-SLOKA (mas.), PUNYA-SLOKĀ (fem.). 'Hymned in holy verse.' An appellation applied to Krishna, Yudhi-shthira, and Nala, also to Draupadī and Sītā.

PURĀ*N*A. 'Old,' hence an ancient legend or tale of olden times. The Purā*n*as succeed the Itihāsas or epic poems, but at a considerable distance of time, and must be distinguished from them. The epics treat of the legendary actions of heroes as mortal men, the Purā*n*as celebrate the powers and works of positive gods, and represent a later and more extravagant development of Hinduism, of which they are in fact the Scriptures. The definition of a Purā*n*a by Amara Sinha, an ancient Sansk*ri*t lexicographer, is a work "which has five distinguishing topics :—(1.) The creation of the universe; (2.) Its destruction and renovation; (3.) The genealogy of gods and patriarchs; (4.) The reigns of the Manus, forming the periods called Manwantaras. (5.) The history of the Solar and Lunar races of kings." These are the Pancha-laksha*n*as or distinguishing marks, but no one of the Purā*n*as answers exactly to the description; some show a partial conformity with it, others depart from it very widely. The Vish*n*u Purā*n*a is the one which best accords with the title. Wilson says, "'A very great portion of the contents of many is genuine and old. The sectarial interpolation or embellishment is always sufficiently palpable to be set aside without injury to the more authentic and primitive material; and the Purā*n*as, although they belong especially to that stage of the Hindu religion in which faith in some one divinity was the prevailing principle, are also a valuable record of the form of Hindu belief which came next in order to that of the Vedas, which grafted hero-worship upon the simpler ritual of the latter, and which had been adopted, and was extensively, perhaps universally, established in India at the time of the Greek invasion." According to the same authority, Pantheism "is one of their invariable characteristics," and underlies their whole teaching, "although the particular divinity who is all things, from whom all things proceed, and to whom all things return, is diversified according to their individual sectarian bias." The Purā*n*as are all written in verse, and their invariable form is that of a dialogue between an exponent and an inquirer, interspersed with the dialogues and observations of other individuals. Thus Pulastya received the Vish*n*u Purā*n*a from Brahmā; he made it known to Parāsara, and Parāsara narrated it to his disciple Maitreya. The Purā*n*as are eighteen in number, and in addition to these there are eighteen Upa Purā*n*as or subordinate works. The Purā*n*as are classified in three categories, according to the prevalence in them of the qualities of purity, gloom, and passion. Those in which the quality of Sattwa or purity prevail are—(1.) Vishnu, (2.) Nāradīya, (3.) Bhāgavata, (4.) Garuda, (5.) Padma, (6.) Varāha. These are Vaishnava Purānas, in which the god Vishnu holds the pre-eminence. The Purānas in which Tamas, the quality of gloom or ignorance, predominates are—(1.) Matsya, (2.) Kūrma, (3.) Linga, (4.) Siva, (5.) Skanda, (6.) Agni. These are devoted to the god Siva. Those in which Rajas or passion prevails relate chiefly to the god Brahmā. They are—(1.) Brahma, (2.) Brahmanda, (3.) Brahma-vaivarta, (4.) Mārkandeya, (5.) Bhavishya, (6.) Vāmana. The works themselves do not fully justify this classification. None of them are devoted exclusively to one god, but Vishnu and his incarnations fill the largest space. One called the Vāyu Purāna is in some of the Purānas substituted for the Agni, and in others for the Siva. This Vāyu is apparently the oldest of them, and may date as far back as the sixth century, and it is considered that some of the others may be as late as the thirteenth or even the sixteenth century. One fact appears certain: they must all have received a supplementary revision, because each one of them enumerates the whole eighteen. The Mārkandeya is the least sectarian of the Purānas; and the Bhāgavata, which deals at length with the incarnations of Vishnu, and particularly with his form Krishna, is the most popular. The most perfect and the best known is the Vishnu, which has been entirely translated into English by Professor Wilson, and a second edition, with many valuable notes, has been edited by Dr. F. E. Hall. The text of the Agni and Mārkandeya Purānas is in course of publication in the *Bibliotheca Indica*. The Purānas vary greatly in length. Some of them specify the number of couplets that each of the eighteen contains. According to the Bhāgavata, the sum total of couplets in the whole eighteen is 400,000; the Skanda is the longest, with 81,000, the Brahma and the Vāmana the shortest, with 10,000 couplets each.

The Upa Purānas are named—(1.) Sanat-kumāra, (2.) Nara-sinha or Nri-sinha, (3.) Nāradīya or Vrihan (old) Nāradīya, (4.) Siva, (5.) Dur-vāsasa, (6.) Kāpila, (7.) Mānava, (8.) Ausanasa, (9.) Vāruna, (10.) Kālikā, (11.) Sāmba, (12.) Nandi, (13.) Saura, (14.) Pārāsara, (15.) Āditya, (16.) Māheswara, (17.) Bhāgavata, (18.)

Vāsish*th*a. These works are not common. Other modern works exist to which the term Purā*n*a has been applied.

An account of each of the eighteen great Purā*n*as is given under its own name.

PURAN-JAYA. 'City-conqueror.' A prince of the Solar race, son of Vikukshi. His story, as told in the Vish*n*u Purā*n*a, is that in the Tretā age there was war between the gods and the Asuras, in which the former were worsted. They had recourse to Vish*n*u for assistance, and he directed them to obtain the aid of Puran-jaya, into whose person he promised to infuse a portion of himself. The prince complied with their wishes, and asked that their chief, Indra, would assume the form of a bull and carry him, the prince, upon his hump. This was done, and thus seated Puran-jaya destroyed all the enemies of the gods. As he rode on the hump he obtained the cognomen of Kakut-stha. In explanation of his title Puran-jaya, the Bhāgavata Purā*n*a says that he took the city of the Daityas situated in the west.

PUROCHANA. The emissary of Dur-yodhana who attempted to burn the Pā*nd*avas in their house and was burnt in his own house by Bhīma. *See* Mahā-bhārata.

PURU. The sixth king of the Lunar race, youngest son of Yayāti and Sarmish*th*ā. He and his brother Yadu were founders of two great branches of the Lunar race. The descendants of Puru were called Pauravas, and of this race came the Kauravas and Pā*nd*avas. Among the Yādavas or descendants of Yadu was K*ri*sh*n*a. *See* Yayāti.

PURUKUTSA. A son of Māndhāt*ri*, into whose person Vish*n*u entered for the purpose of destroying the subterranean Gandharvas, called Mauneyas. He reigned on the banks of the Narmadā, and that river personified as one of the Nāgas was his wife. By her he had a son, Trasadasyu. The Vish*n*u Purā*n*a is said to have been narrated to him by "Daksha and other venerable sages."

PURŪ-RAVAS. In the Vedas, a mythical personage connected with the sun and the dawn, and existing in the middle region of the universe. According to the *Rig*-veda he was son of Ilā, and a beneficent pious prince; but the Mahā-bhārata says, "We have heard that Ilā was both his mother and his father. The parentage usually assigned to him is that he was son of Budha by Ilā, daughter of Manu, and grandson of the moon." Through his mother he received the city of Pratishthāna. (*See* Ilā.) He is the hero of the story and of the drama of Vikrama and Urvasī, or the "Hero and the Nymph." Purū-ravas is the Vikrama or hero, and Urvasī is an Apsaras who came down from Swarga through having incurred the imprecation of Mitra and Varuna. On earth Purū-ravas and she became enamoured of each other, and she agreed to live with him upon certain conditions. "I have two rams," said the nymph, "which I love as children. They must be kept near my bedside, and never suffered to be carried away. You must also take care never to be seen by me undressed; and clarified butter alone must be my food." The inhabitants of Swarga were anxious for the return of Urvasī, and knowing the compact made with Purū-ravas, the Gandharvas came by night and stole her rams. Purū-ravas was undressed, and so at first refrained from pursuing the robbers, but the cries of Urvasī impelled him to seize his sword and rush after them. The Gandharvas then brought a vivid flash of lightning to the chamber which displayed the person of Purū-ravas. So the charm was broken and Urvasī disappeared. Purū-ravas wandered about demented in search of her, and at length found her at Kuru-kshetra bathing with four other nymphs of heaven. She declared herself pregnant, and told him to come there again at the end of a year, when she would deliver to him a son and remain with him for one night. Purū-ravas, thus comforted, returned to his capital. At the end of the year he went to the trysting-place and received from Urvasī his eldest son, Āyus. The annual interviews were repeated until she had borne him five more sons. (Some authorities increase the number to eight, and there is considerable variety in their names.) She then told him that the Gandharvas had determined to grant him any boon he might desire. His desire was to pass his life with Urvasī. The Gandharvas then brought him a vessel with fire and said, "Take this fire, and, according to the precepts of the Vedas, divide it into three fires; then, fixing your mind upon the idea of living with Urvasī, offer oblations, and you shall assuredly obtain your wishes." He did not immediately obey this command, but eventually he fulfilled it in an emblematic way, and "obtained a seat in the sphere of the Gandharvas, and was no more separated from his love." As a son of Ilā, his metronymic is Aila. There is a hymn in the *Ri*g-veda which contains an obscure conversation between Purū-ravas and Urvasī. The above story is first told in the *S*atapatha Brāhma*n*a, and afterwards reappears in the Purā*n*as. The Bhāgavata Purā*n*a says, "From Purū-ravas came the triple Veda in the beginning of the Tretā (age)."

The story is supposed to have a mythic origin. Max Müller considers it "one of the myths of the Vedas which expresses the correlation of the dawn and the sun. The love between the mortal and the immortal, and the identity of the morning dawn and the evening twilight, is the story of Urva*s*ī and Purū-ravas." The word Urva*s*ī, according to the same writer, "was originally an appellation, and meant dawn." Dr. Goldstücker's explanation differs, but seems more apposite. According to this, Purū-ravas is the sun and Urvasī is the morning mist; when Purū-ravas is visible Urva*s*ī vanishes, as the mist is absorbed when the sun shines forth. Urva*s*ī in the story is an Apsaras, and the Apsarases are "personifications of the vapours which are attracted by the sun and form into mists or clouds."

PURUSHA. 'Man.' 1. The original eternal man, the Supreme Being, and soul of the universe. 2. A name of Brahmā.

PURUSHA-NĀRĀYA*N*A. The original male. The divine creator Brahmā.

PURUSHA-SŪKTA. A hymn of the *Ri*g-veda in which the four castes are first mentioned. It is considered to be one of the latest in date. See *Muir's Texts*, i. p. 7.

PURUSHOTTAMA. Literally 'best of men;' but the word Purusha is here used in its mythic sense of soul of the universe, and so the compound means the "supreme soul." It is a title of Vish*n*u, and asserts his right to be considered the Supreme God. So the Hari-vansa says, "Purushottama is whatever is declared to be the highest, Purusha the sacrifice, and everything else which is known by the name of Purusha."

PURUSHOTTAMA - KSHETRA. The sacred territory round about the temple of Jagannātha in Orissa.

PŪRVA-MĪMĀNSĀ. A school of philosophy. *See* Darsana.

PŪSHAN. A deity frequently mentioned in the Vedas, but he is not of a distinctly defined character. Many hymns are addressed to him. The word comes from the root *push*, and the primary idea is that of "nourisher" or Providence. So the

Taittirīya Brahmana says, "When Prajāpati formed living creatures Pūshan nourished them." The account given in Böhtlingk and Roth's Dictionary, and adopted by Dr. Muir, is as follows:—"Pūshan is a protector and multiplier of cattle and of human possessions in general. As a cowherd he carries an ox-goad, and he is drawn by goats. In the character of a Solar deity, he beholds the entire universe, and is a guide on roads and journeys and to the other world. He is called the lover of his sister Sūryā. He aids in the revolution of day and night, and shares with Soma the guardianship of living creatures. He is invoked along with the most various deities, but most frequently with Indra and Bhaga." He is a patron of conjurors, especially of those who discover stolen goods, and he is connected with the marriage ceremonial, being besought to take the bride's hand and bless her. (See *Muir's Texts*, v. 171.) In the Nirukta, and in works of later date, Pūshan is identified with the sun. He is also called the brother of Indra, and is enumerated among the twelve Ādityas. Pūshan is toothless, and feeds upon a kind of gruel, and the cooked oblations offered to him are of ground materials, hence he is called Karambhād. The cause of his being toothless is variously explained. According to the Taittirīya Sanhitā, the deity Rudra, being excluded from a certain sacrifice, shot an arrow at the offering and pierced it. A portion of this sacrifice was presented to Pūshan, and it broke his teeth. In the Mahā-bhārata and in the Purānas the legend takes a more definite shape. "Rudra (*S*iva), of dreadful power, ran up to the gods present at Daksha's sacrifice, and in his rage knocked out the eyes of Bhaga with a blow, and, incensed, assaulted Pūshan with his foot, and knocked out his teeth as he was eating the puro*d*asa offering." In the Purā*n*as it is not *S*iva himself, but his manifestation the Rudras, who disturbed the sacrifice of the gods and knocked Pūshan's teeth down his throat. Pūshan is called Āghri*n*i, 'splendid;' Dasra, Dasma, and Dasma-varchas, 'of wonderful appearance or power,' and Kapardin (q.v.).

PUSHKARA. A blue lotus. A celebrated tank about five miles from Ajmīr. One of the seven Dwīpas. (*See* Dwīpa.) The name of several persons. Of the brother of Nala to whom Nala lost his kingdom and all that he possessed in gambling. Of a son of Bharata and nephew of Rāma-chandra, who reigned over the Gāndhāras.

PUSHKARĀVATĪ. A city of the Gāndhāras not far from the Indus. It is the Πευκελαῶτις of Ptolemy, and the Pousekielofati of Hiouen Thsang.

PUSHPA-DANTA. 'Flower-teeth.' 1. One of the chief attendants of *S*iva. He incurred his master's displeasure by listening to his private conversation with Pārvatī and talking of it afterwards. For this he was condemned to become a man, and so appeared in the form of the great grammarian Kātyāyana. 2. One of the guardian elephants. *See* Loka-pāla.

PUSHPAKA. A self-moving aerial car of large dimensions, which contained within it a palace or city. Kuvera obtained it by gift from Brahmā, but it was carried off by Rāva*n*a, his half-brother, and constantly used by him. After Rāma-chandra had slain Rāva*n*a, he made use of this capacious car to convey himself and Sītā, with Lakshma*n*a and all his allies, back to Ayodhyā; after that he returned it to its owner, Kuvera. It is also called Ratna-varshuka, "that rains jewels."

PUSHPA-K*A*RA*ND*INI. A name of Ujjayinī.

PUSHPA-MITRA. The first of the *S*unga kings, who succeeded the Mauryas, and reigned at Pā*t*ali-putra. In his time the grammarian Patanjali is supposed to have lived.

PUSHPOTKA*T*Ā. A Rākshasī, the wife of Vi*s*ravas and mother of Rāva*n*a and Kumbha-ka*r*na.

PUT. A hell to which childless men are said to be condemned. "A name invented to explain the word *puttra*, son (hell-saver)."

PŪTANĀ. A female demon, daughter of Bali. She attempted to kill the infant K*ri*sh*n*a by suckling him, but was herself sucked to death by the child.

RĀDHĀ. 1. Wife of Adhiratha and foster-mother of Kar*n*a. 2. The favourite mistress and consort of K*ri*sh*n*a while he lived as Go-pāla among the cowherds in V*ri*ndā-vana. She was wife of Ayana-ghosha, a cowherd. Considered by some to be an incarnation of Lakshmī, and worshipped accordingly. Some have discovered a mystical character in Rādhā, and consider her as the type of the human soul drawn to the ineffable god, K*ri*sh*n*a, or as that pure divine love to which the fickle lover returns.

RĀDHEYA. A metronymic of Kar*n*a.

RĀDHIKĀ. A diminutive and endearing form of the name Rādhā.

RĀGA (mas.), RĀGINĪ (fem.). The Rāgas are the musical

modes or melodies personified, six or more in number, and the Rāginīs are their consorts.

RĀGHAVA. Descendant of Raghu, a name of Rāma.

RĀGHAVA-PĀNDAVĪYA. A modern poem by Kavi Rāja, which is in high repute. It is an artificial work, which exhibits extraordinary ingenuity in the employment of words. As its name implies, the poem celebrates the actions of Rāghava, *i.e.*, Rāma, the descendant of Raghu, and also those of the Pā*nd*ava princes. It thus recounts at once in the same words the story of the Rāmāya*n*a and that of the Mahā-bhārata; and the composition is so managed that the words may be understood as applying either to Rāma or the Pā*nd*avas. It has been printed.

RĀGHAVA-VILĀSA. A poem on the life of Rāma by Vi*s*wa-nātha, the author of the Sāhitya-darpa*n*a.

RAGHU. A king of the Solar race. According to the Raghu-van*s*a, he was the son of Dilīpa and great-grandfather of Rāma, who from Raghu got the patronymic Rāghava and the title Raghu-pati, chief of the race of Raghu. The authorities disagree as to the genealogy of Raghu, but all admit him to be an ancestor of Rāma.

RAGHU-PATI. *See* Raghu.

RAGHU-VANSA. 'The race of Raghu.' The name of a celebrated poem in nineteen cantos by Kāli-dāsa on the ancestry and life of Rāma. It has been translated into Latin by Stenzler, and into English by Griffiths. There are other translations and many editions of the text.

RĀHU. Rāhu and Ketu are in astronomy the ascending and descending nodes. Rāhu is the cause of eclipses, and the term is used to designate the eclipse itself. He is also considered as one of the planets, as king of meteors, and as guardian of the south-west quarter. Mythologially Rāhu is a Daitya who is supposed to seize the sun and moon and swallow them, thus obscuring their rays and causing eclipses. He was son of Viprachitti and Sinhikā, and is called by his metronymic Sainhikeya. He had four arms, and his lower part ended in a tail. He was a great mischief-maker, and when the gods had produced the Amrita by churning the ocean, he assumed a disguise, and insinuating himself amongst them, drank some of it. The sun and moon detected him and informed Vish*n*u, who cut off his head and two of his arms, but, as he had secured immortality, his body was placed in the stellar sphere, the upper parts, represented by a dragon's head, being the ascending node, and the lower parts, represented by a dragon's tail, being Ketu the descending node. Rāhu wreaks his vengeance on the sun and moon by occasionally swallowing them. The Vishnu Purāna says, "Eight black horses draw the dusky chariot of Rāhu, and once harnessed are attached to it for ever. On the Parvans (nodes, or lunar and solar eclipses) Rāhu directs his course from the sun to the moon, and back again from the moon to the sun. The eight horses of the chariot of Ketu, swift as the wind, are of the dusky red colour of lac, or of the smoke of burning straw." Rāhu is called Abhra-pisācha, 'the demon of the sky;' Bharanī-bhū, 'born from the asterism Bharanī;' Graha, 'the seizer;' Kabandha, 'the headless.'

RAIBHYA. A sage who was the friend of Bharadwāja. He had two sons, Arvāvasu and Parāvasu. The latter, under the curse of Bharadwāja, killed his father, mistaking him for an antelope, as he was walking about at night covered with an antelope's skin. Arvāvasu retired into the forest to obtain by devotion a remission of his brother's guilt. When he returned, Parāvasu charged him with the crime, and he again retired to his devotions. These so pleased the gods that they drove away Parāvasu and restored Raibhya to life. *See* Yava-krīta.

RAIVATA. 1. Son of Reva or Revata. Also called Kakudmin. He had a very lovely daughter named Revatī, and not deeming any mortal worthy of her, he went to Brahmā to consult him. At the command of that god he bestowed her upon Balarāma. He was king of Ānarta, and built the city of Kusasthalī or Dwārakā in Gujarat, which he made his capital. 2. One of the Manus (the fifth).

RAIVATA, RAIVATAKA. The range that branches off from the western portion of the Vindhya towards the north, extending nearly to the Jumna.

RĀJA-G*RI*HA. The capital of Magadha. Its site is still traceable in the hills between Patna and Gaya.

RĀJANYA. A Vedic designation of the Kshatriya caste.

RĀJARSHI (Rāja-*r*ishi). A *Ri*shi or saint of the regal caste; a Kshatriya who, through pure and holy life on earth, has been raised as a saint or demigod to Indra's heaven, as Viswā-mitra, Purū-ravas, &c.

RĀJA SEKHARA. A dramatist who was the author of the dramas Viddha-Sālabhanjikā and Prāchanda-Pāndava. He was also the writer of Karpūra-Manjarī, a drama entirely in Prākrit. Another play, Bāla-Rāmāyana, is attributed to him. He appears to have been the minister of some Rājput, and to have lived about the beginning of the twelfth century.

RĀJA-SŪYA. 'A royal sacrifice.' A great sacrifice performed at the installation of a king, religious in its nature but political in its operation, because it implied that he who instituted the sacrifice was a supreme lord, a king over kings, and his tributary princes were required to be present at the rite.

RĀJA-TARANGINĪ. A Sanskrit metrical history of Kashmīr by Kalhana Pandit. It commences with the days of fable and comes down to the year 1027 A.D. The author probably lived about 1148 A.D. This is the only known work in Sanskrit which deserves the name of a history. The text has been printed in Calcutta. Troyer published the text with a French translation. Wilson and Lassen have analysed it, and Dr. Bühler has lately reviewed the work in the *Indian Antiquary.*

RAJI. A son of Āyus and father of 500 sons of great valour. In one of the chronic wars between the gods and the Asuras it was declared by Brahmā that the victory should be gained by that side which Raji joined. The Asuras first sought him, and he undertook to aid them if they promised to make him their king on their victory being secured. They declined. The heavenly hosts repaired to him and undertook to make him their Indra. After the Asuras were defeated he became king of the gods, and Indra paid him homage. When he returned to his own city, he left Indra as his deputy in heaven. On Raji's death Indra refused to acknowledge the succession of his sons, and by the help of Brihaspati, who led them astray and effected their ruin, Indra recovered his sovereignty.

RĀKA. A Rākshasī, wife of Visravas and mother of Khara and Sūrpa-nakhā.

RĀKSHASAS. Goblins or evil spirits. They are not all equally bad, but have been classified as of three sorts—one as a set of beings like the Yakshas, another as a sort of Titans or enemies of the gods, and lastly, in the common acceptation of the term, demons and fiends who haunt cemeteries, disturb sacrifices, harass devout men, animate dead bodies, devour human beings, and vex and afflict mankind in all sorts of ways. These last are the Rākshasas of whom Rāva*n*a was chief, and according to some authorities, they are descended, like Rāva*n*a himself, from the sage Pulastya. According to other authorities, they sprang from Brahmā's foot. The Vish*n*u Purā*n*a also makes them descendants of Ka*s*yapa and Kha*s*ā, a daughter of Daksha, through their son Rākshas; and the Rāmāya*n*a states that when Brahmā created the waters, he formed certain beings to guard them who were called Rākshasas (from the root *raksh*, to guard, but the derivation from this root may have suggested the explanation), and the Vish*n*u Purā*n*a gives a somewhat similar derivation. It is thought that the Rākshasas of the epic poems were the rude barbarian races of India who were subdued by the Āryans.

When Hanumān entered the city of Lankā to reconnoitre in the form of a cat, he saw that "the Rākshasas sleeping in the houses were of every shape and form. Some of them disgusted the eye, while some were beautiful to look upon. Some had long arms and frightful shapes; some were very fat and some were very lean: some were mere dwarfs and some were prodigiously tall. Some had only one eye and others only one ear. Some had monstrous bellies, hanging breasts, long projecting teeth, and crooked thighs; whilst others were exceedingly beautiful to behold and clothed in great splendour. Some had two legs, some three legs, and some four legs. Some had the heads of serpents, some the heads of donkeys, some the heads of horses, and some the heads of elephants."—(*Rāmāyana.*)

The Rākshasas have a great many epithets descriptive of their characters and actions. They are called Anu*s*aras, A*s*aras, and Hanūshas, 'killers or hurters;' Ish*t*i-pachas, 'stealers of offerings;' Sandhyā-balas, 'strong in twilight;' Kshapā*t*as, Naktan-charas, Rātri-charas, and *S*amanī-shadas, 'night-walkers;' N*ri*-jagdhas or N*ri*-chakshas, 'cannibals;' Palalas, Palādas, Palan-kashas, Kravyāds, 'carnivorous;' Asra-pas, As*ri*k-pas, Kauna-pas, Kīlāla-pas, and Rakta-pas, 'blood-drinkers;' Danda*s*ukas, 'biters;' Praghasas, 'gluttons;' Malina-mukhas, 'black-faced;' Karbūras, &c. But many of these epithets are not reserved exclusively for Rākshasas.

RĀKSHASA-LOKA. *See* Loka.

RAKTA-VĪJA. An Asura whose combat with the goddess Chāmu*nd*ā (Devī) is celebrated in the Devī-māhātmya. Each drop of his blood as it fell on the ground produced a new Asura, but Chāmu*nd*ā put an end to this by drinking his blood and devouring his flesh.

RĀMA. There are three Rāmas: Para*s*u-rāma, Rāma-chandra, and Bala-rāma; but it is to the second of these that the name is specially applied.

RĀMA, RĀMA-CHANDRA. Eldest son of Da*s*a-ratha, a king of the Solar race, reigning at Ayodhyā. This Rāma is the seventh incarnation of the god Vish*n*u, and made his appearance in the world at the end of the Tretā or second age. His story is briefly told in the Vana Parva of the Mahā-bhārata, but it is given in full length as the grand subject of the Rāmāya*n*a. King Da*s*a-ratha was childless, and performed the a*s*wa-medha sacrifice with scrupulous care, in the hope of obtaining offspring. His devotion was accepted by the gods, and he received the promise of four sons. At this time the gods were in great terror and alarm at the deeds and menaces of Rāva*n*a, the Rākshasa king of Lankā, who had obtained extraordinary power, in virtue of severe penances and austere devotion to Brahmā. In their terror the gods appealed to Vish*n*u for deliverance, and he resolved to become manifest in the world with Da*s*a-ratha as his human father Da*s*a-ratha was performing a sacrifice when Vish*n*u appeared to him as a glorious being from out of the sacrificial fire, and gave to him a pot of nectar for his wives to drink. Da*s*a-ratha gave half of the nectar to Kau*s*alyā, who brought forth Rāma with a half of the divine essence, a quarter to Kaikeyī, whose son Bharata was endowed with a quarter of the deity, and the fourth part to Su-mitrā, who brought forth two sons, Lakshma*n*a and *S*atru-ghna, each having an eighth part of the divine essence. The brothers were all attached to each other, but Lakshma*n*a was more especially devoted to Rāma and *S*atru-ghna to Bharata.

[The two sons of Su-mitrā and the pairing off of the brothers have not passed without notice. The version of the Rāmāya*n*a given by Mr. Wheeler endeavours to account for these circumstances. It says that Da*s*a-ratha divided the divine nectar between his senior wives, Kau*s*alyā and Kaikeyī, and that when the younger, Su-mitrā, asked for some, Da*s*a-ratha desired them to share their portions with her. Each gave her half, so Sumitrā received two quarters and gave birth to two sons: "from the quarter which she received from Kausalyā she gave birth to Lakshmana, who became the ever-faithful friend of Rāma, and from the quarter she received from Kaikeyī she gave birth to Satru-ghna, who became the ever-faithful friend of Bharata." This account is silent as to the superior divinity of Rāma, and according to it all four brothers must have been equals as manifestations of the deity.]

The four brothers grew up together at Ayodhyā, but while they were yet striplings, the sage Viswāmitra sought the aid of Rāma to protect him from the Rākshasas. Dasa-ratha, though very unwilling, was constrained to consent to the sage's request. Rāma and Lakshmana then went to the hermitage of Viswāmitra, and there Rāma killed the female demon Tārakā, but it required a good deal of persuasion from the sage before he was induced to kill a female. Viswāmitra supplied Rāma with celestial arms, and exercised a considerable influence over his actions. Viswāmitra afterwards took Rāma and his brothers to Mithilā to the court of Janaka king of Videha. This king had a lovely daughter named Sītā, whom he offered in marriage to any one who could bend the wonderful bow which had once belonged to Siva. Rāma not only bent the bow but broke it, and thus won the hand of the princess, who became a most virtuous and devoted wife. Rāma's three brothers also were married to a sister and two cousins of Sītā.

This breaking of the bow of Siva brought about a very curious incident, which is probably an interpolation of a later date, introduced for a sectarian purpose. Parasu-rāma, the sixth incarnation of Vishnu, the Brāhman exterminator of the Kshatriyas, was still living upon earth. He was a follower of Siva, and was offended at the breaking of that deity's bow. Notwithstanding that he and Rāma were both incarnations of Vishnu, he challenged Rāma to a trial of strength and was discomfited, but Rāma spared his life because he was a Brāhman.

Preparations were made at Ayodhyā for the inauguration of Rāma as successor to the throne. Kaikeyī, the second wife of Dasa-ratha, and mother of Bharata, was her husband's favourite. She was kind to Rāma in childhood and youth, but she had a spiteful humpbacked female slave named Mantharā. This woman worked upon the maternal affection of her mistress until she aroused a strong feeling of jealousy against Rāma. Kaikeyī had a quarrel and a long struggle with her husband, but he at length consented to install Bharata and to send Rāma into exile for fourteen years. Rāma departed with his wife Sītā and his brother Lakshmana, and travelling southwards, he took up his abode at Chitra-kūta, in the Dandaka forest, between the Yamunā and Godāvarī. Soon after the departure of Rāma, his father Dasa-ratha died, and Bharata was called upon to ascend the throne. He declined, and set out for the forest with an army to bring Rāma back. When the brothers met there was a long contention. Rāma refused to return until the term of his father's sentence was completed, and Bharata declined to ascend the throne. At length it was arranged that Bharata should return and act as his brother's vicegerent. As a sign of Rāma's supremacy Bharata carried back with him a pair of Rāma's shoes, and these were always brought out ceremoniously when business had to be transacted. Rāma passed ten years of his banishment moving from one hermitage to another, and went at length to the hermitage of the sage Agastya, near the Vindhya mountains. This holy man recommended Rāma to take up his abode at Panchāvatī, on the river Godāvarī, and the party accordingly proceeded thither. This district was infested with Rākshasas, and one of them named Sūrpa-nakhā, a sister of Rāvana, saw Rāma and fell in love with him. He repelled her advances, and in her jealousy she attacked Sītā. This so enraged Lakshmana that he cut off her ears and nose. She brought her brothers Khara and Dūshana with an army of Rākshasas to avenge her wrongs, but they were all destroyed. Smarting under her mutilation and with *spretæ injuria formæ*, she repaired to her brother Rāvana in Lankā, and inspired him by her description with a fierce passion for Sītā. Rāvana proceeded to Rāma's residence in an aerial car, and his accomplice Mārīcha having lured Rāma from home, Rāvana assumed the form of a religious mendicant and lulled Sītā's apprehensions until he found an opportunity to declare himself and carry her off by force to Lankā. Rāma's despair and rage at the loss of his faithful wife were terrible. He and Lakshmana went in pursuit and tracked the ravisher. On their way they killed Kabandha, a headless monster, whose disembodied spirit counselled Rāma to seek the aid of Su-grīva, king of the monkeys. The two brothers accordingly went on their way to Su-grīva, and after overcoming some obstacles and assisting Su-grīva to recover Kishkindhyā, his capital, from his usurping brother Bālin, they entered into a firm alliance with him. Through this connection Rāma got the appellations of Kapi-prabhu and Kapi-ratha. He received not only the support of all the forces of Su-grīva and his allies, but the active aid of Hanumān, son of the wind, minister and general of Su-grīva. Hanumān's extraordinary powers of leaping and flying enabled him to do all the work of reconnoitring. By superhuman efforts their armies were transported to Ceylon by "Rāma's bridge," and after many fiercely contested battles the city of Lankā was taken, Rāvana was killed and Sītā rescued. The recovery of his wife filled Rāma with joy, but he was jealous of her honour, received her coldly, and refused to take her back. She asserted her purity in touching and dignified language, and determined to prove her innocence by the ordeal of fire. She entered the flames in the presence of men and gods, and Agni, god of fire, led her forth and placed her in Rāma's arms unhurt. Rāma then returned, taking with him his chief allies to Ayodhyā. Re-united with his three brothers, he was solemnly crowned and began a glorious reign, Lakshma*n*a being associated with him in the government. The sixth section of the Rāmāya*n*a here concludes; the remainder of the story is told in the Uttara-kā*nd*a, a subsequent addition. The treatment which Sītā received in captivity was better than might have been expected at the hands of a Rākshasa. She had asserted and proved her purity, and Rāma believed her; but jealous thoughts would cross his sensitive mind, and when his subjects blamed him for taking back his wife, he resolved, although she was pregnant, to send her to spend the rest of her life at the hermitage of Vālmīki. There she was delivered of her twin sons Kusa and Lava, who bore upon their persons the marks of their high paternity. When they were about fifteen years old they wandered accidentally to Ayodhyā and were recognised by their father, who acknowledged them, and recalled Sītā to attest her innocence. She returned, and in a public assembly declared her purity, and called upon the earth to verify her words. It did so. The ground opened and received "the daughter of the furrow," and Rāma lost his beloved and only wife. Unable to endure life without her, he resolved to follow, and the gods favoured his determination. Time appeared to him in the form of an ascetic and told him that he must stay on earth or ascend to heaven and rule over the gods. Lakshma*n*a with devoted fraternal affection endeavoured to save his brother from what he deemed the baleful visit of Time. He incurred a sentence of death for his interference, and was conveyed bodily to Indra's heaven. Rāma with great state and ceremony went to the river *S*arayū, and walking into the water was hailed by Brahmā's voice of welcome from heaven, and entered "into the glory of Vishnu."

The conclusion of the story as told in the version of the Rāmāya*n*a used by Mr. Wheeler differs materially. It represents that Sītā remained in exile until her sons were fifteen or sixteen years of age. Rāma had resolved upon performing the A*s*wa-medha sacrifice; the horse was turned loose, and *S*atrughna followed it with an army. Ku*s*a and Lava took the horse and defeated and wounded *S*atru-ghna. Rāma then sent Lakshma*n*a to recover the horse, but he was defeated and left for dead. Next Bharata was sent with Hanumān, but they were also defeated. Rāma then set out himself to repair his reverses. When the father and sons came into each other's presence, nature spoke out, and Rāma acknowledged his sons. Sītā also, after receiving an admonition from Vālmīki, agreed to forgive her husband. They returned to Ayodhyā. Rāma performed the A*s*wa-medha, and they passed the remainder of their lives in peace and joy.

The incidents of the first six kā*nd*as of the Rāmāya*n*a supply the plot of Bhava-bhūti's drama Mahā-vīra-charita. The Uttara-kā*nd*a is the basis of his Uttara-rāma-charita. This describes Rāma's jealousy, the banishment of Sītā, and the birth of her sons; but the subsequent action is more human and affecting than in the poem. Rāma repents of his unjust treatment of his wife, and goes forth to seek her. The course of his wanderings is depicted with great poetic beauty, and his meeting with his sons and his reconciliation with Sītā are described with exquisite pathos and tenderness. The drama closes when

"All conspires to make their happiness complete."

The worship of Rāma still holds its ground, particularly in Oude and Bihār, and he has numerous worshippers. "It is noteworthy," says Professor Williams, "that the Rāma legends have always retained their purity, and, unlike those of Brahmā,

Kr*ish*n*a*, *S*iva, and Durgā, have never been mixed up with indecencies and licentiousness. In fact, the worship of Rāma has never degenerated to the same extent as that of some of these other deities." This is true; but it may be observed that Rāma and his wife were pure; there was nothing in their characters suggestive of license; and if "the husband of one wife" and the devoted and affectionate wife had come to be associated with impure ideas, they must have lost all that gave them a title to veneration. The name of Rāma, as 'Rām! Rām!' is a common form of salutation.

RĀMĀYA*N*A. 'The Adventures of Rāma.' The oldest of the Sansk*r*it epic poems, written by the sage Vālmīki. It is supposed to have been composed about five centuries B.C., and to have received its present form a century or two later. The MSS. of the Rāmāya*n*a vary greatly. There are two well-known distinct recensions, the Northern and the Bengal. The Northern is the older and the purer; the additions and alterations in that of Bengal are so numerous that it is not trustworthy, and has even been called "spurious." Later researches have shown that the variations in MSS. found in different parts of India are so diverse that the versions can hardly be classed in a certain number of different recensions. Unfortunately the inferior edition is the one best known to Europeans. Carey and Marshman translated two books of it, and Signor Gorresio has given an Italian translation of the whole. Schlegel published a Latin translation of the first book of the Northern recension. The full texts of both these recensions have been printed, and Mr. Wheeler has given an epitome of the whole work after the Bengal recension. There is also a poetical version by Griffiths.

Besides the ancient Rāmāya*n*a, there is another popular work of comparative modern times called the Adhyātma Rāmāya*n*a. The authorship of it is ascribed to Vyāsa, but it is generally considered to be a part of the Brahmā*nd*a Purā*n*a. It is a sort of spiritualised version of the poem, in which Rāma is depicted as a saviour and deliverer, as a god rather than a man. It is divided into seven books, which bear the same names as those of the original poem, but it is not so long.

The Rāmāya*n*a celebrates the life and exploits of Rāma (Rāma-chandra), the loves of Rāma and his wife Sītā, the rape of the latter by Rāva*n*a, the demon king of Ceylon, the war carried on by Rāma and his monkey allies against Rāva*n*a, ending in the destruction of the demon and the rescue of Sītā, the restoration of Rāma to the throne of Ayodhyā, his jealousy and banishment of Sītā, her residence at the hermitage of Vālmīki, the birth of her twin sons Ku*s*a and Lava, the father's discovery and recognition of his children, the recall of Sītā, the attestation of her innocence, her death, Rāma's resolution to follow her, and his translation to heaven.

The Rāmāya*n*a is divided into seven kā*nd*as or sections, and contains about 50,000 lines. The last of the seven sections is probably of later date than the rest of the work.

1. Bāla-kā*nd*a. The boyhood of Rāma.
2. Ayodhyā-kā*nd*a. The scenes at Ayodhyā, and the banishment of Rāma by his father, King Da*s*a-ratha.
3. Ara*n*ya-kā*nd*a. 'Forest section.' Rāma's life in the forest, and the rape of Sītā by Rāva*n*a.
4. Kishkindhyā-kā*nd*a. Rāma's residence at Kishkindhyā, the capital of his monkey ally, King Su-grīva.
5. Sundara-kā*nd*a. 'Beautiful section.' The marvellous passage of the straits by Rāma and his allies and their arrival in Ceylon.
6. Yuddha-kā*nd*a. 'War section.' The war with Rāva*n*a, his defeat and death, the recovery of Sītā, the return to Ayodhyā and the coronation of Rāma. This is sometimes called the Lankā or Ceylon Kā*nd*a.
7. Uttara-kā*nd*a. 'Later section.' Rāma's life in Ayodhyā, his banishment of Sītā, the birth of his two sons, his recognition of them and of the innocence of his wife, their reunion, her death, and his translation to heaven.

The writer or the compilers of the Rāmāya*n*a had a high estimate of its value, and it is still held in very great veneration. A verse in the introduction says, "He who reads and repeats this holy life-giving Rāmāya*n*a is liberated from all his sins and exalted with all his posterity to the highest heaven;" and in the second chapter Brahmā is made to say, "As long as the mountains and rivers shall continue on the surface of the earth, so long shall the story of the Rāmāya*n*a be current in the world." (For the age of the Rāmāya*n*a, see p. 190.)

RĀMA-GIRI. 'The hill of Rāma.' It stands a short distance north of Nāgpur.

RĀMA-SETU. 'Rāma's bridge,' constructed for him by his

general, Nala, son of Viswa-karma, at the time of his invasion of Ceylon. This name is given to the line of rocks in the channel between the continent and Ceylon, called in maps "Adam's bridge."

RĀMATĀPANĪYOPANISHAD. An Upanishad of the Atharva-veda, in which Rāma is worshipped as the supreme god and the sage Yājnawalkya is his glorifier. It has been printed and translated by Weber in his *Indische Studien*, vol. ix.

RAMBHĀ. An Apsaras or nymph produced at the churning of the ocean, and popularly the type of female beauty. She was sent by Indra to seduce Viswāmitra, but was cursed by that sage to become a stone, and remain so for a thousand years. According to the Rāmāyana, she was seen by Rāvana when he went to Kailāsa, and he was so smitten by her charms that he ravished her, although she told him that she was the wife of Nala-kūvara, son of his brother Kuvera.

RĀMESWARA. 'Lord of Rāma.' Name of one of the twelve great Lingas set up, as is said, by Rāma at Rāmeswaram or Rāmisseram, which is a celebrated place of pilgrimage, and contains a most magnificent temple.

RĀMOPĀKHYĀNA. 'The story of Rāma,' as told in the Vana-parva of the Mahā-bhārata. It relates many, but far from all, of the incidents celebrated in the Rāmāyana; it makes no mention of Vālmīki, the author of that poem, and it represents Rāma as a human being and a great hero, but not a deity.

RANTIDEVA. A pious and benevolent king of the Lunar race, sixth in descent from Bharata. He is mentioned in the Mahā-bhārata and Purānas as being enormously rich, very religious, and charitable and profuse in his sacrifices. The former authority says that he had 200,000 cooks, that he had 2000 head of cattle and as many other animals slaughtered daily for use in his kitchen, and that he fed innumerable beggars daily with beef.

RATI. 'Love, desire.' The Venus of the Hindus, the goddess of sexual pleasures, wife of Kāma the god of love, and daughter of Daksha. She is also called Revā, Kāmi, Prīti, Kāma-patni, 'wife of Kāma;' Kāma-kalā, 'part of Kāma;' Kāma-priyā, 'beloved of Kāma;' Rāga-latā, 'vine of love;' Māyāvatī, 'deceiver;' Kelikilā, 'wanton;' Subhāngī, 'fair-limbed.'

RATNĀVALĪ. 'The necklace.' A drama ascribed to a

king of Kashmīr named *S*rī Harsha Deva. The subject of the play is the loves of Udayana or Vatsa, prince of Kau*s*āmbī, and Vāsava-dattā, princess of Ujjayinī. It was written between 1113 and 1125 A.D., and has been translated by Wilson. There are several editions of the text.

RAUCHYA. The thirteenth Manu. *See* Manu.

RAUDRA. A descendant of Rudra. A name of Kārttikeya, the god of war.

RĀVANA. The demon king of Lankā or Ceylon, from which he expelled his half-brother Kuvera. He was son of Vi*s*ravas by his wife Nikashā, daughter of the Rākshasa Su-mālī. He was half-brother of Kuvera, and grandson of the *Ri*shi Pulastya; and as Kuvera is king of the Yakshas, Rāva*n*a is king of the demons called Rākshasas. Pulastya is said to be the progenitor, not only of Rāva*n*a, but of the whole race of Rākshasas. By penance and devotion to Brahmā, Rāva*n*a was made invulnerable against gods and demons, but he was doomed to die through a woman. He was also enabled to assume any form he pleased. All Rākshasas are malignant and terrible, but Rāva*n*a as their chief attained the utmost degree of wickedness, and was a very incarnation of evil. He is described in the Rāmāya*n*a as having "ten heads (hence his names Da*s*ānana, Da*s*a-kan*th*a, and Pankti-grīva), twenty arms, and copper-coloured eyes, and bright teeth like the young moon. His form was as a thick cloud or a mountain, or the god of death with open mouth. He had all the marks of royalty, but his body bore the impress of wounds inflicted by all the divine arms in his warfare with the gods. It was scarred by the thunderbolt of Indra, by the tusks of Indra's elephant Airāvata, and by the discus of Vish*n*u. His strength was so great that he could agitate the seas and split the tops of mountains. He was a breaker of all laws and a ravisher of other men's wives. . . . Tall as a mountain peak, he stopped with his arms the sun and moon in their course, and prevented their rising." The terror he inspires is such that where he is "the sun does not give out its heat, the winds do not blow, and the ocean becomes motionless." His evil deeds cried aloud for vengeance, and the cry reached heaven. Vish*n*u declared that, as Rāva*n*a had been too proud to seek protection against men and beasts, he should fall under their attacks, so Vish*n*u became incarnate as Rāma-chandra for the express purpose of destroying

Rāva*n*a, and vast numbers of monkeys and bears were created to aid in the enterprise. Rāma's wars against the Rākshasas inflicted such losses upon them as greatly to incense Rāva*n*a. Burning with rage, and excited by a passion for Sītā, the wife of Rāma, he left his island abode, repaired to Rāma's dwelling, assumed the appearance of a religious mendicant, and carried off Sītā to Lankā. Rāva*n*a urged Sītā to become his wife, and threatened to kill and eat her if she refused. Sītā persistently resisted, and was saved from death by the interposition of one of Rāva*n*a's wives. Rāma called to his assistance his allies Su-grīva and Hanumān, with their hosts of monkeys and bears. They built Rāma's bridge, by which they passed over into Lankā, and after many battles and wholesale slaughter Rāva*n*a was brought to bay at the city of Lankā. Rāma and Rāva*n*a fought together on equal terms for a long while, victory sometimes inclining to one sometimes to the other. Rāma with a sharp arrow cut off one of Rāva*n*a's heads, "but no sooner did the head fall on the ground than another sprang up in its room." Rāma then took an arrow which had been made by Brahmā, and discharged it at his foe. It entered his breast, came out of his back, went to the ocean, and then returned clean to the quiver of Rāma. "Rāva*n*a fell to the ground and expired, and the gods sounded celestial music in the heavens, and assembled in the sky and praised Rāma as Vish*n*u, in that he had slain that Rāva*n*a who would otherwise have caused their destruction." Rāva*n*a, though he was chief among Rākshasas, was a Brāhman on his father's side; he was well versed in Sansk*ri*t, used the Vedic ritual, and his body was burnt with Brāhmanical rites. There is a story that Rāva*n*a made each of the gods perform some menial office in his household: thus Agni was his cook, Varu*n*a supplied water, Kuvera furnished money, Vāyu swept the house, &c. The Vish*n*u Purā*n*a relates that Rāva*n*a, "elevated with wine, came on his tour of triumph to the city of Mahishmatī, but there he was taken prisoner by King Kārta-vīrya, and confined like a beast in a corner of his capital." The same authority states that, in another birth, Rāva*n*a was *S*i*s*u-pāla. Rāva*n*a's chief wife was Mandodarī, but he had many others, and they were burnt at his obsequies. His sons were Megha-nāda, also called Indra-jit, Rāva*n*i, and Aksha; Tri-*s*ikha or Tri-*s*iras, Devāntaka, Narāntaka, and Atikāya. *See* Nandī*s*a.

RAVI. The sun. *See* Sūrya.

RE*N*UKĀ. Daughter of King Prasenajit or Re*n*u, wife of Jamad-agni, and mother of Para*s*u-rāma. A sight of the connubial endearments of King Chitra-ratha and his wife inspired her with impure thoughts, and her husband, perceiving that she had "fallen from perfection," desired her sons to kill her. Ruma*n*wat, Su-shena, and Vasu, the three seniors, declined, and their father cursed them so that they became idiots. Para*s*u-rāma, the fourth son, cut off her head, which act so gratified his father that Jamad-agni promised him whatever blessings he desired. Among other things, Para*s*u-rāma asked that his mother might be brought back to life in ignorance of her death and in perfect purity. He also desired that his brothers might be restored to their senses. All this Jamad-agni bestowed. She was also called Konkanā.

REVĀ. The Narmadā river.

REVĀ. 1. Wife of Kar*n*a. 2. A name of Rati.

REVANTA. A son of Sūrya and Sanjnā. He is chief of the Guhyakas, and is also called Haya-vāhana.

REVATĪ. Daughter of King Raivata and wife of Bala-rāma. She was so beautiful that her father, thinking no one upon earth worthy of her, repaired to the god Brahmā to consult him about a husband. Brahmā delivered a long discourse on the glories of Vish*n*u, and directed Raivata to proceed to Dwārakā, where a portion of Vish*n*u was incarnate in the person of Bala-rāma. Ages had elapsed while Raivata was in heaven without his knowledge. When he returned to earth, "he found the race of men dwindled in stature, reduced in vigour, and enfeebled in intellect." He went to Bala-rāma and gave him Revatī, but that hero, "beholding the damsel of excessively lofty height, he shortened her with the end of his ploughshare, and she became his wife." She had two sons. Revatī is said to have taken part with her husband in his drinking bouts.

*RI*BHAVAS. *See R*ibhus.

*RI*BHU. 'Clever, skilful.' An epithet used for Indra, Agni, and the Ādityas. In the Purā*n*ic mythology, *R*ibhu is a "son of the supreme Brahmā, who, from his innate disposition, was of a holy character and acquainted with true wisdom." His pupil was Nidāgha, a son of Pulastya, and he took especial interest in his instruction, returning to him after two intervals of a thousand years "to instruct him further in true wisdom." The Vishnu Purāna, "originally composed by the Rishi (Nārāyana), was communicated by Brahmā to Ribhu." He was one of the four Kumāras (q.v.).

*RI*BHUS. Three sons of Su-dhanwan, a descendant of Angiras, severally named *Ri*bhu, Vibhu, and Vāja. Through their assiduous performance of good works they obtained divinity, exercised superhuman powers, and became entitled to receive praise and adoration. They are supposed to dwell in the solar sphere, and there is an indistinct identification of them with the rays of the sun; but, whether typical or not, they prove the admission, at an early date, of the doctrine that men might become divinities.—*Wilson.* They are celebrated in the *Ri*g-veda as skilful workmen, who fashioned Indra's chariot and horses, and made their parents young again. By command of the gods, and with a promise of exaltation to divine honours, they made a single new sacrificial cup into four. They are also spoken of as supporters of the sky.

*RI*BHUKSHAN. The first of the three *Ri*bhus. In the plural, the three *Ri*bhus.

*RI*CHĪKA. A *Ri*shi descended from Bh*ri*gu and husband of Satyavatī, son of Ūrva and father of Jamad-agni. (*See* Viswāmitra.) In the Mahā-bhārata and Vishnu Purāna it is related that *Ri*chīka was an old man when he demanded in marriage Satyavatī, the daughter of Gādhi, king of Kanya-kubja. Unwilling to give her to so old a man, Gādhi demanded of him 1000 white horses, each of them having one black ear. *Ri*chīka obtained these from the god Varuna, and so gained his wife. According to the Rāmāyana, he sold his son *S*unah-sephas to be a sacrifice.

*RI*DDHI. 'Prosperity.' The wife of Kuvera, god of wealth. The name is also used for Pārvatī, the wife of *S*iva.

*RI*G-VEDA. *See* Veda.

*RI*G-VIDHĀNA. Writings which treat of the mystic and magic efficacy of the recitation of hymns of the *Ri*g-veda, or even of single verses. Some of them are attributed to *S*aunaka, but probably belong only to the time of the Purānas.—*Weber.*

*RI*SHABHA. Son of Nābhi and Meru, and father of a hundred sons, the eldest of whom was Bharata. He gave his kingdom to his son and retired to a hermitage, where he led a life of such severe austerity and abstinence, that he became a mere "collection of skin and fibres, and went the way of all flesh." The Bhāgavata Purāna speaks of his wanderings in the western part of the Peninsula, and connects him with the establishment of the Jain religion in those parts. The name of the first Jain Tīrthakara or saint was Rishabha.

RISHI. An inspired poet or sage. The inspired persons to whom the hymns of the Vedas were revealed, and under whose names they stand. "The seven Rishis" (*saptarshi*), or the Prajā-patis, "the mind-born sons" of Brahmā, are often referred to. In the Satapatha Brāhmana their names are given as Gotama, Bharadwāja, Viswāmitra, Jamad-agni, Vasishtha, Kasyapa, and Atri. The Mahā-bhārata gives them as Marīchi, Atri, Angiras, Pulaha, Kratu, Pulastya, and Vasishtha. The Vāyu Purāna adds Bhrigu to this list, making eight, although it still calls them "seven." The Vishnu Purāna, more consistently, adds Bhrigu and Daksha, and calls them the nine Brahmarshis (*Brahma-rishis*). The names of Gautama, Kanwa, Vālmīki, Vyāsa, Manu, and Vibhāndaka are also enumerated among the great Rishis by different authorities. Besides these great Rishis there are many other Rishis. The seven Rishis are represented in the sky by the seven stars of the Great Bear, and as such are called Riksha and Chitra-sikhandinas, 'having bright crests.'

RISHI-BRĀHMANA. An old Anukramani, or Index of the Sāma-veda.

RISHYA-MŪKA. A mountain in the Dakhin, near the source of the Pampā river and the lake Pampā. Rāma abode there for a time with the monkeys.

RISHYA-SRINGA. 'The deer-horned.' A hermit, the son of Vibhāndaka, descended from Kasyapa. According to the Rāmāyana and Mahā-bharata he was born of a doe and had a small horn on his forehead. He was brought up in the forest by his father, and saw no other human being till he was verging upon manhood. There was great drought in the country of Anga, and the king, Lomapāda, was advised by his Brāhmans to send for the youth Rishya-sringa, who should marry his daughter Sāntā, and be the means of obtaining rain. A number of fair damsels were sent to bring him. He accompanied them back to their city, the desired rain fell, and he married Sāntā. This Sāntā was the adopted daughter of Lomapāda; her real father was

Dasa-ratha, and it was *Ri*shya-*sri*nga who performed that sacrifice for Dasa-ratha which brought about the birth of Rāma.

*RI*TU-PAR*N*A. A king of Ayodhyā, and son of Sarvakāma, into whose service Nala entered after he had lost his kingdom. He was "skilled profoundly in dice."

*RI*TU-SANHĀRA. 'The round of the seasons.' A poem attributed to Kāli-dāsa. This poem was published by Sir W. Jones, and was the first Sansk*ri*t work ever printed. There are other editions. It has been translated into Latin by Bohlen.

ROHI*N*Ī. 1. Daughter of Kasyapa and Surabhi, and mother of horned cattle, including Kāma-dhenu, the cow which grants desires. 2. Daughter of Daksha and fourth of the lunar asterisms, the favourite wife of the moon. 3. One of the wives of Vasu-deva, the father of K*ri*sh*n*a and mother of Bala-rāma. She was burned with her husband's corpse at Dwārakā. 4. K*ri*sh*n*a himself also had a wife so called, and the name is common.

RŌHITA. 'Red.' A red horse; a horse of the sun or of fire. 1. A deity celebrated in the Atharva-veda, probably a form of fire or the sun. 2. Son of King Haris-chandra. He is also called Rohitāswa. The fort of Rohtas is said to derive its name from him. *See* Haris-chandra.

ROMA-HARSHA*N*A. *See* Loma-harsha*n*a.

RUDRA. 'A howler or roarer; terrible.' In the Vedas Rudra has many attributes and many names. He is the howling terrible god, the god of storms, the father of the Rudras or Maruts, and is sometimes identified with the god of fire. On the one hand he is a destructive deity who brings diseases upon men and cattle, and upon the other he is a beneficent deity supposed to have a healing influence. These are the germs which afterwards developed into the god *S*iva. It is worthy of note that Rudra is first called Mahā-deva in the White Yajur-veda. As applied to the god *S*iva, the name of Rudra generally designates him in his destructive character. In the B*ri*had-āra*n*yaka Upanishad the Rudras are "ten vital breaths (*prāna*) with the heart (*manas*) as eleventh." In the Vish*n*u Purā*n*a the god Rudra is said to have sprung from the forehead of Brahmā, and at the command of that god to have separated his nature into male and female, then to have multiplied each of these into eleven persons, some of which were white and gentle, others black and furious. Elsewhere it is said that the eleven Rudras were sons of Kasyapa and Surabhi, and in another chapter of the same Purāna it is represented that Brahmā desired to create a son, and that Rudra came into existence as a youth. He wept and asked for a name. Brahmā gave him the name of Rudra; but he wept seven times more, and so he obtained seven other names: Bhava, Sarva, Īsāna, Pasupati, Bhīma, Ugra, and Mahā-deva. Other of the Purānas agree in this nomenclature. These names are sometimes used for Rudra or Siva himself, and at others for the seven manifestations of him, sometimes called his sons. The names of the eleven Rudras vary considerably in different books.

RUDRA-SĀVARNA. The twelfth Manu. *See* Manu.

RUKMIN. A son of King Bhīshmaka and king of Vidarbha, who offered his services to the Pandavas and Kauravas in turn, but was rejected by both on account of his extravagant boastings and pretensions. He was brother of Rukminī, with whom Krishna eloped. Rukmin pursued the fugitives and overtook them, but his army was defeated by Krishna, and he owed his life to the entreaties of his sister. He founded the city of Bhoja-kata, and was eventually killed by Bala-rāma.

RUKMINĪ. Daughter of Bhīshmaka, king of Vidarbha. According to the Hari-vansa she was sought in marriage by Krishna, with whom she fell in love. But her brother Rukmin was a friend of Kansa, whom Krishna had killed. He therefore opposed him and thwarted the match. Rukminī was then betrothed to Sisu-pāla, king of Chedi, but on her wedding day, as she was going to the temple, "Krishna saw her, took her by the hand, and carried her away in his chariot." They were pursued by her intended husband and by her brother Rukmin, but Krishna defeated them both, and took her safe to Dwārakā, where he married her. She was his principal wife and bore him a son, Pradyumna (q.v.). By him also she had nine other sons and one daughter. "These other sons were Chāru-deshna, Su-deshna, Chāru-deha, Su-shena, Chāru-gupta, Bhadra-chāru, Chāru-vinda, Su-chāru, and the very mighty Chāru; also one daughter, Chāru-matī." At Krishna's death she and seven other of his wives immolated themselves on his funeral pile.

RŪMĀ. Wife of the monkey king Su-grīva.

SABALĀSWAS. Sons of Daksha, one thousand in number,

brought forth after the loss of the Haryaswas. Like their predecessors, they were dissuaded by Nārada from begetting offspring, and "scattered themselves through the regions" never to return.

SACHĪ. Wife of Indra. *See* Indrānī.

SĀDHYAS. A Gana or class of inferior deities; the personified rites and prayers of the Vedas who dwell with the gods or in the intermediate region between heaven and earth. Their number is twelve according to one authority, and seventeen according to another, and the Purānas make them sons of Dharma and Sādhyā, daughter of Daksha.

SAGARA. A king of Ayodhyā, of the Solar race, and son of King Bāhu, who was driven out of his dominions by the Haihayas. Bāhu took refuge in the forest with his wives. Sagara's mother was then pregnant, and a rival wife, being jealous, gave her a drug to prevent her delivery. This poison confined the child in the womb for seven years, and in the interim Bāhu died. The pregnant wife wished to ascend his pyre, but the sage Aurva forbad her, predicting that she would give birth to a valiant universal monarch. When the child was born, Aurva gave him the name of Sagara (*sa*, 'with,' and *gara*, 'poison'). The child grew up, and having heard his father's history, he vowed that he would exterminate the Haihayas and the other barbarians, and recover his ancestral kingdom. He obtained from Aurva the Agneyāstra or fire weapon, and, armed with this, he put nearly the whole of the Haihayas to death and regained his throne. He would also "have destroyed the Sakas, Yavanas, Kāmbojas, Pāradas, and Pahlavas," but they applied to Vasishtha, Sagara's family priest, and he induced Sagara to spare them, but "he made the Yavanas shave their heads entirely; the Sakas he compelled to shave (the upper) half of their heads; the Pāradas wore their hair long; and the Pahlavas let their beards grow in obedience to his commands." Sagara married two wives, Su-mati, the daughter of Kasyapa, and Kesinī, the daughter of Rāja Vidarbha, but having no children, he besought the sage Aurva for this boon. Aurva promised that one wife should have one son; the other, sixty thousand. Kesinī chose the one, and her son was Asamanjas, through whom the royal line was continued. Su-mati had sixty thousand sons. Asamanjas was a wild immoral youth, and his father abandoned him. The other sixty thousand sons followed the courses of their brother, and their impiety was such that the gods complained of them to the sage Kapila and the god Vishnu. Sagara engaged in the performance of an Aswa-medha or sacrifice of a horse, but although the animal was guarded by his sixty thousand sons, it was carried off to Pātāla. Sagara directed his sons to recover it. They dug their way to the infernal regions, and there they found the horse grazing and the sage Kapila seated close by engaged in meditation. Conceiving him to be the thief, they menaced him with their weapons. Disturbed from his devotions, "he looked upon them for an instant, and they were reduced to ashes by the (sacred) flame that darted from his person." Their remains were discovered by Ansumat, the son of Asamanjas, who prayed Kapila that the victims of his wrath might be raised through his favour to heaven. Kapila promised that the grandson of Ansumat should be the means of accomplishing this by bringing down the river of heaven. Ansumat then returned to Sagara, who completed his sacrifice, and he gave the name of Sāgara to the chasm which his sons had dug, and Sāgara means 'ocean.' The son of Ansumat was Dilīpa, and his son was Bhagīratha. The devotion of Bhagīratha brought down from heaven the holy Ganges, which flows from the toe of Vishnu, and its waters having laved the ashes of the sons of Sagara, cleansed them from all impurity. Their Manes were thus made fit for the exequial ceremonies and for admission into Swarga. The Ganges received the name of Sāgara in honour of Sagara, and Bhāgīrathī from the name of the devout king whose prayers brought her down to earth. (*See* Bhāgīrathī.) The Hari-vansa adds another marvel to the story. Sagara's wife Su-mati was delivered of a gourd containing sixty thousand seeds, which became embryos and grew. Sagara at first placed them in vessels of milk, but afterwards each one had a separate nurse, and at ten months they all ran about. The name of Sagara is frequently cited in deeds conveying grants of land in honour of his generosity in respect of such gifts.

SAHA-DEVA. The youngest of the five Pāndu princes, twin son of Mādrī, the second wife of Pāndu, and mythologically son of the Aswins, or more specifically of the Aswin Dasra. He was learned in the science of astronomy, which he had studied under Drona, and he was also well acquainted with the management of cattle. (*See* Mahā-bhārata.) He had a son named Su-hotra by his wife Vijayā.

SAHASRĀKSHA. 'Thousand-eyed.' An epithet of Indra.

SĀHITYA-DARPAṆA. 'The mirror of composition.' A celebrated work on poetry and rhetoric by Viśwanātha Kavi Rāja, written about the fifteenth century. It has been translated into English for the *Bibliotheca Indica.* There are several editions of the text.

ŚAIBYĀ. Wife of Hariś-chandra (q.v.); wife of Jyāmagha (q.v.); wife of Śata-dhanu (q.v.).

SAINDHAVAS. The people of Sindhu or Sindh, of the country between the Indus and the Jhilam.

ŚAIVA PURĀṆA. Same as Śiva Purāṇa.

ŚAKA. An era commencing 78 A.D., and called the era of Śālivāhana. Cunningham supposes its epoch to be connected with a defeat of the Śakas by Śālivāhana.

ŚĀKALA. The city of the Bāhīkas or Madras, in the Panjāb. It has been identified with the Sagala of Ptolemy on the Hyphasis (Byās), south-west of Lahore. Cunningham says it is the Sangala of Alexander.

ŚĀKALYA. An old grammarian and expositor of the Vedas who lived before the time of Yāska. He is said to have divided a Sanhitā of the Veda into five, and to have taught these portions to as many disciples. He was also called Veda-mitra and Deva-mitra.

ŚĀKAPŪṆI, ŚĀKAPŪRṆI. An author who arranged a part of the Ṛig-veda and appended a glossary. He lived before the time of Yāska.

ŚAKAS. A northern people, usually associated with the Yavanas. Wilson says, "These people, the Sakai and Sacæ of classical writers, the Indo-Scythians of Ptolemy, extended, about the commencement of our era, along the West of India, from the Hindu Koh to the mouths of the Indus." They were probably Turk or Tatar tribes, and were among those recorded as conquered by King Sagara, who compelled them to shave the upper half of their heads. They seem to have been encountered and kept back by King Vikramāditya of Ujjayinī, who was called Śakāri, 'foe of the Śakas.'

ŚĀKAṬĀYANA. An ancient grammarian anterior to Yāska

and Pā*n*ini. Part of his work is said to have been lately discovered by Dr. Bühler.

*S*ĀKHĀ. 'Branch, sect.' The *S*ākhās of the Vedas are the different recensions of the same text as taught and handed down traditionally by different schools and teachers, showing some slight variations, the effect of long-continued oral tradition. *See* Veda.

*S*ĀKINĪS. Female demons attendant on Durgā.

*S*AKRA. A name of Indra.

*S*ĀKRĀ*N*Ī. Wife of Indra. *See* Indrā*n*ī.

*S*AKRA-PRASTHA. Same as Indra-prastha.

SĀKTA. A worshipper of the *S*aktis.

*S*AKTI. The wife or the female energy of a deity, but especially of *S*iva. *See* Devī and Tantra.

*S*AKTI, *S*AKTRI. A priest and eldest son of Vasish*t*ha. King Kalmāsha-pāda struck him with a whip, and he cursed the king to become possessed by a man-eating Rākshasa. He himself became the first victim of the monster he had evoked.

*S*AKUNI. Brother of Queen Gāndhārī, and so uncle of the Kaurava princes. He was a skilful gambler and a cheat, so he was selected to be the opponent of Yudhi-sh*t*hira in the match in which that prince was induced to stake and lose his all. He also was known by the patronymic Saubala, from Su-bala, his father.

*S*AKUNTALĀ. A nymph who was the daughter of Viswāmitra by the nymph Menakā. She was born and left in a forest, where she was nourished by birds until found by the sage Ka*n*wa. She was brought up by this sage in his hermitage as his daughter, and is often called his daughter. The loves, marriage, separation, and re-union of *S*akuntalā and King Dushyanta are the subject of the celebrated drama *S*akuntalā. She was mother of Bharata, the head of a long race of kings, who has given his name to India (Bhārata-varsha), and the wars of whose descendants are sung in the Mahā-bhārata. The story of the loves of Dushyanta and *S*akuntalā is, that while she was living in the hermitage of Ka*n*wa she was seen in the forest by King Dushyanta, who fell in love with her. He induced her to contract with him a Gandharva marriage, that is, a simple declaration of mutual acceptance. On leaving her to return to his city, he gave her a ring as a pledge of his love. When the nymph when back to the hermitage, she was so engrossed with thoughts of her husband that she heeded not the approach of the sage Dur-vāsas, who had come to visit Ka*n*wa, so that choleric saint cursed her to be forgotten by her beloved. He afterwards relented, and promised that the curse should be removed as soon as Dushyanta should see the ring. *S*akuntalā, finding herself with child, set off to her husband; but on her way she bathed in a sacred pool, and there lost the ring. On reaching the palace, the king did not recognise her and would not own her, so she was taken by her mother to the forest, where she gave birth to Bharata. Then it happened that a fisherman caught a large fish and in it found a ring which he carried to Dushyanta. The king recognised his own ring, and he soon afterwards accepted *S*akuntalā and her son Bharata. Kāli-dāsa's drama of *S*akuntalā was the first translation made from Sanskrit into English. It excited great curiosity and gained much admiration when it appeared. There are several recensions of the text extant. The text has been often printed, and there are many translations into the languages of Europe. Professor Williams has published a beautifully illustrated translation.

*S*ĀLAGRĀMA. A stone held sacred and worshipped by the Vaish*n*avas, because its spirals are supposed to contain or to be typical of Vish*n*u. It is an ammonite found in the river Gandak, and is valued more or less highly according to the number of its spirals and perforations.

*S*ĀLIVĀHANA. A celebrated king of the south of India, who was the enemy of Vikramāditya, and whose era, the *S*aka, dates from A.D. 78. His capital was Prati-sh*t*hāna on the Godāvarī. He was killed in battle at Kārūr.

*S*ĀLWA. Name of a country in the west of India, or Rājasthān; also the name of its king.

*S*ALYA. King of the Madras, and brother of Mādrī, second wife of Pā*nd*u. In the great war he left the side of the Pā*nd*avas and went over to the Kauravas. He acted as charioteer of Kar*n*a in the great battle. At the death of Kar*n*a he succeeded him as general, and commanded the army on the last day of the battle, when he was slain by Yudhi-sh*t*hira.

SĀMA-VEDA. The third Veda. *See* Veda.

SĀMA-VIDHĀNĀ BRĀHMA*N*A. The third Brāhma*n*a

of the Sāma-veda. It has been edited and translated by Burnell.

SĀMAYACHĀRIKA SŪTRAS. Rules for the usages and practices of everyday life. *See* Sūtras.

*S*ĀMBA. A son of K*r*ish*n*a by Jāmbavatī, but the Linga Purā*n*a names Rukmi*n*ī as his mother. At the swayam-vara of Draupadī he carried off that princess, but he was pursued by Dur-yodhana and his friends and made prisoner. Bala-rāma undertook to obtain his release, and when that hero thrust his ploughshare under the ramparts of Hastinā-pura and threatened it with ruin, the Kauravas gave up their prisoner, and Bala-rāma took him to Dwārakā, There he lived a dissolute life and scoffed at sacred things. The devotions of the three great sages, Vi*s*wāmitra, Dur-vāsas, and Nārada, excited the ridicule of *S*āmba and his boon companions. They dressed *S*āmba up to represent a woman with child and took him to the sages, inquiring whether he would give birth to a boy or a girl. The sages answered, "This is not a woman, but the son of K*r*ish*n*a, and he shall bring forth an iron club which shall destroy the whole race of Yadu, . . . and you and all your people shall perish by that club." *S*āmba accordingly brought forth an iron club, which Ugrasena caused to be pounded and cast into the sea. These ashes produced rushes, and the rushes when gathered turned into clubs, or into reeds which were used as swords. One piece could not be crushed. This was subsequently found in the belly of a fish, and was used to tip an arrow, which arrow was used by the hunter Jaras, who with it unintentionally killed K*r*ish*n*a. Under the curse of Dur-vāsas, *S*āmba became a leper and retired to the Panjāb, where by fasting, penance, and prayer he obtained the favour of Sūrya (the sun), and was cured of his leprosy. He built a temple to the sun on the banks of the Chandra-bhāgā (Chināb), and introduced the worship of that luminary.

*S*ĀMBA-PURĀ*N*A. *See* Purā*n*a.

*S*AMBARA. In the Vedas, a demon, also called a Dasyu, who fought against King Divodāsa, but was defeated and had his many castles destroyed by Indra. He appears to be a mythical personification of drought, of a kindred character to V*r*itra, or identical with him. In the Purā*n*as a Daitya who carried off Pradyumna and threw him into the sea, but was subsequently slain by him. (*See* Pradyumna.) He was also employed by Hiranya-kasipu to destroy Prahlāda.

SAMBHU. A name of Siva; also one of the Rudras.

SAMBŪKA. A Sudra, mentioned in the Raghu-vansā, who performed religious austerities and penances improper for a man of his caste, and was consequently killed by Rāma-chandra.

SAMĪ. The *Acacia suma*, the wood of which is used for obtaining fire by friction. So Agni, or fire, is called Samī-garbha, 'having the Samī for its womb.' It is sometimes personified and worshipped as a goddess, Samī-devī.

SAMPĀTI. A mythical bird who appears in the Rāmāyana as son of Vishnu's bird Garuda, and brother of Jatāyus. According to another account he was son of Aruna and Syenī. He was the ally of Rāma.

SAMVARANA. Son of Riksha, fourth in descent from Ikshwāku, and father of Kuru. According to the Mahā-bhārata he was driven from Hastinā-pura by the Pānchālas, and forced to take refuge among the thickets of the Indus. When the sage Vasishtha joined his people and became the Rāja's family priest, they recovered their country under Kuru.

SAMVARTA. Writer of a Dharma-sāstra or code of law bearing his name.

SAMVAT, SAMVATSARA. 'Year.' The era of Vikramāditya, dating from 57 B.C.

SANAIS-CHARA. 'Slow-moving.' A name of Sani or Saturn.

SANAKA, SANANDA, SANĀTANA, SANAT-KUMĀRA. The four Kumāras or mind-born sons of Brahmā. Some specify seven. Sanat-kumāra (or Sanat-sujāta) was the most prominent of them. They are also called by the patronymic Vaidhātra. *See* Kumāra.

SANAT-KUMĀRA PURĀNA. *See* Purāna.

SANDHYĀ. 'Twilight.' It is personified as the daughter of Brahmā and wife of Siva. In the Siva Purāna it is related that Brahmā having attempted to do violence to his daughter, she changed herself into a deer. Brahmā then assumed the form of a stag and pursued her through the sky. Siva saw this, and shot an arrow which cut off the head of the stag. Brahmā then reassumed his own form and paid homage to Siva. The arrow remains in the sky in the sixth lunar mansion, called Ardrā, and the stag's head remains in the fifth mansion, Mriga-siras.

SANDHYĀ-BALA. 'Strong in twilight.' Rākshasas and other demons, supposed to be most powerful at twilight.

*S*ĀN*D*ILYA. A descendant of *Sand*ila. A particular sage who was connected with the Chhāndogya Upanishad; one who wrote a book of Sūtras, one who wrote upon law, and one who was the author of the Bhāgavata heresy: two or more of these may be one and the same person. The Sūtras or aphorisms have been published in the *Bibliotheca Indica*.

SĀNDĪPANI. A master-at-arms who gave instruction to Bala-rāma and K*r*ish*n*a.

SANDRACOTTUS. *See* Chandra-gupta.

SANGĪTA-RATNĀKARA. A work on singing, dancing, and pantomime, written by *S*ārngi Deva.

SANHITĀ. That portion of a Veda which comprises the hymns. *See* Veda.

SANHITOPANISHAD. The eighth Brāhma*n*a of the Sāma-veda. The text with a commentary has been published by Burnell.

*S*ANI. The planet Saturn. The regent of that planet, represented as a black man in black garments. *S*ani was a son of the sun and Chhāyā, but another statement is that he was the offspring of Bala-rāma and Revatī. He is also known as Āra, Ko*n*a, and Kroda (*cf.* Κρόνος), and by the patronymic *S*aura. His influence is evil, hence he is called Krūra-d*ri*s and Krūra-lochana, 'the evil-eyed one.' He is also Manda, 'the slow;' Pangu, 'the lame;' Sanai*s*-chara, 'slow-moving;' Saptārchī, 'seven-rayed;' and Asita, 'the dark.'

SANJAYA. 1. The charioteer of Dh*ri*ta-rāsh*t*ra. He was minister also, and went as ambassador to the Pā*nd*avas before the great war broke out. He is represented as reciting to Dh*ri*ta-rāsh*t*ra the Bhagavad-gītā. His patronymic is Gāvalga*n*i, son of Gavalga*n*a. 2. A king of Ujjayinī and father of Vāsava-dattā.

SANJNĀ. 'Conscience.' According to the Purā*n*as, she was daughter of Vi*s*wa-karma and wife of the sun. She had three children by him, the Manu Vaivaswata, Yama, and Yamī (goddess of the Yamunā river). "Unable to endure the fervours of her lord, Sanjnā gave him Chhāyā (shade) as his handmaid, and repaired to the forests to practise devout exercises." The sun beheld her engaged in austerities in the form of a mare, and he approached her as a horse. Hence sprang the two Aswins and Revanta. Sūrya then took Sanjnā back to his own dwelling, but his effulgence was still so overpowering, that her father, Viswa-karma, placed the sun upon his lathe, and cut away an eighth part of his brilliancy. She is also call Dyumayī, 'the brilliant,' and Maha-vīryā, 'the very powerful.'

SANKARA. 'Auspicious.' A name of Siva in his creative character or as chief of the Rudras.

SANKARĀCHĀRYA (Sankara + āchārya). The great religious reformer and teacher of the Vedānta philosophy, who lived in the eighth or ninth century. He was a native of Kerala or Malabar, and lived a very erratic life, disputing with heretics and popularising the Vedānta philosophy by his preaching and writings wherever he went. His travels extended as far as Kashmīr, and he died at Kedāranāth in the Himālayas at the early age of thirty-two. His learning and sanctity were held in such high estimation and reverence, that he was looked upon as an incarnation of Siva, and was believed to have the power of working miracles. The god Siva was the special object of his worship, and he was the founder of the great sect of Smārtava Brāhmans, who are very numerous and powerful in the south. He established several maths or monasteries for the teaching and preservation of his doctrines. Some of these still remain. The chief one is at Sringa-giri or Sringiri, on the edge of the Western Ghauts in the Mysore, and it has the supreme control of the Smārtava sect. The writings attributed to him are very numerous; chief among them are his Bhāshyas or commentaries on the Sūtras or aphorisms of Vyāsa, a commentary on the Bhagavad-gītā, some commentaries on the Upanishads, and the Ānanda-laharī, a hymn in praise of Pārvatī, the consort of Siva.

SANKARA-VIJAYA. 'The triumph of Sankara.' A biography of Sankarāchārya relating his controversies with heretical sects and his refutation of their doctrines and superstitions. There is more than one work bearing this name; one by Ānanda Giri, which is published in the *Bibliotheca Indica;* another by Mādhavāchārya; the latter is distinguished as the Sankshepa Sankara-vijaya. The work of Ānanda Giri has been critically examined by Kāshināth Trimbak Telang in the *Indian Antiquary*, vol. v.

SANKARSHANA. A name of Bala-rāma.

SANKHA. Writer of a Dharma-sāstra or law-book bearing

his name. He is often coupled with Likhita, and the two seem to have worked together.

SĀNKHĀYANA. 1. Name of a writer who was the author of the Sānkhāyana Brāhma*n*a of the *Rig*-veda, and of certain *S*rauta-sūtras also called by his name. 2. He is the oldest known writer on the Ars Erotica, and is author of the work called Sānkhāyana Kāma-sūtra.

SĀNKHYA. A school of philosophy. *See* Darsana.

SANKHYA-DAR*S*A*N*A. Kapila's aphorisms on the Sānkhya philosophy. They have been printed.

SĀNKHYA-KĀRIKĀ. A work on the Sānkhya philosophy, written by Īswara K*ri*sh*n*a; translated by Colebrooke and Wilson.

SĀNKHYA-PRAVACHANA. A text-book of the Sānkhya philosophy, said to have been written by Kapila himself. Printed in the *Bibliotheca Indica.*

SĀNKHYA-SĀRA. A work on the Sānkhya philosophy by Vijnāna Bhikshu. Edited by Hall in the *Bibliotheca Indica.*

SANNYĀSĪ. A Brāhman in the fourth and last stage of his religious life. (*See* Brāhman.) In the present day the term has a wider meaning, and is applied to various kinds of religious mendicants who wander about and subsist upon alms, most of them in a filthy condition and with very scanty clothing. They are generally devotees of *S*iva.

*S*Ā*N*TĀ. Daughter of Da*s*a-ratha, son of Aja, but adopted by Loma-pāda or Roma-pāda, king of Anga. She was married to *Ri*shya-*s*ringa.

*S*ĀNTANU. A king of the Lunar race, son of Pratīpa, father of Bhīshma, and in a way the grandfather of Dh*ri*tarāsh*t*ra and Pā*n*du. Regarding him it is said, "Every decrepit man whom he touches with his hands becomes young." (*See* Mahā-bhārata.) He was called Satya-vāch, 'truth-speaker,' and was remarkable for his "devotion and charity, modesty, constancy, and resolution."

*S*ĀNTI-*S*ATAKA. A century of verses on peace of mind. A poem of repute writen by *S*rī *S*ihlana.

SAPTARSHI (Sapta-*ri*shi). The seven great *Ri*shis. *See* *Ri*shi.

SAPTA-*S*ATI. A poem of 700 verses on the triumphs of Durgā. It is also called Devī-māhātmya.

SAPTA-SINDHAVA. 'The seven rivers.' The term frequently occurs in the Vedas, and has been widely known and somewhat differently applied. It was apparently known to the Romans in the days of Augustus, for Virgil says—

> "Ceu septem surgens sedatis amnibus altus
> Per tacitum Ganges."—*Eneid*, ix. 30.

They appear in Zend as the Hapta-heando, and the early Muhammadan travellers have translated the term. But their Saba' Sīn, 'seven rivers,' according to Bīrūnī, applies to the rivers which flow northwards from the mountains of the Hindu Koh, and "uniting near Turmuz, form the river of Balkh (the Oxus)." The hymn in which the names of the rivers have been given has the following description:—"Each set of seven (streams) has followed a threefold course. The Sindhu surpasses the other rivers in impetuosity. . . . Receive favourably this my hymn, O Gangā, Yamunā, Saraswatī, *S*utudri, Parush*n*i; hear, O Marud-v*r*idhā, with the Asiknī and Vitastā, and thou, Ārjīkīyā, with the Sushomā. Unite first in thy course with the Trish*t*āmā, the Susartū, the Rasā, and the Swetī; thou meetest with the Gomatī, and the Krumu with the Kubhā and the Mehatnū." According to this, the "seven rivers" are—(1.) Gangā (Ganges); (2.) Yamunā (Jumna); (3.) Saraswatī (Sarsuti); (4.) *S*utudri (Satlej); (5.) Parush*n*i; (6.) Marud-v*r*idhā; (7.) Ārjīkīyā (the Vi*p*ā*s*ā, Hyphasis Byās). Wilson says "the Parush*n*i is identified with the Irāvatī" (Hydraotes, Rāvi), but in this hymn it is the Marud-v*r*idhā which would seem to be the Irāvatī, because it is said to unite with the Asiknī (Akesines, Chandrabhāga, Chināb) and the Vitastā (Hydaspes or Jhilam). This would leave the Parush*n*i unsettled. The other names, with the exception of the Gomatī (Gūmtī), are not identified. Sushomā has been said to be the Sindhu, but in this hymn the Sindhu is clearly distinct. In the Mahā-bhārata the seven rivers are named in one place Vaswokasārā, Nalinī, Pāvanī, Gangā, Sītā, Sindhu, and Jambū-nadī; and in another, Gangā, Yamunā, Plakshagā, Rathasthā, Saryu (Sarju), Gomatī, and Gandakī (Gandak). In the Rāmāya*n*a and the Purā*n*as the seven rivers are the seven streams into which the Ganges divided after falling from the brow of *S*iva, the Nalinī, Hlādinī, and Pāvanī going east, the Chakshu, Sītā, and Sindhu to the west, while the Ganges proper, the Bhāgīrathī, flowed to the south. The term is also used for the seven great oceans of the world, and for the country of the seven rivers.

SAPTA-VADHRI. A Vedic *Ri*shi. In a hymn he says, "Aswins, by your devices sunder the wickerwork for the liberation of the terrified, imploring *Ri*shi Sapta-vadhri." Concerning this the following old story is told. Sapta-vadhri had seven brothers who determined to prevent his having intercourse with his wife. So they shut him up every night in a large basket, which they locked and sealed, and in the morning they let him out. He prayed to the Aswins, who enabled him to get out of his cage during the night and to return to it at daybreak.

SARABHA. 1. A fabulous animal represented as having eight legs and as dwelling in the Himālayas. It is called also Utpādaka and Kunjarārāti. 2. One of Rāma's monkey allies.

SARA-BHANGA. A hermit visited by Rāma and Sītā in the Da*nd*aka forest. When he had seen Rāma he declared that his desire had been granted, and that he would depart to the highest heaven. He prepared a fire and entered it. His body was consumed, but there came forth from the fire a beautiful youth, and in this form Sara-bhanga departed to heaven.

SĀRADĀ-TILAKA. 1. A mystic poem by Lakshma*n*a. 2. A dramatic monologue by Sankara, not earlier than the twelfth century. 3. Name of a Tantra.

SARADWAT. A *Ri*shi said to be the father of K*ri*pā. He is also called Gautama. *See* K*ri*pā.

SARAMĀ. 1. In the *Ri*g-veda the dog of Indra and mother of the two dogs called, after their mother, Sārameyas, who each had four eyes, and were the watchdogs of Yama. Saramā is said to have pursued and recovered the cows stolen by the Pa*n*is, a myth which has been supposed to mean that Saramā is the same as Ushas, the dawn, and that the cows represent the rays of the sun carried away by night. 2. The wife of Vibhīsha*n*a, who attended upon Sītā, and showed her great kindness when she was in captivity with Rāva*n*a. 3. In the Bhāgavata Purā*n*a, Saramā is one of the daughters of Daksha, and the mother of wild animals.

SĀRAMEYAS. The two children of Saramā, Indra's watchdog; they were the watchdogs of Yama, and each had four eyes. They have been compared with the Greek Hermes.

SARA*N*YŪ. 'The fleet runner.' A daughter of Twash*tri*. She has been identified with the Greek Erinnys. The beginning of this myth is in a hymn of the *Ri*g-veda, which says—"1. Twash*tri* makes a wedding for his daughter. (Hearing) this, the whole world assembles. The mother of Yama, the wedded wife of the great Vivaswat (the sun), disappeared. 2. They concealed the immortal (bride) from mortals. Making (another) of like appearance, they gave her to Vivaswat. Sara*n*yū bore the two A*s*wins, and when she had done so she deserted the two twins." In the Nirukta the story is expanded as follows:—"Sara*n*yū, the daughter of Twash*tri*, bore twins to Vivaswat, the son of Aditi. She then substituted for herself another female of similar appearance, and fled in the form of a mare. Vivaswat in like manner assumed the shape of a horse and followed her. From their intercourse sprang two A*s*wins, while Manu was the offspring of Savar*n*ā (or the female of like appearance)." The B*ri*had-devatā has another version of the same story:—"Twash*tri* had twin children, (a daughter) Sara*n*yū and (a son) Tri-*s*iras. He gave Sara*n*yū in marriage to Vivaswat, to whom she bore Yama and Yamī, who also were twins. Creating a female like herself without her husband's knowledge, and making the twins over in charge to her, Sara*n*yū took the form of a mare and departed. Vivaswat, in ignorance, begot on the female who was left Manu, a royal *Ri*shi, who resembled his father in glory; but discovering that the real Sara*n*yū, Twash*tri*'s daughter, had gone away, Vivaswat followed her quickly, taking the shape of a horse of the same species as she. Recognising him in that form, she approached him with the desire of sexual connection, which he gratified. In their haste his seed fell on the ground, and she, being desirous of offspring, smelled it. From this act sprang the two Kumāras (youths), Nāsatya and Dasra, who were lauded as A*s*wins (sprung from a horse)."—*Muir's Texts*, v. 227. See the Purā*n*ic version under "Sanjnā."

SĀRASWATA. 1. In the Mahā-bhārata the *Ri*shi Sāraswata is represented as being the son of the personified river Saraswatī. In a time of great drought he was fed with fish by his mother, and so was enabled to keep up his knowledge of the Vedas, while other Brāhmans were reduced to such straits for the means of subsistence that study was neglected and the Vedas were lost. When the drought was over, the Brāhmans flocked to him for instruction, and 60,000 acquired a knowledge of the Vedas from him. "This legend," says Wilson, "appears to indicate the revival, or, more probably, the introduction of the Hindu ritual by the race of Brāhmans, or the people called Sāraswata," who dwelt near the Saraswatī river. Sāraswata Brāhmans still dwell in the Panjāb, and are met with in many other parts. 2. The country about the Saraswatī river. 3. A great national division of the Brāhman caste.

SARASWATĪ. 'Watery, elegant.' In the Vedas, Saraswatī is primarily a river, but is celebrated in the hymns both as a river and a deity. The Saraswatī river was one boundary of Brahmāvartta, the home of the early Āryans, and was to them, in all likelihood, a sacred river, as the Ganges has long been to their descendants. As a river goddess, Saraswatī is lauded for the fertilising and purifying powers of her waters, and as the bestower of fertility, fatness, and wealth. Her position as Vāch, the goddess of speech, finds no mention in the *Rig*-veda, but is recognised by the Brāhma*n*as and the Mahā-bhārata. Dr. Muir endeavours to account for her acquisition of this character. He say, "When once the river had acquired a divine character, it was quite natural that she should be regarded as the patroness of the ceremonies which were celebrated on the margin of her holy waters, and that her direction and blessing should be invoked as essential to their proper performance and success. The connection into which she was thus brought with sacred rites may have led to the further step of imagining her to have an influence on the composition of the hymns which formed so important a part of the proceedings, and of identifying her with Vāch, the goddess of speech." In later times Saraswatī is the wife of Brahmā, the goddess of speech and learning, inventress of the Sansk*ri*t language and Deva-nāgarī letters, and patroness of the arts and sciences. "She is represented as of a white colour, without any superfluity of limbs, and not unfrequently of a graceful figure, wearing a slender crescent on her brow and sitting on a lotus."—*Wilson.* The same authority states that "the Vaish*n*avas of Bengal have a popular legend that she was the wife of Vish*n*u, as were also Lakshmī and Gangā. The ladies disagreed; Saraswatī, like the other prototype of learned ladies, Minerva, being something of a termagant, and Vish*n*u finding that one wife was as much as he could manage, transferred

Saraswatī to Brahmā and Gangā to *S*iva, and contented himself with Lakshmī alone. (*See* Vāch.) Other names of Saraswatī are Bhāratī, Brāhmī, Pūt-kārī, *S*āradā, Vāgīswarī. The river is now called Sarsuti. It falls from the Himālayas and is lost in the sands of the desert. In ancient times it flowed on to the sea. A passage in the *Rig*-veda says of it, "She who goes on pure from the mountains as far as the sea."—*Max Müller*, *Veda*, 45. According to the Mahā-bhārata it was dried up by the curse of the sage Utathya (q.v.). *See* Sapta-sindhava.

SARASWATĪ KĀN*T*HĀBHARA*N*A. A treatise on poetical and rhetorical composition generally ascribed to Bhoja Rāja.

SARAYU. The Sarju river or Gogra.

SARMISH*T*HĀ. Daughter of V*ri*shaparvan the Dānava, second wife of Yayāti and mother of Purū. *See* Devayānī.

*S*ĀRNGA. The bow of K*ri*sh*n*a.

SARVA, *S*ARVA. A Vedic deity; the destroyer. Afterwards a name of *S*iva and of one of the Rudras. *See* Rudra.

SARVA-DAR*S*A*N*A SANGRAHA. A work by Mādhavāchārya which gives an account of the Dar*s*a*n*as or schools of philosophy, whether orthodox or heretical. It has been printed.

*S*ARVARĪ. A woman of low caste, who was very devout and looked for the coming of Rāma until she had grown old. In reward of her piety a sage raised her from her low caste, and when she had seen Rāma she burnt herself on a funeral pile. She ascended from the pile in a chariot to the heaven of Vish*n*u.

SARVA-SĀRA. Name of an Upanishad.

*S*A*S*ĀDA. 'Hare-eater.' A name given to Vikukshi (q.v.).

*S*A*S*Ī, *S*A*S*IN. The moon, so called from the marks on the moon being considered to resemble a hare (*sasa*).

*S*ĀSTRA. 'A rule, book, treatise.' Any book of divine or recognised authority, but more especially the law-books.

*S*ATA-DHANU. A king who had a virtuous and discreet wife named *S*aibyā. They were both worshippers of Vish*n*u. One day they met a heretic, with whom *S*ata-dhanu conversed; but the wife "turned away from him and cast her eyes up to the sun." After a time *S*ata-dhanu died and his wife ascended his funeral pile. The wife was born again as a princess with a knowledge of her previous existence, but the husband received the form of a dog. She recognised him in this form and placed the bridal garland on his neck. Then she reminded him of his previous existence and of the fault which had caused his degradation. He was greatly humiliated and died from a broken spirit. After that, he was born successively as a jackal, a wolf, a crow, and a peacock. In each form his wife recognised him, reminded him of his sin, and urged him to make efforts for restoration to his former dignity. At length "he was born as the son of a person of distinction," and *S*aibyā then elected him as her bridegroom; and having "again invested him with the character of her husband, they lived happily together." When he died she again followed him in death, and both "ascended beyond the sphere of Indra to the regions where all desires are for ever gratified." "This legend," says Wilson, "is peculiar to the Vishnu Purā*n*a, although the doctrine it inculcates is to be found elsewhere.

*S*ATA-DHANWAN, *S*ATA-DHANUS. 'Having a hundred bows.' A Yādava and son of H*ri*dika. He killed Satrājit, father of Satya-bhāmā, the wife of K*ri*sh*n*a, in his sleep, and was himself killed in revenge by K*ri*sh*n*a, who struck off his head with his discus.

*S*ATA-DRU. 'Flowing in a hundred (channels).' The name of the river Sutlej, the Zaradrus of Ptolemy, the Hesudrus of Pliny.

*S*ATA-GHNĪ. 'Slaying hundreds.' A missile weapon used by K*ri*sh*n*a. It is described in the Mahā-bhārata as a stone set round with iron spikes, but many have supposed it to be a rocket or other fiery weapon.

*S*ATA-KRATU. 'The god of a hundred rites;' Indra.

*S*ATAPATHA-BRĀHMA*N*A. A celebrated Brāhma*n*a attached to the White Yajur-veda, and ascribed to the *R*ishi Yājnawalkya. It is found in two Sākhās, the Mādhyandina and the Kā*n*wa. This is the most complete and systematic as well as the most important of all the Brāhma*n*as. It has been edited by Weber.

*S*ATA-RŪPĀ. 'The hundred-formed.' The first woman. According to one account she was the daughter of Brahmā, and from their incestuous intercourse the first Manu, named Swāyambhuva, was born. Another account makes her the wife, not the mother, of Manu. The account given by Manu is that Brahmā divided himself into two parts, male and female, and from them sprang Manu. She is also called Sāvitrī. *See* Virāj and Brahmā.

*S*ĀTĀTAPA. An old writer on law.

*S*ĀTA-VĀHANA. A name by which *S*āli-vāhana is sometimes called.

SATĪ. A daughter of Daksha and wife of Rudra, *i.e.*, *S*iva. The Vish*n*u Purā*n*a states that she "abandoned her body in consequence of the anger of Daksha. She then became the daughter of Himavat and Menā; and the divine Bhava again married Umā, who was identical with his (*S*iva's) former spouse." The authorities generally agree that she died or killed herself in consequence of the quarrel between her husband and father; and the Kāsī Kha*nd*a, a modern work, represents that she entered the fire and became a Satī. *See* Pī*th*a-sthāna.

SATRĀJIT, SATRĀJITA. Son of Nighna. In return for praise rendered to the sun he beheld the luminary in his proper form, and received from him the wonderful Syamantaka gem. He lost the gem, but it was recovered and restored to him by K*r*ish*n*a. In return he presented K*r*ish*n*a with his daughter Satya-bhāmā to wife. There had been many suitors for this lady's hand, and one of them, named *S*ata-dhanwan, in revenge for her loss, killed Satrājit and carried off the gem, but he was afterwards killed by K*r*ish*n*a.

*S*ATRU-GHNA. 'Foe destroyer.' Twin-brother of Laksh*m*a*n*a and half-brother of Rāma, in whom an eighth part of the divinity of Vish*n*u was incarnate. His wife was *S*ruta-kīrti, cousin of Sītā. He fought on the side of Rāma and killed the Rākshasa chief Lava*n*a. *See* Da*s*a-ratha and Rāma.

SATYA-BHĀMĀ. Daughter of Satrājita and one of the four chief wives of K*r*ish*n*a. She had ten sons, Bhānu, Subhānu, Swar-bhānu, Prabhānu, Bhānumat, Chandrabhānu, B*r*ihadbhānu, Atibhānu, *S*rībhānu, and Pratibhānu. K*r*ish*n*a took her with him to Indra's heaven, and she induced him to bring away the Pārijāta tree.

SATYA-DH*R*ITI. Son of *S*aradwat and grandson of the sage Gautama. According to the Vish*n*u Purā*n*a he was father by the nymph Urva*s*ī of K*r*ipa and K*r*ipī.

SĀTYAKI. A kinsman of K*r*ish*n*a's, who fought on the side of the Pa*nd*avas, and was K*r*ish*n*a's charioteer. He assassinated K*r*ita-varma in a drinking bout at Dwārakā, and was himself cut down by the friends of his victim. He is also called Dāruka and Yuyudhāna; and *S*aineya from his father, *S*ini.

SATYA-LOKA. *See* Loka.

SATYAVĀN. *See* Sāvitrī.

SATYA-VATĪ. 1. Daughter of Uparichara, king of Chedi, by an Apsaras named Adrikā, who was condemned to live on earth in the form of a fish. She was mother of Vyāsa by the *Ri*shi Parā*s*ara, and she was also wife of King *S*āntanu, mother of Vichitra-vīrya and Chitrāngada, and grandmother of the Kauravas and Pā*nd*avas, the rivals in the great war. The sage Parā*s*ara met her as she was crossing the river Yamunā when she was quite a girl, and the offspring of their illicit intercourse was brought forth on an island (*dwīpa*) in that river, and was hence called Dwaipāyana. (*See* Vyāsa.) She was also called Gandha-kālī, Gandha-vatī, and Kālānganī; and as her mother lived in the form of a fish, she is called Dāsa-nandinī, Dāseyī, Jhajhodarī, and Matsyodarī, 'fish-born.' 2. A daughter of King Gādhi, wife of the Brāhman *Ri*chīka, mother of Jamad-agni and grandmother of Para*s*u-rāma. She was of the Ku*s*ika race, and is said to have been transformed into the Kau*s*ikī river. *See* *Ri*chīka and Viswāmitra.

SATYA-VRATA. 1. Name of the seventh Manu. *See* Manu.

2. A king of the Solar race, descended from Ikshwāku. He was father of Hari*s*-chandra, and is also named Vedhas and Tri-*s*anku. According to the Rāmāya*n*a he was a pious king, and was desirous of performing a sacrifice in virtue of which he might ascend bodily to heaven. Vasish*th*a, his priest, declined to perform it, declaring it impossible. He then applied to Vasish*th*a's sons, and they condemned him to become a Cha*nd*āla for his presumption. In his distress and degradation he applied to Vi*s*wāmitra, who promised to raise him in that form to heaven. Vi*s*wāmitra's intended sacrifice was strongly resisted by the sons of Vasish*th*a, but he reduced them to ashes, and condemned them to be born again as outcasts for seven hundred births. The wrathful sage bore down all other opposition, and Tri-*s*anku ascended to heaven. Here his entry was opposed by Indra and the gods, but Vi*s*wāmitra in a fury declared that he would create "another Indra, or the world should have no Indra at all." The gods were obliged to yield, and it was agreed that

Tri-sanku, an immortal, should hang with his head downwards, and shine among some stars newly called into being by Viswāmitra.

The Vishnu Purāna gives a more simple version. While Satya-vrata was a Chandāla, and the famine was raging, he supported Viswāmitra's family by hanging deer's flesh on a tree on the bank of the Ganges, so that they might obtain food without the degradation of receiving it from a Chandāla: for this charity Viswāmitra raised him to heaven.

The story is differently told in the Hari-vansa. Satya-vrata or Tri-sanku, when a prince, attempted to carry off the wife of a citizen, in consequence of which his father drove him from home, nor did Vasishtha, the family priest, endeavour to soften the father's decision. The period of his exile was a time of famine, and he greatly succoured the wife and family of Viswāmitra, who were in deep distress while the sage was absent far away. He completed his twelve years' exile and penance, and being hungry one day, and having no flesh to eat, he killed Vasishtha's wondrous cow, the Kāma-dhenu, and ate thereof himself, and gave some to the sons of Viswāmitra. In his rage Vasishtha gave him the name Tri-sanku, as being guilty of three great sins. Viswāmitra was gratified by the assistance which Satya-vrata had rendered to his family; "he installed him in his father's kingdom, . . . and, in spite of the resistance of the gods and of Vasishtha, exalted the king alive to heaven."

SĀTYĀYANA. Name of a Brāhmana.

SATYA-YAUVANA. A certain Vidyā-dhara.

SAUBHA. A magical city, apparently first mentioned in the Yajur-veda. An aerial city belonging to Haris-chandra, and according to popular belief still visible occasionally. It is called also Kha-pura, Prati-mārgaka, and Tranga. In the Mahā-bhārata an aerial or self-supporting city belonging to the Daityas, on the shore of the ocean, protected by the Sālwa king.

SAUBHARI. A devout sage, who, when he was old and emaciated, was inspired with a desire of offspring. He went to King Māndhātri, and demanded one of his fifty daughters. Afraid to refuse, and yet unwilling to bestow a daughter upon such a suitor, the king temporised, and endeavoured to evade the request. It was at length settled that, if any one of the daughters should accept him as a bridegroom, the king would consent to the marriage. Saubhari was conducted to the presence of the girls; but on his way he assumed a fair and handsome form, so that all the girls were captivated, and contended with each other as to who should become his wife. It ended by his marrying them all and taking them home. He caused Viswa-karma to build for each a separate palace, furnished in the most luxurious manner, and surrounded with exquisite gardens, where they lived a most happy life, each one of them having her husband always present with her, and believing that he was devoted to her and her only. By his wives he had a hundred and fifty sons; but as he found his hopes and desires for them to daily increase and expand, he resolved to devote himself wholly and solely to penance and the worship of Vishnu. Accordingly, he abandoned his children and retired with his wives to the forest. *See* Vishnu Purāna.

SAUDĀSA. Son of King Sudās. Their descendants are all Saudāsas. *See* Kalmāsha-pāda.

SAUNANDA. A club shaped like a pestle, which was one of the weapons of Bala-rāma.

SAUNAKA. A sage, the son of Sunaka and grandson of Gritsa-mada. He was the author of the Brihad-devatā, an Anukramani, and other works, and he was a teacher of the Atharva-veda. His pupil was Āswalāyana. There was a family of the name, and the works attributed to Saunaka are probably the productions of more than one person.

SAURA PURĀNA. *See* Purāna.

SAURĀSHTRAS. The people of Surāshtra.

SAUTI. Name of the sage who repeated the Mahā-bhārata to the Rishis in the Naimisha forest.

SAUVĪRAS. A people connected with the Saindhavas or people of Sindh, and probably inhabitants of the western and southern parts of the Panjāb. Cunningham says that Sauvīra was the plain country.

SĀVARNA, SĀVARNI. The eighth Manu. The name is used either alone or in combination for all the succeeding Manus to the fourteenth and last. *See* Manu.

SAVARNĀ. Wife of the sun. "The female of like appearance," whom Saranyū, wife of Vivaswat, substituted for herself when she fled. (*See* Saranyū.) Manu was the offspring of

Savarṇā. This is the version given in the Nirukta. In the Vishṇu Purāṇa, Savarṇā is daughter of the ocean, wife of Prāchīnabarhis, and mother of the ten Prachetasas.

SAVITṚI. 'Generator.' 1. A name used in the Vedas for the sun. Many hymns are addressed to him, and he is sometimes distinguished from that deity. 2. One of the Ādityas.

SĀVITRĪ. 1. The holy verse of the Veda, commonly called Gāyatrī. 2. A name of Śata-rūpā, the daughter and wife of Brahmā, who is sometimes regarded as a personification of the holy verse. 3. Daughter of King Aśwa-pati, and lover of Satyavān, whom she insisted on marrying, although she was warned by a seer that he had only one year to live. When the fatal day arrived, Satyavān went out to cut wood, and she followed him. There he fell, dying, to the earth, and she, as she supported him, saw a figure, who told her that he was Yama, king of the dead, and that he had come for her husband's spirit. Yama carried off the spirit towards the shades, but Sāvitrī followed him. Her devotion pleased Yama, and he offered her any boon except the life of her husband. She extorted three such boons from Yama, but still she followed him, and he was finally constrained to restore her husband to life.

SAVYA-SĀCHIN. 'Who pulls a bow with either hand.' A title of Arjuna.

SĀYAṆA. Sāyaṇāchārya, the celebrated commentator on the Ṛig-veda. "He was brother of Mādhavācharya, the prime minister of Vīra Bukka Rāya, Rāja of Vijaya-nagara, in the fourteenth century, a munificent patron of Hindu literature. Both the brothers are celebrated as scholars, and many important works are attributed to them; not only scholia on the Sanhitās and Brāhmaṇas of the Vedas, but original works on grammar and law; the fact, no doubt, being that they availed themselves of those means which their situation and influence secured them, and employed the most learned Brāhmans they could attract to Vijaya-nagara upon the works which bear their name, and to which they also contributed their own labour and learning; their works were, therefore, compiled under peculiar advantages, and are deservedly held in the highest estimation."—*Wilson.*

ŚESHA, ŚESHA-NĀGA. King of the serpent race or Nāgas, and of the infernal regions called Pātāla. A serpent with a thousand heads which is the couch and canopy of Vishṇu whilst sleeping during the intervals of creation. Sometimes *S*esha is represented as supporting the world, and sometimes as upholding the seven Pātālas or hells. Whenever he yawns he causes earthquakes. At the end of each kalpa he vomits venomous fire which destroys all creation. When the gods churned the ocean they made use of *S*esha as a great rope, which they twisted round the mountain Mandara, and so used it as a churn. He is represented clothed in purple and wearing a white necklace, holding in one hand a plough and in the other a pestle. He is also called Ananta, 'the endless,' as the symbol of eternity. His wife was named Ananta-*s*īrshā. He is sometimes distinct from Vāsuki but generally identified with him. In the Purā*n*as he is said to be the son of Ka*s*yapa and Kadru, and according to some authorities he was incarnate in Bala-rāma. His hood is called Ma*n*i-dwīpa, 'the island of jewels,' and his palace Ma*n*i-bhītti, 'jewel-walled,' or Ma*n*i-ma*nd*apa, 'jewel palace.'

SETU-BANDHA. 'Rāma's bridge.' The line of rocks between the continent and Ceylon called in maps "Adam's bridge." It is also know as Samudrāru. There is a poem called Setu-bandha or Setu-kāvya on the subject of the building of the bridge by Rāma's allies.

SHA*D*-DAR*S*ANĀ. *See* Dar*s*ana.

SHA*D*-VIN*S*A. 'Twenty-sixth.' One of the Brāhma*n*as of the Sāma-veda. It is called "the twenty-sixth" because it was added to the Prau*d*ha Brāhma*n*a, which has twenty-five sections.

SHA*T*-PURA. 'The sixfold city,' or 'the six cities' granted by Brahmā to the Asuras, and of which Nikumbha was king. It was taken by K*r*ish*n*a and given to Brahmā-datta, a Brāhman.—*Hari-vansa.*

SIDDHAS. A class of semi-divine beings of great purity and holiness, who dwell in the regions of the sky between the earth and the sun. They are said to be 88,000 in number.

SIDDHĀNTA. Any scientific work on astronomy or mathematics.

SIDDHĀNTA KAUMUDĪ. A modern and simplified form of Pā*n*ini's Grammar by Bha*tt*ojī Dīkshita. It is in print.

SIDDHĀNTA-*S*IROMA*N*I. A work on astronomy by Bhāskarāchārya. It has been printed, and has been translated for the *Bibliotheca Indica.*

SIKHANDIN, SIKHANDINĪ. *Sikhandinī* is said to have been the daughter of Rāja Drupada, but according to another statement she was one of the two wives whom Bhīshma obtained for his brother Vichitra-vīrya. "She (the widow) perished in the jungle, but before her death she had been assured by Parasu-rāma that she should become a man in a future birth, and cause the death of Bhīshma, who had been the author of her misfortunes." Accordingly she was born again as *Sikhandin*, son of Drupada. Bhīshma fell in battle pierced all over by the arrows of Arjuna, but according to this story the fatal shaft came from the hands of *Sikhandin*. *See* Ambā.

SIKSHĀ. Phonetics; one of the Vedāngas. The science which teaches the proper pronunciation and manner of reciting the Vedas. There are many treatises on this subject.

SILPA-SĀSTRA. The science of mechanics; it includes architecture. Any book or treatise on this science.

SINDHU. 1. The river Indus; also the country along that river and the people dwelling in it. From *Sindhu* came the *Hind* of the Arabs, the *Hindoi* or *Indoi* of the Greeks, and our *India*. 2. A river in Mālwa. There are others of the name. *See* Sapta-sindhava.

SINHALA, SINHALA-DWĪPA. Ceylon.

SINHĀSANA DWĀTRINSAT. The thirty-two stories told by the images which supported the throne of King Vikramāditya. It is the Singhāsan Battīsī in Hindustani, and is current in most of the languages of India.

SINHIKĀ. 1. A daughter of Daksha and wife of Kasyapa; also a daughter of Kasyapa and wife of Viprachitti. 2. A Rākshasī who tried to swallow Hanumān and make a meal of him. He allowed her to do so and then rent her body to pieces and departed. Her habit was to seize the shadow of the object she wished to devour and so drag the prey into her jaws.

SIPRĀ. The river on which the city of Ujjayinī stands.

SĪRA-DHWAJA. 'He of the plough-banner.' An epithet for Janaka.

SISUMĀRA. 'A porpoise.' The planetary sphere, which, as explained by the Vishnu Purāna, has the shape of a porpoise, Vishnu being seated in its heart, and Dhruva or the pole star in its tail. "As Dhruva revolves, it causes the sun, moon, and other planets to turn round also; and the lunar asterisms follow in its circular path, for all the celestial luminaries are, in fact, bound to the polar star by aerial cords."

*S*ISU-PĀLA. Son of Dama-ghosha, king of Chedi, by *S*ruta-devā, sister of Vasu-deva; he was therefore cousin of K*ri*sh*n*a, but he was K*ri*sh*n*a's implacable foe, because K*ri*sh*n*a had carried off Rukmi*n*ī, his intended wife. He was slain by K*ri*sh*n*a at the great sacrifice of Yudhi-sh*th*ira in punishment of opprobrious abuse. The Mahā-bhārata states that *S*i*s*u-pāla was born with three eyes and four arms. His parents were inclined to cast him out, but were warned by a voice not to do so, as his time was not come. It also foretold that his superfluous members should disappear when a certain person took the child into his lap, and that he would eventually die by the hands of that same person. K*ri*sh*n*a placed the child on his knees and the extra eye and arms disappeared; K*ri*sh*n*a also killed him. The Vish*n*u Purā*n*a contributes an additional legend about him. "*S*i*s*u-pāla was in a former existence the unrighteous but valiant monarch of the Daityas, Hira*n*ya-ka*s*ipu, who was killed by the divine guardian of creation (in the man-lion Avatāra). He was next the ten-headed (sovereign Rāva*n*a), whose unequalled prowess, strength, and power were overcome by the lord of the three worlds (Rāma). Having been killed by the deity in the form of Rāghava, he had long enjoyed the reward of his virtues in exemption from an embodied state, but had now received birth once more as *S*i*s*u-pāla, the son of Dama-ghosha, king of Chedi. In this character he renewed with greater inveteracy than ever his hostile hatred towards Pu*nd*arīkāksha (Vish*n*u), . . . and was in consequence slain by him. But from the circumstance of his thoughts being constantly engrossed by the supreme being, *S*ī*s*u-pāla was united with him after death, . . . for the lord bestows a heavenly and exalted station even upon those whom he slays in his displeasure." He was called *S*u-nītha, 'virtuous.'

*S*I*S*UPĀLA-BADHA. 'The death of Sī*s*u-pāla;' an epic poem by Māgha, in twenty cantos. It has been often printed, and has been translated into French by Fauche.

SĪTĀ. 'A furrow.' In the Veda, Sītā is the furrow, or husbandry personified, and worshipped as a deity presiding over agriculture and fruits. In the Rāmayā*n*a and later works she is daughter of Janaka king of Videha, and wife of Rāma. The old Vedic idea still adhered to her, for she sprang from a furrow. In the Rāmāyanā her father Janaka says, "As I was ploughing my field, there sprang from the plough a girl, obtained by me while cleansing my field, and known by name as Sītā (the furrow). This girl sprung from the earth grew up as my daughter." Hence she is styled Ayonijā, 'not born from the womb.' She is said to have lived before in the *Kr*ita age as Vedāvatī, and to be in reality the goddess Lakshmī in human form, born in the world for bringing about the destruction of Rāva*n*a, the Rākshasa king of Lankā, who was invulnerable to ordinary means, but doomed to die on account of a woman. Sītā became the wife of Rāma, who won her by bending the great bow of *S*iva. She was his only wife, and was the embodiment of purity, tenderness, and conjugal affection. She accompanied her husband in his exile, but was carried off from him by Rāva*n*a and kept in his palace at Lankā. There he made many efforts to win her to his will, but she continued firm against all persuasions, threats, and terrors, and maintained a dignified serenity throughout. When Rāma had slain the ravisher and recovered his wife, he received her coldly, and refused to take her back, for it was hard to believe it possible that she had retained her honour. She asserted her purity in touching language, and resolved to establish it by the ordeal of fire. The pile was raised and she entered the flames in the presence of gods and men, but she remained unhurt, and the god of fire brought her forth and placed her in her husband's arms. Notwithstanding this proof of her innocence, jealous thoughts passed through the mind of Rāma, and after he had ascended his ancestral throne at Ayodhyā, his people blamed him for taking back a wife who had been in the power of a licentious ravisher. So, although she was pregnant, he banished her and sent her to the hermitage of Vālmīki, where she gave birth to twin sons, Kusa and Lava. There she lived till the boys were about fifteen years old. One day they strayed to their father's capital. He recognised and acknowledged them and then recalled Sītā. She returned and publicly declared her innocence. But her heart was deeply wounded. She called upon her mother earth to attest her purity, and it did so. The ground opened, and she was taken back into the source from which she had sprung. Rāma was now disconsolate and resolved to quit this mortal life. (*See* Rāma.) Sītā had the appellations of Bhūmi-jā, Dharani-sutā, and Pārthivī, all meaning 'daughter of the earth.'

*S*IVA. The name *S*iva is unknown to the Vedas, but Rudra, another name of this deity, and almost equally common, occurs in the Veda both in the singular and plural, and from these the great deity *S*iva and his manifestations, the Rudras, have been developed. In the *Ri*g-veda the word Rudra is used for Agni, and the Maruts are called his sons. In other passages he is distinct from Agni. He is lauded as "the lord of songs, the lord of sacrifices, who heals remedies, is brilliant as the sun, the best and most bountiful of gods, who grants prosperity and welfare to horses and sheep, men, women, and cows; the lord of nourishment, who drives away diseases, dispenses remedies, and removes sin; but, on the other hand he is the wielder of the thunderbolt, the bearer of bow and arrows, and mounted on his chariot is terrible as a wild beast, destructive and fierce." In the Yajur-veda there is a long prayer called *S*atarudriya which is addressed to him and appeals to him under a great variety of epithets. He is "auspicious, not terrible;" "the deliverer, the first divine physician;" he is "blue-necked and red-coloured, who has a thousand eyes and bears a thousand quivers;" and in another hymn he is called "Tryambaka, the sweet-scented increaser of prosperity;" "a medicine for kine and horses, a medicine for men, and a (source of) ease to rams and ewes." In the Atharva-veda he is still the protector of cattle, but his character is fiercer. He is "dark, black, destroying, terrible." He is the "fierce god," who is besought to betake himself elsewhere, "and not to assail mankind with consumption, poison, or celestial fire." The Brāhma*n*as tell that when Rudra was born he wept, and his father, Prajāpati, asked the reason, and on being told that he wept because he had not received a name, his father gave him the name of Rudra (from the root *rud*, 'weep'). They also relate that at the request of the gods he pierced Prajāpati because of his incestuous intercourse with his daughter. In another place he is said to have applied to his father eight successive times for a name, and that he received in succession the names Bhava, Sarva, Pasupati, Ugradeva, Mahāndeva, Rudra, Īsāna, and Asani. In the Upanishads his character is further developed. He declares to the inquiring gods, "I alone was before (all things), and I exist and I shall be. No other transcends me. I am eternal and not eternal, discernible and undiscernible, I am Brahma and I am not Brahma." Again it is said, "He is the only Rudra, he is Īsāna, he is divine, he is Maheswara, he is Mahādeva." "There is only one Rudra, there is no place for a second. He rules this fourth world, controlling and productive; living beings abide with him, united with him. At the time of the end he annihilates all worlds, the protector." "He is without beginning, middle, or end; the one, the pervading, the spiritual and blessed, the wonderful, the consort of Umā, the supreme lord, the three-eyed, the blue-throated, the tranquil. . . . He is Brahmā, he is *S*iva, he is Indra; he is undecaying, supreme, self-resplendent; he is Vish*n*u, he is breath, he is the spirit, the supreme lord; he is all that hath been or that shall be, eternal. Knowing him, a man overpasses death. There is no other way to liberation." In the Rāmāya*n*a *S*iva is a great god, but the references to him have more of the idea of a personal god than of a supreme divinity. He is represented as fighting with Vish*n*u, and as receiving worship with Brahmā, Vish*n*u, and Indra, but he acknowledges the divinity of Rāma, and holds a less exalted position than Vish*n*u. The Mahā-bhārata also gives Vish*n*u or K*r*ish*n*a the highest honour upon the whole. But it has many passages in which *S*iva occupies the supreme place, and receives the homage and worship of Vish*n*u and K*r*ish*n*a. "Mahā-deva," it says, "is an all-pervading god yet is nowhere seen; he is the creator and the lord of Brahmā, Vish*n*u, and Indra, whom the gods, from Brahmā to the Pisāchas, worship." The rival claims of *S*iva and Vish*n*u to supremacy are clearly displayed in this poem; and many of those powers and attributes are ascribed to them which were afterwards so widely developed in the Purā*n*as. Attempts also are made to reconcile their conflicting claims by representing *S*iva and Vish*n*u, *S*iva and K*r*ish*n*a, to be one, or, as it is expressed at a later time in the Hari-vans*a*, there is "no difference between *S*iva who exists in the form of Vish*n*u, and Vish*n*u who exists in the form of *S*iva."

The Purā*n*as distinctly assert the supremacy of their particular divinity, whether it be *S*iva or whether it be Vish*n*u, and they have developed and amplified the myths and allusions of the older writings into numberless legends and stories for the glorification and honour of their favourite god.

The Rudra of the Vedas has developed in the course of ages

into the great and powerful god *S*iva, the third deity of the Hindu triad, and the supreme god of his votaries. He is shortly described as the destroying principle, but his powers and attributes are more numerous and much wider. Under the name of Rudra or Mahā-kāla, he is the great destroying and dissolving power. But destruction in Hindu belief implies reproduction; so as *S*iva or *S*ankara, 'the auspicious,' he is the reproductive power which is perpetually restoring that which has been dissolved, and hence he is regarded as Īswara, the supreme lord, and Mahā-deva, the great god. Under this character of restorer he is represented by his symbol the Linga or phallus, typical of reproduction; and it is under this form alone, or combined with the Yoni, or female organ, the representative of his *S*akti, or female energy, that he is everywhere worshipped. Thirdly, he is the Mahā-yogī, the great ascetic, in whom is centred the highest perfection of austere penance and abstract meditation, by which the most unlimited powers are attained, marvels and miracles are worked, the highest spiritual knowledge is acquired, and union with the great spirit of the universe is eventually gained. In this character he is the naked ascetic Dig-ambara, 'clothed with the elements,' or Dhūr-ja*t*i, 'loaded with matted hair,' and his body smeared with ashes. His first or destructive character is sometimes intensified, and he becomes Bhairava, 'the terrible destroyer,' who takes a pleasure in destruction. He is also Bhūte*s*wara, the lord of ghosts and goblins. In these characters he haunts cemeteries and places of cremation, wearing serpents round his head and skulls for a necklace, attended by troops of imps and trampling on rebellious demons. He sometimes indulges in revelry, and, heated with drink, dances furiously with his wife Devī the dance called Tā*nd*ava, while troops of drunken imps caper around them. Possessed of so many powers and attributes, he has a great number of names, and is represented under a variety of forms. One authority enumerates a thousand and eight names, but most of these are descriptive epithets, as Tri-lochana, 'the three-eyed,' Nīla-kantha, 'the blue-throated,' and Panch-ānana, 'the five-faced.' *S*iva is a fair man with five faces and four arms. He is commonly represented seated in profound thought, with a third eye in the middle of his forehead, contained in or surmounted by the moon's crescent; his matted locks are gathered up into a coil like a horn, which bears upon it a symbol of the river Ganges, which he caught as it fell from heaven; a necklace of skulls (mu*nd*a-mālā), hangs round his neck, and serpents twine about his neck as a collar (nāga-ku*nd*ala); his neck is blue from drinking the deadly poison which would have destroyed the world, and in his hand he holds a tri*s*ūla or trident called Pināka. His garment is the skin of a tiger, a deer, or an elephant, hence he is called K*ri*tti-vāsas; sometimes he is clothed in a skin and seated upon a tiger-skin, and he holds a deer in his hand. He is generally accompanied by his bull Nandi. He also carries the bow Ajagava, a drum (*d*amaru) in the shape of an hour-glass, the Kha*t*wānga or club with a skull at the end, or a cord (pā*s*a) for binding refractory offenders. His Pramathas or attendants are numerous, and are imps and demons of various kinds. His third eye has been very destructive. With it he reduced to ashes Kāma, the god of love, for daring to inspire amorous thoughts of his consort Pārvatī while he was engaged in penance; and the gods and all created beings were destroyed by its glance at one of the periodical destructions of the universe. He is represented to have cut off one of the heads of Brahmā for speaking disrespectfully, so that Brahmā has only four heads instead of five. *S*iva is the great object of worship at Benares under the name of Vi*s*weswara. His heaven is on Mount Kailāsa.

There are various legends respecting *S*iva's garments and weapons. It is said that "he once visited a forest in the form of a religious mendicant, and the wives of the *R*ishis residing there fell in love with his great beauty, which the *R*ishis, perceiving, resented; in order, therefore, to overpower him, they first dug a pit, and by magical arts caused a tiger to rush out of it, which he slew, and taking his skin wore it as a garment; they next caused a deer to spring out upon him, which he took up in his left hand and ever after retained there. They then produced a red-hot iron, but this too he took up and kept in his hand as a weapon. . . . The elephant's skin belonged to an Asura named Gaya, who acquired such power that he would have conquered the gods, and would have destroyed the Munis had they not fled to Benares and taken refuge in a temple of *S*iva, who then destroyed the Asura, and, ripping up his body, stripped off the (elephant) hide, which he cast over his shoulders for a cloak."—*Williams.*

Other names or epithets of *S*iva are Aghora, 'horrible;' Babhru, Bhagavat, 'divine;' Chandra-*s*ekhara, 'moon-crested;' Gangā-dhara, 'bearer of the Ganges;' Girīsa, 'mountain lord;' Hara, 'seizer;' Īsāna, 'ruler;' Ja*t*ā-dhara, 'wearing matted hair;' Jala-mūrtti, 'whose form is water;' Kāla, 'time;' Kālanjara; Kapāla-mālin, 'wearing a garland of skulls;' Mahā-kāla, 'great time;' Mahe*s*a, 'great lord;' M*ri*tyunjaya, 'vanquisher of death;' Pa*s*u-pati, 'lord of animals;' *S*ankara, *S*arva, Sadā*s*iva or *S*ambhu, 'the auspicious;' *S*thānu, 'the firm;' Tryambaka, 'three-eyed;' Ugra, 'fierce;' Virūpāksha, 'of misformed eyes;' Vi*s*wanātha, 'lord of all.'

*S*IVA PURĀNA. *See* Purāna.

*S*IVI. Son of U*s*īnara, and king of the country also called U*s*īnara, near Gandhāra. The great charity and devotion of *S*ivi are extolled in the Mahā-bhārata by the sage Mārka*nd*eya. Agni having assumed the form of a pigeon, was pursued by Indra in the shape of a falcon. The pigeon took refuge in the bosom of *S*ivi, and the falcon would accept nothing from *S*ivi instead of the pigeon but an equal weight of the king's own flesh. *S*ivi cut a piece of flesh from his right thigh and placed it in the balance, but the bird was the heavier. He cut again and again, and still the pigeon drew the scale, until the king placed his whole body in the balance. This outweighed the pigeon and the falcon flew away. On another occasion Vish*n*u went to *S*ivi in the form of a Brāhman and demanded food, but would accept no food but *S*ivi's own son V*ri*had-garbha, whom he required *S*ivi to kill and cook. The king did so, and placed the food before the Brāhman, who then told him to eat it himself. *S*ivi took up the head and prepared to eat. The Brāhman then stayed his hand, commended his devotion, and restoring the son to life, vanished from sight.

SKAMBHA. 'The supporter.' A name sometimes used in the *Ri*g-veda to designate the Supreme Deity. There is considerable doubt and mystery about both this name and deity. "The meaning of the term," says Goldstücker, "is 'the fulcrum,' and it seems to mean the fulcrum of the whole world in all its physical, religious, and other aspects."—*Muir's Texts*, v. 378.

SKANDA. God of war. *See* Kārttikeya.

SKANDA PURĀ*N*A. "The Skanda Purā*n*a is that in which the six-faced deity (Skanda) has related the events of the

Tatpurusha Kalpa, enlarged with many tales, and subservient to the duties taught by Maheswara. It is said to contain 81,800 stanzas: so it is asserted amongst mankind." "It is uniformly agreed," says Wilson, "that the Skanda Purāna, in a collective form, has no existence; and the fragments, in the shape of Sanhitās, Khandas, and Māhātmyas, which are affirmed in various parts of India to be portions of the Purāna, present a much more formidable mass of stanzas than even the immense number of which it is said to consist. The most celebrated of these portions in Hindusthān is the Kāsī Khanda, a very minute description of the temples of Siva in or adjacent to Benares, mixed with directions for worshipping Maheswara, and a great variety of legends explanatory of its merits and of the holiness of Kāsī. Many of them are puerile and uninteresting, but some of them are of a higher character. There is every reason to believe the greater part of the contents of the Kāsī Khanda anterior to the first attack upon Benares by Mahmūd of Ghazni. The Kāsī Khanda alone contains 15,000 stanzas. Another considerable work is the Utkala Khanda, giving an account of the holiness of Orissa." A part of this Purāna has been printed at Bombay.

SMĀRTA. Appertaining to the Smriti. The Smārta-sūtras. *See* Sūtras.

SMRITI. 'What was remembered.' Inspiration, as distinguished from Sruti, or direct revelation. What has been remembered and handed down by tradition. In its widest application, the term includes the Vedāngas, the Sūtras, the Rāmāyana, the Mahā-bhārata, the Purānas, the Dharma-sāstras, especially the works of Manu, Yājnawalkya, and other inspired lawgivers, and the Nīti-sāstras or ethics, but its ordinary application is to the Dharma-sāstras; as Manu says, "By Sruti is meant the Veda, and by Smriti the institutes of law," ii. 10.

SMRITI-CHANDRIKĀ. A treatise on law, according to the Drāvidian or Southern school, by Devana Bhatta.

SOMA. The juice of a milky climbing plant (*Asclepias acida*), extracted and fermented, forming a beverage offered in libations to the deities, and drunk by the Brāhmans. Its exhilarating qualities were grateful to the priests, and the gods were represented as being equally fond of it. This soma juice occupies a large space in the Rig-veda; one Mandala is almost wholly devoted to its praise and uses. It was raised to the position of a deity, and represented to be primeval, all-powerful, healing all diseases, bestower of riches, lord of other gods, and even identified with the Supreme Being. As a personification, Soma was the god who represented and animated the soma juice, an Indian Dionysus or Bacchus.

"The simple-minded Arian people, whose whole religion was a worship of the wonderful powers and phenomena of nature, had no sooner perceived that this liquid had power to elevate the spirits and produce a temporary frenzy, under the influence of which the individual was prompted to, and capable of, deeds beyond his natural powers, than they found in it something divine: it was to their apprehension a god, endowing those into whom it entered with godlike powers; the plant which afforded it became to them the king of plants; the process of preparing it was a holy sacrifice; the instruments used therefor were sacred. The high antiquity of this cultus is attested by the references to it found occurring in the Persian Avesta; it seems, however, to have received a new impulse on Indian territory."—*Whitney.*

In later times, the name was appropriated to the moon, and some of the qualities of the soma juice have been transferred to the luminary, who is Oshadhi-pati, or lord of herbs. So Soma is considered the guardian of sacrifices and penance, asterisms and healing herbs.

In the Purā*n*ic mythology Soma, as the moon, is commonly said to be the son of the *R*ishi Atri by his wife Anasūyā, but the authorities are not agreed. One makes him son of Dharma; another gives his paternity to Prabhākara, of the race of Atri; and he is also said to have been produced from the churning of the ocean in another Manwantara. In the Vish*n*u Purā*n*a he is called "the monarch of Brāhmans;" but the B*ri*had Āra*n*yaka, an older work, makes him a Kshatriya. He married twenty-seven daughters of the *R*ishi Daksha, who are really personifications of the twenty-seven lunar asterisms; but keeping up the personality, he paid such attention to Rohi*n*ī, the fourth of them, that the rest became jealous, and appealed to their father. Daksha's interference was fruitless, and he cursed his son-in-law, so that he remained childless, and became affected with consumption. This moved the pity of his wives, and they interceded with their father for him. He could not recall his curse, but he modified it so that the decay should be periodical, not permanent. Hence the wane and increase of the moon. He performed the Rāja-sūya sacrifice, and became in consequence so arrogant and licentious that he carried off Tārā, the wife of B*ri*haspati, and refused to give her up either on the entreaties of her husband or at the command of Brahmā. This gave rise to a wide-spread quarrel. The sage Usanas, out of enmity to B*ri*haspati, sided with Soma, and he was supported by the Dānavas, the Daityas, and other foes of the gods. Indra and the gods in general sided with B*ri*haspati. There ensued a fierce contest, and "the earth was shaken to her centre." Soma had his body cut in two by *S*iva's trident, and hence he is called Bhagnātmā. At length Brahmā interposed and stopped the fight, compelling Soma to restore Tārā to her husband. The result of this intrigue was the birth of a child, whom Tārā, after great persuasion, declared to be the son of Soma, and to whom the name of Budha was given : from him the Lunar race sprung.

According to the Purā*n*as, the chariot of Soma has three wheels, and is drawn by ten horses of the whiteness of the jasmine, five on the right half of the yoke, and five on the left.

The moon has many names and descriptive epithets, as Chandra, Indu, *S*a*s*ī, 'marked like a hare;' Ni*s*ākara, 'maker of night;' Nakshatra-nātha, 'lord of the constellations;' *S*īta-mārīchi, 'having cool rays;' Sitān*s*u, 'having white rays;' M*ri*-gānka, 'marked like a deer;' *S*iva-sekhara, 'the crest of *S*iva;' Kumuda-pati, 'lord of the lotus;' *S*weta-vājī, 'drawn by white horses.'

SOMADEVA BHA*TT*A. The writer or compiler of the collection of stories called Kathā-sarit-sāgara.

SOMAKA. Grandfather of Drupada, who transmitted his name to his descendants.

SOMA-LOKA. *See* Loka.

SOMA-NĀTHA, SOME*S*WARA. 'Lord of the moon.' The name of a celebrated Lingam or emblem of *S*iva at the city of Somnāth-pattan in Gujarat. It was destroyed by Mahmūd of Ghaznī.

SOMAPAS. 'Soma-drinkers.' A class of Pit*ri*s or Manes who drink the soma juice. *See* Pit*ri*s.

SOMA-VANSA. *See* Chandra-vansa.

SRADDHĀ. 1. Faith, personified in the Vedas and lauded in a few hymns. 2. Daughter of the sage Daksha, wife of the god Dharma, and reputed mother of Kāma-deva, the god of love.

SRADDHA-DEVA, SRĀDDHA-DEVA. Manu is called by the former name in the Brāhmanas, and by the latter in the Mahā-bhārata. The latter is commonly applied to Yama.

SRAUTA. Belonging to the Sruti. *See* Sruti and Sūtra.

SRAUTA-SŪTRA. *See* Sūtra and Vedāngas.

SRĀVASTĪ. An ancient city which seems to have stood near Faizābād in Oude.

SRĪ. 'Fortune, prosperity.' 1. The wife of Vishnu. (*See* Lakshmī.) 2. An honorific prefix to the names of gods, kings, heroes, and men and books of high estimation.

SRĪ BHĀGAVATA. *See* Bhāgavata Purāna.

SRĪ DĀMA CHARITRA. A modern drama in five acts by Sāma Rāja Dīkshita, on the sudden elevation to affluence of Srī Dāman, a friend of Krishna. It is not a good play, "but there is some vivacity in the thoughts and much melody in the style." —*Wilson.*

SRĪ-DHARA SWĀMĪ. Author of several commentaries of repute on the Bhagavad-gītā, Vishnu Purāna, &c.

SRĪ HARSHA. A great sceptical philosopher, and author of the poem called Naishadha or Naishadhīya. There were several kings of the name.

SRĪ HARSHA DEVA. A king who was author of the drama Ratnāvalī.

SRINGA-GIRI. A hill on the edge of the Western Ghāts in Mysore, where there is a math or monastic establishment of Brāhmans, said to have been founded by Sankarāchārya.

SRINGĀRA TILAKA. 'The mark of love.' A work by Rudra Bhatta on the sentiments and emotions of lovers as exhibited in poetry and the drama.

SRINGA-VERA. The modern Sungroor, a town on the left bank of the Ganges and on the frontier of Kosala and the Bhīl country. The country around was inhabited by Nishādas or wild tribes, and Guha, the friend of Rāma, was their chief.

SRĪ-SAILA. The mountain of Srī, the goddess of fortune. It is a holy place in the Dakhin, near the Krishna, and was formerly a place of great splendour. It retains its sanctity but has lost its grandeur. Also called *S*rī-parvata.

*S*RĪ-VATSA. A particular mark, said to be a curl of hair on the breast of Vish*n*u or K*r*ish*n*a, and represented by 

*S*RUTA-BODHA. A work on metres attributed to Kāli-dāsa. It has been edited and translated into French by Lancereau.

*S*RUTA-KĪRTTI. Cousin of Sītā and wife of *S*atru-ghna.

*S*RUTARSHI. A *R*ishi who did not receive the *S*ruti (revelation) direct, but obtained it at second-hand from the Vedic *R*ishis.

*S*RUTI. 'What was heard.' The revealed word. The Mantras and Brāhma*n*as of the Vedas are always included in the term, and the Upanishads are generally classed with them.

STHALĪ-DEVATAS, -DEVATĀS. Gods or goddesses of the soil, local deities.

STHĀNU. A name of *S*iva.

STHĀPATYA-VEDA. The science of architecture, one of the Upa-vedas.

STHŪ*N*Ā, STHU*N*Ā-KAR*N*A. A Yaksha who is represented in the Mahā-bhārata to have changed sexes for a while with *S*ikha*nd*inī, daughter of Drupada.

SU-BĀHU. 'Five-armed.' 1. A son of Dh*r*ita-rāsh*t*ra and king of Chedi. 2. A son of *S*atru-ghna and king of Mathurā.

SU-BALA. 1. A king of Gandhāra, father of Gāndhārī, wife of Dh*r*ita-rāsh*t*ra. 2. A mountain in Lankā on which Hanumān alighted after leaping over the channel.

SU-BHADRĀ. Daughter of Vasu-deva, sister of K*r*ish*n*a, and wife of Arjuna. Bala-rāma, her elder brother, wished to give her to Dur-yodhana, but Arjuna carried her off from Dwārakā at K*r*ish*n*a's suggestion, and Bala-rāma subsequently acquiesced in their union. She was mother of Abhimanyu. She appears especially as sister of K*r*ish*n*a in his form Jagan-nātha, and according to tradition there was an incestuous intimacy between them. When the car of Jagan-nātha is brought out the images of Su-bhadrā and Bala-rāma accompany the idol, and the intimacy of Jagan-nātha and Su-bhadrā is said to provoke taunts and reproaches.

*S*UBHĀNGĪ. 'Fair-limbed.' An epithet of Rati, wife of Kāma, and of Yakshī, wife of Kuvera.

SU-BHĀNU. Son of K*r*ish*n*a and Satya-bhāmā.

SU-BODHINĪ. A commentary by Viśweśwara Bhaṭṭa on the law-book called Mitāksharā.

SU-BRAHMAṆYA. A name of Kārttikeyā, god of war, used especially in the South. *See* Kārttikeya.

SU-CHĀRU. A son of Kṛishṇa and Rukmiṇī.

SU-DARŚANA. A name of Kṛishṇa's chakra or discus weapon. *See* Vajra-nābha.

SUDĀS. A king who frequently appears in the *Ṛig*-veda, and at whose court the rival *Ṛi*shis Vasishṭha and Viśwāmitra are represented as living. He was famous for his sacrifices.

SU-DESHNA. Son of Kṛishṇa and Rukmiṇī.

ŚU-DESHNĀ. 'Good-looking.' 1. Wife of the Rāja of Virāṭa, the patron of the disguised Pāṇḍavas, and mistress of Draupadī. 2. Also the wife of Bālin.

SU-DHARMĀ, SU-DHARMAN. The hall of Indra, "the unrivalled gem of princely courts," which Kṛishṇa commanded Indra to resign to Ugrasena, for the assemblage of the race of Yadu. After the death of Kṛishṇa it returned to Indra's heaven.

ŚŪDRA. The fourth or servile caste. *See* Varṇa.

ŚŪDRAKA. A king who wrote the play called Mṛichchhakaṭī, 'the toy-cart,' in ten acts.

SU-DYUMNA. Son of the Manu Vaivaswata. At his birth he was a female, Ilā, but was afterwards changed into a male and called Su-dyumna. Under the curse of Śiva he again became Ilā, who married Budha or Mercury, and was mother of Purūravas. By favour of Vishṇu the male form was again recovered, and Su-dyumna became the father of three sons. This legend evidently has reference to the origin of the Lunar race of kings.

SU-GRĪVA. 'Handsome neck.' A monkey king who was dethroned by his brother Bālin, but after the latter had been killed, Su-grīva was re-installed by Rāma as king at Kishkindhyā. He, with his adviser Hanumān and their army of monkeys, were the allies of Rāma in his war against Rāvaṇa, in which he was wounded. He is said to have been son of the sun, and from his paternity he is called Ravi-nandana and by other similar names. He is described as being grateful, active in aiding his friends, and able to change his form at will. His wife's name was Rumā.

SUHMA. A country said to be east of Bengal.

SUKA-SAPTATI. 'The seventy (tales) of a parrot.' This is the original of the Tūtī-nāmah of the Persian, from which the Hindustani Totā-kahānī was translated.

SUKRA. The planet Venus and its regent. Sukra was son of Bhrigu and priest of Bali and the Daityas (Daitya-guru). He is also called the son of Kavi. His wife's name was Susumā or Sata-parwā. His daughter Devayānī married Yayāti of the Lunar race, and her husband's infidelity induced Sukra to curse him. Sukra is identified with Usanas, and is author of a code of law. The Hari-vansa relates that he went to Siva and asked for means of protecting the Asuras against the gods, and for obtaining his object he performed "a painful rite, imbibing the smoke of chaff with his head downwards for a thousand years." In his absence the gods attacked the Asuras and Vishnu killed his mother, for which deed Sukra cursed him "to be born seven times in the world of men." Sukra restored his mother to life, and the gods being alarmed lest Sukra's penance should be accomplished, Indra sent his daughter Jayantī to lure him from it. She waited upon him and soothed him, but he accomplished his penance and afterwards married her. Sukra is known by his patronymic Bhārgava, and also as Bhrigu. He is also Kavi or Kāvya, 'the poet.' The planet is called Āsphujit, 'Αφροδίτη; Maghā-bhava, son of Maghā; Shodasānsu, 'having sixteen rays;' and Sweta, 'the white.'

SŪKTA. A Vedic hymn.

SU-MANTRA. The chief counsellor of Rāja Dasa-ratha and friend of Rāma.

SU-MANTU. The collector of the hymns of the Atharva-veda; he is said to have been a pupil of Veda Vyāsa, and to have acted under his guidance.

SUMBHA and NISHUMBHA. Two Asuras, brothers, who were killed by Durgā. These brothers, as related in the Mārkandeya Purāna, were votaries of Siva, and performed severe penance for 5000 years in order to obtain immortality. Siva refused the boon, and they continued their devotions with such increased intensity for 800 years more, that the gods trembled for their power. By advice of Indra, the god of love, Kāma, went to them with two celestial nymphs, Rambhā and Tilottamā, and they succeeded in seducing the two Asuras and holding them in the toils of sensuality for 5000 years. On recovering from their voluptuous aberration they drove the nymphs back to paradise and recommenced their penance. At the end of 1000 years *S*iva blessed them "that in riches and strength they should excel the gods." In their exaltation they warred against the gods, who, in despair, appealed in succession to Brahmā, Vish*n*u, and *S*iva, but in vain. The latter advised them to apply to Durgā, and they did so. She contrived to engage the Asuras in war, defeated their forces, slew their commanders, Cha*nd*a and Mu*nd*a, and finally killed them. *See* Sunda.

SU-MERU. The mountain Meru, actual or personified.

SU-MITRĀ. Wife of Da*s*a-ratha and mother of Lakshma*n*a and *S*atru-ghna. *See* Da*s*a-ratha.

SU-MUKHA. 'Handsome face.' This epithet is used for Garu*d*a and for the son of Garu*d*a.

*S*UNA*H*-*S*EPHAS. The legend of *S*una*h*-sephas, as told in the Aitareya Brāhma*n*a, is as follows:—King Hari*s*-chandra, of the race of Ikshwāku, being childless, made a vow that if he obtained a son he would sacrifice him to Varu*n*a. A son was born who received the name of Rohita, but the father postponed, under various pretexts, the fulfilment of his vow. When at length he resolved to perform the sacrifice, Rohita refused to be the victim, and went out into the forest, where he lived for six years. He then met a poor Brāhman *R*ishi called Ajīgartta, who had three sons, and Rohita purchased from Ajīgartta for a hundred cows, the second son, named *S*una*h*-*s*ephas, to be the substitute for himself in the sacrifice. Varu*n*a approved of the substitute, and the sacrifice was about to be performed, the father receiving another hundred cows for binding his son to the sacrificial post, and a third hundred for agreeing to slaughter him. *S*una*h*-*s*ephas saved himself by reciting verses in honour of different deities, and was received into the family of Vi*s*wāmitra, who was one of the officiating priests. The Rāmāya*n*a gives a different version of the legend. Ambarīsha, king of Ayodhyā, was performing a sacrifice when Indra carried off the victim. The officiating priest represented that this loss could be atoned for only by the sacrifice of a human victim. The king, after a long search, found a Brāhman *R*ishi named *R*ichīka, who had two sons, and the younger, *S*una*h*-*s*ephas, was then sold by his own consent for a hundred thousand cows, ten millions of gold pieces, and heaps of jewels. *S*una*h*-*s*ephas met with his maternal uncle, Viswāmitra, who taught him two divine verses which he was to repeat when about to be sacrificed. As he was bound at the stake to be immolated, he celebrated the two gods Indra and Vishnu with the excellent verses, and Indra, being pleased, bestowed upon him long life. He was afterwards called Devarāta, and is said to have become son of Viswāmitra. The Mahābhārata and the Purānas show some few variations. A series of seven hymns in the *Rig*-veda is attributed to *S*unah-sephas. *See* Muir's *Texts*, i. 355, 407, 413; *Vishnu Purana*, iv. 25; Müller's *Sanskrit Literature*, 408; Wilson's *Rig-veda*, i. 60.

SU-NĀMAN. Son of Ugrasena and brother of Kansa. He was king of the *S*ūrasenas. When Kansa was overpowered in battle by Krishna, Su-nāman went to succour him, but was encountered and slain by Bala-rāma.

SU-NANDĀ. A princess of Chedi who befriended Damayantī when she was deserted by her husband.

SUNDA. Sunda and Upasunda, of the Mahā-bhārata, were two Daityas, sons of Nisunda, for whose destruction the Apsaras Tilottamā was sent down from heaven. They quarrelled for her, and killed each other. *See S*umbha.

SU-PARNAS. 'Fine-winged.' "Beings of superhuman character, as Garuda, and other birds of equally fanciful description; one of those classes first created by the Brahmādikas, and included in the daily presentation of water to deceased ancestors, &c."—*Wilson.*

SU-PĀRSWA. A fabulous bird in the Ramāyana. He was son of Sampāti and nephew of Jatāyus.

SU-PRIYA. 'Very dear.' Chief of the Gandharvas.

*S*ŪRA. A Yādava king who ruled over the *S*ūrasenas at Mathurā; he was father of Vasu-deva and Kuntī, and grandfather of Krishna.

SURĀ. Wine or spirituous liquor, personified as Surā-devī, a goddess or nymph produced at the churning of the ocean.

SURABHI. The 'cow of plenty,' produced at the churning of the ocean, who granted every desire, and is reverenced as "the fountain of milk and curds." *See* Kāma-dhenu and Nandinī.

SURAS. In the Vedas, a class of beings connected with Sūrya, the sun. The inferior deities who inhabit Swarga; a god in general. According to some, the word is allied to *swar*, 'heaven;' others think it to have sprung from the derivation assigned to *asura*, and as *a-sura* is said to signify 'not a god,' *sura* has come to mean 'god.'

SU-RASĀ. A Rākshasī, mother of the Nāgas. When Hanumān was on his flight to Lankā against Rāva*n*a, she tried to save her relative by swallowing Hanumān bodily. To avoid this Hanumān distended his body and continued to do so, while she stretched her mouth till it was a hundred leagues wide. Then he suddenly shrank up to the size of a thumb, darted through her, and came out at her right ear.

*S*ŪRASENAS. Name of a people, the Suraseni of Arrian. Their capital was Mathurā on the Yamunā, which Manu calls *S*ūrasena.

*S*ŪRPA-NAKHĀ. 'Having nails like winnowing-fans.' Sister of Rāva*n*a. This Rākshasī admired the beauty of Rāma and fell in love with him. When she made advances to Rāma he referred her to Lakshma*n*a, and Lakshma*n*a in like manner sent her back to Rāma. Enraged at this double rejection, she fell upon Sītā, and Rāma was obliged to interfere forcibly for the protection of his wife. He called out to Lakshma*n*a to disfigure the violent Rākshasī, and Lakshma*n*a cut off her nose and ears. She flew to her brothers for revenge, and this brought on the war between Rāma and Rāva*n*a. She descanted to Rāva*n*a on the beauty of Sītā, and instigated his carrying her off, and finally she cursed him just before the engagement in which he was killed.

SŪRYA. The sun or its deity. He is one of the three chief deities in the Vedas, as the great source of light and warmth, but the references to him are more poetical than precise. Sometimes he is identical with Savit*ri* and Āditya, sometimes he is distinct. "Sometimes he is called son of Dyaus, sometimes of Aditi. In one passage, Ushas, the dawn, is his wife, in another he is called the child of the dawns; he moves through the sky in a chariot drawn by seven ruddy horses or mares." Sūrya has several wives, but, according to later legends, his twin sons the A*s*wins, who are ever young and handsome and ride in a golden car as precursors of Ushas, the dawn, were born of a nymph called A*s*winī, from her having concealed herself in the form of a mare. In the Rāmāya*n*a and Purā*n*as, Sūrya is said to be the son of Ka*s*yapa and Aditi, but in the Rāmāya*n*a he is otherwise referred to as a son of Brahmā. His wife was Sanjnā, daughter of Viswa-karma, and by her he had three children, the Manu Vaivaswata, Yama, and the goddess Yamī, or the Yamunā river. His effulgence was so overpowering that his wife gave him Chhāyā (shade) for a handmaid, and retired into the forest to devote herself to religion. While thus engaged, and in the form of a mare, the sun saw her and approached her in the form of a horse. Hence sprang the two Aswins and Revanta. Sūrya brought back his wife Sanjnā to his home, and her father, the sage Viswa-karma, placed the luminary on his lathe and cut away an eighth of his effulgence, trimming him in every part except the feet. The fragments that were cut off fell blazing to the earth, and from them Viswa-karma formed the discus of Vishnu, the trident of Siva, the weapon of Kuvera, the lance of Kārttikeya, and the weapons of the other gods. According to the Mahā-bhārata, Karna was his illegitimate son by Kuntī. He is also fabled to be the father of Sani and the monkey chief Sugrīva. The Manu Vaivaswata was father of Ikshwāku, and from him, the grandson of the sun, the Sūrya-vansa, or Solar race of kings, draws its origin. In the form of a horse Sūrya communicated the White Yajur-veda to Yājnawalkya, and it was he who bestowed on Satrājit the Syamantaka gem. A set of terrific Rākshasas called Mandehas made an attack upon him and sought to devour him, but were dispersed by his light. According to the Vishnu Purāna he was seen by Sattrājita in "his proper form," "of dwarfish stature, with a body like burnished copper, and with slightly reddish eyes." Sūrya is represented in a chariot drawn by seven horses, or a horse with seven heads, surrounded with rays. His charioteer is Aruna or Vivaswat, and his city Vivaswatī or Bhāswatī. There are temples of the sun, and he receives worship. The names and epithets of the sun are numberless. He is Savitri, 'the nourisher;' Vivaswat, 'the brilliant;' Bhāskara, 'light-maker;' Dina-kara, 'day-maker;' Arha-pati, 'lord of day;' Loka-chakshuh, 'eye of the world;' Karma-sākshī, 'witness of the deeds (of men);' Graha-rāja, 'king of the constellations;' Gabhastimān, 'possessed of rays;' Sahasra-kirana, 'having a thousand rays;' Vikarttana, 'shorn of his beams' (by Viswa-karma); Mārtanda, 'descended from Mritanda,' &c. Sūrya's wives are called Savarnā, Swātī, and Mahā-vīryā.

SŪRYA-KĀNTA. 'The sun-gem.' A crystal supposed to be formed of condensed rays of the sun, and though cool to the touch, to give out heat in the sun's rays. There is a similar moon-stone. It is also called Dahanopala. *See* Chandra-kānta.

SŪRYA SIDDHĀNTA. A celebrated work on astronomy, said to have been revealed by the sun (Sūrya). It has been edited in the *Bibliotheca Indica* by Hall, and there are other editions. It has been translated by Whitney and Burgess.

SŪRYA-VANSA. The Solar race. A race or lineage of Kshatriyas which sprank from Ikshwāku, grandson of the sun. Rāma was of this race, and so were many other great kings and heroes. Many Rājputs claim descent from this and the other great lineage, the Lunar race. The Rāna of Udaypur claims to be of the Sūrya-vansa, and the Jhārejas of Cutch and Sindh assert a descent from the Chandra-vansa. There were two dynasties of the Solar race. The elder branch, which reigned at Ayodhyā, descended from Ikshwāku through his eldest son, Vikukshi. The other dynasty, reigning at Mithilā, descended from another of Ikshwāku's sons, named Nimi. The lists of these two dynasties on the opposite page are taken from the Vishnu Purāna. The lists given by other authorities show some discrepancies, but they agree in general as to the chief names.

SU-SARMAN. A king of Tri-gartta, who attacked the Rāja of Virāta, and defeated him and made him prisoner, but Bhīma rescued the Rāja and made Su-sarman prisoner.

SUSHENA. 1. A son of Krishna and Rukminī. 2. A physician in the army of Rāma, who brought the dead to life and performed other miraculous cures.

SUSHNA. An Asura mentioned in the *Rig*-veda as killed by Indra.

SUSRUTA. A medical writer whose date is uncertain, but his work was translated into Arabic before the end of the eighth century. The book has been printed at Calcutta. There is a Latin translation by Hepler and one in German by Vullers.

SŪTA. 'Charioteer.' A title given to Karna.

SU-TĪKSHNA. A hermit sage who dwelt in the Dandaka forest, and was visited by Rāma and Sītā.

SŪTRA. 'A thread or string.' A rule or aphorism. A verse expressed in brief and technical language,—a very favourite form among the Hindus of embodying and transmitting rules. There are Sūtras upon almost every subject, but "the Sūtras" generally signify those which are connected with the Vedas, viz.,

THE SŪRYA-VANSA OR SOLAR RACE.

IKSHWĀKU.

Dynasty of Ayodhyā.

Vikukshi.
Kakutstha.
Anenas.
P*ri*thu.
Vi*s*waga*s*wa.
Ardra.
Yuvanā*s*wa.
*S*rāvasta.
B*ri*hadaswa.
Kuvalayā*s*wa (called Dhundhumāra).
D*ri*dhā*s*wa.
Harya*s*wa.
Nikumbha.
Sanhatā*s*wa.
Kri*s*ā*s*wa.
Prasenajit.
Yuvanā*s*wa.
Māndhāt*ri*.
Purukutsa.
Trasadasyu.
Sambhūta.
Anara*n*ya.

P*ri*shada*s*wa.
Harya*s*wa.
Sumanas.
Tridhanwan.
Trayāru*n*a.
Satyavrata (Trisanku).
Hari*s*chandra.
Rohitā*s*wa.
Harita.
Chunchu.
Vijaya.
Ruruka.
V*ri*ka.
Bāhuka.
Sagara.
Asamanjas.
An*s*umat.
Dilīpa.
Bhagīratha.
*S*ruta.
Nābhāga.
Ambarīsha.
Sindhudwīpa.

Ayutāyus.
*R*itupar*n*a.
Sarvakāma.
Sudāsa.
Saudāsa (Kalmāsha-pāda).
A*s*maka.
Mūlaka (Nārīkavacha).
Da*s*aratha.
Ilavila.
Vi*s*wasaha.
Kha*t*wānga.
Dīrgha-bāhu.
Raghu.
Aja.
Da*s*aratha.
RĀMA.
Ku*s*a.
Atithi.
Nishadha.
Nala.
Nabhas.
Pu*nd*arīka.

Kshema-dhanwan.
Devānika.
Ahīnagu.
Pāripātra
Dala.
Chhala.
Uktha.
Vajranābha.
*S*ankhanābha.
Dhyushitā*s*wa.
Vi*s*wasaha.
Hira*n*yanābha.
Pushya.
Dhruvasandhi.
Sudar*s*ana.
Agnivar*n*a.
*S*īghra.
Maru.
Prasu*s*ruta.
Susandhi.
Amarsha.
Mahaswat.
Vi*s*rutavat.
B*ri*hadbala.

Dynasty of Mithilā.

Nimi.
Janaka.
Udāvasu.
Nandivardhana.
Suketu.
Devarāta.
B*ri*haduktha (or B*ri*hadratha).
Mahāvīrya.
Satyadh*ri*ti.
Dh*ri*sh*t*aketu.
Harya*s*wa.
Maru.
Pratibandhaka.
K*ri*taratha.
K*ri*ta.
Vibudha.
Mahādh*ri*ti.
K*ri*tirāta.
Mahāroman.

Suvar*n*aroma.
Hraswaroma.
Sīradhwaja (father of Sītā).
Bhānumat.
*S*atadyumna.
*S*uchi.
Ūrjavāha.
Satyadhwaja.
Ku*n*i.
Anjana.
*R*itujit.
Arish*t*anemi.
*S*rutāyus.
Supār*s*wa.
Sanjaya.
Kshemāri.
Anenas.
Mīnaratha.
Satyaratha.
Sātyarathi.
Upagu.
*S*ruta.

*S*āswata.
Sudhanwan.
Subhāsa.
Su*s*ruta.
Jaya.
Vijaya.
*R*ita.
Sunaya.
Vītahavya.
Dh*ri*ti.
Bahulā*s*wa.
K*ri*ti.

the Kalpa Sūtras, relating to ritual; the G*ri*hya Sūtras, to domestic rites; and the Sāmayachārika Sūtras, to conventional usages. The Kalpa Sūtras, having especial reference to the Veda or *S*ruti, are called *S*rauta; the others are classed as Smārta, being derived from the Sm*ri*ti. The Sūtras generally are anterior to Manu, and are probably as old as the sixth century B.C. Several have been published in the *Bibliotheca Indica.*

*S*UTUDRĪ. The river Satlej. *See S*ata-dru.

SU-VAHU. A Rākshasa, son of Tārakā. He was killed by Rāma.

SU-VELA. One of the three peaks of the mountain Trikū*t*a, on the midmost of which the city of Lankā was built.

SU-YODHANA. 'Fair fighter.' A name of Dur-yodhana.

SWADHĀ. 'Oblation.' Daughter of Daksha and Prasūti according to one statement, and of Agni according to another. She is connected with the Pit*ri*s or Manes, and is represented as wife of Kavi or of one class of Pit*ri*s, and as mother of others.

SWĀHĀ. 'Offering.' Daughter of Daksha and Prasūti. She was wife of Vahni or Fire, or of Abhimānī, one of the Agnis.

*S*WA-PHALKA. Husband of Gāndinī and father of Akrūra. He was a man of great sanctity of character, and where "he dwelt famine, plague, death, and other visitations were unknown." His presence once brought rain to the kingdom of Kā*s*ī-rāja, where it was much wanted.

SWAR. *See* Vyāh*ri*ti.

SWARGA. The heaven of Indra, the abode of the inferior gods and of beatified mortals, supposed to be situated on Mount Meru. It is called also Sairibha, Mi*s*rakā-vana, Tāvisha, Tridivam, Tri-pish*t*apam, and Ūrdhwa-loka. Names of heaven or paradise in general are also used for it.

SWAR-LOKA. *See* Loka.

SWĀROCHISHA. Name of the second Manu. *See* Manu.

SWASTIKA. A mystical religious mark placed upon persons or things. It is in the form of a Greek cross with the ends bent round 

SWAYAM-BHŪ. 'The self-existent.' A name of Brahmā, the creator.

SWĀYAM-BHUVA. A name of the first Manu (q.v.).

*S*WETA-DWĪPA. 'The white island or continent.' Colonel Wilford attempted to identify it with Britain.

*S*WETA-KETU. A sage who, according to the Mahā-bhārata, put a stop to the practice of married women consorting with other men, especially with Brāhmans. His indignation was aroused at seeing a Brāhman take his mother by the hand and invite her to go away with him. The husband saw this, and told his son that there was no ground of offence, for the practice had prevailed from time immemorial. *S*weta-ketu would not tolerate it, and introduced the rule by which a wife is forbidden to have intercourse with another man unless specially appointed by her husband to raise up seed to him.

SWETĀ*S*WATARA. An Upanishad attached to the Yajur-veda. It is one of the most modern. Translated by Dr. Roer for the *Bibliotheca Indica.*

*S*YĀLA. 'A brother-in-law.' A Yādava prince who insulted the sage Gārgya, and was the cause of his becoming the father of Kāla-yavana, a great foe of K*r*ish*n*a and the Yādava family.

*S*YĀMĀ. 'The black.' A name of *S*iva's consort. *See* Devī.

SYAMANTAKA. A celebrated gem given by the sun to Satrājita. "It yielded daily eight loads of gold, and dispelled all fear of portents, wild beasts, fire, robbers, and famine." But though it was an inexhaustible source of good to the virtuous wearer, it was deadly to a wicked one. Satrājita being afraid that K*r*ish*n*a would take it from him, gave it to his own brother, Prasena, but he, being a bad man, was killed by a lion. Jāmbavat, king of the bears, killed the lion and carried off the gem, but K*r*ish*n*a, after a long conflict, took it from him, and restored it to Satrājita. Afterwards Satrājita was killed in his sleep by *S*ata-dhanwan, who carried off the gem. Being pursued by K*r*ish*n*a and Bala-rāma, he gave the gem to Akrūra and continued his flight, but he was overtaken and killed by K*r*ish*n*a alone. As K*r*ish*n*a did not bring back the jewel, Bala-rāma suspected that he had secreted it, and consequently he upbraided him and parted from him, declaring that he would not be imposed upon by perjuries. Akrūra subsequently produced the gem, and it was claimed by K*r*ish*n*a, Bala-rāma, and Satya-bhāmā. After some contention it was decided that Akrūra should keep it, and so "he moved about like the sun wearing a garland of light."

SYĀVĀSWA. Son of Archanānas. Both were Vedic *Ri*shis. In a hymn he says, "*S*a*s*īyasī has given me cattle, comprising horses and cows and hundreds of sheep." The story told in explanation is that Archanānas, having seen the daughter of Rāja Rathavīti, asked her in marriage for his son *S*yāvā*s*wa. The king was inclined to consent, but the queen objected that no daughter of their house had ever been given to any one less saintly than a *Ri*shi. To qualify himself *S*yāvā*s*wa engaged in austerities and begged alms. Among others, he begged of *S*a*s*ī-yasī, wife of Rāja Taranta. She took him to her husband, with whose permission she gave him a herd of cattle and costly ornaments. The Rāja also gave him whatever he asked for, and sent him on to his younger brother, Purumīlha. On his way he met the Maruts, and lauded them in a hymn, for which they made him a *Ri*shi. He then returned to Rathavīti, and received his daughter to wife.

TĀ*D*AKĀ. *See* Tārakā.

TAITTIRĪYA. This term is applied to the Sanhitā of the Black Yajur-veda. (*See* Veda.) It is also applied to a Brāhma*n*a, to an Āra*n*yaka, to an Upanishad, and a Prāti*s*ākhya of the same Veda. All these are printed, or are in course of printing, in the *Bibliotheca Indica*, and of the last there is a translation in that serial.

TAKSHA, TAKSHAKA. Son of Bharata, and nephew of Rāma-chandra. The sovereign of Gāndhāra, who resided at and probably founded Taksha-*s*ilā or Taxila, in the Panjāb.

TAKSHAKA. 'One who cuts off; a carpenter.' A name of Vi*s*wa-karma. A serpent, son of Kadru, and chief of snakes.

TAKSHA-*S*ILĀ. A city of the Gāndhāras, situated in the Panjāb. It was the residence of Taksha, son of Bharata and nephew of Rāma-chandra, and perhaps took its name from him. It is the Taxila of Ptolemy and other classical writers. Arrian describes it as "a large and wealthy city, and the most populous between the Indus and Hydaspes." It was three days' journey east of the Indus, and General Cunningham has found its remains at Sāhh-dharī, one mile north-east of Kala-kīsarāī.

TĀLAJANGHA. Son of Jaya-dhwaja, king of Avanti, of

the Haihaya race, and founder of the Tāla-jangha tribe of Haihayas. *See* Haihaya.

TĀLA-KETU. 'Palm-banner.' An appellation of Bhīshma; also of an enemy killed by K*ri*sh*n*a. Bala-rāma had the synonymous appellation Tāla-dhwaja.

TĀLAM. The throne of Durgā.

TALAVAKĀRA. A name of the Kena Upanishad.

TĀMASA. The fourth Manu. *See* Manu.

TAMASĀ. The river "Tonse," rising in the *R*iksha mountains, and falling into the Ganges.

TĀMRA-LIPTA. The country immediately west of the Bhāgīrathī; Tamlook, Hijjali, and Midnapore. Its inhabitants are called Tāmra-liptakas.

TĀMRA-PAR*N*A, TĀMRA-PAR*N*Ī. Ceylon, the ancient Taprobane. There was a town in the island called Tāmra-par*n*ī, from which the whole island has been called by that name.

TA*ND*U. One of *S*iva's attendants. He was skilled in music, and invented the dance called Tā*nd*ava. *See S*iva.

TĀ*ND*YA, TĀ*ND*AKA. The most important of the eight Brāhma*n*as of the Sāma-veda. It has been published in the *Bibliotheca Indica.*

TANTRA. 'Rule, ritual.' The title of a numerous class of religious and magical works, generally of later date than the Purā*n*as, and representing a later development of religion, although the worship of the female energy had its origin at an earlier period. The chief peculiarity of the Tantras is the prominence they give to the female energy of the deity, his active nature being personified in the person of his *S*akti, or wife. There are a few Tantras which make Vish*n*u's wife or Rādhā the object of devotion, but the great majority of them are devoted to one of the manifold forms of Devī, the *S*akti of *S*iva, and they are commonly written in the form of a dialogue between these two deities. Devī, as the *S*akti of *S*iva, is the especial energy concerned with sexual intercourse and magical powers, and these are the leading topics of the Tantras. There are five requisites for Tantra worship, the five Mākāras or five *m*'s—(1.) Madya, wine; (2.) Mānsa, flesh; (3.) Matsya, fish; (4.) Mudrā, parched grain and mystic gesticulations; (5.) Maithuna, sexual intercourse. Each *S*akti has a twofold nature, white and black, gentle and ferocious. Thus Umā and Gaurī are gentle forms of the *S*akti of *S*iva, while Durgā and Kālī are fierce forms. The *S*āktas or worshippers of the *S*aktis are divided into two classes, Dakshināchārīs and Vāmāchārīs, the right-handed and the left-handed. The worship of the right-hand *S*āktas is comparatively decent, but that of the left hand is addressed to the fierce forms of the *S*aktis, and is most licentious. The female principle is worshipped, not only symbolically, but in the actual woman, and promiscuous intercourse forms part of the orgies. Tantra worship prevails chiefly in Bengal and the Eastern provinces.

TAPAR-LOKA, TAPO-LOKA. *See* Loka.

TAPATĪ. The river Tapti personified as a daughter of the Sun by Chhāyā. She was mother of Kuru by Samvara*n*a.

TĀRĀ. Wife of the monkey king Bālin, and mother of Angada. After the death of Bālin in battle she was taken to wife by his brother, Su-grīva.

TĀRĀ, TĀRAKĀ. Wife of B*ri*haspati. According to the Purā*n*as, Soma, the moon, carried her off, which led to a great war between the gods and the Asuras. Brahmā put an end to the war and restored Tārā, but she was delivered of a child which she declared to be the son of Soma, and it was named Budha. *See* B*ri*haspati.

TĀRAKA. Son of Vajrānaka. A Daitya whose austerities made him formidable to the gods, and for whose destruction Skanda, the god of war, was miraculously born.

TĀRAKĀ. A female Daitya, daughter of the Yaksha Su-ketu or of the demon Sunda, and mother of Mārīcha. She was changed into a Rākshasī by Agastya, and lived in a forest called by her name on the Ganges, opposite the confluence of the Sarju, and she ravaged all the country round. Vi*s*wāmitra desired Rāma-chandra to kill her, but he was reluctant to kill a woman. He resolved to deprive her of the power of doing harm, and cut off her two arms. Lakshma*n*a cut off her nose and ears. She, by the power of sorcery, assailed Rāma and Lakshma*n*a with a fearful shower of stones, and at the earnest command of Vi*s*wāmitra, the former killed her with an arrow.—*Rāmāyana.*

TĀRAKĀ-MAYA. The war which arose in consequence of Soma, the moon, having carried off Tārā, the wife of B*ri*haspati.

TĀRKSHYA. An ancient mythological personification of the sun in the form of a horse or bird. In later times the name is applied to Garu*d*a.

TATWA SAMĀSA. A text-book of the Sānkhya philosophy, attributed to Kapila himself.

TELINGA. The Telugu country, stretching along the coast from Orissa to Madras.

TILOTTAMĀ. Name of an Apsaras. She was originally a Brāhman female, but for the offence of bathing at an improper season she was condemned to be born as an Apsaras, for the purpose of bringing about the mutual destruction of the two demons Sunda and Upasunda.

TIMIN, TIMIN-GILA. The Timin is a large fabulous fish. The Timin-gila, 'swallower of the Timin,' is a still larger one; and there is one yet larger, the Timin-gila-gila or Timi-timin-gila, 'swallower of the Timin-gila.' *Cf.* the Arabic Tinnīn, sea-serpent. It is also called Samudrāru.

TISHYA. The Kali Yuga or fourth age.

TITTIRI. 'A partridge.' An ancient sage who was the pupil of Yāska, and is an authority referred to by Pā*n*ini. Some attribute the Taittirīya Sanhitā of the Yajur-veda to him. *See* Veda.

TOSALAKA. An athelete and boxer who was killed by K*ri*sh*n*a in the public arena in the presence of Kan*s*a.

TRAIGARTTAS. The people of Tri-gartta (q.v.).

TRASADASYU. A royal sage and author of hymns. According to Sāya*n*a, he was son of Purukutsa. When Purukutsa was a prisoner, "his queen propitiated the seven *R*ishis to obtain a son who might take his father's place. They advised her to worship Indra and Varu*n*a, in consequence of which Trasadasyu was born." He was renowned for his generosity. According to the Bhāgavata Purā*n*a he was father of Purukutsa.

TRETĀ YUGA. The second age of the world, a period of 1,296,000 years. *See* Yuga.

TRI-BHUVANA, TRI-LOKA. The three worlds, Swarga, Bhūmi, Pātāla—heaven, earth, and hell.

TRI-DA*S*A. 'Three times ten, thirty.' In round numbers, the thirty-three deities—twelve Ādityas, eight Vasus, eleven Rudras, and two A*s*wins.

TRI-GARTTA. 'The country of the three strongholds,' lately identified with the northern hill state of Kotoch, which is still called by the people "the country of Traigart."—*Wilson.* General Cunningham, however, clearly identifies it with the Jālandhar Doāb and Kāngra.

TRI-JA*T*Ā. An amiable Rākshasī who befriended Sītā when she was the captive of Rāva*n*a in Ceylon. She is also called Dharma-jnā.

TRI-KĀ*ND*A *S*ESHA. A Sanskrit vocabulary in three chapters, composed as a supplement to the Amara-kosha. It has been printed in India.

TRI-KŪ*T*A. 'Three peaks.' 1. The mountain on which the city of Lankā was built. 2. A mountain range running south from Meru.

TRI-LOCHANA. 'Three-eyed,' *i.e.*, *S*iva. The Mahā-bhārata relates that the third eye burst from *S*iva's forehead with a great flame when his wife playfully placed her hands over his eyes after he had been engaged in austerities in the Himālaya. This eye has been very destructive. It reduced Kāma, the god of love, to ashes.

TRI-MŪRTI. 'Triple form.' The Hindu triad. This was foreshadowed in the Vedic association of the three gods Agni, Vāyu, and Sūrya. The triad consists of the gods Brahmā, *S*iva, and Vish*n*u, the representatives of the creative, destructive, and preservative principles. Brahmā is the embodiment "of the Rajo-gu*n*a, the quality of passion or desire, by which the world was called into being; *S*iva is the embodied Tamo-gu*n*a, the attribute of darkness or wrath, and the destructive fire by which the earth is annihilated; and Vish*n*u is the embodied Satwa-gu*n*a, or property of mercy and goodness by which the world is preserved. The three exist in one and one in three, as the Veda is divided into three and is yet but one; and they are all Ā*s*rita, or comprehended within that one being who is Parama or 'supreme,' Guhya or 'secret,' and Sarvātmā, 'the soul of all things.'"—*Wilson.*

The Padma Purā*n*a, which is a Vaish*n*ava work and gives the supremacy to Vish*n*u, says, "In the beginning of creation, the great Vish*n*u, desirous of creating the whole world, became threefold: creator, preserver, and destroyer. In order to create this world, the supreme spirit produced from the right side of his body himself as Brahmā; then in order to preserve the world he produced from the left side of his body Vish*n*u; and in order to destroy the world he produced from the middle of his body the eternal *S*iva. Some worship Brahmā, others Vish*n*u, others *S*iva; but Vish*n*u, one yet threefold, creates, preserves, and destroys, therefore let the pious make no difference between the three." The representation of the Tri-mūrti is one body with three heads: in the middle Brahmā, on the right Vish*n*u, and on the left *S*iva. The worship of Brahmā is almost extinct, but Vish*n*u and *S*iva receive unbounded adoration from their respective followers, and each is elevated to the dignity of the supreme being.

T*RIN*ĀVARTTA. A demon who assumed the form of a whirlwind and carried off the infant K*ri*sh*n*a, but was overpowered and killed by the child.

TRI-PĀDA. 'Three-footed.' Fever personified as having three feet, symbolising the three stages of fever—heat, cold, and sweat.

TRI-PURA. 'Triple city.' 1. According to the Hari-van*s*a it was aerial, and was burnt in a war with the gods. 2. A name of the demon Bā*n*a, because he received in gift three cities from *S*iva, Brahmā, and Vish*n*u. He was killed by *S*iva. His name at full length is Tripurāsura. The name is also applied to *S*iva.

TRI-PURI. The capital city of the Chedis, now traceable in the insignificant village of Tewar, on the banks of the Narmadā.

TRI-*S*ANKU. *See* Satya-vrata.

TRI-*S*IRAS. 'Three-headed.' 1. In the Vedas, a son of Twash*tri*; also called Vi*s*wa-rūpa. 2. Fever personified as a dæmon with three heads, typical of the three stages of heat, cold, and sweating. 3. Kuvera, god of wealth. 4. An Asura killed by Vish*n*u. 5. A son or a friend of Rāva*n*a killed by Rāma.

TRI-*S*ŪLA. 'A trident.' The trident of *S*iva.

TRITA, TRITA ĀPTYA. A minor deity mentioned occasionally in the *Ri*g-veda, and generally in some relation to Indra. Thus "Indra broke through the defences of Vala, as did Trita through the coverings (of the well)." In explanation of this and similar allusions, a legend is told by the commentator to the effect, that Ekata, Dwita, and Trita (first, second, and third), were three men produced in water by Agni, for the purpose of rubbing off the remains of an oblation of clarified butter. Agni threw the cinders of the offerings into water, and from them sprang the three brothers, who, from their origin in water (*āp*), were called Āptyas. Trita went one day to draw water from a well and fell into it. The Asuras then heaped coverings over the mouth of it to prevent his getting out, but he broke through them with ease. The Nītī-manjarī tells the story differently. Ekata, Dwita, and Trita were travelling in a desert and suffered from thirst. They came to a well from which Trita drew water and gave it to his brothers. In order to appropriate his property the two brothers threw him into the well, placed a cart-wheel over it, and there left him. Trita prayed earnestly to the gods, and with their help he escaped.

T*RI*TSUS. A people frequently mentioned in the Veda. Sāya*n*a says they were "priests who were Vasish*t*ha's disciples." Vasish*t*ha himself is said to have belonged to the tribe.

TRI-VE*N*Ī. 'The triple braid.' A name of Prayāga. It is so called because the Ganges and Jumna here unite, and the Saraswatī is supposed to join them by an underground channel.

TRI-VIKRAMA. A name of Vish*n*u used in the *Ri*g-veda, and referring to three steps or paces which he is represented as taking. These steps, according to the opinion of a commentator, are "the three periods of the sun's course,—his rising, culminating, and setting." An old commentator says, "Vish*n*u stepped by separate strides over the whole universe. In three places he planted his step, one step on the earth, a second in the atmosphere, and a third in the sky, in the successive forms of Agni, Vāyu, and Sūrya." The great commentator Sāya*n*a, a comparatively modern writer, understands these steps as being the three steps of Vish*n*u in the Vāmana or dwarf incarnation, and no doubt they were the origin of this fiction.

TRYAMBAKA. 'Three-eyed,' or 'Having three wives or sisters.' 1. A name of *S*iva. 2. One of the Rudras. 3. Name of one of the twelve great Lingas. *See* Linga.

TRYARU*N*A. A king, son of Triv*ri*shan, of the race of Ikshwāku. He was riding in a chariot which Vri*s*a, his purohita or family priest, was driving. The vehicle passed over and killed a Brāhman boy, and a question arose as to who was responsible for the death. The question was referred to an assembly of the Ikshwākus, and they decided it against Vri*s*a. The purohit by his prayers then restored the boy to life, and being very angry with them for what he deemed partiality, "fire henceforth ceased to perform its functions in their dwellings, and the cooking of their food and other offices ceased." The Ikshwākus appeased him, and upon his prayers the use of fire was restored to them. This story is told by Sāyana in elucidation of a Vedic allusion, and he quotes the *S*ātyāyana Brāhma*n*a as the authority.

TUKHĀRAS. A northern tribe from whom Tukhāristān obtained its name. They are probably the tribe of *S*akas, by whom Bactria was taken from the Greeks. They are also called Tushāras.

TULĀDHĀRA. A trading Vai*s*ya mentioned in the Mahābhārata as very virtuous and learned, to whom Jājali, an arrogant Brāhman, was sent by a voice from the sky to learn wisdom.

TULUNGA. Tuluva, or the country where the Tulu language is spoken, on the western coast below Goa.

TUMBURU. Name of a Gandharva. *See* Virādha.

TU*ND*A. A demon slain by Nahusha, the son of Āyus. He had a son named Vitu*nd*a, who was killed by Bhagavatī (Durgā).

TURANGĀ-VAKTRA. 'Horse-faced people.' *See* Kinnaras.

TURUSHKAS. Turks; the people of Turkistan. The Indo-Scythians, who, under Kanishka and other kings of the race, held Northern India.

TURVA*S*A, TURVA*S*U. Son of Yayāti by Devayānī. He refused to bear the curse of premature decrepitude passed upon his father, and so his father cursed him that his posterity should "not possess dominion." His father gave him a part of his kingdom, but after some generations, his line merged into that of his brother Puru, who bore for a time the curse passed upon his father.

TUSHĀRA. *See* Tukhāra.

TUSHITAS. A ga*n*a or class of subordinate deities, thirty-six in number, but sometimes reduced to twelve, and identified with the Ādityas.

TWASH*TRI*. In the *Ri*g-veda this deity is the ideal artist, the divine artisan, the most skilful of workmen, who is versed in all wonderful and admirable contrivances, and corresponds in many respects with Hephaistos and Vulcan. He sharpens and carries the great iron axe, and he forges the thunderbolts of Indra. He is the beautiful, skilful worker, the omniform, the archetype of all forms, the vivifier and the bestower of long life. He imparts generative power and bestows offspring. He forms husband and wife for each other, even from the womb. He develops the seminal germ in the womb, and is the shaper of all forms, human and animal. He has generated a strong man, a lover of the gods, a swift horse, and has created the whole world. As the *S*atapatha Brāhma*n*a expresses it, "He has produced and nourishes a great variety of creatures; all worlds (or beings) are his, and are known to him; he has given to heaven and earth and to all things their forms." He created Brahmanaspati above all creatures, and generated Agni along with heaven and earth, the waters and the Bh*ri*gus. He is master of the universe, the first-born protector and leader, and knows the region of the gods. He is supplicated to nourish the worshipper and protect his sacrifice. He is the bestower of blessings, and is possessed of abundant wealth, and grants prosperity. He is asked, like other gods, to take pleasure in the hymns of his worshippers and to grant them riches. He is associated with the *Ri*bhus, and is represented as sometimes envying and sometimes admiring their skill. He is represented as being occasionally in a state of hostility with Indra, and he had a son named Vi*s*wa-rūpa (omniform) or Tri-*s*iras, who had three heads, six eyes, and three mouths, who was especially obnoxious to Indra, and was slain by him. He had a daughter, Sara*n*yū, whom he married to Vivaswat, and she was the mother of the A*s*wins. In the Purā*n*as Twash*tri* is identified with Vi*s*wakarman, the artisan of the gods, and sometimes also with Prajāpati. One of the Ādityas and one of the Rudras bear this name, as also did a prince descended from Bharata.

UCHCHAI*H*-*S*RAVAS. The model horse. The white horse of Indra, produced at the churning of the ocean. It is fed on ambrosia, and is held to be the king of horses.

UCHCHHISH*T*A. The remains of a sacrifice, to which divine powers are ascribed by the *Ri*g-veda.

UDAYA-GIRI PARVATA. The eastern mountain from behind which the sun rises.

UDAYANA. 1. A prince of the Lunar race, and son of Sahasrānīka, who is the hero of a popular story. He was king of Vatsa, and is commonly called Vatsa-rāja. His capital was Kau*s*āmbī. Vāsava-dattā, princess of Ujjayinī, saw him in a dream and fell in love with him. He was decoyed to that city, and there kept in captivity by the king, Cha*nd*asena; but when he was set at liberty by the minister, he carried off Vāsava-dattā from her father and a rival suitor. 2. A name of Agastya.

UDDHAVA. The friend and counsellor of K*r*ish*n*a. According to some he was K*r*ish*n*a's cousin, being son of Devabhāga, the brother of Vasu-deva. He was also called Pavanavyādhi.

UDGĀT*RI*. A priest whose duty it is to chaunt the prayers or hymns from the Sāma-veda.

UDRANKA. Haris-chandra's aerial city. *See* Saubha.

UGRA. A name of Rudra, or of one of his manifestations. *See* Rudra.

UGRASENA. A king of Mathurā, husband of Kar*n*ī, and father of Kan*s*a and Devaka. He was deposed by Kan*s*a, but K*r*ish*n*a, after killing the latter, restored Ugrasena to the throne. *See* Kan*s*a.

UJJAYANĪ. The Greek Οζήνη and the modern Oujein or Ujjein. It was the capital of Vikramāditya and one of the seven sacred cities. Hindu geographers calculate their longitude from it, making it their first meridian.

ULŪKA. 'An owl' Son of Kitava. He was king of a country and people of the same name. He was an ally of the Kauravas, and acted as their envoy to the Pā*nd*avas.

ULŪPĪ. A daughter of Kauravya, Rāja of the Nāgas, with whom Arjuna contracted a kind of marriage. She was nurse to her step-son, Babhru-vāhana, and had great influence over him. According to the Vish*n*u Purā*n*a she had a son named Irāvat.

UMĀ. 'Light.' A name of the consort of *S*iva. The earliest known mention of the name is in the Kena Upanishad, where she appears as a mediatrix between Brahmā and the other gods, and seems to be identified with Vāch. *See* Devī.

UMĀ-PATI. 'Husband of Umā,' that is to say, *S*iva.

UPANISHADS. 'Esoteric doctrine.' The third division of the Vedas attached to the Brāhma*n*a portion, and forming part of the *S*ruti or revealed word. The Upanishads are generally written in prose with interspersed verses, but some are wholly in verse. There are about 150 of these works, probably even more. They are of later date than the Brāhma*n*as, but it is thought that the oldest may date as far back as the sixth century B.C. The object of these treatises is to ascertain the mystic sense of the text of the Veda, and so they enter into such abstruse questions as the orgin of the universe, the nature of the deity, the nature of soul, and the connection of mind and matter. Thus they contain the beginnings of that metaphysical inquiry which ended in the full development of Hindu philosophy. The Upanishads have "one remarkable peculiarity, the total absence of any Brahmanical exclusiveness in their doctrine. They are evidently later than the older Sanhitās and Brāhma*n*as, but they breathe an entirely different spirit, a freedom of thought unknown in any earlier work except the *R*ig-veda hymns themselves. The great teachers of the higher knowledge and Brāhmans are continually represented as going to Kshatriya kings to become their pupils."—*Professor Cowell.* The *R*ig-veda has the Upanishad called Aitareya attached to the Aitareya Brāhma*n*a. The Taittirīya Sanhitā of the Yajur has an Upanishad of the same name. The Vājasaneyī Sanhitā has the Īsa, and attached to the *S*atapatha Brāhma*n*a it has the B*ri*had Āra*n*yaka, which is the most important of them. The Sāma-veda has the Kena and Chhāndogya. All these have been translated into English. The Atharva-veda has the Ka*th*a, Pra*s*na, Mu*nd*aka, Māndukya, and others, altogether fifty-two in number. These are the most important of the Upanishads. Many of the Upanishads have been printed, and several of them translated in the *Bibliotheca Indica*, and by Poley. There is a catalogue by Müller in the *Zeitschrift des D. M. G.*, vol. xix.

UPAPLAVYA. Matsya, the capital of the king of Virā*t*a.

UPA-PURĀ*N*AS. Secondary or subordinate Purā*n*as. *See* Purā*n*a.

UPARICHARA. A Vasu or demigod, who, according to the Mahā-bhārata, became king of Chedi by command of Indra. He had five sons by his wife; and by an Apsaras, named Adrikā, condemned to live on earth in the form of a fish, he had a son named Matsya (fish), and a daughter, Satya-vatī, who was the mother of Vyāsa.

UPA*S*RUTI. A supernatural voice which is heard at night revealing the secrets of the future.

UPASUNDA. A Daitya, son of Nisunda, brother of Sunda, and father of Mūka. *See* Sunda.

UPA-VEDAS. Subordinate or inferior Vedas. These are sciences which have no connection whatever with the *S*ruti or revealed Veda. They are four in number—(1.) Āyur-veda, medicine; (2.) Gāndharva-veda, music and dancing; (3.) Dhanur-veda, archery, military science; (4.) Sthāpatya-veda, architecture.

UPENDRA. A title given to K*r*ish*n*a by Indra.

URAGAS. The Nāgas or serpents inhabiting Pātāla.

ŪRMILĀ. Daughter of Janaka, sister of Sītā, wife of Laksh-ma*n*a, and mother of Gandharvī Somadā.

ŪRVA. Father of *R*ichīka and grandfather of Jamad-agni.

URVA*S*Ī. A celestial nymph, mentioned first in the *Rig-veda*. The sight of her beauty is said to have caused the generation, in a peculiar way, of the sages Agastya and Vasish*t*ha by Mitra and Varu*n*a. A verse says, "And thou, O Vasish*t*ha, art a son of Mitra and Varu*n*a." She roused the anger of these two deities and incurred their curse, through which she came to live upon the earth, and became the wife or mistress of Purū-ravas. The story of her amour with Purū-ravas is first told in the *S*atapatha Brāhma*n*a. The loves of Purū-ravas, the Vikrama or hero, and of Urva*s*ī, the nymph, are the subject of Kālidāsa's drama called Vikramorva*s*ī. *See* Purū-ravas.

U*S*ANAS. 1. The planet Venus or its regent, also called *S*ukra (q.v.). 2. Author of a Dharma-sāstra or law-book.

ŪSHĀ. A Daitya princess, daughter of Bā*n*a and grand-daughter of Bali. She is called also Prīti-jushā. She fell in love with a prince whom she saw in a dream, and was anxious to know if there were such a person. Her favourite companion, Chitra-lekhā, drew the portraits of many gods and men, but Ūshā's choice fell upon Aniruddha, son of Pradyumna and grandson of K*r*ish*n*a. Chitra-lekhā, by her magic power, brought Aniruddha to Ūshā. Her father, on hearing of the youth's being in the palace, endeavoured to kill him, but he defended himself successfully. Bā*n*a, however, kept Aniruddha, "binding him in serpent bonds." K*r*ish*n*a, Pradyumna, and Bala-rāma went to the rescue; and although Bā*n*a was supported by *S*iva and by Skanda, god of war, his party was defeated, and Aniruddha was carried back to Dwārakā with his wife Ūshā.

USHAS. The dawn, the ἠώς of the Greeks and Aurora of the Latins. She is the daughter of heaven and sister of the Ādityas. This is one of the most beautiful myths of the Vedas, and is enveloped in poetry. Ushas is the friend of men, she smiles like a young wife, she is the daughter of the sky, she goes to every house, she thinks of the dwellings of men, she does not despise the small or the great, she brings wealth; she is always the same, immortal, divine, age cannot touch her; she is the young goddess, but she makes men grow old. "All this," adds Max Müller, "may be simply allegorical language. But the transition from Devī, 'the bright,' to Devī, the goddess, is so easy; the daughter of the sky assumes so readily the same personality which is given to the sky, Dyaus, her father, that we can only guess whether, in every passage, the poet is speaking of a bright apparition or of a bright goddess, of a natural vision or a visible deity." She is called Ahanā and Dyotanā, 'the illumer.'

USHMAPAS. The Pitris or a class of Pitris (q.v.).

USIJ. Mentioned in the *Rig*-veda as the mother of Kakshīvat. A female servant of the queen of the Kalinga Rāja. The king desired his queen to submit to the embraces of the sage Dīrgha-tamas, in order that he might beget a son. The queen substituted her bondmaid Usij. The sage, cognisant of the deception, sanctified Usij, and begat upon her a son, Kakshīvat, who, through his affiliation by the king, was a Kshatriya, but, as the son of Dīrgha-tamas, was a Brāhman. This story is told in the Mahā-bhārata and some of the Purānas.

UTATHYA. A Brāhman of the race of Angiras, who married Bhadrā, daughter of Soma, a woman of great beauty. The god Varuna, who had formerly been enamoured of her, carried her off from Utathya's hermitage, and would not give her up to Nārada, who was sent to bring her back. Utathya, greatly enraged, drank up all the sea, still Varuna would not let her go. At the desire of Utathya, the lake of Varuna was then dried up and the ocean swept away. The saint then addressed himself to the countries and to the river:—"Saraswatī, disappear into the deserts, and let this land, deserted by thee, become impure." "After the country had become dried up, Varuna submitted himself to Utathya and brought back Bhadrā. The sage was pleased to get back his wife, and released both the world and Varuna from their sufferings."

UTKALA. The modern Orissa. It gives its name to one of the five northern nations of Brāhmans. *See* Brāhman.

UTTAMAUJAS. A warrior of great strength, and an ally of the Pāndavas.

UTTĀNA-PAD. 'Outstretched, supine.' In the Vedas, a peculiar creative source from which the earth sprang. Supposed to refer to the posture of a woman in parturition.

UTTĀNA-PĀDA. A son of Manu and *S*ata-rūpā. By his wife Su-n*r*itā he had four sons, Dhruva, Kīrtimān, Ayushmān, and Vasu. Some of the Purā*n*as gave him another wife, Su-ruchi, and a son, Uttama. *See* Dhruva.

UTTARA (mas.), UTTARĀ (fem.). A son and daughter of the Rāja of Virā*t*a. Uttara was killed in battle by *S*alya. The daughter married Abhimanyu, son of Arjuna.

UTTARA-KURU. A region lying far to the north. (*See* Jambu-dwīpa.) (Plural.) The inhabitants of this region.

UTTARA MĪMĀNSĀ. A school of philosophy. *See* Dar*s*ana.

UTTARA-NAISHADA-CHARITA. A poem on the life of Nala, king of Nishada, written about the year 1000 A.D. by *S*rī Harsha, a celebrated sceptical philosopher. It has been printed in the *Bibliotheca Indica.*

UTTARA-RĀMA-CHARITA. 'The later chronicle of Rāma. A drama by Bhava-bhūti on the latter part of Rāma's life. The second part of King Rāma, as the Mahā-vīra-charita is the first. The drama is based on the Uttara Kā*nd*a of the Rāmāya*n*a, and quotes two or three verses from that poem. It was probably written about the beginning of the eighth century. It has been translated in blank verse by Wilson, and more literally by Professor C. H. Tawney. There are several editions of the text.

VA. A name of Varu*n*a; also name of his dwelling.

VĀCH. 'Speech.' In the *Ri*g-veda, Vāch appears to be the personification of speech by whom knowledge was communicated to man. Thus she is said to have "entered into the *Ri*shis," and to make whom she loves terrible and intelligent, a priest and a *Ri*shi. She was "generated by the gods," and is called "the divine Vāch," "queen of the gods," and she is described as "the melodious cow who milked forth sustenance and water," "who yields us nourishment and sustenance." The Brāhma*n*as associate her with Prajāpati in the work of creation. In the Taittirīya Brāhma*n*a she is called "the mother of the Vedas," and "the wife of Indra, who contains within herself all worlds." In the *S*atapatha Brāhma*n*a she is represented as entering into a sexual connection with Prajāpati, who, "being desirous of creating, connected himself with various spouses," and among them, "through his mind, with Vāch," from whom "he created the waters;" or, as this last sentence is differently translated, "He created the waters from the world [in the form] of speech (Vāch)." In the Kathaka Upanishad this idea is more distinctly formulated:—"Prajāpati was this universe. Vāch was a second to him. He associated sexually with her; she became pregnant; she departed from him; she produced these creatures; she again entered into Prajāpati."

The Aitareya Brāhma*n*a and the *S*atapatha Brāhma*n*a have a story of the Gandharvas having stolen the soma juice, or, as one calls it, "King Soma," and that as the Gandharvas were fond of women, Vāch was, at her own suggestion, "turned into a female" by the gods and *R*ishis, and went to recover it from them.

In the Atharva-veda she is identified with Virāj, and is the daughter of Kāma (desire). "That daughter of thine, O Kāma, is called the cow, she whom sages denominate Vāch-Virāj."

The Mahā-bhārata also calls her "the mother of the Vedas," and says, "A voice derived from Brahmā entered into the ears of them all; the celestial Saraswatī was then produced from the heavens." Here and "in the later mythology, Saraswatī was identified with Vāch, and became under different names the spouse of Brahmā and the goddess of wisdom and eloquence, and is invoked as a muse," generally under the name of Saraswatī, but sometimes as Vāch.

The Bhāgavata Purā*n*a recognises her as "the slender and enchanting daughter" of Brahmā, for whom he had a passion, and from whom mankind was produced, that is the female Virāj. (*See* Virāj and *S*ata-rūpa.) Saraswatī, as wife of Brahmā and goddess of wisdom, represents perhaps the union of power and intelligence which was supposed to operate in the work of creation. According to the Padma Purā*n*a, Vāch was daughter of Daksha, wife of Kasyapa, and mother of the Gandharvas and Apsarases.

VĀ*D*AVA, VĀ*D*AVĀNALA. The submarine fire which "devours the water of the ocean," causing it to throw off the vapours which are condensed into rain and snow. The word is also written Va*d*ava and Ba*d*ava. *See* Aurva.

VĀHANA. 'A vehicle.' Most of the gods are represented as having animals as their vāhanas. Brahmā has the Hansa, swan or goose; Vish*n*u has Garu*d*a, half eagle, half man; *S*iva, the bull Nandi; Indra, an elephant; Yama, a buffalo; Kārttikeya, a peacock; Kāma-deva, the marine monster Makara, or a parrot; Agni, a ram; Varuna, a fish; Ganesa, a rat; Vāyu, an antelope; *S*ani, or Saturn, a vulture; Durgā, a tiger.

VAHNI. Fire. *See* Agni.

VĀHUKA. 'Charioteer.' A name and office assumed by Nala in his time of disguise.

VAIBHOJAS. The Mahā-bhārata says, "The descendants of Druhyu are the Vaibhojas." "A people unacquainted with the use of cars or beasts of burthen, and who travel on rafts; they have no kings."—*Wilson.*

VAIBHRĀJA. A celestial grove; the grove of the gods on Mount Supārswa, west of Meru.

VAIDARBHA. Belonging to the country of Vidarbha or Birār. The people of that country.

VAIDEHA. Belonging to the country of Videha or Tirhoot, &c. The king or the people of the country. Janaka was called Vaideha and Sītā was Vaidehī.

VAIDYA-NĀTHA. 'Lord of physicians.' A title of *S*iva. Name of one of the twelve great Lingas. *See* Linga.

VAIJAYANTA. The palace or the banner of Indra.

VAIJAYANTĪ. 1. The necklace of Vishnu, composed of five precious gems, pearl, ruby, emerald, sapphire, and diamond; it "is the aggregate of the five elemental rudiments." 2. A law-book current in the south. It is a commentary by Nanda Pa*nd*ita on the Vish*n*u Sm*ri*ti.

VAIKARTTANA. A name of Kar*n*a from his putative father, Vikarttana, the sun.

VAIKUN*T*HA. The paradise of Vish*n*u, sometimes described as on Mount Meru, and at others as in the Northern Ocean. It is also called Vaibhra. Vish*n*u himself is sometimes designated by this term.

VAINATEYA. A name of Vish*n*u's bird Garu*d*a.

VAIRĀJ. Manu the son of Virāj.

VAIRĀJAS. Semi-divine beings or Manes unconsumable by fire, who dwell in Tapo-loka, but are capable of translation to Satya-loka. The Kā*s*ī-kha*nd*a explains this term as the Manes of "ascetics, mendicants, anchorets, and penitents, who have completed a course of rigorous austerities." *See* Pit*ri*s.

VAIROCHANA. A name of Bali.

VAISĀLĪ. A city founded by Visāla, son of T*ri*nabindu. This is "a city of considerable renown in Indian tradition, but its site is a subject of some uncertainty." It was a celebrated place among the Buddhists, and would seem to have been situated on the left bank of the Ganges. General Cunningham places it about 27 miles north of Patna. It is frequently confounded with Visālā, *i.e.*, Ujjayinī.

VAISAMPĀYANA. A celebrated sage who was the original teacher of the Black Yajur-veda. He was a pupil of the great Vyāsa, from whom he learned the Mahā-bhārata, which he afterwards recited to King Janamejaya at a festival. The Hari-vansa is also represented as having been communicated by him.

VAISESHIKA. The Atomic school of philosophy. *See* Darsana.

VAISRAVANA. Patronymic of Kuvera.

VAISWĀNARA. A name by which Agni is occasionally known in the *R*ig-veda.

VAISYA. The third or trading and agricultural caste. *See* Varna.

VAITĀNA SŪTRA. The ritual of the Atharva-veda. The text has been published by Dr. Garbe.

VAITARA*N*Ī. '(The river) to be crossed,' that is, the river of hell, which must be crossed before the infernal regions can be entered. This river is described as being filled with blood, ordure, and all sorts of filth, and to run with great impetuosity. A second river stated by the Mahā-bhārata to be in the country of the Kalingas; it must be the river of the same name (vulg. "Byeturnee") somewhat higher up in Cuttack.

VAIVASWATA. Name of the seventh Manu; he was son of Sūrya and father of Ikshwāku, the founder of the Solar race of kings.

VĀJASANEYĪ-SANHITĀ. The body of hymns forming the White Yajur-veda. *See* Veda.

VĀJIN. A priest of the White Yajur-veda.

VAJRA. 1. The thunderbolt of Indra, said to have been made of the bones of the *R*ishi Dadhīchi. It is a circular weapon, with a hole in the centre, according to some, but others represent it as consisting of two transverse bars. It has many names:—Asani, Abhrottha, 'sky-born;' Bahu-dāra, 'much cleaving;' Bhidira or Chhidaka, 'the splitter;' Dambholi and Jasuri, 'destructive;' Hrādin, 'roaring;' Kulisa, 'axe;' Pavi, 'pointed;' Phena-vāhin, 'foam-bearing; Shat-kona, 'hexagon;' Sambha and Swaru. 2. Son of Aniruddha. His mother is sometimes said to be Aniruddha's wife Su-bhadrā, and at others the Daitya princess Ūshā. Krishna just before his death made him king over the Yādavas at Indra-prastha. *See* the next.

VAJRA-NĀBHA. The celebrated chakra (discus) of Krishna. According to the Mahā-bhārata it was given to him by Agni for his assistance in defeating Indra and burning the Khāndava forest.

VAKA. 'A crane.' A great Asura who lived near the city of Eka-chakrā, and forced the Rāja of the place to send him daily a large quantity of provisions, which he devoured, and not only the provisions, but the men who carried them. Under the directions of Kuntī, her son Bhīma took the provisions, and when the demon struck him, a terrific combat followed; each one tore up trees by the roots and belaboured the other, till Bhīma seized the demon by the legs and tore him asunder. Kuvera is sometimes called by this name.

VĀLA-KHILYAS. 1. Eleven hymns of an apocryphal or peculiar character interpolated in the *Rig*-veda. 2. "Pigmy sages no bigger than a joint of the thumb, chaste, pious, resplendent as the rays of the sun." So described by the Vishnu Purāna, which says that they were brought forth by Samnati (humility), wife of Kratu, and were 60,000 in number. They are able to fly swifter than birds. The *Rig*-veda says that they sprang from the hairs of Prajāpati (Brahmā). They are the guards of the chariot of the sun. They are also called Kharwas. Wilson says "they are not improbably connected with the character of Däumling, Thaumlin, Tamlane, Tom-a-lyn, or Tom Thumb."

VĀLMĪKI. The author of the Rāmāyana, which he in Vedic phrase is said to have "seen." He himself is represented as taking part in some of the scenes he describes. He received the banished Sītā into his hermitage at Chitra-kūta, and educated her twin sons Kusa and Lava. "Tradition has marked a hill in the district of Banda in Bundlekand as his abode." The invention of the sloka is attributed to him, but it cannot be his, because the metre is found in the Vedas.

VĀMĀCHĀRĪS. Followers of the left-hand sect. *See* Tantra.

VĀMA-DEVA. 1. A Vedic *Rishi*, author of many hymns. In one of his hymns he represents himself as speaking before his birth, saying, "Let me not come forth by this path, for it is difficult (of issue): let me come forth obliquely from the side." Sāya*n*a, the commentator, says in explanation, "The *Ri*shi Vāma-deva, whilst yet in the womb, was reluctant to be born in the usual manner, and resolved to come into the world through his mother's side. Aware of his purpose, the mother prayed to Aditi, who thereupon came with her son Indra to expostulate with the *Ri*shi." [This story accords with that told by the Buddhists of the birth of Buddha.] In the same hymn Vāma-deva says, "In extreme destitution I have cooked the entrails of a dog," and Manu cites this to show that a man is not rendered impure even by eating the flesh of dogs for the preservation of his life. In another hymn he says, "As a hawk I came forth with speed;" and a commentator explains, "Having assumed the form of a hawk, he came forth from the womb by the power of Yoga, for he is considered to have been endowed with divine knowlege from the period of his conception." 2. A Vedic sage mentioned in the Mahā-bhārata as possessor of two horses of marvellous speed called Vāmyas. 3. A name of *S*iva; also of one of the Rudras.

VĀMANA. The dwarf incarnation of Vish*n*u. *See* Avatāra.

VĀMANA PURĀ*N*A. "That in which the four-faced Brahmā taught the three objects of existence, as subservient to the greatness of Tri-vikrama (Vish*n*u), which treats also of the *S*iva kalpa, and which consists of 10,000 stanzas, is called the Vāmana Purā*n*a." It contains an account of the dwarf incarnation of Vish*n*u, and "extends to about 7000 stanzas, but its contents scarcely establish its claim to the character of a Purā*n*a." "It is of a more tolerant character than the (other) Purā*n*as, and divides its homage impartially between *S*iva and Vish*n*u with tolerable impartiality. It has not the air of any antiquity, and its compilation may have amused the leisure of some Brāhman of Benares three or four centuries ago."—*Wilson.*

VĀNA-PRASTHA. 'A dweller in the worlds.' A Brāhman in the third stage of his religious life, passing his time as an anchorite in the woods. *See* Brāhman.

VANA-CHARAS (mas.), VANE-CHARĪS (fem.). Wanderers of the woods. Fauns, Dryads, or sylvan guardians.

VAN*S*A. A race or family. Lists of the *Ri*shis or successive teachers of the Vedas which are found attached to some of the Brāhma*n*as are called Van*s*as.

VAN*S*A-BRĀHMA*N*A. The eighth Brāhma*n*a of the Sāma-veda. It has been edited by Burnell.

VAPUSHMAT. A man who killed King Marutta of the Solar race. Dama, son or grandson of Marutta, in retaliation killed Vapushmat. With his blood he made the funeral offerings to the Manes of Marutta, and with the flesh he fed the Brāhmans who were of Rākshasa descent.

VARA-DĀ. 'Bestower of boons.' A name of Devī, also of Saraswatī.

VARĀHA. The boar incarnation of Vish*n*u. *See* Avatāra.

VĀRĀHA-KALPA. The present kalpa or year of Brahmā. *See* Kalpa.

VARĀHA MIHĪRA. An astronomer who was one of "the nine gems" of the court of Vikramāditya. (*See* Nava-ratna.) He was author of B*ri*hat-sanhitā and B*ri*haj-jātaka. His death is placed in *S*aka 509 (A.D. 587).

VARĀHA PURĀ*N*A. "That in which the glory of the great Varāha is predominant, as it was revealed to Earth by Vish*n*u, in connexion, wise Munis, with the Mānava kalpa, and which contains 24,000 verses, is called the Varāha Purā*n*a;" but this description differs so from the Purā*n*a which bears the name in the present day, that Wilson doubts its applying to it. The known work "is narrated by Vish*n*u as Varāha, or in the boar incarnation, to the personified Earth. Its extent, however, is not half that specified, little exceeding 10,000 stanzas. It furnishes also itself evidence of the prior currency of some other work similarly denominated." "It may perhaps be referred to the early part of the twelfth century."

VĀRĀ*N*ASĪ. The sacred city of Benares; also called Kā*s*ī.

VĀRA*N*ĀVATA. The city in which the Pā*nd*avas dwelt in exile.

VARARUCHI. A grammarian who is generally supposed to be one with Kātyāyana (q.v.). There was another Vararuchi who was one of "the nine gems" at the court of Vikramāditya.

VARDDHA-KSHATRĪ. A patronymic of Jayad-ratha.

VĀRKSHĪ. Daughter of a sage, who is instanced in the Mahā-bhārata as being a virtuous woman, and wife of ten husbands.

VARNA. 'Class or caste.' The Chatur-varna, or four castes, as found established in the code of Manu, are—

1. Brāhman. The sacerdotal and learned class, the members of which may be, but are not necessarily priests.

2. Kshatriya. The regal and warrior caste.

3. Vaisya. Trading and agricultural caste.

4. Sūdra. Servile caste, whose duty is to serve the other three.

The first three castes were called dwi-ja, "twice born or regenerate," from their being entitled to investiture with the sacred thread which effects a second birth. The Brāhmans maintain that their caste alone remains, that the other three have been lost or degraded, and it is generally believed that there are no pure Kshatriyas or Vaisyas now existing. The numerous castes which have sprung up from the intercourse of people of different castes or from other causes are called Varna-sankara, 'mixed castes.'

VARSHA. A region. Nine varshas are enumerated as situated between the great mountain ranges of the earth :—(1.) Bhārata-varsha, India; (2.) Kim-purusha or Kin-nara; (3.) Hari; (4.) Ramyaka; (5.) Hiran-maya; (6.) Uttara-kuru; (7.) Ilāvrita; (8.) Bhadrāswa; (9.) Ketu-māla.

VĀRSHNEYA. A name of Krishna as a descendant of Vrishni. Name of King Nala's charioteer.

VĀRTTIKAS. Supplementary rules or notes to the grammar of Pānini by later grammarians, as Kātyāyana, Patanjali, &c. Kātyāyana is the chief of these annotators, and is called Vārttika-kāra, 'the annotator.'

VARUNA. Similar to Οὐρανός. 'The universal encompasser, the all-embracer.' One of the oldest of the Vedic deities, a personification of the all-investing sky, the maker and upholder of heaven and earth. As such he is king of the universe, king of gods and men, possessor of illimitable knowledge, the supreme deity to whom especial honour is due. He is often associated with Mitra, he being the ruler of the night and Mitra of the day; but his name frequently occurs alone, that of Mitra only seldom. In later times he was chief among the lower celestial deities called Ādityas, and later still he became a sort of Neptune, a god of the seas and rivers, who rides upon the Makara. This character he still retains. His sign is a fish.

He is regent of the west quarter and of one of the Nakshatras or lunar mansions. According to the Mahā-bhārata he was son of Kardama and father of Pushkara. The Mahā-bhārata relates that he carried off Bhadrā, the wife of Utathya (q.v.), a Brāhman, but Utathya obliged him to submit and restore her. He was in a way the father of the sage Vasish*th*a (q.v.). In the Vedas, Varu*n*a is not specially connected with water, but there are passages in which he is associated with the element of water both in the atmosphere and on the earth, in such a way as may account for the character and functions ascribed to him in the later mythology.

Dr. Muir thus sums up in the words of the hymns the functions and attributes of Varu*n*a :—"The grandest cosmical functions are ascribed to Varu*n*a. Possessed of illimitable resources (or knowledge), this divine being has meted out (or fashioned) and upholds heaven and earth, he dwells in all worlds as sovereign ruler; indeed the three worlds are embraced within him. He made the golden and revolving sun to shine in the firmament. The wind which resounds through the atmosphere is his breath. He has opened out boundless paths for the sun, and has hollowed out channels for the rivers, which flow by his command. By his wonderful contrivance the rivers pour out their waters into the one ocean but never fill it. His ordinances are fixed and unassailable. They rest on him unshaken as on a mountain. Through the operation (of his laws) the moon walks in brightness, and the stars which appear in the nightly sky mysteriously vanish in daylight. Neither the birds flying in the air, nor the rivers in their ceaseless flow can attain a knowledge of his power or his wrath. His messengers behold both worlds. He knows the flight of birds in the sky, the paths of ships on the ocean, the course of the far-travelling wind, and beholds all the things that have been or shall be done. No creature can even wink without him. He witnesses men's truth and falsehood. He instructs the *Ri*shi Vasish*th*a in mysteries; but his secrets and those of Mitra are not to be revealed to the foolish." "He has unlimited control over the destinies of mankind. He has a hundred thousand remedies, and is supplicated to show his wide and deep benevolence and drive away evil and sin, to untie sin like a rope and remove it. He is entreated not to steal away, but to prolong life, and to spare the suppliant who daily transgresses his laws. In many places mention is made of the bonds or nooses with which he seizes and punishes transgressors. Mitra and Varu*n*a conjointly are spoken of in one passage as being barriers against falsehood, furnished with many nooses, which the hostile mortal cannot surmount; and, in another place, Indra and Varu*n*a are described as binding with bonds not formed of rope. On the other hand, Varu*n*a is said to be gracious even to him who has committed sin. He is the wise guardian of immortality, and a hope is held out that he and Yama, reigning in blessedness, shall be beheld in the next world by the righteous."

"The attributes and functions ascribed to Varu*n*a impart to his character a moral elevation and sanctity far surpassing that attributed to any other Vedic deity."

The correspondence of Varu*n*a with Ouranos has been already noted, but "the parallel will not hold in all points. There is not in the Vedic mythology any special relation between Varu*n*a and P*ri*thivī (the earth) as husband and wife, as there is between Ouranos and Gaia in the theogony of Hesiod; nor is Varu*n*a represented in the Veda, as Ouranos is by the Greek poet, as the progenitor of Dyaus (Zeus), except in the general way in which he is said to have formed and to preserve heaven and earth" (*Muir's Texts*, v. 58). Manu also refers to Varu*n*a as "binding the guilty in fatal cords."

In the Purā*n*as, Varu*n*a is sovereign of the waters, and one of his accompaniments is a noose, which the Vedic deity also carried for binding offenders: this is called Nāga-pā*s*a, Pulakānga, or Vi*s*wa-jit. His favourite resort is Pushpa-giri, 'flower mountain,' and his city Vasudhā-nagara or Sukhā. He also possesses an umbrella impermeable to water, formed of the hood of a cobra, and called Ābhoga. The Vish*n*u Purā*n*a mentions an incident which shows a curious coincidence between Varu*n*a and Neptune. At the marriage of the sage *Ri*chīka, Varu*n*a supplied him with the thousand fleet white horses which the bride's father had demanded of him. Varu*n*a is also called Prachetas, Ambu-rāja, Jala-pati, Ke*s*a, 'lord of the waters;' Ud-dāma, 'the surrounder;' Pā*s*a-bh*ri*t, 'the noose-carrier;' Viloma, Vāri-loma, 'watery hair;' Yāda*h*-pati, 'king of aquatic animals. His son is named Agasti.

VARU*N*ĀNĪ, VARU*N*Ī. Wife of Varu*n*a and goddess of

wine. She is said to have sprung from the churning of the ocean. The goddess of wine is also called Madā and Surā.

VASANTA. Spring and its deified personification.

VASANTA-SENĀ. The heroine of the drama called M*ri*chchhaka*t*ī, 'the toy cart.'

VĀSAVA-DATTĀ. A princess of Ujjayinī, who is the heroine of a popular story by Subandhu. The work has been printed by Dr. F. Hall in the *Bibliotheca Indica.* He considers it to have been written early in the seventh century. *See* Udayana.

VASISH*T*HA. 'Most wealthy.' A celebrated Vedic sage to whom many hymns are ascribed. According to Manu he was one of the seven great *R*ishis and of the ten Prajāpatis. There was a special rivalry between him and the sage Vi*s*wāmitra, who raised himself from the Kshatriya to the Brāhman caste. Vasish*t*ha was the possessor of a "cow of plenty," called Nandinī, who had the power of granting him all things (*vasu*) he desired, hence his name. A law-book is attributed to him, or to another of the same name. Though Vasish*t*ha is classed among the Prajāpatis who sprang from Brahmā, a hymn in the *R*ig-veda and the commentaries thereon assign him a different origin, or rather a second birth, and represent him and the sage Agastya to have sprung from Mitra and Varu*n*a. The hymn says, "Thou, O Vasish*t*ha, art a son of Mitra and Varu*n*a, born a Brāhman from the soul of Urva*s*ī. All the gods placed in the vessel thee the drop which had fallen through divine contemplation." The comment on this hymn says, "When these two Ādityas (Mitra and Varu*n*a) beheld the Apsaras Urva*s*ī at a sacrifice their seed fell from them. . . . It fell on many places, into a jar, into water, and on the ground. The Muni Vasish*t*ha was produced on the ground, while Agastya was born in the jar."

There is a peculiar hymn attributed to Vasish*t*ha in the *R*ig-veda (Wilson, iv. 121), beginning "Protector of the dwelling," which the commentators explain as having been addressed by him to a house-dog which barked as he entered the house of Varu*n*a by night to obtain food after a three days' fast. By it the dog was appeased and put to sleep, "wherefore these verses are to be recited on similar occasions by thieves and burglars."

In the same Veda and in the Aitareya Brāhma*n*a, Vasish*t*ha appears as the family priest of King Sudās, a position to which his rival Vi*s*wāmitra aspired. This is amplified in the Mahā-bhārata, where he is not the priest of Sudās but of his son Kalmāsha-pāda, who bore the patronymic Saudāsa. It is said that his rival Viswāmitra was jealous, and wished to have this office for himself, but the king preferred Vasishtha. Vasishtha had a hundred sons, the eldest of whom was named Saktri. He, meeting the king in the road, was ordered to get out of the way; but he civilly replied that the path was his, for by the law a king must cede the way to a Brāhman. The king struck him with a whip, and he retorted by cursing the king to become a man-eater. Viswāmitra was present, but invisible, and he maliciously commanded a man-devouring Rākshasa to enter the king. So the king became a man-eater, and his first victim was Saktri. The same fate befell all the hundred sons, and Vasishtha's grief was boundless. He endeavoured to destroy himself in various ways. He cast himself from the top of Mount Meru, but the rocks he fell upon were like cotton. He passed through a burning forest without harm. He threw himself into the sea with a heavy stone tied to his neck, but the waves cast him on dry land. He plunged into a river swollen by rain, but although he had bound his arms with cords, the stream loosened his bonds and landed him unbound (*vipāsa*) on its banks. From this the river received the name of Vipāsā (Byās). He threw himself into another river full of alligators, but the river rushed away in a hundred directions, and was consequently called Sata-dru (Sutlej). Finding that he could not kill himself, he returned to his hermitage, and was met in the wood by King Kalmāsha-pāda, who was about to devour him, but Vasishtha exorcised him and delivered him from the curse he had borne for twelve years. The sage then directed the king to return to his kingdom and pay due respect to Brāhmans. Kalmāsha-pāda begged Vasishtha to give him offspring. He promised to do so, and "being solicited by the king to beget an heir to the throne, the queen became pregnant by him and brought forth a son at the end of twelve years."

Another legend in the Mahā-bhārata represents Viswāmitra as commanding the river Saraswatī to bring Vasishtha, so that he might kill him. By direction of Vasishtha the river obeyed the command, but on approaching Viswāmitra, who stood ready armed, it promptly carried away Vasishtha in another direction.

The enmity of Vasishtha and Viswāmitra comes out very

strongly in the Rāmāyana. Viswāmitra ruled the earth for many thousand years as king, but he coveted the wondrous cow of plenty which he had seen at Vasishtha's hermitage, and attempted to take her away by force. A great battle followed between the hosts of King Viswāmitra and the warriors produced by the cow to support her master. A hundred of Viswāmitra's sons were reduced to ashes by the blast of Vasishtha's mouth, and Viswāmitra being utterly defeated, he abdicated and retired to the Himālaya. The two met again after an interval and fought in single combat. Viswāmitra was again worsted by the Brahmānical power, and "resolved to work out his own elevation to the Brahmānical order," so as to be upon an equality with his rival. He accomplished his object and became a priest, and Vasishtha suffered from his power. The hundred sons of Vasishtha denounced Viswāmitra for presuming, though a Kshatriya, to act as a priest. This so incensed Viswāmitra that he "by a curse doomed the sons of Vasishtha to be reduced to ashes and reborn as degraded outcasts for seven hundred births." Eventually, "Vasishtha, being propitiated by the gods, became reconciled to Viswāmitra, and recognised his claim to all the prerogatives of a Brāhman *R*ishi, and Viswāmitra paid all honour to Vasishtha.

A legend in the Vishnu Purāna represents Vasishtha as being requested by Nimi, a son of Ikshwāku, to officiate at a sacrifice which was to last for a thousand years. The sage pleaded a prior engagement to Indra for five hundred years, but offered to come at the end of that period. The king made no remark, and Vasishtha, taking silence as assent, returned as he had proposed. He then found that Nimi had engaged the *R*ishi Gautama to perform the sacrifice, and this so angered him that he cursed the king to lose his corporeal form. Nimi retorted the curse, and in consequence "the vigour of Vasishtha entered into the vigour of Mitra and Varuna. Vasishtha, however, received from them another body when their seed had fallen from them at the sight of Urvasī."

In the Mārkandeya Purāna he appears as the family priest of Haris-chandra. He was so incensed at the treatment shown to that monarch by Viswāmitra, that he cursed that sage to be transformed into a crane. His adversary retorted by dooming him to become another bird, and in the forms of two monstrous birds they fought so furiously that the course of the universe was disturbed, and many creatures perished. Brahmā at length put an end to the conflict by restoring them to their natural forms and compelling them to be reconciled.

According to the Vishnu Purāna, Vasishtha had for wife Ūrjā, one of the daughters of Daksha, and by her he had seven sons. The Bhāgavata Purāna gives him Arundhatī for wife. The Vishnu Purāna also makes him the family priest "of the house of Ikshwāku;" and he was not only contemporary with Ikshwāku himself, but with his descendants down to the sixty-first generation. "Vasishtha, according to all accounts (says Dr. Muir), must have been possessed of a vitality altogether superhuman," for it appears that the name Vasishtha is "used not to denote merely a person belonging to a family so called, but to represent the founder of the family himself as taking part in the transactions of many successive ages."

"It is clear that Vasishtha, although he is frequently designated in post-vedic writings as a Brāhman, was, according to some authorities, not really such in any proper sense of the word, as in the accounts which are given of his birth he is declared to have been either a mind-born son of Brahmā, or the son of Mitra and Varuna and the Apsaras Urvasī, or to have had some other supernatural origin" (*Muir*, i. 337). Vasishtha's descendants are called Vāsishthas and Vāshkalas.

VĀSTOSH-PATI. 'House protector.' One of the later gods of the Veda, represented as springing from Brahmā's dalliance with his daughter. He was the protector of sacred rites and guardian of houses.

VASU. The Vasus are a class of deities, eight in number, chiefly known as attendants upon Indra. They seem to have been in Vedic times personifications of natural phenomena. They are Āpa (water), Dhruva (pole-star), Soma (moon), Dhara (earth), Anila (wind), Anala (fire), Prabhāsa (dawn), and Pratyūsha (light). According to the Rāmāyana they were children of Aditi.

VASU-DEVA. Son of Sura, of the Yādava branch of the Lunar race. He was father of Krishna, and Kuntī, the mother of the Pāndava princes, was his sister. He married seven daughters of Āhuka, and the youngest of them, Devakī, was the mother of Krishna. After the death of Krishna and Bala-rāma he also died, and four of his wives burnt themselves with his corpse. So says the Mahā-bhārata, but according to the Vishnu Purāna he and Devakī and Rohinī burnt themselves at Dwārakā. He received the additional name of Ānaka-dundubhi, because the gods, conscious that he was to be the putative father of the divine Krishna, sounded the drums of heaven at his birth. He was also called Bhū-kasyapa and Dundu, 'drum.'

VĀSU-DEVA. A name of Krishna, derived from that of his father, Vasu-deva; but as that is incompatible with his claims to divinity, the Mahā-bhārata explains that he is so called "from his dwelling (*vasanāt*) in all beings, from his issuing as a Vasu from a divine womb." The name was assumed by an impostor named Paundraka, who was killed by Krishna. *See* Paundraka.

VĀSUKI. King of the Nāgas or serpents who live in Pātāla. He was used by the gods and Asuras for a coil round the mountain Mandara at the churning of the ocean. *See* Sesha.

VASU-SENA. A name of Karna.

VĀTA. 'Wind.' Generally the same as Vāyu, but the name is sometimes combined in the Veda with that of Parjanya, and Parjanya-vātā and Vāyu are then mentioned distinctively.

VĀTĀPI. Vātāpi and Ilwala, two Rākshasas, sons either of Hrāda or Viprachitti. They are mentioned in the Rāmāyana as dwelling in the Dandaka forest. Vātāpi assumed the form of a ram which was offered in sacrifice and afterwards eaten by Brāhmans. Ilwala then called upon him to come forth, and accordingly he tore his way out of the stomachs of the Brāhmans. He tried the same trick upon Agastya, but that austere sage ate and digested him. Ilwala, as before, called his brother to come forth, and assaulted the sage, who told him that his brother would never return. Then Ilwala was burnt up by fire from the eyes of Agastya. The Mahā-bhārata's story varies slightly.

VATA-VĀSIN. 'Dwelling in fig-trees' (*vata*). Yakshas.

VATSA, VATSA-RĀJA. King of Vatsa, the capital of which was Kausāmbī. A title of the prince Udayana. There are many persons named Vatsa.

VĀTSYĀYANA. A sage who wrote upon erotic subjects, and was author of the Kāma-sūtras and Nyāya-bhāsha. He is also called Malla-nāga.

VĀYU. 'Air, wind.' The god of the wind, Eolus. In the

Vedas he is often associated with Indra, and rides in the same car with him, Indra being the charioteer. The chariot has a framework of gold which touches the sky, and is drawn by a thousand horses. There are not many hymns addressed to him. According to the Nirukta there are three gods specially connected with each other. "Agni, whose place is on earth; Vāyu or Indra, whose place is in the air; and Sūrya, whose place is in the heaven." In the hymn Purusha-sūkta Vāyu is said to have sprung from the breath of Purusha, and in another hymn he is called the son-in-law of Twash*tri*. He is regent of the north-west quarter, where he dwells.

According to the Vish*n*u Purā*n*a he is king of the Gandharvas. The Bhāgavata Purā*n*a relates that the sage Nārada incited the wind to break down the summit of Mount Meru. He raised a terrible storm which lasted for a year, but Vish*n*u's bird, Garu*d*a, shielded the mountain with his wings, and all the blasts of the wind-god were in vain. Nārada then told him to attack the mountain in Garu*d*a's absence. He did so, and breaking off the summit of the mountain, he hurled it into the sea, where it became the island of Lankā (Ceylon).

Vāyu is the reputed father of Bhīma and of Hanumat, and he is said to have made the hundred daughters of King Ku*s*anābha crooked because they would not comply with his licentious desires, and this gave the name Kanyā-kubja, 'hump-backed damsel,' to their city.

Other names of Vāyu (wind) are Anila, Marut, Pavana Vāta, Gandha-vaha, 'bearer of perfumes;' Jala-kāntāra, 'whose garden is water;' Sadā-gata, Satata-ga, 'ever moving,' &c.

VĀYU PURĀ*N*A. "The Purā*n*a in which Vāyu has declared the laws of duty, in connection with the *S*weta kalpa, and which comprises the Māhātmya of Rudra, is the Vāyu Purā*n*a; it contains twenty-four thousand verses." No MS. containing this number of verses has yet been discovered, but there are indications of the work being imperfect. The Purā*n*a is divided into four sections, the first beginning with the creation, and the last treating of the ages to come. It is devoted to the praise of *S*iva, and is connected with the *S*iva Purā*n*a, for when one of them is given in a list of Purā*n*as the other is omitted.

VEDA. Root, *vid*, 'know.' 'Divine knowledge.' The Vedas are the holy books which are the foundation of the Hindu religion. They consist of hymns written in an old form of Sansk*ri*t, and according to the most generally received opinion they were composed between 1500 and 1000 B.C. But there is no direct evidence as to their age, and opinions about it vary considerably. Some scholars have thought that the oldest of the hymns may be carried back a thousand years farther. It seems likely that some of the hymns were composed before the arrival of the Aryan immigrants in India, and there is no doubt that the hymns vary greatly in age and spread over a very considerable period.

There are various statements as to the origin of the Vedas. One is that the hymns emanated like breath from Brahma, the soul of the universe. It is agreed that they were revealed orally to the *Ri*shis or sages whose names they bear; and hence the whole body of the Veda is known as *S*ruti, 'what was heard.'

The Vedas are now four in number:—(1.) *Ri*g, (2.) Yajur, (3.) Sāma, (4.) Atharva; but the Atharva is of comparatively modern origin. The other three are spoken of by Manu as the "three Vedas," and are said by him to have been "milked out, as it were," from fire, air, and the sun. In reality the *Ri*g-veda is *the* Veda, the original work; for the Yajur and the Sāma are merely different arrangements of its hymns for special purposes.

Each Veda is divided into two parts, Mantra and Brāhma*n*a. The Mantra, or 'instrument of conveying thought,' consists of prayer and praise embodied in the metrical hymns. The Brāhma*n*a, a collective term for the treatises called Brāhma*n*as, is of later date than the Mantra. It is written in prose, and contains liturgical and ritualistic glosses, explanations, and applications of the hymns illustrated by numerous legends. To the Brāhma*n*as are added the Āra*n*yakas and Upanishads, mystical treatises in prose and verse, which speculate upon the nature of spirit and of God, and exhibit a freedom of thought and speculation which was the beginning of Hindu philosophy. All the Vedic writings are classified in two great divisions, exoteric and esoteric: the Karma-kā*nd*a, 'department of works,' the ceremonial; and the Jnāna-kā*nd*a, 'department of knowledge.' The hymns and prayers of the Mantra come under the first, the philosophical speculations of the Brāhma*n*as, and especially of the Upanishads, under the second division. All are alike *S*ruti or revelation. *See* Brāhma*n*a, Upanishad, &c.

The Mantra or metrical portion is the most ancient, and the

book or books in which the hymns are collected are called Sanhitās. The *Rig*-veda and the Sāma-veda have each one Sanhitā; the Yajur-veda has two Sanhitās.

As before stated, the *Rig*-veda is the original Veda from which the Yajur and Sāman are almost exclusively derived. It consists of 1017 Sūktas or hymns, or with eleven additional hymns called Vālakhilyas of an apocryphal character, 1028. These are arranged in eight Ash*t*akas, 'octaves,' or Kha*nd*as, 'sections,' which are again subdivided into as many Adhyāyas, 'chapters,' 2006 Vargas or 'classes,' 10,417 *Ri*ks or 'verses,' and 153,826 Padas or 'words.' There is another division, which runs concurrently with this division, in ten Ma*nd*alas, 'circles' or 'classes,' and 85 Anuvākas or 'sections.' The total number of hymns is the same in both arrangements. It is a generally received opinion that the hymns of the tenth Ma*nd*ala are later in date than the others.

A few hymns of the *Rig*-veda, more especially some of the later hymns in the tenth Ma*nd*ala, appear to contain some vague, hazy conception of one Supreme Being; but as a whole they are addressed directly to certain personifications of the powers of nature, which personifications were worshipped as deities having those physical powers under their control. From these powers the Vedic poets invoked prosperity on themselves and their flocks; they extolled the prowess of these elemental powers in the struggles between light and darkness, warmth and cold, and they offered up joyous praise and thanksgiving for the fruits of the earth and personal protection. Chief among the deities so praised and worshipped were Agni, Indra, and Sūrya. More hymns are addressed to Agni (Ignis), 'fire,' than to any other deity, and chiefly in its sacrificial character, though it receives honour also for its domestic uses. Indra was honoured as the god of the atmosphere, who controlled the rains and the dew, so all-important to an agricultural people. Sūrya, 'the sun,' was 'the source of heat,' but he shared this honour with Agni, the sun being considered a celestial fire. Among the most ancient of the myths was that of Dyaus-pitar, 'heavenly father,' the regent of the sky. Others were Aditi, 'the infinite expanse;' Varu*n*a (Οὐρανός), 'the investing sky,' afterwards god of the waters; Ushas (ἠώς), 'the dawn,' daughter of the sky; the two A*s*wins, 'twin sons of the sun,' ever young and handsome, and riding in a golden car as precursors of the dawn. P*ri*thivī, 'the broad one,' as the earth was called, received honour as the mother of all beings. There were also the Maruts or storm-gods, personifications of the wind, the especial foes of V*ri*tra, the spirit of drought and ungenial weather, who was in constant conflict with Indra; Rudra, the howling, furious god, who ruled the tempest and the storm; Yama, the god of the dead and judge of departed spirits, also received his meed of reverence; last, though apparently not least in the estimation of the Aryan worshippers, was Soma, the personification of the fermented juice of the plant so named. This exhilarating liquid was alike acceptable to the gods and their worshippers, and many hymns are addressed to it as a deity.

To each hymn of the *Ri*g-veda there is prefixed the name of the *Ri*shi to whom it was revealed, as Vasish*th*a, Vi*s*wāmitra, Bharadwāja, and many others; and these sages are frequently spoken of as authors of the hymns bearing their names. It is quite unknown when the hymns were first committed to writing. They were transmitted orally from generation to generation, and continued to be so handed down even after they had been collected and arranged by K*ri*sh*n*a Dwaipāyana, 'the arranger.' The oral teaching of the Vedas produced what are called the *S*ākhās or 'schools' of the Vedas. Different learned men, or bodies of men, became famous for their particular versions of the text, and taught these versions to their respective pupils. These different versions constitute the *S*ākhās; they present, as might be expected, many verbal variations, but no very material discrepancies.

"The poetry of the *Ri*g-veda," says Professor Cowell, "is remarkably deficient in that simplicity and natural pathos or sublimity which we naturally look for in the songs of an early period of civilisation. The language and style of most of the hymns is singularly artificial. . . . Occasionally we meet with fine outbursts of poetry, especially in the hymns addressed to the dawn, but these are never long sustained; and as a rule we find few grand similes or metaphors." A similar opinion is expressed by Professor Williams, who finds them "to abound more in puerile ideas than in striking thoughts and lofty conceptions."

The Yajur or second Veda is composed almost exclusively of

hymns taken from the *Rig*, but it contains some prose passages which are new. Many of the hymns show considerable deviations from the original text of the *Rig*. These differences may perhaps be attributable either to an original difference of the traditional text or to modifications required by the ritualistic uses of the Yajur. The Yajur-veda is the priests' office-book, arranged in a liturgical form for the performance of sacrifices. As the manual of the priesthood, it became the great subject of study, and it has a great number of different *S*ākhās or schools. It has two Sanhitās, one called the Taittirīya Sanhitā, the other Vājasaneyī Sanhitā, commonly known as the Black and White Yajur. Of these, the former is the more ancient, and seems to have been known in the third century B.C. These Sanhitās contain upon the whole the same matter, but the arrangement is different. The White Yajur is the more orderly and systematic, and it contains some texts which are not in the Black.

The Sanhitā of the Taittirīya or Black Yajur is arranged in 7 Kā*nd*as or books, 44 Pra*s*nas or chapters, 651 Anuvākas or sections, and 2198 Ka*nd*ikās or pieces, "fifty words as a rule forming a Ka*nd*ikā." The Sanhitā of the Vājasaneyī or White Yajur is in 40 Adhyāyas or chapters, 303 Anuvākas, and 1975 Ka*nd*ikās.

How the separation into two Sanhitās arose has not been ascertained. It probably originated in a schism led by the sage Yājnawalkya; but if it did not, it produced one, and the adherents of the two divisions were hostile to each other and quarrelled like men of different creeds. In later days a legend was invented to account for the division, which is thus given by the Vish*n*u and Vāyu Purā*n*as: The Yajur-veda, in twenty-seven branches (*S*ākhās), was taught by Vai*s*ampāyana to his disciple Yājnawalkya. Vai*s*ampāyana had the misfortune to kill his sister's child by an accidental kick, and he then called upon his disciples to perform the appropriate expiatory penance. Yājnawalkya refused to join the "miserable inefficient Brāhmans," and a quarrel ensued. The teacher called upon the disciple to give up all that he had learnt from him; and the disciple, with the same quick temper, vomited forth the Yajur texts which he had acquired, and they fell upon the ground stained with blood. The other pupils were turned into partridges (Tittiri), and they picked up the disgorged texts; hence the part of the Veda which was thus acquired was called Taittirīya and Black. Yājnawalkya sorrowfully departed, and by the performance of severe penances induced the Sun to impart to him those Yajur texts which his master had not possessed. The Sun then assumed the form of a horse (Vājin), and communicated to him the desired texts. The priests of this portion of the Veda were called Vājins, while the Sanhitā itself was called Vājasaneyī, and also White (or bright), because it was revealed by the sun. The statement that Yājnawalkya received this Veda from the sun is, however, earlier than the Purā*n*as, for it is mentioned by the grammarian Kātyāyana. A more reasonable and intelligible explanation is, that Vājasaneyī is a patronymic of Yājnawalkya, the offspring of Vājasani, and that Taittirīya is derived from Tittiri, the name of a pupil of Yāska's. Weber, the man best acquainted with this Veda, says, "However absurd this legend (of the Purā*n*as) may be, a certain amount of sense lurks beneath its surface. The Black Yajur is, in fact, a motley undigested jumble of different pieces; and I am myself more inclined to derive the name Taittirīya from the variegated partridge (Tittiri) than from the *R*ishi Tittiri." Goldstücker's view is, that the "motley character of the Black Yajur-veda arises from the circumstance that the distinction between the Mantra and Brāhma*n*a portions is not so clearly established in it as in the other Vedas, hymns and matter properly belonging to the Brāhma*n*as being there intermixed. This defect is remedied in the White Yajur-veda, and it points, therefore, to a period when the material of the old Yajur was brought into a system consonant with prevalent theories, literary and ritualistic."

The Sāma-veda Sanhitā is wholly metrical. It contains 1549 verses, only seventy-eight of which have not been traced to the *R*ig-veda. The readings of the text in this Veda frequently differ, like those of the Yajur, from the text as found in the *R*ig, and Weber considers that the verses "occurring in the Sāma Sanhitā generally stamp themselves as older and more original by the greater antiquity of their grammatical forms." But this opinion is disputed. The verses of the Sāma have been selected and arranged for the purpose of being chaunted at the sacrifices or offerings of the Soma. Many of the invocations are addressed to Soma, some to Agni, and some to Indra. The Mantra or metrical part of the Sāma is poor in literary and historical interest, but its Brāhma*n*as and the other literature belonging to it are full and important.

There were different sets of priests for each of the three Vedas. Those whose duty it was to recite the *Ri*g-veda were called Hot*ri*s or Bahv*ri*chas, and they were required to know the whole Veda. The priests of the Yajur, who muttered its formulas in a peculiar manner at sacrifices, were called Adhwaryus, and the chaunters of the verses of the Sāman were called Udgāt*ri*s.

The Atharva-veda, the fourth Veda, is of later origin than the others. This is acknowledged by the Brāhmans, and is proved by the internal evidence of the book itself. It is supposed to date from about the same period as the tenth Ma*nd*ala of the *Ri*g-veda, and as Manu speaks of only "the three Vedas," the Atharva could hardly have been acknowledged in his time. Professor Whitney thinks its contents may be later than even the tenth Ma*nd*ala of the *Ri*g, although these two "stand nearly connected in import and origin." There are reasons for supposing it to have had its origin among the Saindhavas on the banks of the Indus. One-sixth of the whole work is not metrical, "and about one-sixth (of the hymns) is also found among the hymns of the *Ri*g-veda, and mostly in the tenth book of the latter; the rest is peculiar to the Atharva." The number of the hymns is about 760, and of the verses about 6000. Professor Whitney, the editor of the Atharva, speaks of it thus: "As to the internal character of the Atharva hymns, it may be said of them, as of the tenth book of the *Ri*g, that they are productions of another and a later period, and the expressions of a different spirit from that of the earlier hymns in the other Vedas. In the latter, the gods are approached with reverential awe indeed, but with love and confidence also; a worship is paid them that exalts the offerer of it; the demons embraced under the general name Rākshasa are objects of horror whom the gods ward off and destroy; the divinities of the Atharva are regarded rather with a kind of cringing fear, as powers whose wrath is to be deprecated and whose favour curried, for it knows a whole host of imps and hobgoblins, in ranks and classes, and addresses itself to them directly, offering them homage to induce them to abstain from doing harm. The Mantra prayer, which in the older Veda is the instrument of devotion, is here rather the tool of superstition; it wrings from the unwilling hands of the gods the favours which of old their good-will to men induced them to grant, or by simple magical power obtains the fulfilment of the utterer's wishes. The most prominent characteristic feature of the Atharva is the multitude of incantations which it contains; these are pronounced either by the person who is himself to be benefited, or more often by the sorcerer for him, and are directed to the procuring of the greatest variety of desirable ends; most frequently perhaps long life or recovery from grievous sickness is the object sought; then a talisman, such as a necklace, is sometimes given, or in very numerous cases some plant endowed with marvellous virtues is to be the immediate external means of the cure; farther, the attainment of wealth or power is aimed at, the downfall of enemies, success in love or in play, the removal of petty pests, and so on, even down to the growth of hair on a bald pate. There are hymns, too, in which a single rite or ceremony is taken up and exalted, somewhat in the same strain as the Soma in the Pāvamanya hymns of the *Rig*. Others of a speculative mystical character are not wanting; yet their number is not so great as might naturally be expected, considering the development which the Hindu religion received in the periods following after that of the primitive Veda. It seems in the main that the Atharva is of popular rather than of priestly origin; that in making the transition from the Vedic to modern times, it forms an intermediate step rather to the gross idolatries and superstitions of the ignorant mass than to the sublimated Pantheism of the Brāhmans." Such is the general character of the fourth Veda, but Max Müller has translated a hymn in his *Ancient Sanskrit Literature*, of which Professor Wilson said in the *Edinburgh Review*, "We know of no passage in Vedic literature which approaches its simple sublimity." This hymn is addressed to Varu*n*a, "the great one who rules over these worlds, and beholds all as if he were close by; who sees all that is within and beyond heaven and earth," &c.

This Veda is also called the Brāhman Veda, "because it claims to be the Veda for the chief sacrificial priest, the Brāhman." It has a Brāhma*n*a called Gopa*th*a and many Upanishads. An entirely new recension of this Veda has lately been found in Kashmīr. It is in the hands of Professor Roth, and is believed to show many important variations.

The whole of the *Rig*-veda, with the commentary of Sāyana, has been magnificently printed in six large quarto vols. under the editorship of Max Müller, at the expense of the Government of India. Editions of the text separately in the Sanhitā and in the Pada forms have been published by him; also another edition with the Sanhitā and Pada texts on opposite pages. There is also a complete edition of the text in Roman characters by Aufrecht, and a portion of the text was published by Roer in the *Bibliotheca Indica.* Dr. Rosen published the first Ashtaka of the text, with a Latin translation, in 1838. Four volumes of Wilson's incomplete translation have appeared. There is a French translation by Langlois, and Max Müller has printed a critical translation of twelve hymns to the Maruts. There are other translations of portions. Translations by Ludwig and by Grassmann have also lately appeared. The text, with an English and Marāthī translation, is appearing in monthly parts at Bombay.

The Sanhitā of the Black Yajur-veda has been published by Roer and Cowell in the *Bibliotheca Indica.* The White has been printed by Weber, and another edition has been published in Calcutta.

Of the Sāma Sanhitā, the text and a translation have been published by Dr. Stevenson. Benfey has also published the text with a German translation and a glossary; and an edition with the commentary of Sāyana is now coming out in the *Bibliotheca Indica* (vol. i.).

The text of the Atharva-veda Sanhitā has been printed by Roth and Whitney, and a part of it also by Aufrecht.

VEDA-MĀTRI. 'Mother of the Vedas.' The Gāyatrī.

VEDĀNGAS. (Veda + angas.) 'Members of the Veda.' The Shad-angas or six subjects necessary to be studied for the reading, understanding, and proper sacrificial employment of the Vedas:—

1. *Sikshā.* Phonetics or pronunciation, embracing accents, quantity, and euphony in general.

2. *Chhandas.* Metre.

3. *Vyākarana.* Grammar. Said to be represented by Pānini, but rather by older grammars culminating in his great work.

4. *Nirukta.* Etymology or glossary, represented by the glossary of Yāska.

5. *Jyotisha.* Astronomy. Such knowledge of the heavenly bodies as was necessary for compiling a calendar fixing the days

and hours suitable for the performance of Vedic sacrifices and ceremonies.

6. *Kalpa.* Ceremonial. Rules for applying the Vedas to the performance of sacrifices. These rules are generally written in the form of Sūtras or short aphorisms, and so they are known as the Kalpa-sūtras or *S*rauta-sūtras.

VEDĀNTA. The orthodox school of philosophy. *See* Dar*s*ana.

VEDĀNTA-PARIBHĀSHĀ. A modern text-book on the Vedānta philosophy.

VEDĀNTA-SĀRA. 'Essence of the Vedānta.' A short popular work on the Vedānta philosophy. It has been translated by Ballantyne, and also by Böhtlingk, Roer, and Frank.

VEDĀNTA-SŪTRA. The aphorisms of Bādarāya*n*a on the Vedānta philosophy. They are commonly called Brahma-sūtras, and a translation under that name by the Rev. K. M. Banerjea is progressing in the *Bibliotheca Indica.* There is a French translation by Poley.

VEDĀRTHA-PRAKĀ*S*A. 'Elucidation of the meaning of the Veda.' This is the name of Sāya*n*a's great commentary on the *Ri*g-veda. Also of a commentary on the Taittirīya Sanhitā by Mādhavāchārya.

VEDAVATĪ. The 'vocal daughter' of the *R*ishi Ku*s*a-dhwaja, son of B*ri*haspati. When Rāva*n*a was passing through a forest in the Himālaya he met with Vedavatī, a damsel of great beauty dressed in ascetic garb. He fell in love and tried to win her. She told him that gods and Gandharvas had sought to woo her, but her father would give her to no one but Vish*n*u, whom he desired for his son-in-law. Provoked at this resolution, *S*ambhu, king of the Daityas, slew her father; but she remained firm to her father's wish, and practised austerities to gain Vish*n*u for her spouse. Nothing daunted, Rāva*n*a urgently pressed his suit, and boasted that he was superior to Vish*n*u. He then touched her hair with the tip of his finger. This greatly incensed her, and she forthwith cut off her hair, and said she would enter into the fire before his eyes, adding, "Since I have been insulted in the forest by thee who art wicked-hearted, I shall be born again for thy destruction." So she entered the blazing fire, and celestial flowers fell all around. It was she who was born again as Sītā, and was the moving cause of Rāva*n*a's death, though Rāma was the agent.—*Muir's Texts,* ii. 498, iv. 458.

VEDA-VYĀSA. 'The arranger of the Vedas.' *See* Vyāsa.

VEDODAYA. 'Source of the Veda.' An epithet of the sun as the source of the Sāma-veda.

VEGAVAT. 'Swift.' 1. A son of Krishna. 2. A Dānava who fought on the side of the Sālwas against Krishna, and was killed by Samba.

VENA. Son of Anga, and a descendant of Manu Swāyambhuva. When he became king he issued this proclamation:—"Men must not sacrifice or give gifts or present oblations. Who else but myself is the enjoyer of sacrifices? I am for ever the lord of offerings." The sages remonstrated respectfully with him, but in vain; they admonished him in stronger terms; but when nothing availed, they slew him with blades of consecrated grass. After his death the sages beheld clouds of dust, and on inquiry found that they arose from bands of men who had taken to plundering because the country was left without a king. As Vena was childless, the sages, after consultation, rubbed the thigh (or, according to the Hari-vansa, the right arm) of the dead king to produce a son. From it there came forth "a man like a charred log, with flat face, and extremely short." The sages told him to sit down (Nishīda). He did so, and thus became a Nishāda, from whom "sprang the Nishādas dwelling in the Vindhya mountains, distinguished by their wicked deeds." The Brāhmans then rubbed the right hand of Vena, and from it "sprang the majestic Prithu, Vena's son, resplendent in body, glowing like the manifested Agni." The above is the story as told, with little variation, in the Mahā-bhārata, the Vishnu and Bhāgavata Puranas, and the Hari-vansa. The Padma Purāna says that Vena began his reign well, but fell into the Jaina heresy. For this the sages pummelled him until the first of the Nishādas came forth from his thigh and Prithu from his right arm. Being freed from sin by the birth of the Nishāda, he retired to a hermitage on the Narmadā, where he engaged in penance. Vishnu was thus conciliated, and granted him the boon of becoming one with himself. *See* Prithi.

VENĪ-SANHĀRA. 'The binding of the braid.' A drama by Bhatta Nārāyana. The plot is taken from the Mahā-bhārata. Draupadī, the wife of the Pāndu princes, was dragged by the hair of her head into the hall of the Kauravas by Duh-sāsana, and she vowed that it should remain dishevelled until the insult was avenged. After the death of the Kauravas she again braided her hair. Wilson has given an analysis of the drama. There are several editions of the text.

VENKA*T*A, VENKA*T*ĀDRI. A hill which was a seat of the worship of Vish*n*u. It is the modern Tripati.

VETĀLA. A ghost or goblin; a sprite who haunts cemeteries and animates dead bodies.

VETĀLA-PANCHAVIN*S*ATĪ. The twenty-five stories of the Vetāla. It is the Baitāl Pachīsī of Hindustani, and has been translated into all the languages of India. The work is ascribed to an author named Jambhala-datta.

VETRAVATĪ. The river Betwa, which rises in the Vindhyas and falls into the Jumna below Kalpi.

VIBHĀ*N*DAKA. Son of Ka*s*yapa. An ascetic who retired from the world and lived in the forest with his infant son *R*ishya-*sr*inga (q.v.). A sage of this name is sometimes classed among the great *R*ishis.

VIBHĪSHANA. 'Terrible.' A younger brother of Rāva*n*a. He, like his brother, propitiated Brahmā, and obtained a boon. His was that he should never commit an unworthy action even in the greatest extremity. He was virtuous, and opposed to the practices of the Rākshasas. This led to a quarrel between him and Rāva*n*a, who kicked him from his seat. He flew off to Kailāsa, and under the advice of *S*iva he went and allied himself with Rāma-chandra, who received and embraced him as a friend. After the defeat and death of Rāva*n*a he was raised by Rāma to the throne of Lankā.

VICHITRA-VĪRYA. Name of a king. *See* Mahā-bhārata.

VIDAGDHA-MĀDHAVA. A drama in seven acts by Rūpa on the loves of K*ri*sh*n*a and Rādhā, written in 1533 A.D. "It is weak as a drama, and its literary merits are small."

VIDARBHA. Birar, and probably including with it the adjoining district of Beder, which name is apparently a corruption of Vidarbha. The capital was Ku*nd*ina-pura, the modern "Kundapur," about forty miles east of Amarāvatī.

VIDDHA-*S*ĀLABHANJIKĀ. 'The statue.' A comedy of domestic intrigue by Rāja *S*ekhara. It was probably written earlier than the tenth century.

VIDEHA. An ancient country, of which the capital was Mithilā. It corresponds with the modern Tirhut or North Bihar.

VIDHĀTRI. 'Creator.' A name of Brahmā, of Vishnu, and of Viswa-karmā.

VIDURA. A son of Vyāsa by a Sūdra slave girl, who took the place of his consort. Vidura was called Kshattri, a term ordinarily applied to the child of a Sūdra father and Brāhman mother. He enjoyed the character of the "wisest of the wise," and gave good advice to both Kauravas and Pāndavas, but in the war he sided with the latter. *See* Mahā-bhārata.

VIDŪRA. A mountain in Ceylon, probably Adam's Peak.

VIDVAN-MODA-TARANGINĪ. 'Fountain of pleasure to the learned.' A philosophical work by Rāma-deva, translated into English by Rāja Kālī Krishna.

VIDYĀ-DHARA (mas.), VIDYĀ-DHARĪ (fem.). 'Possessors of knowledge.' A class of inferior deities inhabiting the regions between the earth and sky, and generally of benevolent disposition. They are attendants upon Indra, but they have chiefs and kings of their own, and are represented as intermarrying and having much intercourse with men. They are also called Kāma-rūpin, 'taking shapes at will;' Khechara and Nabhas-chara, 'moving in the air;' Priyam-vada, 'sweet-spoken.'

VIDYĀRANYA, VIDYĀRANYA-SWĀMĪ. 'Forest of learning.' A title of Mādhavāchārya, as patron of the city of Vidyā-nagara, afterwards altered to Vijaya-nagara, the capital of the last great Hindu dynasty of the Dakhin.

VĪJA-GANITA. A work on algebra, translated by Colebrooke and by Strachey. It is a chapter of the work called Siddhānta-siromani, written by Bhāskarāchārya. There are several editions of the text.

VIJAYA-NAGARA. The capital of the last great Hindu dynasty of the south. It was originally called Vidyā-nagara, 'city of learning,' after the great scholar and minister Mādhavāchārya, entitled Vidyāranya, 'forest of learning.' But in the days of its glory the Vidyā was altered to Vijaya, 'victory.'

VIJNĀNESWARA. Author of the law-book called Mitāksharā.

VIKARNA. A son of Dhrita-rāshtra.

VIKRAMĀDITYA. A celebrated Hindu king who reigned at Ujjayinī. He is said to have been the son of a king named Gardabhila. His name has been given to the Samvat era, commencing 57 B.C. He was a great patron of learning, and his court was made illustrious by the Nava-ratna, or nine gems of literature, who flourished there. He is a great hero of romance, and many improbable stories are told of him. His real position is uncertain. He appears to have driven out the *S*akas, and to have established his authority over Northern India. He is said to have fallen in battle with his rival *S*ālivāhana, king of the Dakhin, who also has an era called *S*aka dating from 78 A.D.

VIKRAMORVA*S*Ī. 'The hero and the nymph.' A celebrated drama by Kālidāsa, translated in Wilson's *Hindu Theatre.* There are many editions and translations. *See* Purū-ravas.

VIKUKSHI. A king of the Solar race, who succeeded his father, Ikshwāku. He received the name of *S*a*s*āda, 'hare-eater.' He was sent by his father to hunt and obtain flesh suitable for offerings. Being weary and hungry he ate a hare, and Vasish*th*a, the priest, declared that this act had defiled all the food, for what remained was but his leavings.

VIMADA. In the *Ri*g-veda it is said the A*s*wins gave a bride to the youthful Vimada, and the commentator explains that Vimada had won his bride at a swayam-vara, but was stopped on the way home by his unsuccessful competitors. The A*s*wins came to his succour, repulsed the assailants, placed the bride in their chariot, and carried her to the home of the prince.

VINATĀ. A daughter of Daksha, one of the wives of Ka*s*yapa, and mother of Garu*d*a. According to the Bhāgavata Purā*n*a she was the wife of Tārkshya or Garu*d*a.

VINDA. Vinda and Anuvinda were joint kings of Avanti, and fought in the great war.

VINDHYA. The mountains which stretch across India, and divide what Manu calls the Madhya-de*s*a or 'middle land,' the land of the Hindus, from the south, that is, they divide Hindustān from the Dakhin. The mountain is personified, and according to a legend he was jealous of the Himālaya, and called upon the sun to revolve round him as he did round Meru. When the sun refused the mountain began to raise its head to obstruct that luminary, and to tower above Himālaya and Meru. The gods invoked the aid of Agastya, the spiritual guide of Vindhya. That sage called upon the mountain to bow down before him, and afford him an easy passage to and from the south. It obeyed, and Agastya passed over. But he never returned, and so the mountain remains in its humbled condition, far inferior to the Himālaya.

VINDHYĀVALĪ. Wife of Bali the Asura.

VINDHYA-VĀSINĪ. 'The dweller in the Vindhyas.' The wife of *S*iva. *See* Devī.

VIPĀS, VIPĀSĀ. The river Byās, the Hyphasis or Bibasis of the classical writers. A legend relates that it obtained its name through the sage Vasish*t*ha, who, wishing to commit suicide, bound his limbs with cords and threw himself into the water. The river, declining to drown him, cast him unbound (*vipāsa*) on its bank.

VIPRACHITTI. Son of Ka*s*yapa and Danu. He is chief of the Dānavas.

VĪRA-BHADRA. A son or emanation of *S*iva, created from his mouth, and having, according to the Vāyu Purā*n*a, "a thousand heads, a thousand eyes, a thousand feet, wielding a thousand clubs, a thousand shafts; holding the shell, the discus, the mace, and bearing a blazing bow and battle-axe; fierce and terrific, shining with dreadful splendour, and decorated with the crescent moon; clothed in a tiger's skin, dripping with blood, having a capacious stomach and a vast mouth armed with formidable tusks," &c., &c. The object of his creation was to stop Daksha's sacrifice, and harry away the gods and others who were attending. He is an especial object of worship in the Mahratta country, and there are sculptures of him in the caves of Elephanta and Ellora, where he is represented with eight hands.

VĪRA-CHARITA. A book of tales by Ananta, which describes the feuds between the descendants of Vikramāditya and *S*ālivāhana.

VIRĀDHA. A horrible man-eating Rākshasa, son of Kāla and *S*atahradā. By penance he had obtained from Brahmā the boon of invulnerability. He is described as "being like a mountain peak, a man-eater, loud-voiced, hollow-eyed, large-mouthed, huge, huge-bellied, horrible, rude, long, deformed, of dreadful aspect, wearing a tiger's skin, dripping with fat, wetted with blood, terrific to all creatures, like death with open mouth, bearing three lions, four tigers, two wolves, ten deer, and the great head of an elephant with the tusks, and smeared with fat, on the point of an iron pike, shouting with a loud voice." Rāma, with Lakshma*n*a and Sītā, encountered him in the Da*n*daka forest, when he foully abused and taunted the brothers, and seized upon Sītā. The brothers proved with their arrows that he was not invulnerable, but he caught them, threw them over his shoulders, and ran off with them as if they had been children. They broke both his arms, threw him down, beat him with their fists, and dashed him to the earth, but they could not kill him, so they dug a deep hole and buried him alive. After his burial there arose from the earth a beautiful person, who said that he was a Gandharva who had been condemned by Kuvera to assume the shape of a Rākshasa, from which Rāma had enabled him to escape. He was also called Tumburu.

VIRĀJ. Manu thus describes Virāj :—" Having divided his body into two parts, the lord (Brahmā) became with the half a male, and with the (other) half a female ; and in her he created Virāj. Know that I (Manu), whom that male Virāj himself created, am the creator of all this world." (*See* Manu.) One passage in the *Ṛig*-veda says, " From him (Purusha) sprang Virāj, and from Virāj (sprang) Purusha " (*Muir's Texts*, v. 50, 369), like as Aditi is said to have sprung from Daksha, and Daksha from Aditi. Virāj, the male half of Brahmā, is supposed to typify all male creatures; and *S*ata-rūpā, the female half, all female forms.

VĪRA-MITRODAYA. A law-book by Mitra-mi*s*ra, of authority in the Benares School. It is in the form of a commentary on the Mitāksharā. The text is in print.

VIRĀ*T*A. A country in the vicinity of the modern Jaypur. The present town of Baira*t* is 105 miles south of Delhi. Its king was called Rāja of Virā*t*a or Rāja Virā*t*a. It was at his court that the Pā*nd*ava princes and Draupadī lived in disguise. They rendered him great services against his enemies, and he fought on their side in the great war and was killed by Dro*n*a. *See* Matsya.

VIROCHANA. A Dānava, son of Prahlāda, and father of Bali. He is also called Dri*s*ana. When the earth was milked, Virochana acted as the calf of the Asuras. *See* Pri*t*hi.

VIRŪPĀKSHA. 'Deformed as to the eyes.' A name of *S*iva, who has three eyes. Also one of the Rudras. Also a Dānava, son of Ka*s*yapa.

VI*S*ĀKHA-DATTA. Author of the drama " Mudrā-rākshasa." He is said to be of royal descent, but his family has not been identified.

VI*S*ĀLĀ. A name of the city Ujjayinī.

VISH*N*U. Root, *vish*, 'to pervade.' The second god of the Hindu triad. In the *Ri*g-veda Vish*n*u is not in the first rank of gods. He is a manifestation of the solar energy, and is described as striding through the seven regions of the universe in three steps, and enveloping all things with the dust (of his beams). These three steps are explained by commentators as denoting the three manifestations of light—fire, lightning, and the sun; or the three places of the sun—its rising, culmination, and setting. In the Veda he is occasionally associated with Indra. He has very little in common with the Vish*n*u of later times, but he is called "the unconquerable preserver," and this distinctly indicates the great preserving power which he afterwards became.

In the Brāhma*n*as Vish*n*u acquires new attributes, and is invested with legends unknown to the Vedas, but still very far distant from those of the Purā*n*as. In Manu, the name is mentioned, but not as that of a great deity. In the Mahā-bhārata and in the Purā*n*as he is the second member of the triad, the embodiment of the Satwa-gu*n*a, the quality of mercy and goodness, which displays itself as the preserving power, the self-existent, all-pervading spirit. As such, his votaries associate him with the watery element which spread everywhere before the creation of the world. In this character he is called Nārāya*n*a, 'moving in the waters,' and is represented pictorially in human form slumbering on the serpent *S*esha and floating on the waters. This, too, is the position he assumes during the periods of temporary annihilation of the universe.

The worshippers of Vish*n*u recognise in him the supreme being from whom all things emanate. In the Mahā-bhārata and in the Purā*n*as he is the Prajāpati (creator) and supreme god. As such, he has three Avasthas or conditions:—1. That of Brahmā, the active creator, who is represented as springing from a lotus which grew from Vish*n*u's navel while he was sleeping afloat upon the waters. 2. Vish*n*u himself, the preserver, in an Avatāra or incarnate form, as in K*ri*sh*n*a. 3. *S*iva or Rudra, the destructive power, who, according to a statement of the Mahā-bhārata, sprang from his forehead. But though the Mahā-bhārata generally allows Vish*n*u the supremacy, it does not do so invariably and exclusively. There are passages which uphold *S*iva as the greatest of the gods, and represent Vish*n*u as paying him homage. The *S*aiva Purā*n*as of course make *S*iva supreme.

Vishnu's preserving and restoring power has been manifested to the world in a variety of forms called Avatāras, literally 'descents,' but more intelligibly 'incarnations,' in which a portion of his divine essence was embodied in a human or supernatural form possessed of superhuman powers. All these Avatāras became manifest for correcting some great evil or effecting some great good in the world. The Avatāras are ten in number, but the Bhāgavata Purāna increases them to twenty-two, and adds that in reality they are innumerable. All the ten Avatāras are honoured, but the seventh and eighth, Rāma and Krishna, are honoured as great mortal heroes and receive worship as great gods. Krishna is more especially looked upon as a full manifestation of Vishnu, and as one with Vishnu himself, and he is the object of a widely extended and very popular worship. *See* Avatāra.

The holy river Ganges is said to spring from the feet of Vishnu.

As preserver and restorer, Vishnu is a very popular deity, and the worship paid to him is of a joyous character. He has a thousand names (Sahasra-nāma), the repetition of which is a meritorious act of devotion. His wife is Lakshmī or Srī, the goddess of fortune, his heaven is Vaikuntha, and his vehicle is the bird Garuda. He is represented as a comely youth of a dark-blue colour, and dressed like an ancient king. He has four hands. One holds the Panchajanya (q.v.), a Sankha or conch-shell; another the Su-darsana or Vajra-nābha, a chakra or quoit weapon; the third, a Gadā or club called Kaumodakī; and the fourth, a Padma or lotus. He has a bow called Sārnga, and a sword called Nandaka. On his breast are the peculiar mark or curl called Srī-vatsa and the jewel Kaustubha, and on his wrist is the jewel Syamantaka. He is sometimes represented seated on a lotus with Lakshmī beside him, or reclining on a leaf of that plant. Sometimes he is portrayed reclining on the serpent Sesha, and at others as riding on his gigantic bird Garudā.

Of the thousand names of Vishnu the following are some of the most common:—Achyuta, 'unfallen, imperishable;' Ananta, 'the endless;' Ananta-sayana, 'who sleeps on the serpent Ananta;' Chatur-bhuja, 'four-armed;' Dāmodara, 'bound round the belly with a rope,' as Krishna; Govinda or Gopāla, 'the cowkeeper' (Krishna); Hari; Hrishikesa, 'lord of the organs of sense;' Jala-sayin, 'who sleeps on the waters;' Janārddana, 'whom men worship;' Kesava, 'the hairy, the radiant;' Kirītin, 'wearing a tiara;' Lakshmīpati, 'lord of Lakshmī;' Madhusūdana, 'destroyer of Madhu;' Mādhava, 'descendant of Madhu;' Mukunda, 'deliverer;' Murāri, 'the foe of Mura;' Nara, 'the man;' Nārāyana, 'who moves in the waters;' Panchāyudha, 'armed with five weapons;' Padma-nābha, 'lotus-navel;' Pītāmbara, 'clothed in yellow garments;' Purusha, 'the man, the spirit;' Purushottama, 'the highest of men, the supreme spirit;' Sārngin or Sārngi-pāni, 'carrying the bow Sārnga;' Vāsudeva, Krishna, son of Vasudeva; Vārshneya, 'descendant of Vrishni;' Vaikuntha-nātha, 'lord of Vaikuntha (paradise);' Yajnesa, Yajneswara, 'lord of sacrifice.'

VISHNU. Author of a Dharma-sāstra or law-book.

VISHNU PURĀNA. This Purāna generally stands third in the lists, and is described as "that in which Parāsara, beginning with the events of the Varāha Kalpa, expounds all duties, is called the Vaishnava, and the learned know its extent to be 23,000 stanzas." The actual number of stanzas does not amount to 7000, and there is nó appearance of any part being wanting. The text is in print.

Wilson, the translator of this Purāna, says, "Of the whole series of Purānas the Vishnu most closely corresponds to the definition of a Pancha-lakshana Purāna, or one which treats of five specified topics (Primary Creation, Secondary Creation, Genealogies of Gods and Patriarchs, Reigns of the Manus, History). It comprehends them all; and although it has infused a portion of extraneous and sectarial matter, it has done so with sobriety and judgment, and has not suffered the fervour of its religious zeal to transport it to very wide deviations from the prescribed path. The legendary tales which it has inserted are few, and are conveniently arranged, so that they do not distract the attention of the compiler from objects of more permanent interest and importance." The whole work has been translated with numerous elucidatory notes by Wilson, and a second edition has been published with additional valuable notes by Dr. F. Hall.

VISMĀPANA. 'Astounding.' The aerial city of the Gandharvas, which appears and disappears at intervals.

VISRAVAS. Son of the Prajāpati Pulastya, or, according to a statement of the Mahā-bhārata, a reproduction of half

Pulastya himself. By a Brahmanī wife, daughter of the sage Bharadwāja, named I*d*avi*d*ā or Ilavi*d*ā, he had a son, Kuvera, the god of wealth. By a Rākshasī named Nikashā or Kaikasī, daughter of Sumāli, he had three sons, Rāva*n*a, Kumbha-kar*n*a, and Vibhīshana and a daughter named Sūrpa-nakhā. The Vish*n*u Purā*n*a substitutes Ke*s*inī for Nikashā. The account given by the Mahā-bhārata is that Pulastya, being offended with Kuvera for his adulation of Brahmā, reproduced half of himself as Vi*s*ravas, and Kuvera to recover his favour gave him three Rākshasī handmaids: Pushpotka*t*ā, the mother of Rāva*n*a and Kumbhakar*n*a; Mālinī, the mother of Vibhīshana; and Rākā, the mother of Khara and Sūrpa-nakhā.

VI*S*WA-DEVAS, VI*S*WE-DEVAS. 'All the gods.' In the Vedas they form a class nine in number. All the deities of inferior order. They are addressed in the Veda as "preservers of men, bestowers of rewards." In later times, a class of deities particularly interested in exequial offerings. The accounts of them are rather vague. They are generally said to be ten in number, but the lists vary, both as to the number and the names. The following is one list:—(1.) Vasu, (2.) Satya, (3.) Kratu, (4.) Daksha, (5.) Kāla, (6.) Kāma, (7.) Dh*ri*ti, (8.) Kuru, (9.) Purū-ravas, (10.) Mādravas. Two others are sometimes added, Rochaka or Lochana and Dhuri or Dhwani. *See* Vish*n*u Purā*n*a, Hall's edition, vol. iii. pp. 178, 188, 189.

VI*S*WA-KARMĀ, VI*S*WA-KARMAN. 'Omnificent.' This name seems to have been originally an epithet of any powerful god, as of Indra and Sūrya, but in course of time it came to designate a personification of the creative power. In this character Vi*s*wa-karmā was the great architect of the universe, and is described in two hymns of the *Ri*g-veda as the one "all-seeing god, who has on every side eyes, faces, arms, and feet, who, when producing heaven and earth, blows them forth (or shapes them) with his arms and wings; the father, generator, disposer, who knows all worlds, gives the gods their names, and is beyond the comprehension of mortals." In these hymns also he is said to sacrifice himself or to himself, and the Nirukta explains this by a legend which represents that "Vi*s*wa-karmā, son of Bhuvana, first of all offered up all worlds in a Sarva-medha (general sacrifice), and ended by sacrificing himself."

In the Epic and Purā*n*ic periods Vi*s*wa-karmā is invested

with the powers and offices of the Vedic Twash*tri*, and is sometimes so called. He is not only the great architect, but the general artificer of the gods and maker of their weapons. It was he who made the Agneyastra or "fiery weapon," and it was he who revealed the Sthāpatya-veda, or science of architecture and mechanics. The Mahā-bhārata describes him as "the lord of the arts, executor of a thousand handicrafts, the carpenter of the gods, the fashioner of all ornaments, the most eminent of artisans, who formed the celestial chariots of the deities, on whose craft men subsist, and whom, a great and immortal god, they continually worship."

In the Rāmāya*n*a, Vi*s*wa-karmā is represented as having built the city of Lankā for the Rākshasas, and as having generated the ape Nala, who constructed Rāma's bridge from the continent to Ceylon.

The Purā*n*as make Vi*s*wa-karmā the son of Prabhāsa, the eighth Vasu, by his wife "the lovely and virtuous Yoga-siddhā." His daughter Sanjnā was married to Sūrya, the sun; but as she was unable to endure his effulgence, Vi*s*wa-karmā placed the sun upon his lathe and cut away an eighth part of his brightness. The fragments fell to the earth, and from these Vi*s*wa-karmā formed "the discus of Vish*n*u, the trident of *S*iva, the weapon of Kuvera the god of wealth, the lance of Kārttikeya god of war, and the weapons of the other gods." Vi*s*wa-karmā is also represented as having made the great image of Jagan-nātha.

In his creative capacity he is sometimes designated Prajāpati. He also has the appellations Kāru, 'workman;' Takshaka, 'woodcutter;' Deva-vardhika, 'the builder of the gods;' Sudhanwan, 'having a good bow.'

VI*S*WĀMITRA. A celebrated sage, who was born a Kshatriya, but by intense austerities raised himself to the Brāhman caste, and became one of the seven great *R*ishis. According to the *R*ig-veda he was son of a king named Ku*s*ika, a descendant of Ku*s*a, but later authorities make him the son of Gāthin or Gādhi, king of Kanyā-kubja, and a descendant of Puru; so Vi*s*wāmitra is declared in the Hari-van*s*a to be "at once a Paurava and a Kau*s*ika" by lineage. According to some, Gādhi was of the Ku*s*ika race, descended from Ku*s*ika. Vi*s*wāmitra is called Gādhi-ja and Gādhi-nandana, 'son of Gādhi.' The story of Viswāmitra's birth, as told in the Vishnu Purāna, is that Gādhi had a daughter named Satyavatī, whom he gave in marriage to an old Brāhman of the race of Bhrigu named *R*ichīka. The wife being a Kshatriya, her husband was desirous that she might bear a son having the qualities of a Brāhman, and he gave her a dish of food which he had prepared to effect this object. He also gave her mother a dish intended to make her conceive a son with the character of a warrior. At the instigation of the mother the dishes were exchanged, so the mother gave birth to Viswāmitra, the son of a Kshatriya with the qualities of a Brāhman; and Satyavatī bore Jamad-agni, the father of Parasu-rāma, the warrior Brāhman and destroyer of the Kshatriyas.

The most noteworthy and important feature in the legends of Viswāmitra is the active and enduring struggle between him and the Brāhman *R*ishi Vasishtha, a fact which is frequently alluded to in the *Rig*-veda, and is supposed to typify the contentions between the Brāhmans and the Kshatriyas for the superiority. Both these *R*ishis occupy a prominent position in the *Rig*-veda, Viswāmitra being the *R*ishi of the hymns in the third Mandala, which contains the celebrated verse Gāyatrī, and Vasishtha of those of the seventh. Each of them was at different times the Purohita or family priest of King Su-dās, a position of considerable importance and power, the possession of which stimulated if it did not cause their rivalry. The two sages cursed each other, and carried their enmity into deeds of violence. Viswāmitra's hundred sons are represented as having been eaten or burnt up by the breath of Vasishtha. On the other hand, the hundred sons of Vasishtha were, according to one legend, eaten up by King Kalmāsha-pāda, into whom a man-eating Rākshasa had entered under the influence of Viswāmitra, or, according to another legend, they were reduced to ashes by Viswāmitra's curse "and reborn as degraded outcasts for seven hundred births." The Aitareya Brāhmana states that Viswāmitra had a hundred sons, but that when he adopted his nephew *S*unah-*s*ephas he proposed to make him the eldest of his sons. Fifty of them assented, and them Viswāmitra blessed that they should "abound in cattle and sons;" the other and elder fifty dissented, and them he cursed "that their progeny should possess the furthest ends (of the country)," and from them have descended many of the border tribes and most of the

Dasyus. The Māha-bhārata has a legend of Viswāmitra having commanded the river Saraswatī to bring his rival Vasish*t*ha that he might kill him, and of having turned it into blood when it flowed in another direction and carried Vasish*t*ha out of his reach.

Viswāmitra's relationship to Jamad-agni naturally places him in a prominent position in the Rāmāya*n*a. Here the old animosity between him and Vasish*t*ha again appears. He as a king paid a visit to Vasish*t*ha's hermitage, and was most hospitably entertained; but he wished to obtain Vasish*t*ha's wondrous cow, the Kāma-dhenu, which had furnished all the dainties of the feast. His offers were immense, but were all declined. The cow resisted and broke away when he attempted to take her by force, and when he battled for her, his armies were defeated by the hosts summoned up by the cow, and his "hundred sons were reduced to ashes in a moment by the blast of Vasish*t*ha's mouth." A long and fierce combat followed between Vasish*t*ha and Viswāmitra, in which the latter was defeated; the Kshatriya had to submit to the humiliation of acknowledging his inferiority to the Brāhman, and he therefore resolved to work out his own elevation to the Brāhmanical order.

While he was engaged in austerities for accomplishing his object of becoming a Brāhman he became connected with King Tri-sanku. This monarch was a descendant of King Ikshwāku, and desired to perform a sacrifice in virtue of which he might ascend bodily to heaven. His priest, Vasish*t*ha, declared it to be impossible, and that priest's hundred sons, on being applied to, refused to undertake what their father had declined. When the king told them that he would seek some other means of accomplishing his object, they condemned him to become a Cha*nd*āla. In this condition he had resort to Viswāmitra, and he, taking pity on him, raised him to heaven in his bodily form, notwithstanding the opposition of the sons of Vasish*t*ha. The Hari-vansa version of this story is different. Tri-sanku, also called Satya-vrata, had attempted the abduction of the young wife of a citizen. For this his father banished him, and condemned him to "the performance of a silent penance for twelve years." During his exile there was a famine, and Tri-sanku succoured and supported the wife and family of Viswāmitra, who were reduced to the direst extremity in that sage's absence.

Vasish*th*a, the family priest, had done nothing to assuage the wrath of the aggrieved father, and this offended Tri-*s*anku. At the end of his penance, being in want of meat, he killed Vasish*th*a's wonder-working cow and partook of her flesh; for this act Vasish*th*a gave him the name of Tri-*s*anku, 'guilty of three sins.' Vi*s*wāmitra was grateful for the assistance rendered by Tri-*s*anku, and gave him the choice of a boon. He begged that he might ascend bodily to heaven. Vi*s*wāmitra then installed Tri-*s*anku in his father's kingdom, "and in spite of the resistance of the gods and of Vasish*th*a he exalted the king alive to heaven."

The Māha-bhārata and the Rāmāya*n*a tell the story of Vi*s*wāmitra's amour with Menakā. His austerities had so alarmed the gods that Indra sent this Apsaras to seduce Vi*s*wāmitra "by the display of her charms and the exercise of all her allurements." She succeeded, and the result was the birth of *S*akuntalā. Vi*s*wāmitra at length became ashamed of his passion, and "dismissing the nymph with gentle accents, he retired to the northern mountains, where he practised severe austerities for a thousand years." He is said also to have had an amour with the nymph Rambhā.

The result of the struggle between Vasish*th*a and Vi*s*wāmitra is thus told in the Rāmāya*n*a:—"Vasish*th*a, being propitiated by the gods, became reconciled to Vi*s*wāmitra, and recognised his claim to all the prerogatives of a Brāhman *R*ishi. . . . Vi*s*wāmitra, too, having attained the Brahmānical rank, paid all honour to Vasish*th*a."

The Rāmāya*n*a gives many particulars of Vi*s*wāmitra's connection with Rāma. It was Vi*s*wāmitra who prevailed upon King Da*s*a-ratha to send his son Rāma for the protection of the Brāhmans against the attacks of Rāva*n*a and his Rākshasas. He acted as his guru, and returned with Rāma to Ayodhyā, where the prince obtained the hand of Sītā.

In the Mārka*nd*eya and other Purā*n*as the story is told of Vi*s*wāmitra's implacable persecution of King Hari*s*-chandra (*see* Hari*s*-chandra), one result of which was that Vasish*th*a and Viswāmitra cursed each other so that they were turned into birds, and fought together most furiously till Brahmā put an end to the conflict, restored them to their natural forms, and compelled them to be reconciled.

VI*S*WA-RŪPA. 'Wearing all forms, omnipresent, universal;' a title of Vish*n*u.

VI*S*WĀVASU. A chief of the Gandharvas in Indra's heaven.

VI*S*WE*S*WARA. 'Lord of all.' A name of *S*iva. The celebrated Linga or emblem of *S*iva at Benares. *See* Linga.

VĪTA-HAVYA. A king of the Haihayas. His sons attacked and slew all the family of Divodāsa, king of Kāsī. A son, named Pratardana (q.v.), was subsequently born to Divodāsa, and he attacked the Haihayas and compelled Vīta-havya to fly to the sage Bh*r*igu for protection. Pratardana pursued him, and demanded that he should be given up. Then "Vīta-havya, by the mere word of Bh*r*igu, became a Brāhman *R*ishi and an utterer of the Veda" (Mahā-bhārata). His son, G*r*itsa-mada, was a highly honoured *R*ishi, and author of several hymns in the *R*ig-veda. He was the founder of the tribe of Haihayas called Vīta-havyas.

VITASTĀ. The classic Hydaspes, the Behat of later days, and the modern Jhelam.

VIVĀDA-BHANGĀR*N*AVA. A code of Hindu law according to the Bengal school, composed by Jagan-nātha Tarkālankāra at the end of the last century. It has been translated by Colebrooke, and is commonly known as *Colebrooke's Digest.*

VIVĀDA-CHANDRA. A law-book of the Benares school by Lakhimā Devī, a learned lady.

VIVĀDA-CHINTĀMA*N*I. A law-book of the Mithilā school by Vāchaspati Mis*r*a. The text is in print.

VIVĀDA-RAṬNĀKARA. A law-book of the Benares school by Chande*s*wara, who lived about 1314 A.D.

VIVĀDA-TĀ*N**D*AVA. A law-book of the Benares school by Ratnākara.

VIVASWAT. 'The bright one.' The sun. (*See* Sūrya.) Used sometimes perhaps for the firmament.

VIVINDHAYA. A Dānava killed in battle by Chārudesh*n*a, son of K*r*ish*n*a. *See* Mahā-bhārata.

VOPA-DEVA. A grammarian of great repute, who lived about the thirteenth century A.D. at Deva-giri, and wrote the Mugdha-bodha.

VRAJA. A pastoral district about Āgra and Mathurā, where K*r*ish*n*a passed his boyhood with the cowherds.

VRĀTYA. "Persons whom the twice-born beget on women of their own classes, but who omit the prescribed rites and have abandoned the Gāyatrī, are to be designated as Vrātyas." —*Manu.*

V*RI*DDHA. 'Old.' An epithet frequently found prefixed to the books of ancient writers, and evidently implying that there are one or more versions or recensions—as V*ri*ddha Manu, V*ri*ddha Hārita. *See* Dharma-*s*āstra.

V*RI*HAT-KATHĀ. 'Great story.' A large collection of tales from which the Kathā-sarit-sāgara was drawn. There is a critical examination of this work by Dr. Bühler in the *Indian Antiquary*, vol. i.

V*RI*HAT-SANHITĀ. The astronomical work of Varāha Mihira.

V*RI*HAN NĀRADĪYA PURĀ*N*A. An Upa-purā*n*a. *See* Purā*n*a.

V*RI*HASPATI. *See* B*ri*haspati.

V*RI*KODARA. 'Wolf belly.' An epithet of Bhīma.

V*RI*NDĀ-VANA. A wood in the district of Mathurā where K*ri*sh*n*a passed his youth, under the name of Gopāla, among the cowherds.

V*RI*SH*N*I. A descendant of Yadu, and the ancestor from whom K*ri*sh*n*a got the name Vārsh*n*eya.

V*RI*SH*N*IS, V*RI*SH*N*AYAS. The descendants of V*ri*sh*n*i, son of Madhu, whose ancestor was the eldest son of Yadu. K*ri*sh*n*a belonged to this branch of the Lunar race.

V*RI*TRA. In the Vedas he is the demon of drought and ungenial weather, with whom Indra, the god of the firmament, is constantly at war, and whom he is constantly overpowering, and releasing the rain. Sometimes called V*ri*trāsura.

V*RI*TRA-HAN. The slayer of V*ri*tra. A title of Indra.

VYĀ*D*I. An old grammarian and lexicographer, somewhat later in time than Pā*n*ini. A story in the V*ri*hat-kathā represents him as contemporary with Vararuchi.

VYĀH*RI*TIS. Three mystical words said by Manu to have been milked from the Vedas by Prajāpati—the word *bhūr*, from the *Ri*g-veda; the word *bhuvah*, from the Yajur-veda; and the word *swar*, from the Sāma-veda (*Manu*, ii. 76). The *S*atapatha Brāhma*n*a defines them as "three luminous essences" which Prajāpati produced from the Vedas by heating them.

"He uttered the word *bhūr*, which became this earth; *bhuvah*, which became this firmament; and *swar*, which became that sky." A fourth word, *mahar*, is sometimes added, and is probably intended to represent the Atharva-veda. *See* Loka.

VYĀKARAṆA. 'Grammar.' One of the Vedāngas. The science of grammar has been carefully studied among the Hindus from very ancient times, and studied for its own sake as a science rather than as a means of acquiring or regulating language. The grammar of Pāṇini is the oldest of those known to survive, but Pāṇini refers to several grammarians who preceded himself. One of them was named Śākaṭāyana, a portion of whose work is said to have been discovered lately.

VYĀSA. 'An arranger.' This title is common to many old authors and compilers, but it is especially applied to Veda-vyāsa the arranger of the Vedas, who, from the imperishable nature of his work, is also called Śāśwatas, 'the immortal.' The name is given also to the compiler of the Mahā-bhārata, the founder of the Vedānta philosophy, and the arranger of the Purāṇas; all these persons being held to be identical with Veda-vyāsa. But this is impossible, and the attribution of all these works to one person has arisen either from a desire to heighten their antiquity and authority, or from the assumed identity of several different "arrangers." Veda-vyāsa was the illegitimate son of the Ṛishi Parāśara and Satyavatī, and the child, who was of a dark colour, was brought forth on an island (dwīpa) in the Yamunā. Being illegitimate he was called Kānīna, the 'bastard;' from his complexion he received the name Kṛishṇa, and from his birthplace he was called Dwaipāyana. His mother afterwards married King Śāntanu, by whom she had two sons. The elder was killed in battle, and the younger, named Vichitra-vīrya, died childless. Kṛishṇa Dwaipāyana preferred a life of religious retirement, but in accordance with law and at his mother's request, he took the two childless widows of her son, Vichitra-vīrya. By them he had two sons, Dhṛita-rāshṭra and Pāṇḍu, between whose descendants the great war of the Mahā-bhārata was fought.

The Purāṇas mention no less than twenty-eight Vyāsas, incarnations of Vishṇu or Brahmā, who descended to the earth in different ages to arrange and promulgate the Vedas.

VYAVAHĀRA-CHINTĀMAṆI. A law-book of the Benares school by Vāchaspati Miśra.

VYAVAHĀRA-MAYŪKHA. A law-book of the Mahratta school by Nīlakan*th*a Bha*tt*a. Translated by Borrodaile.

VYAVAHĀRA-TATWA. A modern work on law according to the Bengal school by Raghunandana, who is also called Smārta-Bha*tt*āchārya.

YĀDAVA. A descendant of Yadu. The Yādavas were the celebrated race in which K*ri*sh*n*a was born. At the time of his birth they led a pastoral life, but under him they established a kingdom at Dwārakā in Gujarat. All the Yādavas who were present in that city after the death of K*ri*sh*n*a perished in it when it was submerged by the ocean. Some few were absent, and perpetuated the race, from which many princes and chiefs still claim their descent. The great Rājas of Vijaya-nagara asserted themselves as its representatives. The Vish*n*u Purā*n*a says of this race, "Who shall enumerate the whole of the mighty men of the Yādava race, who were tens of ten thousands and hundreds of hundred thousands in number?"

YADU. Son of King Yayāti of the Lunar race, and founder of the line of the Yādavas in which K*ri*sh*n*a was born. He refused to bear the curse of decrepitude passed upon his father by the sage *S*ukra, and in consequence he incurred the paternal curse, "Your posterity shall not possess dominion." Still he received from his father the southern districts of his kingdom, and his posterity prospered.

YĀJA. A Brāhman of great sanctity, who, at the earnest solicitation of King Drupada, and for the offer of ten millions of kine, performed the sacrifice through which his "altar-born" children, Dh*ri*sh*t*a-dyumna and Draupadī, came forth from the sacrificial fire.

YAJNA. 'Sacrifice.' Sacrifice personified in the Purā*n*as as son of Ruchi and husband of Dakshi*n*ā. He had the head of a deer, and was killed by Vīra-bhadra at Daksha's sacrifice. According to the Hari-van*s*a he was raised to the planetary sphere by Brahmā, and made into the constellation M*ri*ga-*s*iras (deer-head).

YAJNA-DATTA-BADHA. 'The death of Yajna-datta.' An episode of the Rāmāya*n*a. It has been translated into French by Chézy.

YAJNA-PARIBHĀSHĀ. A Sūtra work by Āpastambha.

YAJNA-SENA. A name of Drupada.

YĀJNAWALKYA. A celebrated sage, to whom is attributed the White Yajur-veda, the *S*atapatha Brāhma*n*a, the B*ri*had Āra*n*yaka, and the code of law called Yājnawalkya-sm*ri*ti. He lived before the grammarian Kātyāyana, and was probably later than Manu; at any rate, the code bearing his name is posterior to that of Manu. He was a disciple of Bāshkali, and more particularly of Vai*s*ampāyana. The Mahā-bhārata makes him present at the Rāja-sūya sacrifice performed by Yudhi-sh*th*ira; and according to the *S*atapatha Brāhma*n*a he flourished at the court of Janaka, king of Videha and father of Sītā. Janaka had long contentions with the Brāhmans, in which he was supported, and probably prompted, by Yājnawalkya. This sage was a dissenter from the religious teaching and practices of his time, and is represented as contending with and silencing Brāhmans at the court of his patron. A Brāhman named Vidagdha *S*ākalya was his especial adversary, but he vanquished him and cursed him, so that "his head dropped off, and his bones were stolen by robbers." Yājnawalkya also is represented as inculcating the duty and necessity of religious retirement and meditation, so he is considered as having been the originator of the Yoga doctrine, and to have helped in preparing the world for the preaching of Buddha. He had two wives, Maitreyī and Kātyāyanī, and he instructed the former in his philosophical doctrine. Max Müller quotes a dialogue between them from the *S*atapatha Brāhma*n*a (*Ancient Sanskrit Literature*, p. 22), in which the sage sets forth his views.

The White Yajur-veda originated in a schism, of which Yājnawalkya was a leader, if not the author. He was the originator and compiler of this Veda, and according to some it was called Vājasaneyī Sanhitā, from his surname Vājasaneya. *See* Veda.

What share Yājnawalkya had in the production of the *S*atapatha Brāhma*n*a and B*ri*had Āra*n*yaka is very doubtful. Some part of them may, perhaps, have sprung directly from him, and they were probably compiled under his superintendence; but it may be, as some think, that they are so called because they treat of him and embody his teaching. One portion of the B*ri*had Āra*n*yaka, called the Yājnawalkīya Kā*nd*a, cannot have been his composition, for it is devoted to his glorification and honour, and was probably written after his death.

The Smriti, or code of law which bears the name of Yājnawalkya, is posterior to that of Manu, and is more precise and stringent in its provisions. Its authority is inferior only to that of Manu, and as explained and developed by the celebrated commentary Mitāksharā, it is in force all over India except in Bengal proper, but even there the original text-book is received. The second century A.D. has been named as the earliest date of this work. Like Manu, it has two recensions, the Brihad and Vriddha, perhaps more. The text has been printed in Calcutta, and has been translated into German by Stenzler and into English by Roer and Montriou.

YAJUR or YAJUSH. The second Veda. *See* Veda.

YAKSHAS. A class of supernatural beings attendant on Kuvera, the god of wealth. Authorities differ as to their origin. They have no very special attributes, but they are generally considered as inoffensive, and so are called Punya-janas, 'good people,' but they occasionally appear as imps of evil. It is a Yaksha in whose mouth Kāli-dāsā placed his poem Megha-dūta (cloud messenger).

YAKSHA-LOKA. *See* Loka.

YAKSHĪ, YAKSHINĪ. 1. A female Yaksha. 2. Wife of Kuvera. 3. A female demon or imp attendant on Durgā.

YAMA. 'Restrainer.' Pluto, Minos. In the Vedas Yama is god of the dead, with whom the spirits of the departed dwell. He was the son of Vivaswat (the Sun), and had a twin-sister named Yamī or Yamunā. These are by some looked upon as the first human pair, the originators of the race; and there is a remarkable hymn, in the form of a dialogue, in which the female urges their cohabitation for the purpose of perpetuating the species. Another hymn says that Yama "was the first of men that died, and the first that departed to the (celestial) world." He it was who found out the way to the home which cannot be taken away: "Those who are now born (follow) by their own paths to the place whither our ancient fathers have departed." "But," says Dr. Muir, "Yama is nowhere represented in the *Rig*-veda as having anything to do with the punishment of the wicked." So far as is yet known, "the hymns of that Veda contain no prominent mention of any such penal retribution. . . . Yama is still to some extent an object of terror. He is represented as having two insatiable dogs with four eyes and wide nostrils, which guard the road to his abode, and which the departed are advised to hurry past with all possible speed. These dogs are said to wander about among men as his messengers, no doubt for the purpose of summoning them to their master, who is in another place identified with death, and is described as sending a bird as the herald of doom."

In the epic poems Yama is the son of the Sun by Sanjnā (conscience), and brother of Vaivaswata (Manu). Mythologically he was the father of Yudhi-sh*t*hira. He is the god of departed spirits and judge of the dead. A soul when it quits its mortal form repairs to his abode in the lower regions; there the recorder, Chitra-gupta, reads out his account from the great register called Agra-sandhānī, and a just sentence follows, when the soul either ascends to the abodes of the Pit*r*is (Manes), or is sent to one of the twenty-one hells according to its guilt, or it is born again on earth in another form. Yama is regent of the south quarter, and as such is called Dakshinā*s*ā-pati. He is represented as of a green colour and clothed with red. He rides upon a buffalo, and is armed with a ponderous mace and a noose to secure his victims.

In the Purā*n*as a legend is told of Yama having lifted his foot to kick Chhāyā, the handmaid of his father. She cursed him to have his leg affected with sores and worms, but his father gave him a cock which picked off the worms and cured the discharge. Through this incident he is called *S*īr*n*a-pāda, 'shrivelled foot.'

Yama had several wives, as Hemamālā, Su-*s*īlā, and Vijayā. He dwells in the lower world, in his city Yama-pura. There, in his palace called Kālīchī, he sits upon his throne of judgment, Vichāra-bhū. He is assisted by his recorder and councillor, Chitra-gupta, and waited upon by his two chief attendants and custodians, Chanda or Mahā-chanda, and Kāla-pursusha. His messengers, Yama-dūtas, bring in the souls of the dead, and the door of his judgment-hall is kept by his porter, Vaidhyata.

Yama has many names descriptive of his office. He is M*r*ityu, Kāla, and Antaka, 'death;' K*r*itānta, 'the finisher;' *S*amana, 'the settler;' Da*n*dī or Da*n*da-dhara, 'the rod-bearer;' Bhīma-*s*āsana, 'of terrible decrees;' Pā*s*ī, 'the noose-carrier;' Pit*r*i-pati, 'lord of the manes;' Preta-rāja, 'king of the ghosts;' *S*rāddha-deva, 'god of the exequial offerings;' and especially

Dharma-rāja, 'king of justice.' He is Audumbara, from Udumbara, 'the fig-tree,' and from his parentage he is Vaivaswata. There is a Dharma-*s*āstra which bears the name of Yama.

YAMA-VAIVASWATA. Yama as son of Vivaswat.

YAMĪ. The goddess of the Yamunā river. Sister of Yama (q.v.).

YAMUNĀ. The river Jumna, which rises in a mountain called Kalinda (Sun). The river Yamunā is personified as the daughter of the Sun by his wife Sanjnā. So she was sister of Yama. Bala-rāma, in a state of inebriety, called upon her to come to him that he might bathe, and as she did not heed, he, in a great rage, seized his ploughshare-weapon, dragged her to him and compelled her to follow him whithersoever he wandered through the wood. The river then assumed a human form and besought his forgiveness, but it was some time before she could appease him. Wilson thinks that "the legend probably alludes to the construction of canals from the Jumna for the purposes of irrigation." The river is also called Kālindī, from the place of its source, Sūrya-jā, from her father, and Tri-yāmā.

YĀSKA. The author of the Nirukta, the oldest known gloss upon the text of the Vedic hymns. Yāska lived before the time of Pā*n*ini, who refers to his work, but he was not the first author who wrote a Nirukta, as he himself refers to several predecessors. *See* Nirukta.

YASODĀ. Wife of the cowherd Nanda, and foster-mother of K*r*ish*n*a.

YĀTUS, YĀTU-DHĀNAS. Demons or evil spirits of various forms, as dogs, vultures, hoofed-animals, &c. In ancient times the Yātus or Yātu-dhānas were distinct from the Rākshasas though associated with them, but in the epic poems and Purā*n*as they are identified. Twelve Yātu-dhānas are named in the Vāyu Purā*n*a, and they are said to have sprung from Ka*s*yapa and Su-rasā. They are associated with the Dasyus, and are thought to be one of the native races which opposed the progress of the immigrant Āryans.

YAVA-KRĪ, YAVA-KRĪTA. 'Bought with barley.' Son of the sage Bharadwāja. He performed great penances in order to obtain a knowledge of the Vedas without study, and having obtained this and other boons from Indra, he became arrogant and treated other sages with disrespect. He made love to the wife of Parāvasu, son of his father's friend, Raibhya. That sage in his anger performed a sacrifice which brought into being a fearful Rākshasa who killed Yava-krīta at his father's chapel. Bharadwāja, in grief for his son, burnt himself upon the funeral pile. Before his death he cursed Parāvasu to be the death of his father, Raibhya, and the son killed his father in mistake for an antelope. All three were restored to life by the gods in recompense of the great devotions of Arvāvasu, the other son of Raibhya (q.v.).—*Mahā-bhārata.*

YAVANAS. Greeks, Ἰάονες, the Yavans of the Hebrew. The term is found in Pāṇini, who speaks of the writing of the Yavanas. The Purāṇas represent them to be descendants of Turvasu, but they are always associated with the tribes of the north-west frontier, and there can be no doubt that the Macedonian or Bactrian Greeks are the people most usually intended by the term. In the Bactrian Pāli inscriptions of King Priyadarsī the word is contracted to Yona, and the term Yona-rāja "is associated with the name of Antiochus, probably Antiochus the Great, the ally of the Indian prince Sophagasenas, about B.C. 210." The Purāṇas characterise them as "wise and eminently brave." They were among the races conquered by King Sagara, and "he made them shave their heads entirely." In a later age they were encountered on the Indus by Pushpa-mitra, a Mauryan general, who dethroned his master and took the throne. In modern times the term has been applied to the Muhammadans.

YAYĀTI. The fifth king of the Lunar race, and son of Nahusha. He had two wives, Devayānī and Sarmishṭhā, from the former of whom was born Yadu, and from the latter Puru, the respective founders of the two great lines of Yādavas and Pauravas. In all he had five sons, the other three being Druhyu, Turvasu, and Anu. He was a man of amorous disposition, and his infidelity to Devayānī brought upon him the curse of old age and infirmity from her father, Sukra. This curse Sukra consented to transfer to any one of his sons who would consent to bear it. All refused except Puru, who undertook to resign his youth in his father's favour. Yayāti, after a thousand years spent in sensual pleasures, renounced sensuality, restored his vigour to Puru, and made him his successor. This story of Puru's assuming Yayāti's decrepitude is first told in the

Mahā-bhārata. The above is the version of the Vishnu Purāna. In the Padma it is told in a different manner. Yayāti was invited to heaven by Indra, who sent Mātali, his charioteer, to fetch his guest. On their way they held a philosophical discussion, which made such an impression on Yayāti that, when he returned to earth, he, by his virtuous administration, rendered all his subjects exempt from passion and decay. Yama complained that men no longer died, and so Indra sent Kāma-deva, god of love, and his daughter, Asruvindumatī, to excite a passion in the breast of Yayāti. He became enamoured, and in order to become a fit husband for his youthful charmer he made application to his sons for an exchange of their youth and his decrepitude. All refused but Puru, whose manly vigour his father assumed. After awhile the youthful bride, at the instigation of Indra, persuaded her husband to return to heaven, and he then restored to Puru his youth. The Bhāgavata Purāna and the Hari-vansa tell the story, but with variations. According to the latter, Yayāti received from Indra a celestial car, by means of which he in six nights conquered the earth and subdued the gods themselves. This car descended to his successors, but was lost by Jamamejaya through the curse of the sage Gārgya. Yayāti, after restoring his youth to Puru, retired to the forest with his wife and gave himself up to mortification. Abstaining from food, he died and ascended to heaven. He and his five sons are all called Rājarshis.

YAYĀTI-CHARITRA. A drama in seven acts on the life of Yayāti. It is attributed to Rudra-deva. The subject is Yayāti's intrigue with Sarmishthā.

YOGA. A school of philosophy. *See* Darsana and Yājnawalkya.

YOGA-NIDRĀ. 'The sleep of meditation.' Personified delusion. The great illusory energy of Vishnu and the illusory power manifested in Devī as Mahā-māyā, the great illusion.

YOGINĪ. A sorceress. The Yoginīs are eight female demons attendant on Durgā. Their names are Mārjanī, Karpūra-tilakā, Malaya-gandhinī Kaumudikā, Bherundā, Mātālī, Nāyakī, and Jayā or Subhāchāra; Su-lakshanā, Su-nandā.

YONI. The female organ. Alone, or in combination with the Linga, it is an object of worship by the followers of the Saktis.

YUDHI-SH*T*HIRA. The eldest of the five Pā*nd*u princes, mythologically the son of Dharma, the god of justice. With the Hindus he is the favourite one of the five brothers, and is represented as a man of calm, passionless judgment, strict veracity, unswerving rectitude, and rigid justice. He was renowned as a ruler and director, but not as a warrior. Educated at the court of his uncle, Dh*ri*ta-rāsh*t*ra, he received from the family preceptor, Dro*n*a, a military training, and was taught the use of the spear. When the time came for naming the Yuva-rāja or heir-apparent to the realm of Hastinā-pura, the Mahā-rāja Dh*ri*ta-rāsh*t*ra selected Yudhi-sh*t*hira in preference to his own eldest son, Dur-yodhana. A long-standing jealousy between the Pā*nd*ava and Kaurava princes then broke forth openly. Dur-yodhana expostulated with his father, and the end was that the Pā*nd*avas went in honourable banishment to the city of Vāra*n*āvata. The jealousy of Dur-yodhana pursued them, and his emissaries laid a plot for burning the brothers in their dwelling-house. Yudhi-sh*t*hira's sagacity discovered the plot and Bhīma frustrated it. The bodies of a Bhil woman and her five sons were found in the ruins of the burnt house, and it was believed for a time that the Pā*nd*avas and their mother had perished. When Draupadī had been won at the swayam-vara, Yudhi-sh*t*hira, the eldest of the five brothers, was requested by his juniors to make her his wife, but he desired that she should become the wife of Arjuna, by whose prowess she had been won. Through the words of their mother, Kuntī, and the decision of the sage Vyāsa, the princess became the common wife of the five brothers. An arrangement was made that Draupadī should dwell in turn with the five brothers, passing two days in the separate house of each, and that under pain of exile for twelve years no one of the brothers but the master of the house should enter while Draupadī was staying in it. The arms of the family were kept in the house of Yudhi-sh*t*hira, and an alarm of robbery being raised, Arjuna rushed there to procure his weapons while Draupadī was present. He thus incurred the pain of exile, and departed, though Yudhi-sh*t*hira endeavoured to dissuade him by arguing that the elder brother of a fatherless family stood towards his juniors in the position of a father. After the return of the Pā*nd*avas from exile and their establishment at Indra-prastha, the rule of Yudhi-sh*t*hira is described as having been most excellent and prosperous. The Rāja "ruled his country with great justice, protecting his subjects as his own sons, and subduing all his enemies round about, so that every man was without fear of war or disturbance, and gave his whole mind to the performance of every religious duty. And the Rāja had plenty of rain at the proper season, and all his subjects became rich; and the virtues of the Rāja were to be seen in the great increase of trade and merchandise, in the abundant harvests and the prolific cattle. Every subject of the Rāja was pious; there were no liars, no thieves, and no swindlers; and there were no droughts, no floods, no locusts, no conflagrations, no foreign invasions, and no parrots to eat the grain. The neighbouring Rājas, despairing of conquering Rāja Yudhi-sh*t*hira, were very desirous of securing his friendship. Meanwhile Yudhi-sh*t*hira, though he would never acquire wealth by unfair means, yet prospered so exceedingly that had he lavished his riches for a thousand years no diminution would ever have been perceived." After the return of his brother Arjuna from exile, Yudhi-sh*t*hira determined to assert his supremacy by performing the Rāja-sūya sacrifice, and this led to a war with Jarāsandha, Rāja of Magadha, who declined to take part in it, and was in consequence defeated and killed. The dignity which Yudhi-sh*t*hira had gained by the performance of the sacrifice rekindled the jealousy of Dur-yodhana and the other Kauravas. They resolved to invite their cousins to a gambling match, and to cheat Yudhi-sh*t*hira of his kingdom. Yudhi-sh*t*hira was very unwilling to go, but could not refuse his uncle's invitation. *S*akuni, maternal uncle of Dur-yodhana, was not only a skilful player but also a dexterous cheat. He challenged Yudhi-sh*t*hira to throw dice with him, and Yudhi-sh*t*hira, after stipulating for fair-play, began the game. He lost his all, his kingdom, his brothers, himself, and his wife, all of whom became slaves. When Draupadī was sent for as a slave and refused to come, Duh-*s*āsana dragged her into the hall by the hair, and both he and Dur-yodhana grossly insulted her. Bhīma was half mad with rage, but Yudhi-sh*t*hira's sense of right acknowledged that Draupadī was a slave, and he forbade Bhīma and his brothers to interfere. When the old Mahā-rāja Dh*ri*ta-rāsh*t*ra was informed of what had passed, he came into the assembly, and declaring that his sons had acted wrongfully, he sent Draupadī and her husbands away, imploring them to forget what had passed. Dur-yodhana was very wroth, and induced the Mahā-rāja to allow another game to avoid war, the condition being that the losers should go into exile for thirteen years, and should remain concealed and undiscovered during the whole of the thirteenth year. The game was played, and loaded dice gave *S*akuni the victory, so the Pā*nd*avas went again into exile. During that time they rendered a service to Dur-yodhana by rescuing him and his companions from a band of marauders who had made them prisoners. When Jayad-ratha, king of Sindhu, was foiled in his attempt to carry off Draupadī, the clemency of Yudhi-sh*t*hira led him to implore his brothers to spare their captive's life. As the thirteenth year of exile approached, in order to keep themselves concealed, the five brothers and Draupadī went to the country of Virā*t*a and entered into the service of the Rāja. Yudhi-sh*t*hira's office was that of private companion and teacher of dice-playing to the king. Here Yudhi-sh*t*hira suffered his wife Draupadī to be insulted, and dissuaded his brothers from interfering, lest by so doing they should discover themselves. When the term of exile was concluded, Yudhi-sh*t*hira sent an envoy to Hastinā-pura asking for a peaceful restoration to the Pā*nd*avas of their former position. The negotiations failed, and Yudhi-sh*t*hira invited K*r*ish*n*a to go as his representative to Hastinā-pura. Notwithstanding Yudhi-sh*t*hira's longing for peace the war began, but even then Yudhi-sh*t*hira desired to withdraw, but was overruled by K*r*ish*n*a.

Yudhi-sh*t*hira fought in the great battle, but did not distinguish himself as a soldier. The version of the Mahā-bhārata given in Mr. Wheeler's work makes him guilty of downright cowardice. At the instigation of K*r*ish*n*a he compassed the death of Dro*n*a by conveying to that warrior false intelligence of the death of his son A*s*watthāman, and his character for veracity was used to warrant the truth of the representation. His conscience would not allow him to tell a downright lie, but it was reconciled to telling a lying truth in killing an elephant named A*s*watthāman, and informing the fond father that A*s*watthāman was dead. He retreated from a fight with Kar*n*a, and afterwards reproached Arjuna for not having supported him and Bhīma. This so irritated Arjuna that he would have killed him on the spot had not K*r*ish*n*a interposed. After the great battle was over Krishna saluted him king, but he showed great disinclination to accept the dignity. His sorrow for those who had fallen was deep, especially for Karna, and he did what he could to console the bereaved Dhrita-rāshtra and Gāndharī, as well as the many other sufferers. He was made king, and was raised to the throne with great pomp, he acting as ruler under the nominal supremacy of the old King Dhrita-rāshtra. There, after an interval, he asserted his universal supremacy by performing the great Aswa-medha sacrifice. The death of Krishna at Dwārakā and regrets for the past embittered the lives of the Pāndavas, and they resolved to withdraw from the world. Yudhi-shthira appointed Parīkshit, grandson of Arjuna, to be his successor, and the five brothers departed with Draupadī to the Himālayas on their way to Swarga. The story of this journey is told with great feeling in the closing verses of the Mahā-bhārata. *See* Mahā-bhārata.

Yudhi-shthira had a son named Yaudheya by his wife Devikā; but the Vishnu Purāna makes the son's name Devaka and the mother's Yaudheyī.

YUGA. An age of the world. Each of these ages is preceded by a period called its Sandhyā or twilight, and is followed by another period of equal length called Sandhyānsa, 'portion of twilight,' each being equal to one-tenth of the Yuga. The Yugas are four in number, and their duration is first computed by years of the gods:—

1.	Krita Yuga,	4000	
	Sandhyā,	400	
	Sandhyānsa,	400	
			4,800
2.	Tretā Yuga,	3000	
	Sandhyā,	300	
	Sandhyānsa,	300	
			3,600
3.	Dwāpara Yuga,	2000	
	Sandhyā,	200	
	Sandhyānsa,	200	
			2,400
4.	Kali Yuga,	1000	
	Sandhyā,	100	
	Sandhyānsa,	100	
			1,200
			12,000

But a year of the gods is equal to 360 years of men, so

4800	×	360	=	1,728,000
3600	×	360	=	1,296,000
2400	×	360	=	864,000
1200	×	360	=	432,000
		Total,	.	4,320,000

years, forming the period called a Mahā-yuga or Manwantara. Two thousand Mahā-yugas or 8,640,000,000 years make a Kalpa or night and a day of Brahmā.

This elaborate and practically boundless system of chronology was invented between the age of the *Rig*-veda and that of the Mahā-bhārata. No traces of it are to be found in the hymns of the *Rig*, but it was fully established in the days of the great epic. In this work the four ages are described at length by Hanūmat, the learned monkey chief, and from that description the following account has been abridged:—

The K*r*ita is the age in which righteousness is eternal, when duties did not languish nor people decline. No efforts were made by men, the fruit of the earth was obtained by their mere wish. There was no malice, weeping, pride, or deceit; no contention, no hatred, cruelty, fear, affliction, jealousy, or envy. The castes alike in their functions fulfilled their duties, were unceasingly devoted to one deity, and used one formula, one rule, and one rite. Though they had separate duties, they had but one Veda and practised one duty.

In the Tretā Yuga sacrifice commenced, righteousness decreased by one-fourth; men adhered to truth, and were devoted to a righteousness dependent on ceremonies. Sacrifices prevailed with holy acts and a variety of rites. Men acted with an object in view, seeking after reward for their rites and their gifts, and were no longer disposed to austerities and to liberality from a simple feeling of duty.

In the Dwāpara Yuga righteousness was diminished by a half. The Veda became fourfold. Some men studied four Vedas, others three, others two, others one, and some none at all. Ceremonies were celebrated in a great variety of ways. From the decline of goodness only few men adhered to truth. When men had fallen away from goodness, many diseases, desires, and calamities, caused by destiny, assailed them, by which they were severely afflicted and driven to practise austerities. Others desiring heavenly bliss offered sacrifices. Thus men declined through unrighteousness.

In the Kali Yuga righteousness remained to the extent of one-fourth only. Práctices enjoined by the Vedas, works of righteousness, and rites of sacrifice ceased. Calamities, diseases, fatigue, faults, such as anger, &c., distresses, hunger, and fear prevailed. As the ages revolve righteousness declines, and the people also decline. When they decay their motives grow weak, and the general decline frustrates their aims.—*Muir*, i. 144.

In the K*ri*ta Yuga the duration of life was four thousand years, in the Tretā three thousand, in the Dwāpara two thousand. In the Kali Yuga there is no fixed measure. Other passages of the Mahā-bhārata indicate "that the K*ri*ta Yuga was regarded as an age in which Brāhmans alone existed, and that Kshatriyas only began to be born in the Tretā."

YUGAN-DHARA. A city in the Panjāb. A people dwelling there and in the vicinity.

YUVANĀ*S*WA. A king of the Solar race, father of Māndhāt*ri*. A legend represents this son as being conceived by and born of his father.

YUVA-RĀJA. 'Young king.' The heir-apparent to a throne.

YUYUDHĀNA. A name of Sātyaki.

YUYUTSU. A son of Dh*ri*ta-rāsh*t*ra by a Vāi*s*ya handmaid. On the eve of the great battle he left the side of the Kauravas and joined the Pā*nd*avas. When Yudhi-sh*th*ira retired from the world he established Yuyutsu in the kingdom of Indraprastha.

SANSKRIT INDEX.

GENERAL INDEX.

THE END.